N. P. Iloeje B.Sc , Dip Ed., F.R.G.S..

A New Geography
of West Africa

NEW REVISED EDITION

Longman

Acknowledgements

The publishers are grateful to the following for permission to reproduce photographs in the text: AAA for pages 31, 46 top, 68, 129 right and 140; Africa Magazine for page 56; Paul Almasy for pages 45 left, 46 bottom, 95 top and 135 top; Black Star/Georg Gerster for page 179; Cadbury Brothers, Bournville for pages 47 bottom right, 77 right and 78 left; J. Allan Cash for pages 42, 81 and 89 left; Rapho Guillermet Pictures/Marc & Evelyne Bernheim, N.Y. for page 97; Professor R.J. Harrison-church for page 111 bottom; Hoa-Qui for pages 11, 45 right, 47 bottom left, 50 bottom, 72, 85 bottom right, 95 bottom, 103 top, 115 top, 116 bottom, 117, 125, 134 and 142 bottom; Alan Hutchison Library for page 55; Paul Iloeje for pages 50 top, 73 right, 85 top left, 116 top and 133 top; Ministry of Information and Home Affairs, Enugu for page 147; Nigeria Magazine for page 59 bottom; Picturepoint for pages 51 and 78 right; John Topham Picture Library for pages 59 top (Central Press), 86 right and 110 bottom; Transafrica Pix for pages 37 right, 64 and 148.

And in the colour section: AAA for K; J. Allan Cash for O; Bruce Coleman Limited for D; Hoa-Qui for E, I, M and P; Alan Hutchison Library for N; Picturepoint for G, H, J and L; John Topham Picture Library for F (Claude Pavard); Transafrica Pix for B and C. Photograph A is a Longman Group photo.

The cover aerial photograph of Abidjan was kindly supplied by Hoa-Qui.

We are grateful to the following for permission to reproduce copyright material:
University of Cambridge Local Examinations Syndicate for a question from G.C.E. 'O' level Geography Paper, November 1970; University of London University Entrance and School Examinations Council for a question from G.C.E. 'O' level Geography Paper, January 1971 and Question 6 from G.C.E. 'O' level Geography Paper 2, Section B, November 1976; The West African Examinations Council for Question 4 SC/GCE 'O' level Geography Paper 2, November 1972; Question 4, Section 2 SCG/GCE 'O' level Geography Paper 2, November 1974; Question 1B and Question 3aii, Section 2 SC/GCE 'O' level Geography Paper 2, June 1975; Question 3 SC/GCE 'O' level Geography Paper 2, November 1975; Question 1b, 3b, Section II, and 4 SC/GCE 'O' level Geography Paper 2, June 1976; Question 4, 4 Section II SC/GCE 'O' level Geography Paper 2, November 1976; Question 2 and 4 SC/GCE 'O' level Geography Paper 1, June 1977; Question 1b and 6, Section B SC/GCE 'O' level Geography Paper 2, June 1977; Question 1, Section 2, 4b and 5, Section B SC/GCE 'O' level Geography Paper 2, November 1977.

Longman Group UK Limited,
Longman House, Burnt Mill, Harlow,
Essex CM20 2JE, England
and Associated Companies throughout the world

First published 1972
New revised edition 1980
Sixth impression 1986

Produced by Longman Group (FE) Ltd
Printed in Hong Kong

ISBN 0-582-60379-X

Contents

What this book is all about

The purpose and scope of the book

West Africa is made up of peoples with languages, customs and ways of life different from our own. If we knew more about their ways of life and how they resemble or differ from our own, we would be in a better position to understand them. The main aim of this book is, therefore, to help West Africans to get to know one another better, know their countries a little more intimately, and so to promote a closer understanding between the nations of West Africa. The book also has a more immediate purpose.

Students and teachers alike have long felt the need for a good and up-to-date book on West Africa which adequately covers the syllabus for the West African School Certificate and for teachers' examinations. This book is an attempt to satisfy that need. It covers the syllabus in full, devoting special attention to the human geography of the region. In particular, unlike the practice common in existing English textbooks at this level of dismissing all French-speaking West African countries in a few pages, each country, whether French-speaking or English-speaking, receives due attention and adequate treatment equal to its importance.

The book is divided into three parts. It starts with a general study of the historical and physical background of the geography of West Africa in Part One, and continues in Part Two with a country by country study. In Part Three the major economic activities studied in Part Two are selected and viewed in their West African context. The final chapter offers a brief survey of West African current affairs.

What is new in this new edition?

This new edition contains new trends and features on the West African scene which have occurred since the first edition of the book was published. These include the independent status of the former Portuguese West African territories, new international groupings like the ECOWAS and the river basin authorities, and changes in the patterns of population, economic activities, production and trade. Current statistics reflecting these changes have been added to replace outdated ones, and a new theory of plate tectonics has been included in Chapter 2 to explain the origin of West Africa.

In this edition too, some maps and diagrams have been modified, others updated, new photographs, more illustrations and sample studies added, to introduce greater variety to the book.

Part Three has been updated and expanded considerably since the emphasis in the West African School Certificate Syllabus is now on general regional studies. Thus the former Chapter 20 has been divided into the present Chapters 20 and 21 in order to accommodate more facts on farming, and a new Chapter 24 has been added on population and population trends. Soil erosion and drought, and their effects on West African agriculture, have been more effectively dealt with, and new trends in both mining and manufacturing industries, and in regional and external trade have also been discussed. A section on port development has been included.

There is also a new introduction in style. Interposed within the text in most chapters are relevant revision exercises which provide not only convenient breaks at the middle of the chapter, but drills, meant to consolidate what has been studied before, and prepare the student for what comes next.

The preparatory exercises at the beginning of the chapters have been further simplified where necessary, while more recent examination questions have been included at the end of each chapter, and at the close of the book.

Finally, it is hoped that the introduction of colour

in this edition will improve considerably the freshness and attractiveness of the book and therefore enhance its appeal and comprehension.

Two ways of using this book and enjoying doing so

There are two ways of using the book. For the student who is studying West Africa for the first time and who has enough time to devote to the region, and in fact for someone who would like to study the region with greater interest and relaxation, he should study Part One, then Part Two, noting in particular the sample studies and detailed treatment of certain topics in this part. Part Three then becomes easy, and he should use it to tie up, in their West African context, the economic activities of the individual countries studied in Part Two. This is the best way of getting the maximum satisfaction out of the book.

However, for the student who is revising the region or who has limited time to devote to it, and for purposes of only satisfying the current West African School Certificate syllabus on the region, a different approach is possible. The student may wish to study Part One and then go straight to Part Three, using Part Two as reference and for studying, in depth, specific selected topics which have wide West African significance. Examples of such topics are cocoa production (Ghana), the Kainji or Volta project (Nigeria and Ghana respectively), petroleum production (Nigeria), groundnut production (Senegambia), iron ore mining (Liberia and Mauritania) and balanced and planned economy (Ivory Coast).

Whichever of the two methods is used, the student should find the book enjoyable to read. The exercises at the beginning, middle and end of each chapter provide useful drills and should not be missed out. Those at the close of the book can be reserved for final revision a month or so before the examination.

Acknowledgements

During my field study tours to the various countries of West Africa to collect the first hand information I needed to write this book, I had the opportunity of exchanging views and checking my impressions and interpretations of the geography of the countries with accepted authorities on it. Among them were Dr George Benneh of the University of Ghana and Professor Willi Schultze, formerly of the University of Liberia. My sincere gratitude goes to them, no less than to various ministries and organizations, too numerous to mention here, which placed their valuable publications at my disposal.

I also received much encouragement from a number of geography teachers both in Nigeria and abroad who have expressed the desire to see a suitable book produced on the subject at School Certificate level. To these I am deeply indebted.

Finally, I acknowledge with thanks the critical comments on the manuscript made by Dr P. Mitchell, formerly of the University of Sierra Leone and now of the Centre of West African Studies at Birmingham, Mr P. Amenechi, formerly Senior Geography Master at St Gregory's College, Lagos and Mr T. Uboegbulam, former Senior Geography Master at Queen's School, Enugu and now Lecturer at the A.I.C.E., Owerri, Dr Charles Toupet of the University of Dakar and Mr M. Senior, former geography master at Mfantsipim Secondary School, Cape Coast, Ghana. Their comments were of much help to me in ensuring that the facts contained in the book are as internationally acceptable as they are of the right standard for secondary schools and colleges.

N. P. Iloeje
Enugu.

PART ONE

West Africa – a study of its historical and physical geography

1 Before we really start

Preparation

Prepare yourself for studying this chapter by doing the following exercises:

1. Take a look at the photographs in this book. Do any of them show people, scenes or activities in or near your area?
2. Find your town or village in a map of your country. In which state or region of your country is it?
3. Show your country on an atlas map of West Africa. Is it one of the large, medium sized or small countries?
4. Name other countries of West Africa. Note the positions of latitudes 5°N and 20°N, longitudes 20°W, 0° and 15°E, the Sahara Desert and the Atlantic Ocean.

Where West Africa is

Before we begin to study the geography of a place, we first of all need to find where the place is. We do this

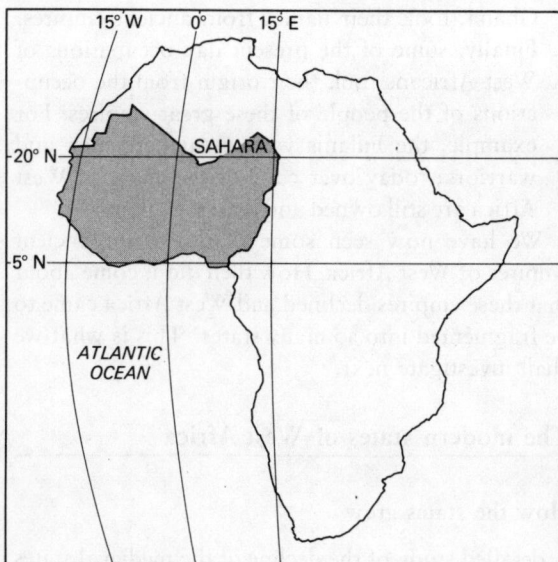

1.1 Where West Africa is.

by defining its position, using lines of latitude and longitude and by working out where it is in relation to places we know already. Then we go on to trace its growth, estimate its present size and meet its peoples. This is what we shall do in this chapter.

Drawing the precise boundaries of West Africa is not a straightforward task. The northern and eastern boundaries are not so easy to define. Some writers use the Sahara Desert in the north, but the limit of this desert is constantly shifting. Others use the 250 mm isohyet. This line is not fixed either and changes each year. In the east, the crest of Mandara-Bamenda-Cameroun Mountains is often used, but this line splits Cameroun into two, assigning Western Cameroun to the region, but leaving Eastern Cameroun out of it! Even in the west and south, where it would appear that West Africa ends in the Atlantic Ocean, it is difficult to say exactly how far from the shoreline the permanent boundary is. This is because the limits of territorial waters are often the subject of international squabbles, followed by agreements or, often, disagreements!

All we can say is that West Africa is *roughly* bounded in the north by latitude 25°N, in the east by longitude 15°E, and in the west and south by the Atlantic Ocean as shown in Figure 1.1, and then stop at that. The countries conventionally included within the region can be seen in Figure 1.3.

The ancient empires of West Africa

West Africa was not always made up of the many countries you saw in Figure 1.3. It was a land of great empires which grew strong and declined at different times in history.

The first of these empires was the Ghana Empire which flourished about the 8th century, but which probably started much earlier. The most recent was

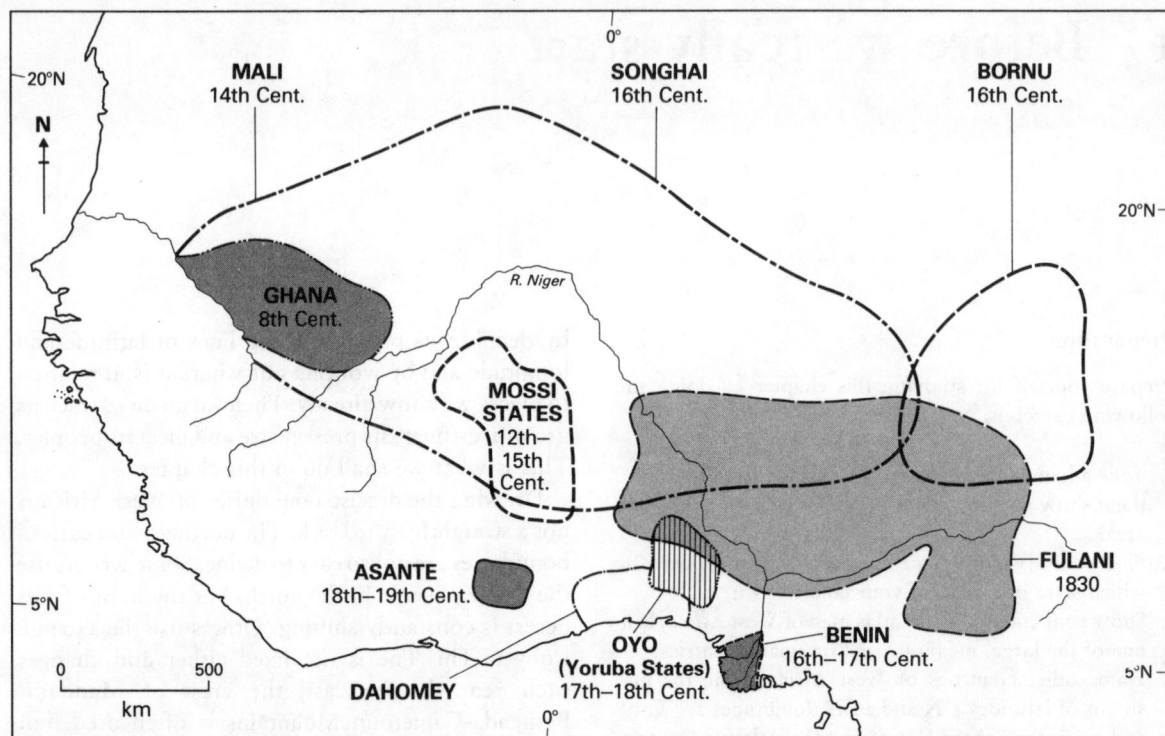

1.2 The ancient kingdoms and empires of West Africa.

the Fulani Empire which reached its maximum limit in 1830. These and others, with which you should be familiar, are shown in Figure 1.2.

Though we normally talk about these empires in our history lessons, their mention here is relevant because of the geographical significance which they have:

1. You will notice from the map that the very large ones – Songhai, Bornu, Fulani and Ghana – are all located in the north while in the south we find the small ones like Asante and Benin. This is because those in the north had earlier contacts with North Africa and the Middle East and therefore the growth influences of these civilizations, and their location in the savanna zone, allowed them freer movement and greater possibilities of territorial expansion. Conversely, those in the south were far from these earlier civilizations, and were tucked away in the forest which restricted their freedom of movement and limited their expansion.
2. Their study shows that West Africans had their own political organizations, culture and civilizations even before the 'white' man came.
3. By comparing Figures 1.2 and 1.3 we see that the

present boundaries are entirely artificial bearing no relation whatsoever to the original boundaries, nor, in fact, being consistent with any other natural feature.
4. Some of the modern states, notably Mali and Ghana, took their names from ancient empires.
5. Finally, some of the present day occupations of West Africans took their origin from the occupations of the people of these great empires. For example, the Fulanis were great herdsmen and warriors; today over 90% of the cattle in West Africa are still owned and reared by them.

We have now seen some of the major ancient empires of West Africa. How then did it come about that these empires declined and West Africa came to be fragmented into so many states? This is what we shall investigate next.

The modern states of West Africa

How the states grew

A detailed study of the decline of the medieval states in West Africa, and the growth of the modern states

Country	Area in '000 sq. km.	Population in '000	Year of census or estimate	Density per sq. km.
Nigeria	923.3	79,500	(1976)	86.1
Benin	115.8	3,112	(1977)	26.9
Togo	56.0	2,312	(1977)	41.3
Ghana	238.5	9,866	(1975)	41.4
Ivory Coast	322.5	6,673	(1975)	20.7
Liberia	113.4	1,603	(1976)	14.1
Sierra Leone	71.7	3,002	(1974)	41.9
Guinea	245.9	5.143	(1972)	20.9
Guinea Bissau	36.1	800	(1975)	22.2
Senegal	196.2	5,100	(1976)	26.0
The Gambia	10.5	494	(1973)	47.0
Mauritania	1,030.7	1,400	(1977)	1.4
Mali	1,240.0	6,308	(1976)	5.1
Upper Volta	274.0	6,173	(1976)	22.5
Niger	1,267.0	4,852	(1975)	3.8
Off shore Islands	1.4	450	1972 } 1973 }	321.4
TOTAL	6,1430	136,788		22.3

Countries of West Africa by area and population

strictly belongs to your history lesson. However, a summary of it here is not out of place because it too provides a background to the geographical study of the region. The reasons for the decline of the medieval states revolve around three major factors: (i) inter-state wars which resulted in one state conquering, and therefore annexing, and superseding, the other; (ii) the slave trade both across the Atlantic and across the Sahara which disrupted the political stability of the states; and (iii) the deliberate policy of wars of aggression, followed by annexation of parts or whole of the states by European powers, which created new states out of the old ones.

With the decline of these medieval states and annexation by European powers, one competing against the other for more territory, came the famous 'scramble for Africa' of the 19th century. It was a free-for-all affair – all European powers cutting off and claiming ownership of bits and pieces of the continent (including West Africa), depending on whichever power came first or whichever was able to edge its neighbour out!

To prevent this scramble resulting in an open conflict among themselves, the European powers agreed to meet in Berlin, capital of Germany, to hold

talks on the issue. They did so and held the famous 'Berlin Conference of 1884'. During this conference they carved Africa up and shared it out among themselves – with utter disregard for either the wishes of the people or existing political boundaries. And so it came that the West African mainland was shaped into the 15 countries you see in Figure 1.3 (though some with slightly different boundaries which were adjusted later). The nations of West Africa were thus shared among Britain, France, Germany, Spain and Portugal. Only Liberia remained self-governing.

The 15 countries on the mainland of West Africa have a total area of 6 142 000 square kilometres. The main off-shore islands are Fernando Po, São Tomé, Principé, Annobon and Cape Verde Islands which add another 1 400 square kilometres to the aggregate area of the region. These countries were ruled for over half a century before they started, one by one, to shake off the chains of colonialism and gain independence.

The year 1960 was critical in the political history of West African countries. In that year, as you can see from the map, most of them became independent. Only Liberia, Ghana and Guinea were independent before then. Sierra Leone and The Gambia gained this status in 1961 and 1964 respectively while the former Portuguese territories of Guinea Bissau and

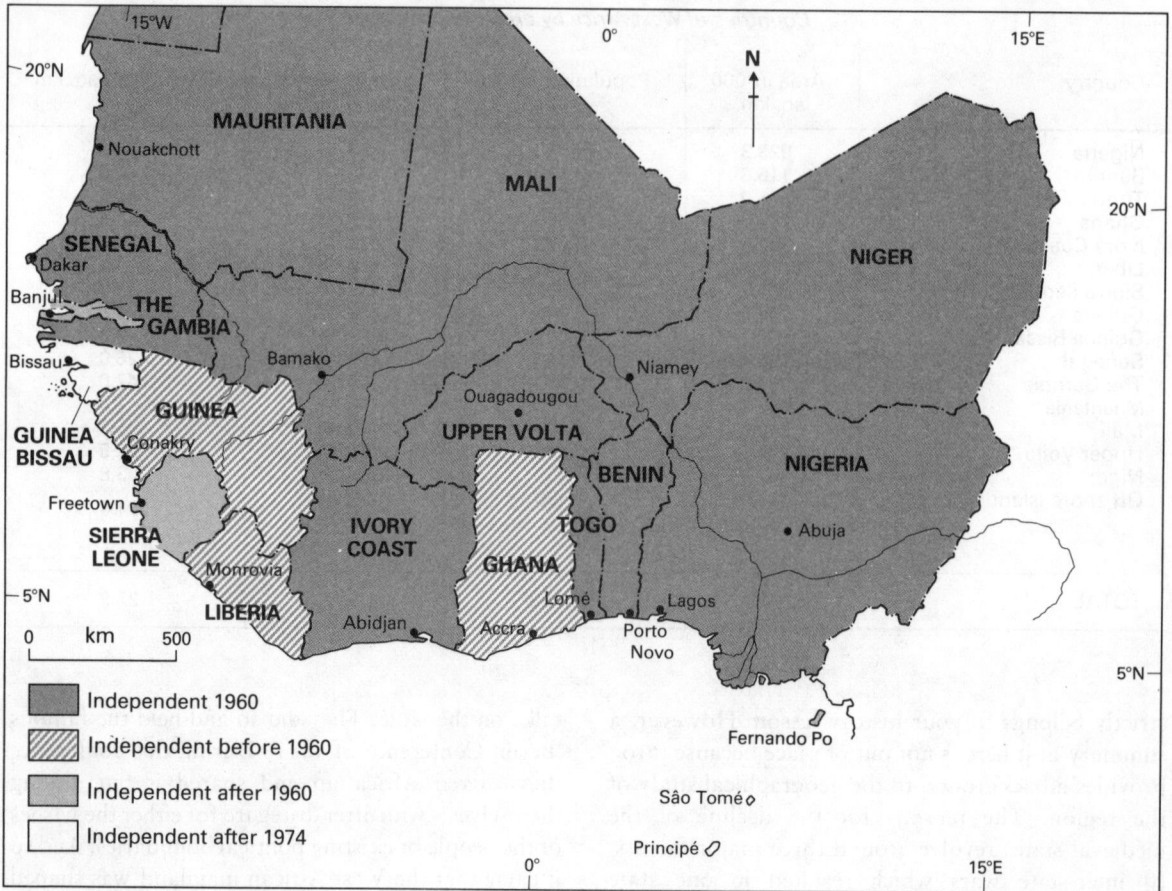

1.3 The modern states of West Africa.

Cape Verde Islands attained independence in 1974 and 1975 respectively. And so in 1975, colonialism was wiped out completely from the face of West Africa.

How large the states are

The table on page 3 shows the area and population figures of the countries of West Africa. Figures 1.4, 1.5 and 1.6 show the areas, populations and population densities in diagrams.

See whether you are able to answer the following questions on these illustrations yourself, stating the exact figures or quantities in each case.

1. Which is the largest country in area? How much of the area of West Africa as a whole is this country?
2. Which is the largest country by population? What percentage of the population of West Africa does this country have?

3. Which are the smallest countries – both in area and in population?
4. Which country has the highest population density? Which has the lowest? What are the densities of each?

There are also other facts which can be deduced from the illustrations.

1. The English speaking countries have more aggregate population than the French speaking countries – 94.5 million as against 41.59 million. They also have higher population densities. This is because during the scramble for Africa, discussed above, the British quickly annexed the already densely populated parts and thus claimed them at the Berlin Conference. Today these countries generally have more varied resources and therefore higher population growth potential.
2. Niger, Mali and Mauritania (all French speaking) are remarkable for their wide areas but very low population densities. This is chiefly because they

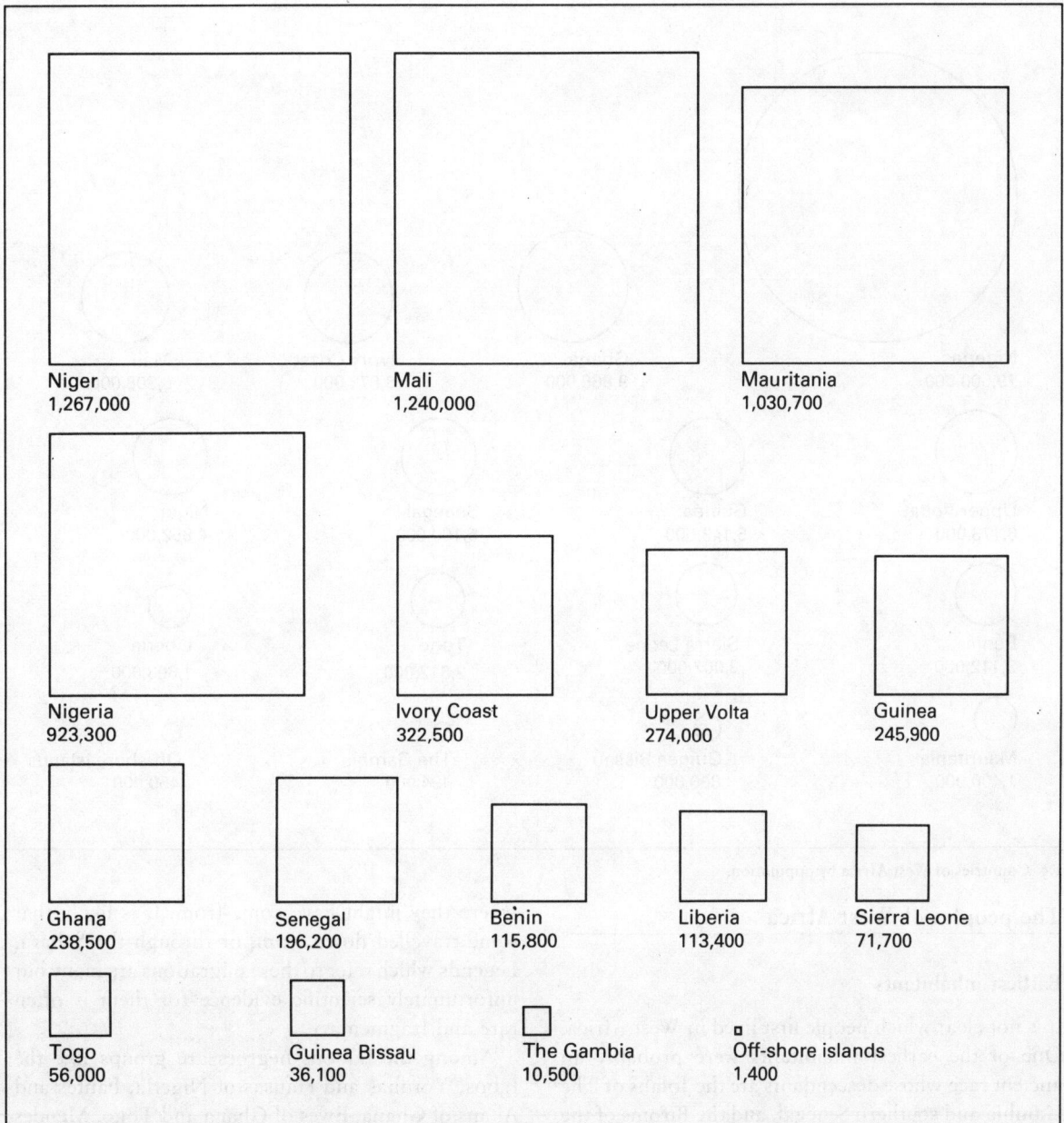

1.4 Countries of West Africa by area (in sq km).

Niger
1,267,000

Mali
1,240,000

Mauritania
1,030,700

Nigeria
923,300

Ivory Coast
322,500

Upper Volta
274,000

Guinea
245,900

Ghana
238,500

Senegal
196,200

Benin
115,800

Liberia
113,400

Sierra Leone
71,700

Togo
56,000

Guinea Bissau
36,100

The Gambia
10,500

Off-shore islands
1,400

are located on the edge of the Sahara Desert.
3. Though not shown in the illustrations, over 100 000 foreigners, mostly French, live in the French speaking countries. Not so many live in the English speaking countries. This is not surprising since the French, and later some of the French speaking countries, notably Ivory Coast and Senegal, maintain an open door policy to French immigration and settlement. It is therefore common to find French people in Ivory Coast running cafés and wayside inns – a situation rare in Ghana or Nigeria.

Nigeria
79,500,000

Ghana
9,866,000

Ivory Coast
6,673,000

Mali
6,308,000

Upper Volta
6,173,000

Guinea
5,143,000

Senegal
5,100,000

Niger
4,852,000

Benin
3,112,000

Sierra Leone
3,002,000

Togo
2,312,000

Liberia
1,603,000

Mauritania
1,400,000

Guinea Bissau
800,000

The Gambia
494,000

Off-shore islands
450,000

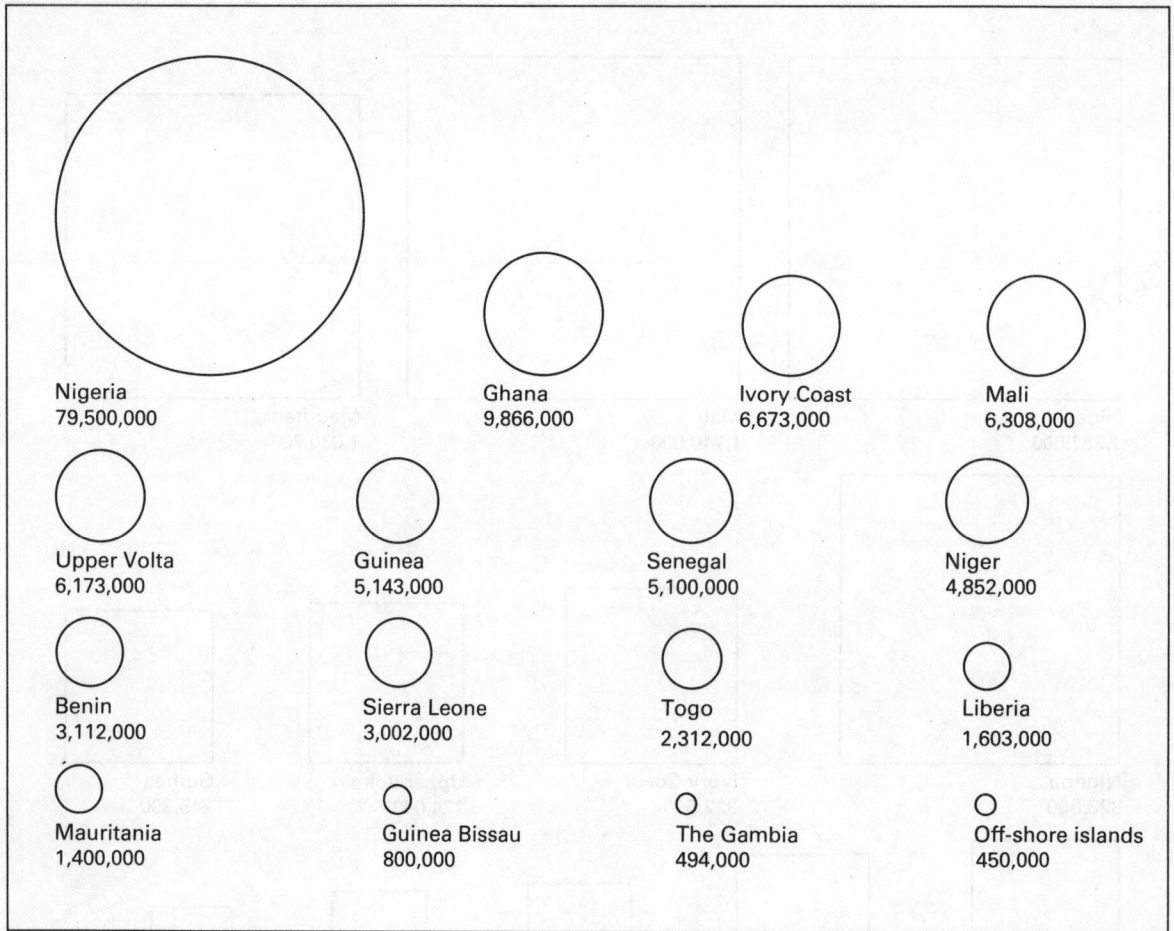

1.5 Countries of West Africa by population.

The peoples of West Africa

Earliest inhabitants

It is not clear which people first lived in West Africa. One of the earliest inhabitants were probably an ancient race whose descendants are the Jolahs of The Gambia and southern Senegal, and the Biroms of the Jos Plateau in Nigeria. They are short in stature, and it seems likely that they occupied larger areas than they now do, but were driven to their present remote and restricted areas by numerically and militarily stronger peoples who arrived later.

Negroes

The bulk of the 122 million or more West Africans are however negroes. There is little doubt that they have lived here for quite a long time. What is not clear is

where they might have come from. It is likely that some travelled down from, or through the Sahara. Legends which refer to these migrations are many but unfortunately scientific evidence for them is often rare and fragmentary.

Among the famous negroes are groups like the Igbos, Yorubas and Hausas of Nigeria, Fantes and Akans of Ghana, Ewes of Ghana and Togo, Mendes of Sierra Leone, Mandigoes of Guinea and Wolofs of Senegal and The Gambia. They are mainly farmers and traders and have contributed immensely to the economic development of the region.

Hamites

West African hamites are represented by the Fulani people and the Arabs. They entered the region from the north in more recent times and occupied the savanna and sahel regions of the interior where the

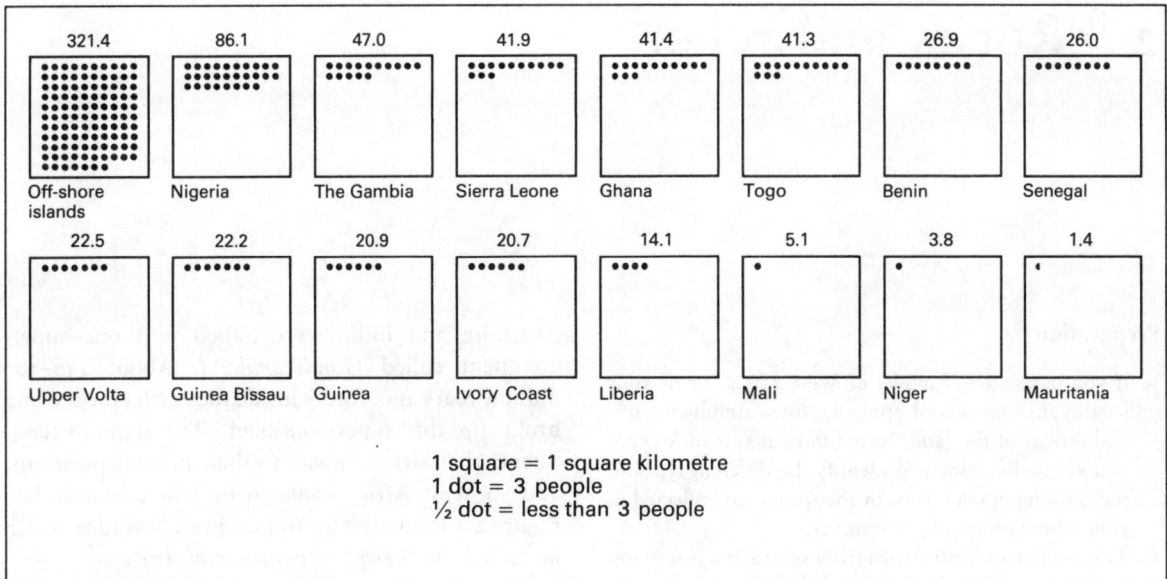

1.6 Countries of West Africa by population density.

Fulanis are the main nomadic herdsmen. In Senegal, Guinea and Sierra Leone, however, the Fulanis (called Peuls in the French speaking countries) have settled in the coastal areas.

Many hamites have retained their tall and elegant features, and sometimes their original language, culture and occupations as well. But many, by inter-marriage, have lost their characteristics and can scarcely be distinguished from the other peoples.

Foreigners

The foreign elements to the West African population are the Europeans, Americans and Asiatics. A number came in from the south, but relatively few, notably the French among the Europeans, have come to settle. They live mainly in towns, and engage principally in trade, administration, professional work and private business.

Summary

No detailed work has been attempted in this introductory chapter. All we have done here is to define the boundaries of West Africa, recall some of the empires which reigned over the region in the past, trace how these declined and gave way to the modern states, saying how these historical events affect, and are affected by, the geography of West Africa. We finally took a bird's eye view of the size, population and population densities of the modern West African states, and introduced ourselves to the peoples of West Africa to find out who they are.

Now see how much of this you are able to remember. If there are points you are not sure of, read the relevant sections in the chapter once more and then answer the questions on them.

Revision exercises

1. How large is West Africa – in area and population?
2. How do we define its boundaries? Why is it difficult to define the boundaries exactly?
3. Which great empires reigned over parts of West Africa in the past, and where were they located?
4. How did West Africa come to be fragmented into so many states?
5. How do you relate the events in questions 3 and 4 to the geography of the region?
6. Name the major peoples who inhabit West Africa. Where did they come from?
7. What general features on the population of West Africa do you deduce from Table 1 and Figures 1.4–1.6 of this chapter?
8. Give one reason why so many French people live in Ivory Coast and Senegal.

2   Rocks and relief

Preparation

1. If you have a relief model of West Africa, or of your locality, in your school, study it. Note carefully the ups and downs of the land. Name three major rock types you know. Examine and identify the different types of rocks found in your area, or the specimens collected in your school geography laboratory.
2. Trace a map of West Africa from your atlas. Insert and name your country in it.

Before studying the relief of West Africa, and to help us to understand it a little better, we will take a look at the origin of the region and the types of rocks found in the area.

The origin of West Africa

Early in this century, a German geologist, Alfred Wegner, stated his theory that hundreds of millions of years ago, Africa, South America, Antarctica,

Australia and India were joined into one super-continent called *Gondwanaland*. About 150–200 million years ago, forces inside the earth cracked and broke up this super-continent. The separate continents then drifted away to their present positions, and so West Africa came to be where it is today. Figure 2.1 is an attempt to interpret this idea which he called the *theory of continental drift*.

There is evidence to show that this is what might have happened. Look at the maps of Africa and South America, for instance, and see how the 'bulge' of South America tends to fit into the 'dent' of West Africa and how other parts of the eastern outline of South America fit almost exactly into the western outline of Africa. Besides this, similar rocks and similar remains of old plants and animals are found in Brazil and West Africa which today are separated by the vast Atlantic Ocean. In view of these facts to support the case, one can say that there is clearly some sense in what Wegner said, and that this is probably how Africa really came to be a separate continent.

More recently, in 1972, an American geologist, Dewey, threw more light on this theory in trying to explain why the continents drift. He said that the rocks of the continents are light and actually rest on the heavier rocks of the earth's crust. This crust is not in one piece round the earth, but is divided into a number of separate parts called *tectonic plates*. These plates in turn 'float' on partially molten rocks underneath, called the mantle. This is shown in Figure 2.2.

Since the plates float, they tend to move sideways. When two adjacent plates move apart, the continental rocks resting on them crack, and each portion is carried along as a 'passenger' by the plate on which it rests. So when the continents above drift apart, it is actually the tectonic plates underneath them floating on the mantle that have drifted apart.

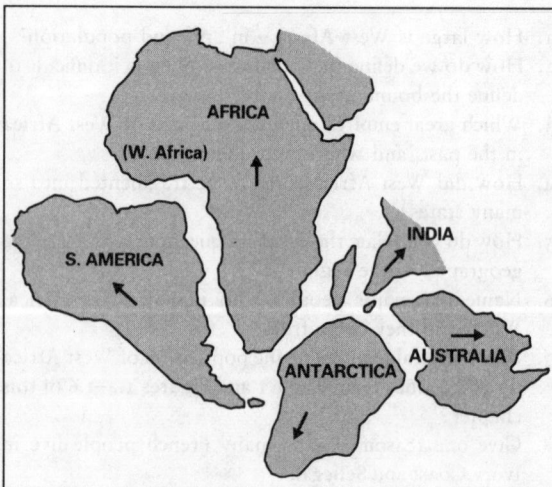

2.1 The breaking up of Gondwanaland.

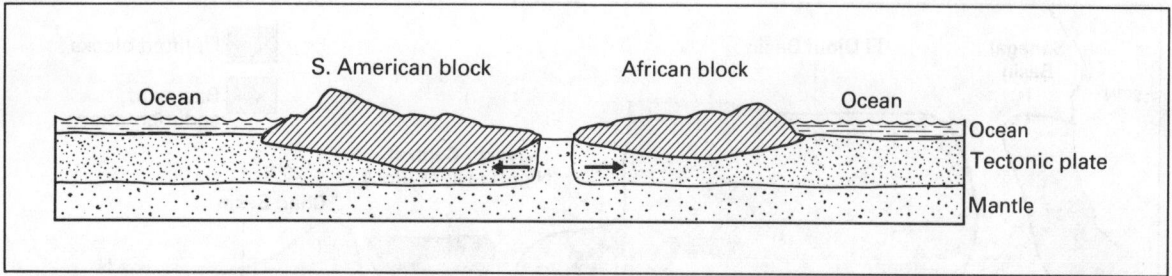

2.2 The theory of plate tectonics.

This theory which helps to explain why the continents drift is called the theory of *plate tectonics*.

As shown in the figure above, the South American plate carries on it the South American Continent. The African plate carries the African Continent. As both plates moved apart some 150–200 million years ago, South America and Africa, which were once one continent, cracked and drifted apart, each being carried away by its own tectonic plate.

Having seen how West Africa came to be, let us now study the rocks that make up the sub-continent.

Present day rocks and structure

Look at Figure 2.3. You will see that there are four major rock types in West Africa – probably more than you can find in your school area.

The most widespread rocks of all are the *basement complex rocks*. They are old, hard rocks chiefly made up of granites.

The rocks are found in all the continents of Gondwanaland, and as we saw above, this is one reason for thinking that these continents might have been joined together at one time.

Covering the basement complex rocks in places are *sedimentary rocks*. They are much younger and consist of hardened sediments deposited millions of years ago. The older ones among them are made of limestones, the younger ones of sandstones and clays.

Recent deposits appear widely in four principal areas – Senegal, mid-Niger, Chad and the Niger Delta. The deposits are principally made up of sands, clays and alluvium.

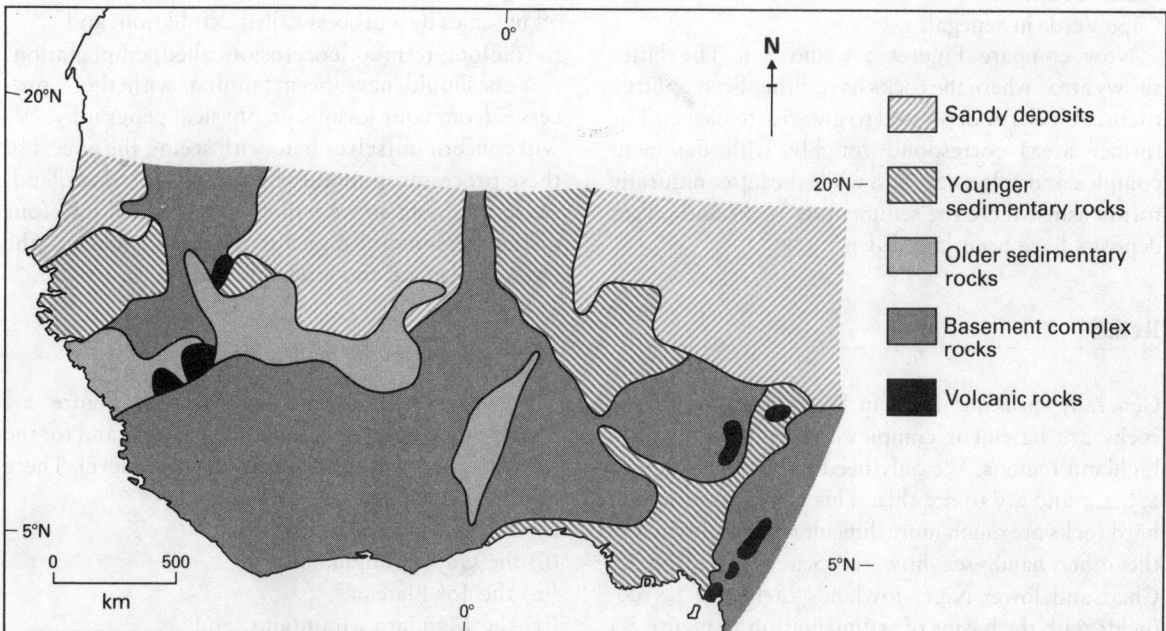

2.3 The rock types in West Africa.

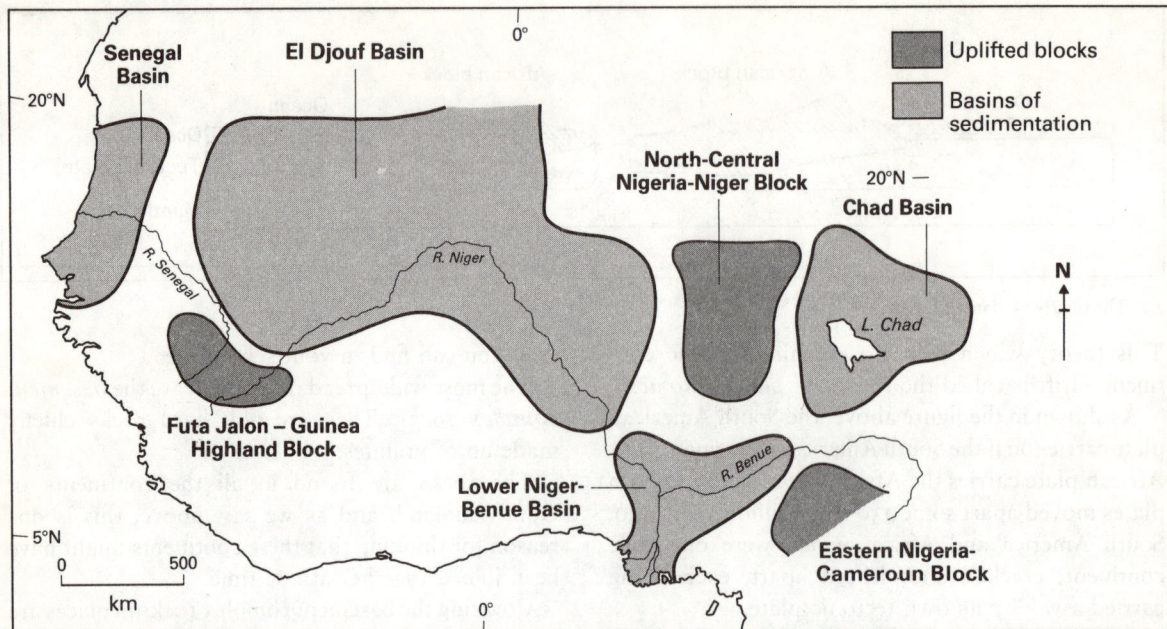

2.4 The structure of West Africa.

Volcanic activity punctured the West African rocks in many places and poured out *volcanic rocks* made up of lava and other materials from beneath the earth. That is why today we find these rocks in the Adamawa, Biu and Jos areas in Nigeria, in the island chain of Fernando Po, Príncipe and Sâo Tomé, and in Cape Verde in Senegal.

Now compare Figures 2.3 and 2.4. The latter shows areas where the rocks have either been uplifted to form blocks or depressed to give rise to basins. The former areas correspond roughly with basement complex and volcanic areas, while the latter naturally form basins where the sedimentary rocks and recent deposits have been laid down.

Relief

Generally speaking, areas in West Africa where the rocks are basement complex are uplifted to form highland regions. We only need to compare Figures 2.3, 2.4 and 2.5 to see this. This is because the old, hard rocks are much more difficult to wear down. On the other hand, see how the Senegal, mid-Niger, Chad and lower-Niger lowlands in Figure 2.5 co-incide with the basins of sedimentation in Figure 2.4 where younger sedimentary rocks are found.

The face of West Africa is being continuously modified by a number of factors. Four of them are:
(i) earth movements, principally volcanic action,
(ii) rivers which erode rocks from the highlands and deposit the fragments on the lowlands,
(iii) semi-arid rock weathering which peels the rocks off in scales by a process called exfoliation, and
(iv) the long-term cycle of erosion called pediplanation.

You should have been familiar with these pro-cesses from your lessons on physical geography. We will concern ourselves here with seeing the effects of these processes in modifying the West African land-scape. In doing so we will divide the relief into four distinct regions: the high mountains and plateaus, the interior plateau, the lowlands and the coastline.

The high mountains and plateaus

These can easily be distinguished in Figure 2.5 because they stand out clearly in isolation, and for the most part are over 1 000 metres above sea level. There are five principal ones:
(i) the Futa Jalon Plateau,
(ii) the Guinea Highlands,
(iii) the Jos Plateau,
(iv) the Mandara Mountains, and
(v) the Adamawa-Bamenda Highlands.

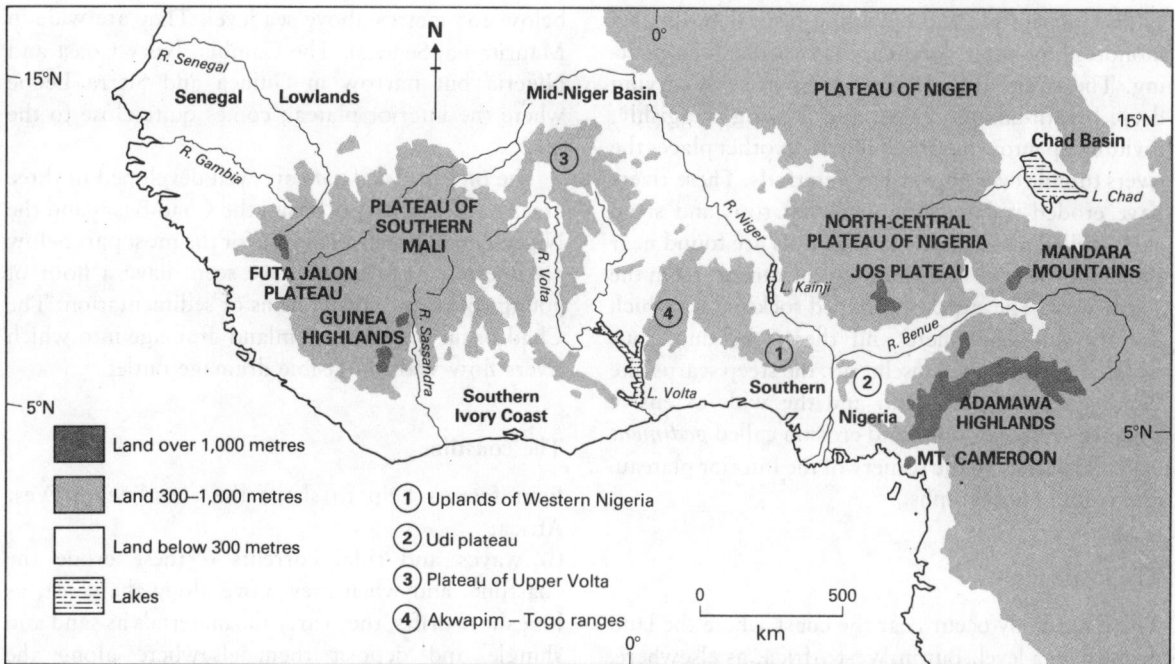

2.5 The relief of West Africa.

The high mountains and plateaus rise steeply from the surrounding plains. See for example, the almost vertical slopes of the Futa Jalon Plateau in Figure 2.6. Those of the Jos Plateau are even steeper and more impressive. All but the Futa Jalon Plateau are made up chiefly of granites with some volcanic rocks. Weathering by exfoliation has produced numerous isolated granite hills called *inselbergs* on them.

Many of the famous rivers in West Africa rise from these plateaus and carve deep 'V'-shaped valleys on them. The Senegal, Casamance and Gambia Rivers rise from the Futa Jalon; the sources of the Niger and Sassandra lie in the heart of the Guinea Highlands; the Jos Plateau is a centre of drainage dispersal for rivers like the Gongola, Kaduna and Sokoto; the Yesderam rises in the Mandara Mountains, and the Adamawa-Bamenda Highlands contain the head-waters of the Benue, Cross, Katsina Ala and other rivers. Trace the courses of these rivers in your atlas. We shall learn more about them in Chapter 4.

The interior plateau

This is perhaps the most striking relief region in West Africa. Like the high plateaus, it is chiefly made up of basement complex rocks. But, unlike them, it is more

2.6 The Futa Jalon Plateau.

extensive and averages only 500 metres above sea level. River erosion has chopped it into blocks such as the North-Central Plateau of Nigeria, the Plateau of southern Mali and Upper Volta, the Akwapim-Togo-Atakora Ranges which continue eastwards to the uplands of western Nigeria, and the Udi Plateau. All these are shown in Figure 2.5. The last is the only one made up of sedimentary rocks.

The interior plateau has often been described as monotonous, but its landscape is varied and fascinating. The rivers named above cross it, both carving deep, breath-taking gorges, and flowing sluggishly, dividing up into separate channels. In other places the rivers tumble over impressive waterfalls. These rivers have eroded isolated hills with flat tops and steep sides, called mesas. Such tabular hills are found near Bamako (Mali) as one flies in to the airport from the south-west. The curiously shaped rock pillars which dot the landscape here and there, the numerous isolated dome-shaped inselbergs, the steep scarps like Bandiagara Scarp of Mali and the wide extensive concave surface of semi-arid erosion called *pediment* – all add variety to the scenery of the interior plateau. (See colour photographs.)

The lowlands

These normally occur near the coast where the land drops to sea level. But in West Africa, as elsewhere, they are sometimes found in the interior. Hence we have both the coastal and the interior lowlands.

In West Africa the *coastal lowlands* are generally below 200 metres above sea level. They are wide in Mauritania, Senegal, The Gambia, Ivory Coast and Nigeria but narrow in Guinea and Sierra Leone where the interior plateau comes quite close to the sea.

The *interior lowlands* are well developed in three areas – the mid-Niger Basin, the Chad Basin and the Niger-Benue Valley. They lie for the most part below 300 metres, and, as we have seen, have a floor of young rocks and form basins of sedimentation. The Chad Basin is a basin of inland drainage into which rivers flow with no visible drainage outlet.

The coastline

Four factors help to shape the coastline of West Africa:

(i) waves and tidal currents – these erode the coastline, and when they move along the coast, as longshore drifts, they carry the materials as sand and shingle and deposit them elsewhere along the shoreline,

(ii) rivers – these deposit sediments they have brought from inland along the coast,

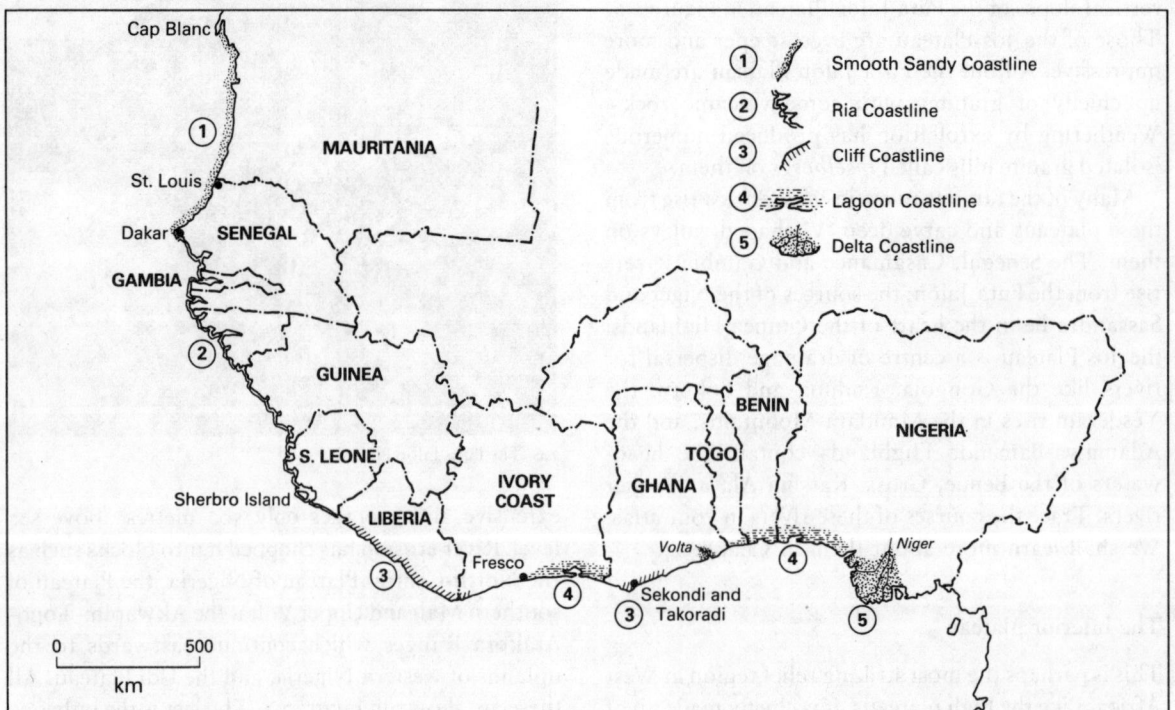

2.7 The West African coastline.

(iii) the nature of the relief and rocks near the coast – hard rocks near the coast are less easily eroded than soft ones, and

(iv) the rising or falling of the land relative to the sea level.

These factors have given West Africa five distinct types of coastline shown in Figure 2.7 and described below.

1. Between Cape Blanco in the north-west and Dakar, the sands from the Sahara and the sea, deposited respectively by winds and waves, are being pressed smoothly into position by waves to form a *smooth sandy coastline*. In the region of the Senegal estuary, the sand has been shifted southwards by longshore drift across the estuary to form a continuously elongating sand spit. This spit has blocked the former estuary pushing it many kilometres southwards. Behind the spit are many lagoons, which are silting up in places to give rise to mangrove swamps. See Figure 2.8 and point to the spit, the estuary, the lagoons and the swamps. How far has the spit moved between 1658 and 1884? How far south of St Louis is the tip now?

2. Between Dakar and Shebro Island in Sierra Leone the level of the land has fallen relative to the sea level; here the sea has rushed in to drown many of the river estuaries, thus giving rise to a *ria coastline*. Recall the characteristics of a ria. The wide mouths of the Gambia and Sierra Leone Rivers and the inlets along the coast of Guinea Bissau are typical examples of such rias.

3. Where hard rocks occur close to the sea in West Africa, waves have cut low but steep cliffs along the coast. We find such a *cliff coastline* in Liberia and Ghana, particularly in the regions of Monrovia and Sekondi respectively. Along the cliff coastline of Sekondi erosion has not only formed low cliffs at the coast, but has also cut off a small chunk of the land to form a small island called the Nkontompo Stack. The stack is separated from the mainland by a few metres only.

4. The coasts of Ivory Coast (east of Fresco), Togo, Benin and Nigeria west of the delta are low and sandy, have numerous lagoons and either submerged or exposed sand bars. Such a coastline is called a *lagoon coastline*. Some of the lagoons, like the Porto Novo lagoon in Benin and the Lagos Lagoon and Kuramo Waters in Nigeria, are elongated and lie parallel to the coast. These are parts of the sea cut off by the sand bars. Others like the Lake Ahémé in Togo or the northern branches of the Porto Novo Lagoon and Kuramo Waters are transverse to the coast and represent drowned river estuaries. See these in a large scale atlas map of this coast.

5. Finally, the Volta and Niger Rivers carry down tonnes of mud, clay and silt and deposit them as alluvium near the coast. Their mouths are blocked by these alluvial sediments and so they are forced to break into several shallow channels called distributaries.

The deposits and distributaries together form the delta which gives rise to a *delta coastline*. The Niger Delta is one of the best examples of this feature in the world.

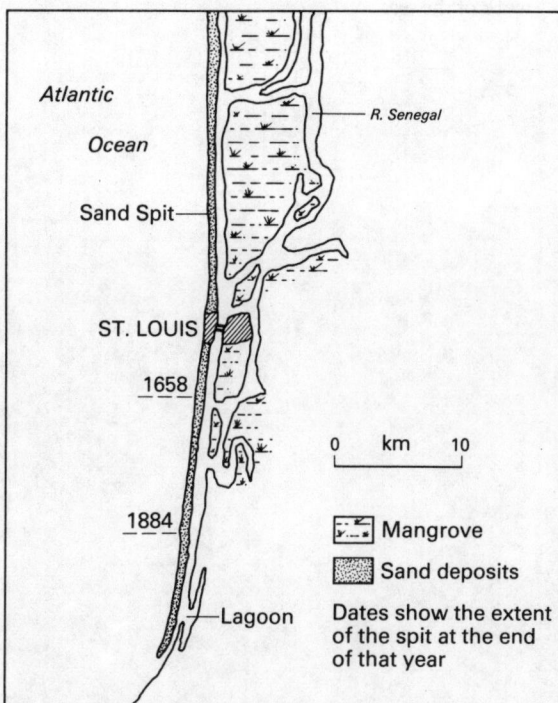

2.8 The West African coast in the region of Senegal estuary.

The importance of relief

It is important to learn about the relief of West Africa, not only to know what it is like, but also because it has a remarkable influence on the other aspects of the geography of the region. For example, the high mountains and plateaus attract heavy rainfall and keep the areas on the lee side comparatively dry. Minerals are generally, though not invariably, associated with the highlands. Sedimentary rock minerals like petroleum are also found in the basins of sedimentation. Remote, mountainous districts are often sparsely populated, though, like the Jos and Adamawa plateaus of Nigeria, they can form a place of refuge for oppressed groups of people. Rugged relief is a hindrance to communication, but its features often attract tourists.

The nature of the West African coastline is even more significant because of its influence in the location of ports. Rias form excellent natural harbours because they have sheltered inlets. The natural harbour of Freetown is the best example in West Africa. Lagoon coasts can form good harbours, as at Abidjan and Lagos, for the same reason, but it is often necessary to cut the sand-bars and dredge the lagoons to allow big ships in. On the other hand, the low cliff coastlines of Liberia and Ghana required strong breakwaters before the artificial harbours of Monrovia, Takoradi and Tema could be built there. The smooth sandy coast north of Dakar is even more difficult. St Louis harbour has been silted up almost completely by continued sand deposition, and it cost Mauritania a lot of money before it could build a badly needed new port out of the sandy wastes near Nouakchott.

Summary

We began this chapter by studying the possible origin of West Africa and the nature of its rocks, and dwelt in more detail on the relief of the region with particular reference to the coastline. We finished with an account of the influence of the relief on other features of the geography of West Africa since this is one of the reasons for studying the relief. Now try your hand at the questions that follow.

Revision exercises

1. Describe the theories of continental drift and plate tectonics. How do these help us to understand the origin of West Africa?
2. Divide the mainland of West Africa into its principal relief regions. Comment on the features of each, showing how these are related to the rocks found in the area.
3. Comment on the nature of the West African coastline. How does this nature influence shipping and the development of ports?
4. Illustrating your answer with examples from West Africa and with the aid of diagrams, write an explanatory account of coastal landforms produced by the work of the sea.

3 Weather and climate

Preparation

1. Copy the monthly figures of temperature, rainfall and wind direction recorded over a period of one year in your school or in an approved weather station near your school. Draw graphs, like those in Figure 3.8 to show these temperature and rainfall distributions.
2. Calculate the annual range of temperature and the total rainfall for that year.
3. During which months do the wet and dry seasons occur?
4. Name the prevailing winds during these seasons and state their directions.

Weather is the word used to describe the day to day changes in the conditions of the atmosphere. Climate refers to the average weather conditions of an area over a long period.

The chief elements of weather and climate are temperature, winds and rainfall, but pressure, humidity and cloud cover are also important. These elements vary from place to place and also at different times of the year.

You know that the sun shines directly over the Equator in March during its apparent passage northwards. (The earth, of course, moves round the sun, but to us it seems as if it is the sun which is moving.) It reaches the Tropic of Cancer in June, then turns round on its apparent journey southwards until it passes the Equator again in September and performs another turn in December over the Tropic of Capricorn. This movement determines the broad pattern of the weather and climate of West Africa. A number of local factors however, such as relief, the distribution of land and sea and ocean currents, combine to add some variations to the climate.

We shall therefore discuss the broad pattern of the climate, noting and accounting for the seasonal changes and local variations as we go along, and finish with a study of the climatic regions of West Africa.

The pattern of climate

The climatic year is normally divided into two – the period when the sun is in the northern hemisphere and the period when it is in the southern hemisphere. In temperate lands, where this movement causes wide variations in temperature, the terms 'summer' and 'winter' are used to describe these seasons. But in a tropical land, like West Africa, the changes are reflected more in the rainfall than in the temperature. Hence we use the terms 'wet season' and 'dry season' to describe the two periods. The wet season lasts from April to September with a peak in June and July, and the dry season lasts from October to March with December and January being the driest months. Each of these seasons has a set of climatic conditions associated with it.

The wet season climate

Figures 3.1 and 3.2 describe the temperature, pressure and winds at the height of the wet season in West Africa. As the sun moves northwards from the Equator to the Tropic of Cancer it passes over successive latitudes of the West African region. This is when West Africa has its highest temperatures because the sun is overhead at noon at that time. The hottest months are March and April for places in the south like Abidjan and Accra where the sun passes over first, and May and June for places in the north like Agades and Ouagadougou where the sun arrives much later. The sun arrives at the Tropic of Cancer in June, but its full effect is not felt until July. Temperatures are highest in the northern landmass where an average of over 30°C is recorded, whereas in the south the moderating influence of the sea keeps the average temperature as low as below 25°C (Figure 3.1).

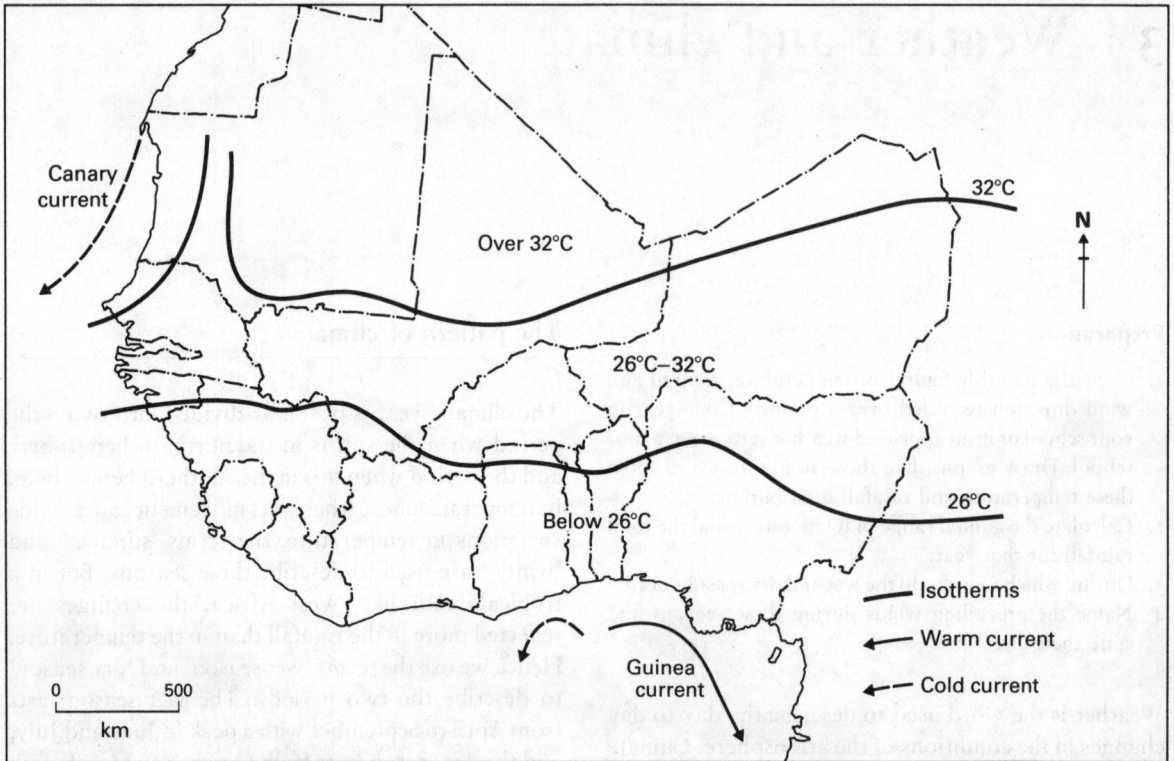

3.1 July temperature conditions in West Africa.

Table 1

Seasonal distribution of rainfall for selected stations

Station	Latitude	April–September		October–March	
		Amount (in mm)	% of Annual	Amount (in mm)	% of Annual
Agades	17°N	157.5	100	0.0	0
Ouagadougou	12°N	825	95	40	5
Conakry	10°N	3 715	88	515	12
Abidjan	5°N	1 300	67.5	627.5	32.5

The temperature distribution is reflected in the pressure. The high temperatures in the Sahara are the principal cause of the belt of low pressure which prevails over it, whereas in the south we have high pressure over the Atlantic, as shown in Figure 3.2.

This pressure distribution in turn has its effect on the winds experienced in West Africa during this season. An air mass – the *tropical maritime air mass* – is progressively drawn in from the south-west to the low pressure area as the sun moves northwards. In mid-July it prevails all over the region and it becomes the dominant factor which determines the weather and climate of West Africa during this season.

This tropical maritime air mass carries a lot of moisture from over the Atlantic Ocean and on arriving in West Africa increases the moisture content or *humidity* of the air, and therefore its cloud cover. Relative humidities can remain at over 90% for many days. Clothes fail to dry quickly and everywhere the atmosphere is wet and muggy. This moisture condenses on being forced to rise either by convection or over a barrier of highlands or an air mass, and then falls back as rain.

It is therefore during this wet season that West Africa experiences its heaviest rainfall. In fact much of the rainfall shown in Figure 3.3 falls during this season, as Table 1 shows clearly. The moisture also tends to lower the temperatures by shielding the sun's rays away. That is why the temperatures in West Africa fall slightly with the onset of the rains.

The rainfall is not evenly distributed over the region. Most coastal areas, being nearer the sea,

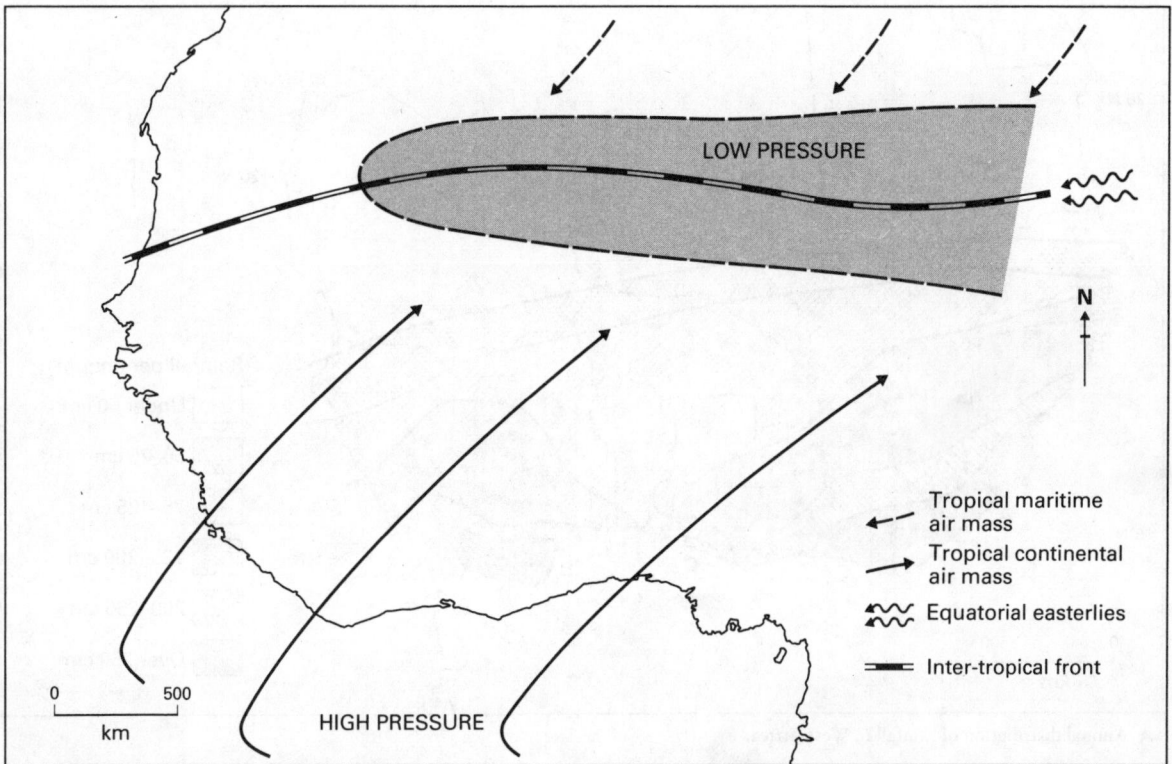

3.2 July pressure and air masses in West Africa.

receive heavier rainfall than the interior. Thus Abidjan registers 1 300 mm during this season, but Agades only 157.5 mm. The Sahara fringes are remarkably dry because they lie in the interior, and are also in the rain shadow of the highlands, and in the zone from which the winds blow away for most of the year.

The coasts of Guinea, Sierra Leone, Liberia, and the Niger delta run nearly at right angles to the wind direction. The first three areas are backed by the Futa Jalon and the Guinea Highlands. The last is washed by the warm Guinea current and is covered with swamps, both of which supply a great deal of water vapour to the air by evaporation. For these reasons these areas record the heaviest rainfall in West Africa.

On the other hand, notice how comparatively dry the coasts of Ghana and Togo and the coast north of Dakar are. The dryness of the former can be ascribed to four points; to the presence of a cool, upwelling current south of Accra, to the fact that the coast is parallel to the direction of the wind, to the rain-shadow effect caused by the coast west of Cape Three Points and to the low, flat Accra Plains. All these are

factors which give little incentive to rising air masses and they therefore reduce rainfall possibilities.

The coast north of Dakar is dry because winds generally blow off-shore there. When they do blow on-shore, as during the wet season, their surface layers, which are in immediate contact with the cold Canary current, are cooled and so become heavy; this makes the air mass stable and therefore less likely to give rise to rainfall since convectional currents do not have the chance to develop.

The length of the wet season varies over West Africa. Study Figure 3.4. How many months does the season last in the south, and how many does it last in the north? Why is it so? In the heart of the Sahara, the wet season is virtually unknown.

We have described the rainfall pattern during this season at some length because it is of such importance to the geography of West Africa. Before we leave it, therefore, we must state the reasons for its importance.

1. The arrival of the rain brings welcome relief from the great heat of March and April. This can be seen clearly in Figure 3.8 where the temperature

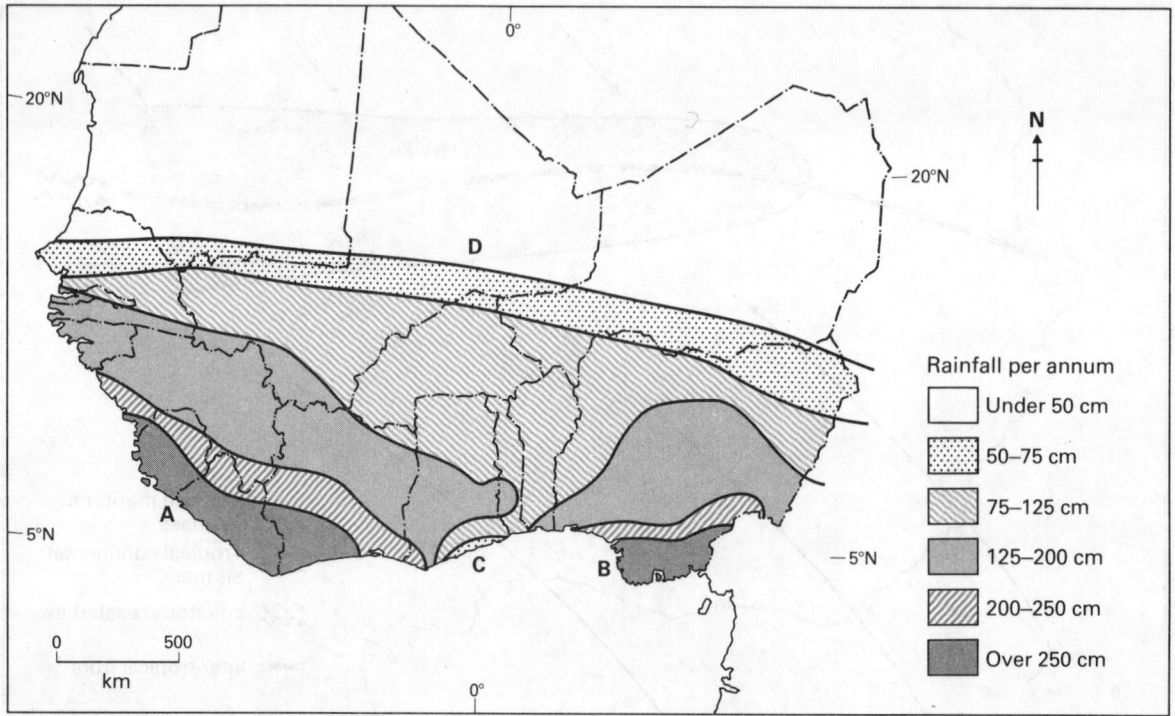

3.3 Annual distribution of rainfall in West Africa.

Rainfall per annum

☐ Under 50 cm
▫ 50–75 cm
▨ 75–125 cm
▦ 125–200 cm
▧ 200–250 cm
■ Over 250 cm

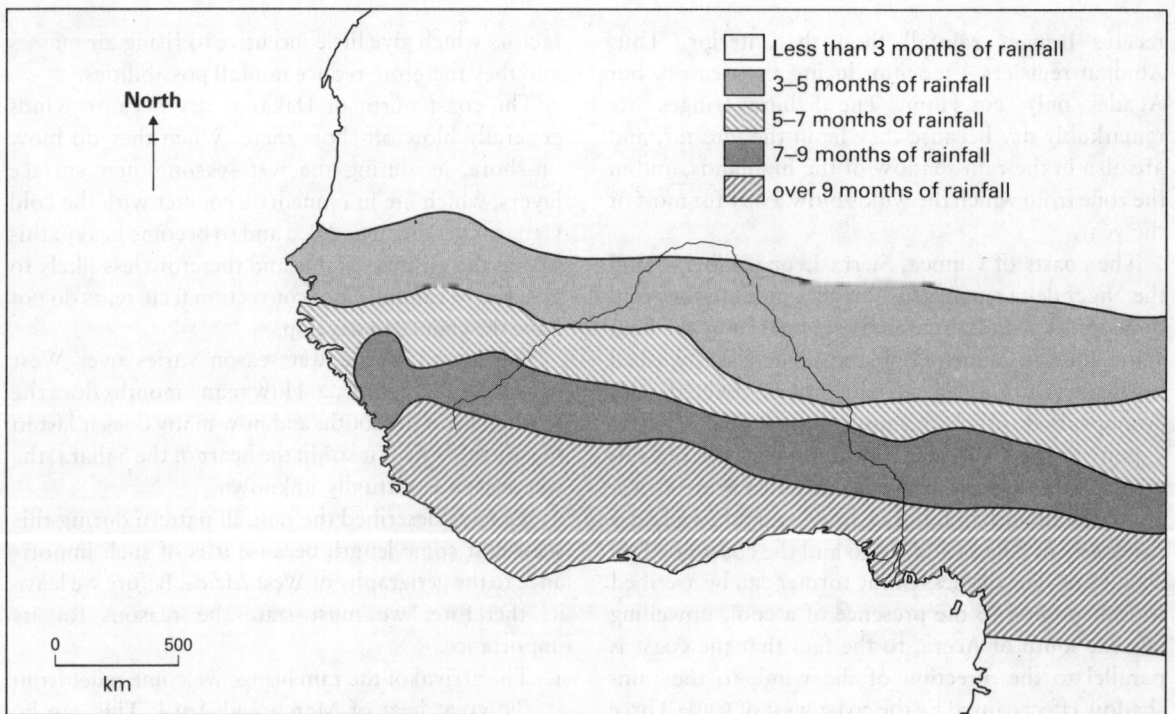

Less than 3 months of rainfall
3–5 months of rainfall
5–7 months of rainfall
7–9 months of rainfall
over 9 months of rainfall

3.4 The length of the wet season in West Africa.

graphs for all the stations fall as the rainfall increases.

2. The nature of a season or a climatic region is determined by the amount of rain that falls, and we use both the amount of rainfall and the length of the rainy season to demarcate climatic regions in West Africa.

3. Its uneven distribution causes variations in the density and appearance of the plant cover from place to place and at different times of the year. The vegetational belts of West Africa run generally east to west and plant cover decreases in density from south to north in sympathy with the trend and decreasing intensity of rainfall. A comparison of Figures 3.3 and 5.1 will show this.

4. Rainfall helps to form soil by causing the rocks to disintegrate and the vegetation to rot. But sadly enough it also destroys soil through erosion and leaching.

5. It has an important relevance in agriculture, for it influences the growing seasons, the types of crops grown and the farm routine that is practised.

The dry season climate

We have seen that West Africa has its highest temperatures when the sun passes over it between March and June. It crosses the latitudes of West Africa once more between June and September on its way southwards, but its effect on temperatures this time is diminished by the rainfall and cloud cover.

The dry season really sets in about October and lasts till about April of the following year. Temperatures then are low, because the sun is in the southern hemisphere. There is a complete reversal in the distribution of temperatures over West Africa, for it is now cooler in the north (below 20°C) than in the south (over 25°C), as shown in Figure 3.5. Notice carefully the cooling effect of the Canary current on the temperatures of the coast north of Cape Verde. In this season also, the atmosphere is dry and the nights are longer. Clouds are virtually absent, so heat is lost rapidly by radiation during the nights; hence nights are usually cool.

The pressure system also reverses, for there is now

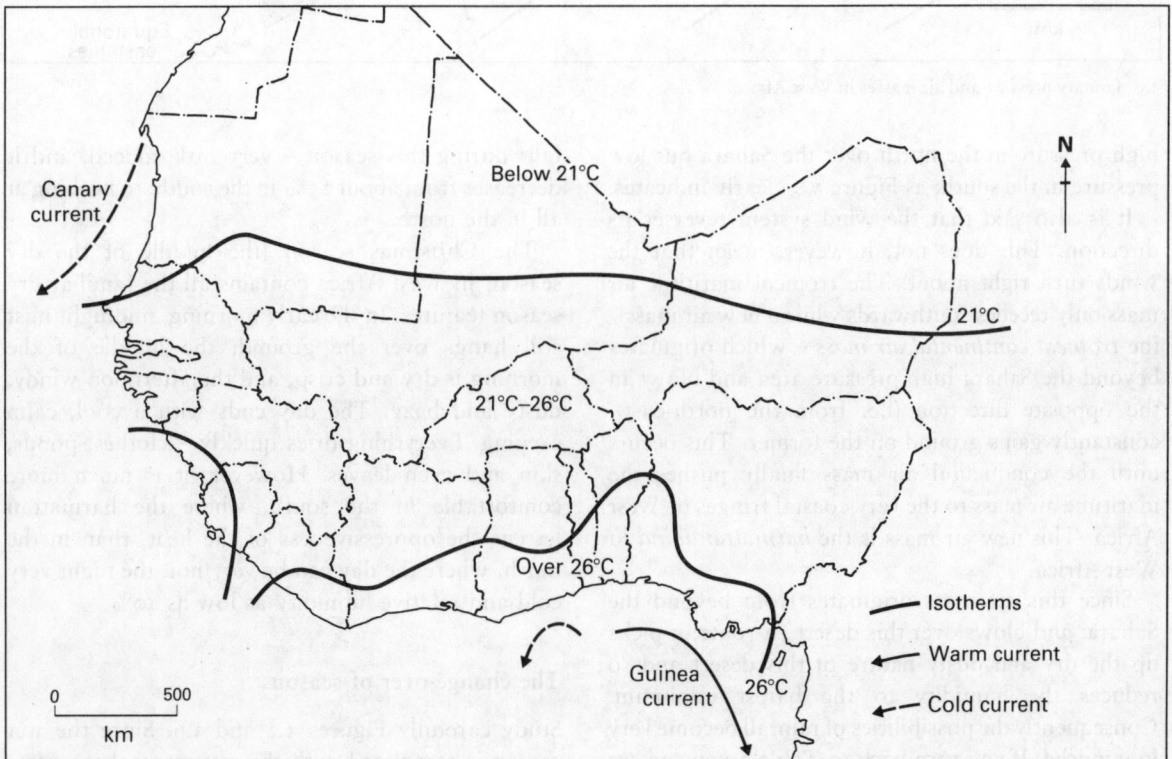

3.5 January temperature conditions in West Africa.

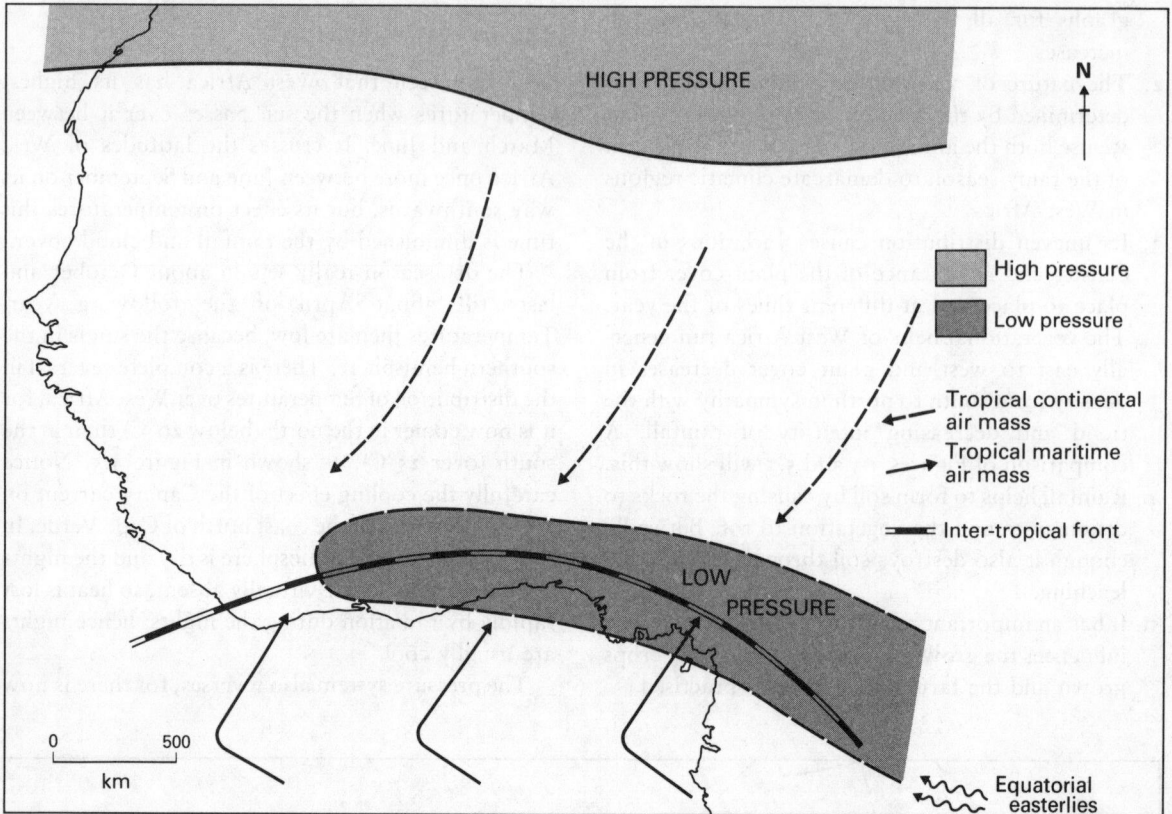

3.6 January pressure and air masses in West Africa.

high pressure in the north over the Sahara but low pressure in the south, as Figure 3.6 clearly indicates.

It is also said that the wind system reverses its direction. This does not, however, mean that the winds turn right about. The tropical maritime air mass only recedes southwards while a new air mass – the *tropical continental air mass* – which originates beyond the Sahara high pressure area and blows in the opposite direction (i.e. from the north-east), constantly gains ground on the former. This occurs until the continental air mass finally pushes the maritime air mass to the very coastal fringes of West Africa. This new air mass is the *harmattan wind* in West Africa.

Since this air mass originates from beyond the Sahara, and blows over this desert en-route, it picks up the dry and dusty nature of this desert and so reduces the humidity to the barest minimum. Consequently the possibilities of rainfall become very low indeed. If you turn back to Table 1 you can see clearly how much of the rain recorded in Figure 3.3

falls during this season – very little indeed, and it decreases from about 25% in the south, to nothing at all in the north.

The Christmas season (the middle of the dry season) in West Africa contains all the familiar dry season features. In the early morning, midnight mist still hangs over the ground; the middle of the morning is dry and crisp, and the afternoon windy, dusty and hazy. The day ends with a cool, calm evening. Everything dries quickly – clothes, ponds, skin and even leaves. However, it is much more comfortable in the south, where the harmattan lessens the oppressiveness of the heat, than in the north, where the day can be very hot, the night very cold and relative humidity as low as 10%.

The change-over of seasons

Study carefully Figures 3.2 and 3.6. Since the wet season is associated with the wet tropical maritime air mass and the dry season with the tropical continental air mass, the change-over of seasons occurs when one air mass is giving way to the other. This happens at the boundary of these two air masses where they meet along a vertical or slanting plane called the *inter-tropical front*. This front, together with the weather conditions associated with it, moves northwards and southwards in response to the advance and retreat of the air masses.

But this is not the only thing that happens along this front. There is a cool easterly air mass giving the *equatorial easterlies* which blow in the upper atmosphere over the front. This air mass generally stays above the others, but it sometimes dives down and undercuts either the tropical maritime or tropical continental air mass, forcing the other up very violently. When the maritime air mass is the victim of this under-cut, as in Figure 3.7, rapid upward moving air currents are formed, the moisture in them suddenly condenses and sets free electricity charges in the atmosphere. These give rise to a combination of thunder, lightning, strong winds and a brief but torrential downpour of rain. We call this a *line squall*. This is why we have heavy but brief thunderstorms at the beginning and the end of the rainy season.

When it is the dry continental air mass that is undercut, however, the result is a whirlwind which blows spirally upwards carrying paper, dry leaves and dust with it. We refer to this wind as a *dust devil*. Dust devils occur most regularly in the early harmattan season.

Now before we go on to the climatic regions, see how much of what we have learnt of the pattern of climate you can remember:

1. During which months is the wet season in West Africa?
2. Which are the dominant air masses in the wet season, dry season and change-over of seasons in West Africa? Where do they come from?
3. What type of weather does each of the air masses bring to the region?
4. Why is the wet season in West Africa longer in the south than in the north?
5. What time of the year is shown in Figure 3.2? Describe the temperature, pressure, winds, humidity and rainfall during this season.
6. Describe how a line squall occurs. How does it differ from a dust devil?

Climatic regions

A climatic region is an area over which the climate follows more or less the same pattern throughout the year. The graphs in Figure 3.8 help us to divide West Africa into climatic regions.

There is one important feature in figure which deserves our attention and which will help us in the study of climatic regions. You will notice that stations like Abidjan, Ibadan and Accra have

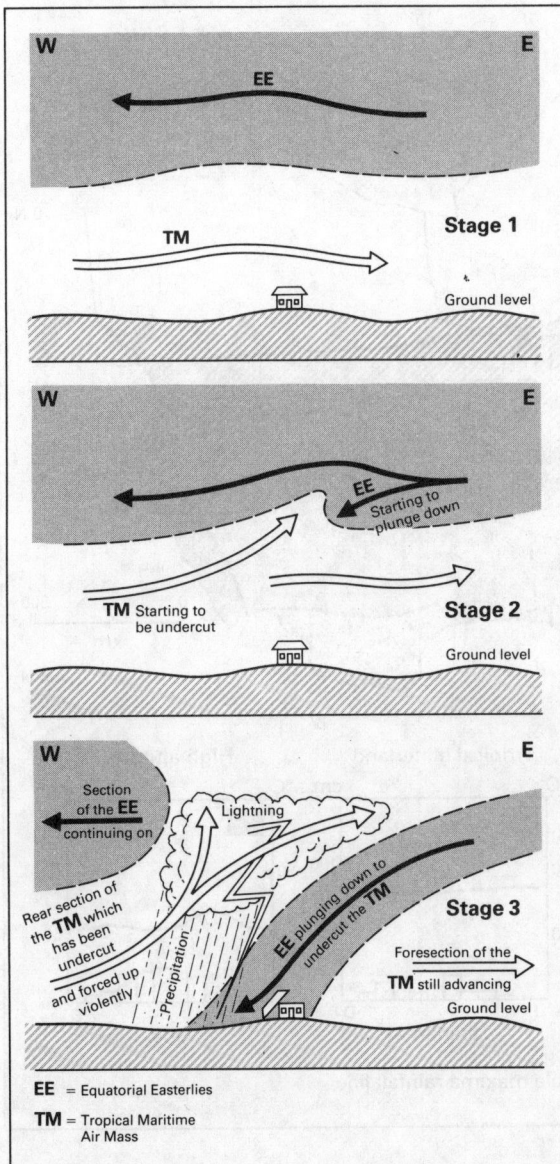

3.7 The formation of line squalls over West Africa.

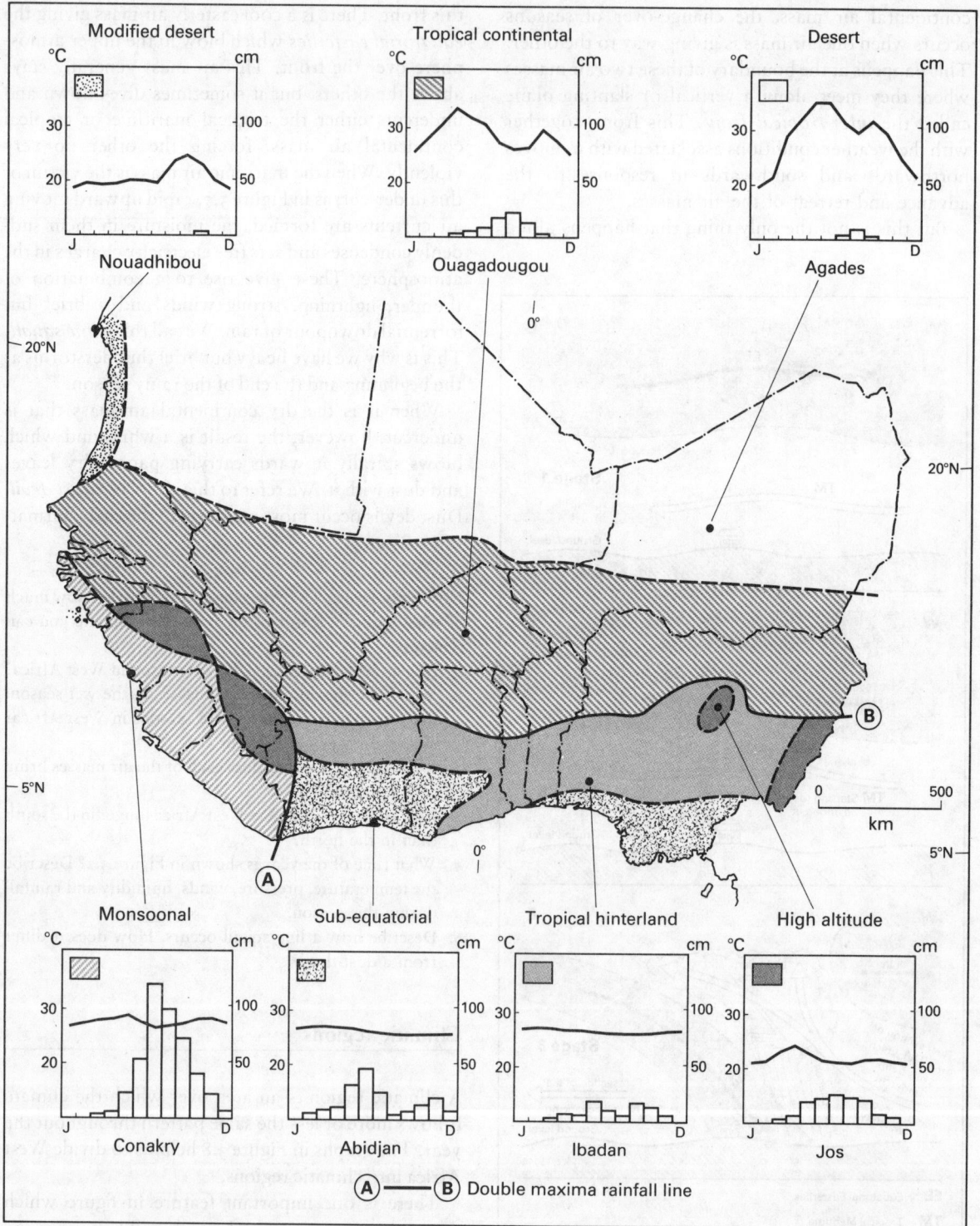

3.8 Climatic data and types for selected stations in West Africa.

maximum rainfall twice in the year – once in June and July and the other about September and October, while the others have it only once in July and August. This is also shown in the rainfall graphs in Figure 3.8. Can we find an explanation for this?

The belt of heavy rainfall follows the sun but lags a little behind it. The sun passes over the latitudes of Abidjan, Ibadan and Accra on its way northwards and takes a long time to come back to them again, since they are far away from the turning point at the Tropic of Cancer. For this reason the two periods of heavy rain associated with the overhead sun are far apart and very distinct in these places. Between these times, during the period normally referred to as the *August break*, the southwest winds sweep right across the southern latitudes with little incentive to rise by convection.

In places further north, and nearer the Tropic of Cancer however, the sun returns no sooner than it leaves, bringing with it again the belt of heavy rainfall. As a result, the two periods of maximum rainfall come so close together that they merge into one continuous period of heavy rainfall. The places in the south are said to have *double maxima rainfall* while those in the north have *single maximum rainfall*. The critical line which divides them is known as the *double maxima rainfall line*. This is shown clearly as AB in Figure 3.8.

Let us now see how this line, among other features, helps us to distinguish the climatic regions of West Africa. Study Figure 3.8.

South of the line there are two principal climatic regions, both with double maxima rainfall. These are:

1. The *sub-equatorial region*, typified by Abidjan. Here the temperatures and humidities are high, the annual range of temperature is low and sea breezes are prominent along the coastal margins. Rain falls nearly all the year round with a high annual total over 1500 mm.

2. The *tropical hinterland*, with the same temperature and rainfall pattern but lower humidities, since it is further inland. It has less rainfall – 1000 mm to 1500 mm per annum, and some 8 months of wet season and 4 months of dry season. (Compare the graphs of Ibadan and Abidjan.)

North of the double maxima rainfall line there are four main regions:

3. The *monsoon region* of Liberia, Sierra Leone and Guinea. This has a similar temperature pattern, with a low annual range, as the first two regions, but the rainfall is characteristically heavy with a single peak. It has a short spell of 2–3 months of dry season from about December to February. See the figures and graphs for Conakry.

4. The *tropical continental region*, situated in the heart of West Africa. This region has moderately high ranges of temperature (8°C) for Ouagadougou, restricted rainfall (250 mm to 1000 mm per annum) with clear single maximum. The dry season here varies from 4–9 months. Name one country which lies wholly within this region in Figure 3.8, and parts of other countries which lie in the region.

5. *The desert region* has extremes of annual and daily temperatures and perennial aridity. The figures and graphs for Agades testify to this. Rainfall here is less than 250 mm per annum.

6. *The modified desert region* lies along the coast of Mauritania. It is desert, since it is characterised by aridity, but modified because the cool Canary currents of the Atlantic Ocean wash the coast and keep the temperatures low, as is clearly indicated in the graph for Nouadhibou. (Compare it with the graph for Agades.) Since there is a tendency to 'winter' rainfall the region is sometimes said to have a modified Mediterranean type of climate.

Finally, we must mention:

7. *The high altitude regions* of Futa Jalon, Guinea, Jos and Adamawa. Temperatures here are low and fairly equable because of the altitude, and the rainfall is high, over 250 mm higher than the surrounding area. The rainfall is largely of the relief type with variable maxima (that is, some years have double or multiple, other years single).

Summary

We dealt with the two major seasons in West Africa – the wet and the dry. The former corresponds roughly with the time the sun is in the northern hemisphere and the latter with when it is in the southern. Each of these seasons has its characteristic temperature, pressure, wind system, humidity and rainfall, the last of which is the most vital element. The change-over from one season to the other is marked by line squalls and dust devils. The three air masses which are associated with these seasons are dominant factors in the climate of West Africa.

Changes in rainfall and temperature ranges over West Africa help us to distinguish seven climatic types. Each has a pattern of climate which distinguishes it from that of the adjacent regions. Two have double maxima rainfall, four single maximum and one – the montane type – variable maxima rainfall.

Revision exercises

1. Explain how *three* of the following factors influence the climate of West Africa.
   (a) Ocean currents
   (b) Relief
   (c) Vegetation
   (d) Distance from the sea
   (e) Migration of the overhead sun.
   (*WASC 1975*) (For the purpose of this exercise explain how all the five factors influence the climate.)
2. Explain the following:
   (a) why vegetation belts in West Africa run generally east and west;
   (b) why rainfall along the south-east coast of Ghana and south-west Togo is generally low;
   (c) line squalls.
   (*WASC 1976 adapted*)
3. (a) What criteria would you use in dividing West Africa into climatic regions?
   (b) Draw a map of West Africa to show its main climatic regions.
   (c) Choose any two of these regions, trace and account for the weather and climatic changes experienced throughout the year.
   (*Teachers Grade II Cert. Exam. Enugu 1971*)
4. Explain any *four* of the following:
   (a) The 'intertropical zone of convergence' moves south in January and north in July;
   (b) The south-west coast of West Africa receives heavy rainfall;
   (c) The annual range of temperature in West Africa increases from south to north;
   (d) The relative humidity in West Africa increases from north to south;
   (e) Accra has an annual rainfall of 30″ (700 mm) while Jos has 56″ (1400 mm).
   (*WASC June, 1979*)
   (For the purpose of this exercise explain all five)

4 Water drainage and river systems

Preparation

1. Observe a stream or river in your locality immediately after a heavy storm. What is the name of the stream or river? See how the flood water is drained into it and then carried away. Is the water clean or muddy? Why is this?
2. How and why do the volume and appearance of the stream and river differ during the wet season, and the dry season?
3. What is the source of the supply of drinking water in your district? Do you sometimes suffer from a shortage of water? Can you say why?
4. Study Figure 2.5 again. Trace the principal rivers of West Africa. Which is the longest river? Which of them flow(s) through your own country?

The water you observed in your home area flows down the slope into the nearby stream. It finds its way into a river not very far away. It is then carried into one of the major West African rivers which finally empties it into one of the West African lakes or into the Atlantic Ocean. Some of the rain water seeps into the ground, becomes underground water and may find its way out through a spring and into a river. This is the way your home area is drained.

It is the way much of West Africa is also drained. Since rivers play the most vital rôle in this process, we shall consider the general characteristics of West African rivers and describe the specific features of the more important ones. To complete the picture, we shall end up with a review of their economic importance.

General characteristics of West African rivers

1. West African rivers are fed by flood and springs, and these depend on rainfall. It is obvious, therefore, that the volume of the rivers varies with the quantity of the supply of rain water. Thus, in the wet season the rivers swell in volume, whereas in the dry season they dwindle in size exposing pebbles and bare rocks in their beds. Some, particularly the small ones in the north, dry up almost completely, leaving nothing but shallow pools, sand, pebbles and rocks where in the wet season there was a voluminous river with raging torrents. Under these conditions, navigation on the rivers is obviously greatly impeded as boats cannot sail comfortably on fast flowing or shallow rivers.

2. There is yet another way in which the rivers of West Africa are affected by climatic factors. The high temperatures and humidity make the rocks weather easily. Flood water then sweeps the weathered materials down into the rivers. That is why they change appearance with the seasons. They look brown and muddy in the wet season when they are in flood, and carry a lot of weathered material, but relatively clean and almost sparkling in the dry season. Do you find that this is true of the river or stream in your area?

3. Some rivers in West Africa received more flood water and more tributaries; they flow faster and therefore are more powerful than others. Many of these cut into the valleys of the weaker ones and may 'behead' them. This process is called *river capture*. Look out for examples of these captures when we discuss the individual rivers.

4. West African rivers do not all flow smoothly. This is obvious because the surface and rocks over which they flow are not uniform. Their courses are interrupted by *gorges*, *rapids* and *waterfalls*, particularly where they cross mountain ranges and hard rocks. Their mouths are often choked with *deltas* and *sand bars* as we saw in Chapter 2. You know of the Niger and Volta deltas, and you have probably heard of the Bamako Rapids on the Niger and the Shiroro Gorge on the Kaduna River in Nigeria. If you are not sure of their locations,

look them up now in your atlas.

5. Some of the rivers never find their way to the sea. They flow into an inland lake, itself without a visible outlet to the sea. The Yobe, Hadejia and Yedseram which flow into Lake Chad are typical examples, and the basin they flow in is called a *basin of inland drainage*.

6. Because of the interruptions and the fluctuations in their volume, West African rivers have been said to be of limited use for navigation. Consequently, earlier writers seem to have underrated their economic value, which is indeed, considerable as we shall see below.

The major rivers

Of the rivers in West Africa, some are long like the Niger, the Volta and the Senegal, which rise from the interior highlands and flow into the sea. Others are short. They rise from the interior plateau, tumble over their edge and flow swiftly into the Atlantic Ocean. Then, as we saw above there are rivers of inland drainage.

The major West African river is the River Niger, which Mungo Park sailed down in 1895. Unfortunately, he could not travel the whole length of the river. He did not start from the source, nor could he go beyond the Bussa Rapids. Let us imagine, though, that we can travel from one end of the river to the other and explore for ourselves its characteristics.

The Niger flows through many countries in West Africa. It rises in the Guinea Highlands, collects its main headwaters, the Milo and Tinkisso, in Guinea, flows through the arid country of Mali, then southeastwards through the south-western end of Niger. It finally crosses Nigeria from north-west to south. In the last country it collects its main tributary, the Benue, and enters the Atlantic by a delta.

Its length of 4 160 kilometres (it is the longest river in West Africa and the third longest in Africa) is divided into five sections (see Figure 4.1).

1. The upper section above Sansanding is young and

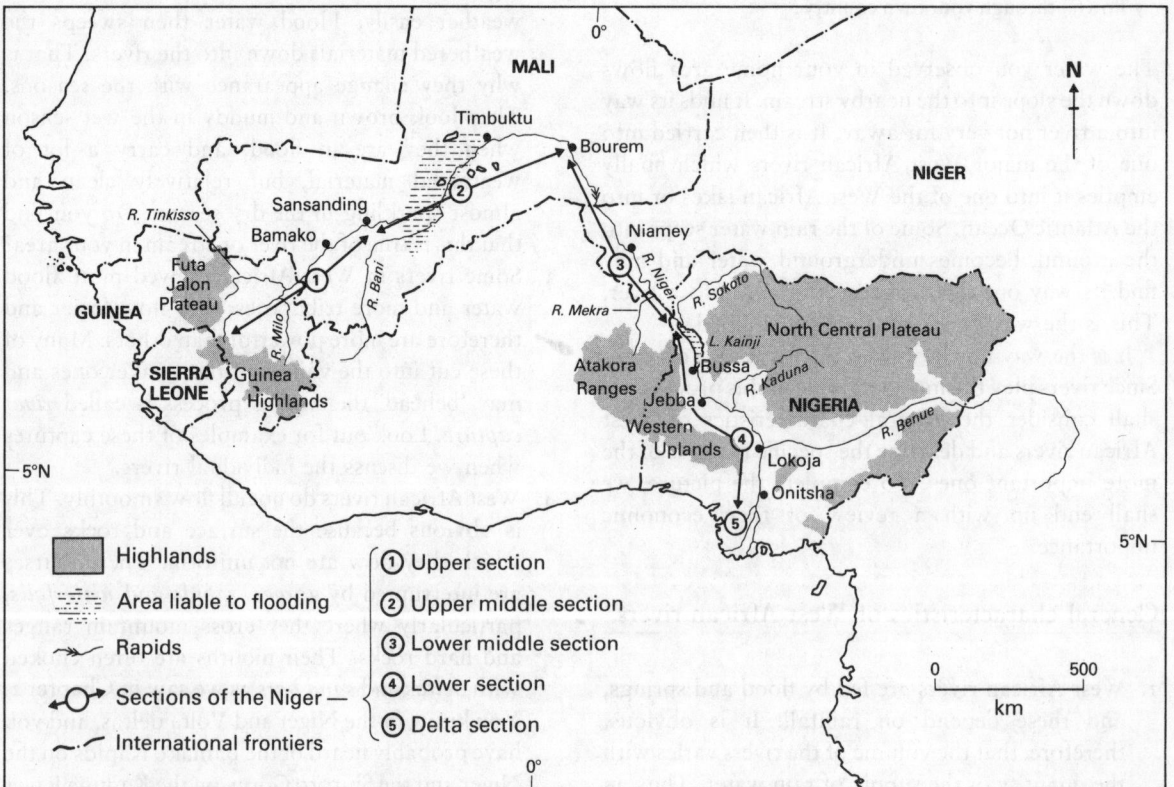

4.1   The course of the River Niger.

flows swiftly in parts. Its valley here is deep and 'V'-shaped.

2. The upper middle section flows sluggishly in a wide open valley and ends at the angular bend at Bourem, where it is probable that the lower section of the river captured the upper section (see Figure 4.2).

3. The lower middle section ends at the Nigerian frontier. It is young with many gorges, and it crosses the Atakora Ranges by many hair-pin bends. In these parts it is obviously not navigable.

4. The lower section includes the Kainji Lake below which are the Kainji Dam and power station. It ends at the apex of the delta. This section is voluminous, navigable and fed by many large tributaries including the Benue, Sokoto and Kaduna.

5. Finally, the river splits up into distributaries in the delta and enters the sea by many mouths.

The River Volta, with an overall length of 1 600 kilometres, is the second longest river in West Africa. It rises from the Sikasso Plateau of Upper Volta and flows through Ghana to the sea. It has many angular bends. Some of these mark probable elbows of capture as the one shown on Figure 4.3. It then flows through the 400 kilometre artificial Lake Volta (the largest artificial lake in Africa), over the dam at Akosombo and through a small delta to the sea. It is Ghana's chief river.

The third longest river in West Africa is the River Senegal. Like the Niger and the Volta, it is an international river, for it rises from the Futa Jalon Plateau in Guinea, flows northwards through Mali, then westwards through Senegal where it enters the sea by a shallow sand-choked estuary.

The River Gambia, like the Senegal, rises from the Futa Jalon Plateau. It flows across Senegal and then into the Gambia where it bends many times before it enters the sea by a wide, deep, drowned estuary called the Gambia River.

All these rivers drain into the open sea. The rivers of Lake Chad, however, are peculiar in that they drain into an inland lake – Lake Chad – which, as we saw above, has no visible outlet to the sea. Some of these rivers are the Hadejia, Yedseram, Logone and Shari. They are called rivers of inland drainage, and the lake is called a lake of inland drainage. Both the rivers and the lake are extremely shallow because:
(i) they are located on the edge of the Sahara where there is little rainfall but intense heat and therefore much evaporation;
(ii) sand is blown into them by the winds from the desert, and
(iii) the lake itself is known to be discharging water via an underground channel to an oasis deep in the heart of the Sahara.

The short rivers of West Africa include the Cross and Imo of Nigeria, the Pra and Tano of Ghana, and Sassandra of Ivory Coast, the Rokel of Sierra Leone and the Konkouré of Guinea. Look them up in your atlases and trace their courses.

The economic importance of the rivers

Our studies of the rivers of West Africa cannot be complete, even at this stage, without a mention of the ways in which they are of use to man. As well as their navigational uses, which as we have seen are limited by the terrain through which they flow, there are other ways in which they are of value to man.

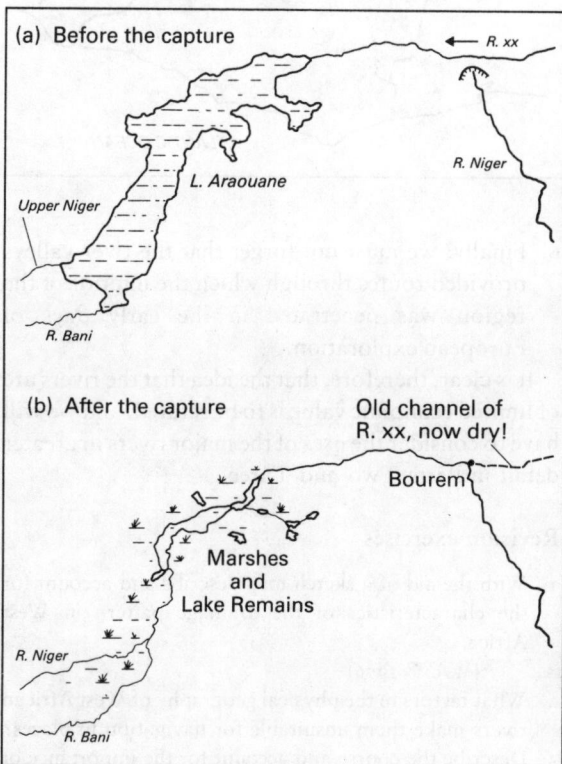

4.2 The Niger capture at Bourem.

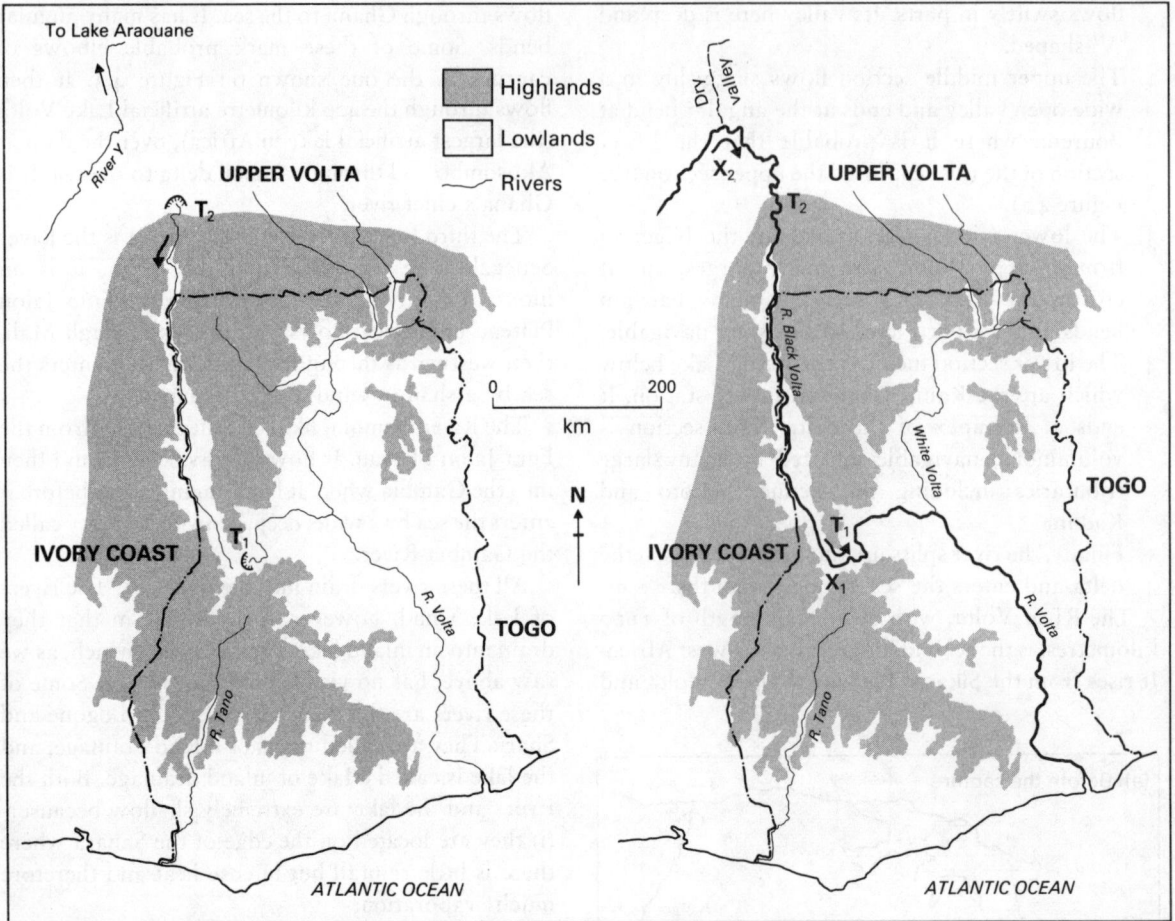

4.3 The captures of the River Volta.

1. They offer possibilities for the production of hydro-electricity. Already the Niger has been dammed at Kainji, the Volta at Akosombo and others elsewhere for this purpose (see Chapter 23).

2. The dry areas of the region can be irrigated with waters from these rivers (see Chapter 20).

3. They provide drinking water for man and his livestock – so important in the arid lands of West Africa.

4. Fresh water fish are caught from them and are used as food and as a trading commodity.

5. They form the nuclei for the integrated development activities of the many river basin development authorities in West Africa, e.g. the Senegal, mid-Niger, Cross River and Chad Basin Development Authorities. The activities of these authorities will be described in detail in Parts Two and Three of this book.

6. Finally, we must not forget that the river valleys provided routes through which the interior of the region was penetrated in the early days of European exploration.

It is clear, therefore, that the idea that the rivers are of limited economic value is to be refuted, and we will have to consider the uses of the major rivers in greater detail in Parts Two and Three.

Revision exercises

1. With the aid of a sketch map describe and account for the characteristics of the drainage pattern in West Africa.

   (*WASC 1976*)

2. What factors in the physical geography of West African rivers make them unsuitable for navigation in places?

3. Describe the course and account for the importance of any one major river of West Africa.

5 Vegetation and plant species

Preparation

1. Make a list of the local, English or French names of five or more plants which grow in your area. Do any of them change appearance at different times of the year? If they do, in what ways do they change, and why?
2. Study once more Figure 3.3 which shows the annual distribution of rainfall. What similarities do you notice between this figure and Figure 5.1 in this chapter?
3. Prepare an outline map of West Africa. Insert the boundaries of your own country, and locate your own town or village in it. Locate one other country in the heart of the region.

The word, vegetation, is used to describe the trees and grasses which grow on the earth. Over West Africa, vegetation changes from place to place and also at different times of the year. In this chapter we shall find out how and why these changes take place, and examine how man has made use of the vegetation cover to satisfy his economic needs.

To observe the changes properly we must travel across West Africa from south to north, and stay in each vegetational region for at least the twelve months of the year. It would take us some seven years to cover all the vegetational belts. Let us however,

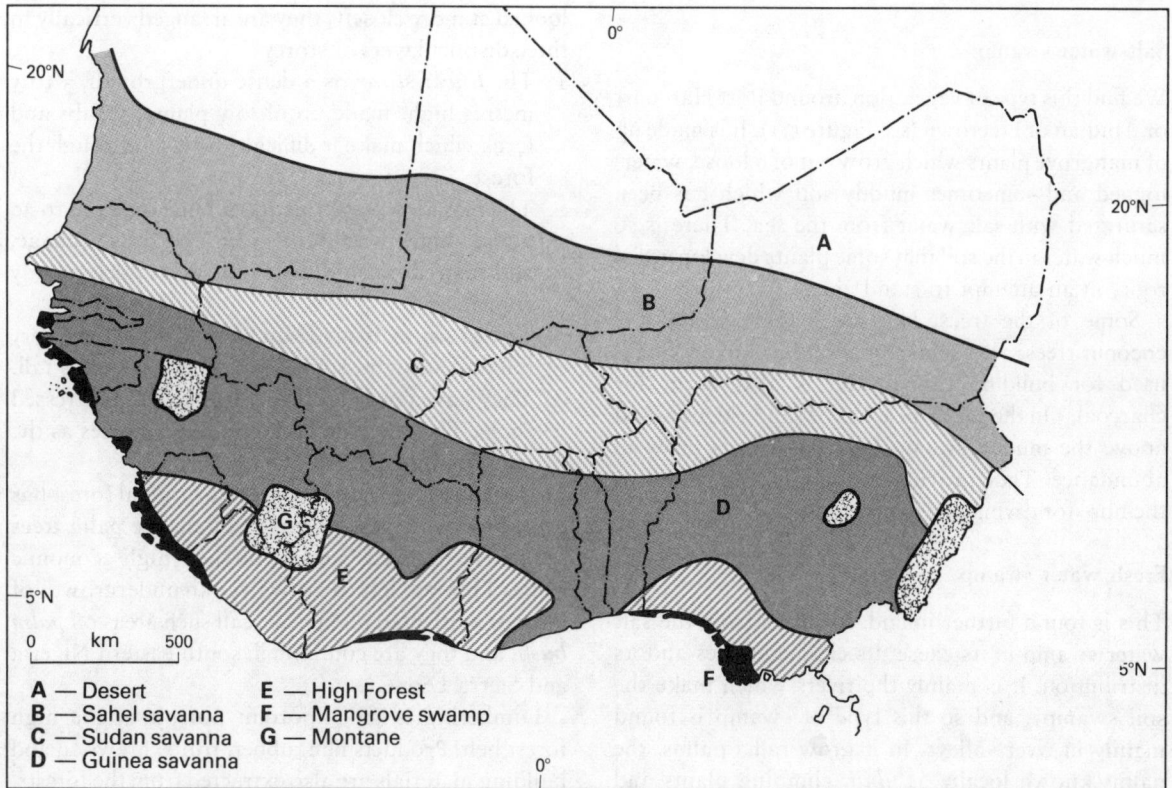

A — Desert
B — Sahel savanna
C — Sudan savanna
D — Guinea savanna
E — High Forest
F — Mangrove swamp
G — Montane

5.1 Vegetational cover of West Africa.

imagine that we can do this within 30 minutes. What do we discover?

We find that the vegetation changes very broadly from forest and swamps in the south, to grassland or savannas in the heart of the region, and finally to desert in the extreme north and montane vegetation on the high plateaus.

We do not, however, notice exactly where the changes take place because they are very gradual, and distinct boundaries do not generally exist. But we can observe general differences in the characteristics of each region as we will now describe.

Forests and swamps

These are found in the southern parts of West Africa, in the areas with sub-equatorial and monsoon types of climate (see Chapter 3). The soils here are generally wet, deep and loamy and have plenty of rotten organic matter, so luxuriant vegetation grows. They comprise the salt and fresh water swamps and the high forest.

Salt water swamp

We find this type of vegetation around Port Harcourt or Abidjan or Freetown (see Figure 5.1). It is made up of mangrove plants which grow out of a loose, water-logged and sometimes muddy soil which has been saturated with salt water from the sea. There is so much water in the soil that some plants develop aerial roots in an attempt to stand above the water.

Some of the trees, like the mangrove and the coconut trees, are useful to man. Mangrove wood is used for building canoes and is also burnt for charcoal. On the sandy beaches or sand ridges raised above the muddy swamp lands, coconuts grow in abundance. They provide the nuts used for food or the fibre for drying and export as copra.

Fresh water swamp

This is found further inland. It differs from the salt water swamp in its cause, its characteristics and its distribution. It is mainly the rivers which make the soil swampy, and so this type of swamp is found mainly in river valleys. In it grow raffia palms, the palms known locally as *ubili*, climbing plants and fresh water ferns.

The raffia palm is tapped for a sweet wine called *tombo* or *ngwo*. Its leaves are used for roofing houses. The ubili is used for building because it has straight, tough and termite-proof trunks. The climbing plants are used for tie-ties, while the swamps themselves, particularly those along the Great Scarcies River in Sierra Leone and the Anambra and Cross rivers in Nigeria may form excellent rice fields.

The high forest

If we stop in a place near Benin in Nigeria, Tarkwa in southern Ghana, Agboville in southern Ivory Coast or in the interior of Liberia, we shall be right in the heart of the high forest. See, in Figure 5.1, how it is located in two blocks separated by the tongue of guinea savanna which comes down to the coast in south-eastern Ghana and southern Togo. Can you say why the two blocks are separated in this way? Compare this figure again with Figure 3.3.

Let us see what the vegetation is like. Many plant species, including parasites, climbers and creepers, can be found in any one area of the high forest. But looked at more closely, they are arranged vertically in three distinct layers or storeys.

1. The *lower storey* is a dense undergrowth, 3 to 5 metres high, made up of low plants, shrubs and ferns which make it difficult to travel through the forest.
2. The *middle storey* consists of huge trees, 20 to 30 metres high, with dark green and dense foliage, and many branches which grow on thick woody trunks.
3. The *top storey* is made up of trees which are very tall and straight, sometimes up to 60 metres tall. They have few leaves, grey trunks and buttressed roots. They include such economic species as the *walnut*, the *iroko* and the *obeche*.

There are many areas where the original forest has been cleared. In these areas, though, the palm trees are rarely touched because of their high economic value. They are left to grow over an undergrowth of ferns or cultivated plants. We call such areas *oil palm bush*, and they are common in south-eastern Nigeria and Sierra Leone.

Lumbering is an important pursuit in the high forest belt. Products like rubber, fruits, firewood and building materials are also extracted from the forests. The oil palm yields oil, kernels, palm wine and building materials. In addition, other tree crops like cocoa and coffee, and root crops such as cassava and yams grow well in the forest belt.

Grasslands or savannas

Our journey northwards brings us into the heart of the savanna country. Savanna is the name given to tropical grassland in Africa. The savanna lands correspond roughly with areas which have the tropical hinterland and continental types of climate because the light rainfall, low relative humidities, wide ranges of temperature and well pronounced dry season encourage the growth of grass. But some trees grow as well. In fact, centuries ago, many more trees grew there than can be seen now. But man and his animals have cleared much of the former vegetation so that the trees and grass that remain now are only survivals of the original plant cover.

See the extent of the grass-lands in Figure 5.1. What parts of which countries do they cover? You can see that if we stop in places such as near Kano (Nigeria) or Tamale (Ghana) or Ouagadougou (Upper Volta), or even north of Dakar which is very near the coast, and look around the countryside we shall be able to study at first hand the characteristics of this vegetation.

We shall find three types of savanna grassland – guinea, sudan and sahel.

Guinea savanna

This is found in a continuous belt which stretches from southern Senegal, covering nearly the whole of Guinea, through northern Ghana to central Nigeria. It is the broadest belt of vegetation in West Africa. It is sometimes called the *parkland savanna* or *savanna woodland* because, in addition to its very tall grasses, it contains trees like the oil bean, shea butter and locust bean trees.

5.2 Guinea savanna in the dry season. What suggests that this photograph was taken in the dry season? Would it be easy or difficult to build a road here? Why?

The vegetation changes with the seasons. In the wet season the grass and the leaves are fresh and green. But in the dry season they wither and die leaving only the trees which later lose their leaves through withering or bush fire.

Bush fires and drought are a great nuisance, but nature provides the plants with ways of resisting them, and of new growth even after they have been burnt or dried up. The tops of the grasses may be burnt, but the roots remain alive, so they sprout up again with the first drops of rain. Some trees have thick barks which restrict transpiration and protect them from bush fires; others develop long tap roots which help them reach the very low water table, even in the dry season.

The vegetation is however not uniformly thick in the guinea savanna region. Along the water courses where the soil is wet, denser and darker vegetation called *fringing forest* is found. In Gambia, the Casamance district of southern Senegal and in northern Guinea, rainfall is relatively heavy in the wet season. As a result the plant cover is denser than elsewhere in the guinea savanna land. The vegetation even develops two distinct layers – a lower layer, 4–6 metres high, and a canopy, 15–20 metres high. This variety of the guinea savanna is often referred to as the *Casamance woodland.*

On the other hand there are two areas where the vegetation is not as dense as normal. We mentioned the dry coastal belt of Accra when dealing with the climate (chapter 3). The soils here are thin and the vegetation has been burnt away over many centuries. Therefore it consists of very tough, short and prickly shrubs interspersed with innumerable ant hills. At the southern verge of the grassland the trees have been cut principally to clear the land for cultivation or for settlement. Here the grassland has become more open than immediately north of it, and is called *derived savanna.*

Sudan savanna

This lies to the north of the guinea savanna in a drier but parallel belt of land which stretches right across West Africa from central Senegal to northern Nigeria.

Since it is drier with an annual rainfall of less than 1 000 mm, shorter grasses grow there than in the guinea savanna region. But the grass is also kept short by the cattle, which graze in greater numbers in this belt than in any other in West Africa.

Some trees also grow in this region. These include the dum palm, the silk cotton tree and the famous baobab tree which stores water in its trunk. Fringing forests are also found here, and the grass in western Senegal is more luxuriant because this area is more humid.

Sahel savanna

This is the northern belt of savanna, found in areas where the rainfall is less than 500 mm per annum, and the dry season is at least ten months long. The belt borders on the desert region (see Figure 5.1) and so no trees grow there except isolated stands of thorny shrubs like the acacia, and a few gum arabic trees and date palms. Elsewhere we find short, miserable looking grasses, generally less than one metre high, scattered widely over the sandy or rocky plain. The area is so open that a Land Rover or a reasonably strong car can drive through the countryside from village to village without any need for roads!

Looking at these three types of grasslands as a group, we see that they are all useful to man, though the last is the least so. Crops like millet, maize, guinea corn, cotton and groundnuts grow best in the savannas. Over 90% of the cattle in West Africa are reared here. Tree crops like the shea butter and kapok are grown in these areas, while gum arabic and dates are collected from those areas of the sahel savanna region where these trees occur. Where irrigated, large quantities of cotton and rice are grown, and the open savannas formed the homes of large mediaeval empires in West Africa as we saw in Chapter 1.

Montane vegetation and desert

If we are well equipped with strong boots, good protective clothing, a strong vehicle and an adequate supply of drinking water, we will then be able to travel into the desert or climb some of the mountains to see what the vegetation is like in these remote places.

Montane vegetation

Scarcely any mountain in West Africa is high enough

to reproduce the whole range of montane vegetation. Yet in the highlands of Guinea and the mountains of Fernando Po, we find rain forest on the lower slopes, mist forest between 1000 metres and 2000 metres, and thin temperate forest and grass beyond this level. On the plateaus of Futa Jalon and Jos and in north eastern Nigeria, the vegetation cover changes from guinea savanna at the foothills to poor savanna with herbs and sedges above. In either case the gradation is due to the fact that with increasing altitude, exposure increases, the temperature falls and the soil becomes thinner.

The desert

This type of landscape is found in northern Mali, Niger and Mauritania. Much of the desert is sandy, except in those areas where rocks and pebbles are the dominant feature. Other exceptions are oases where underground water is so near the surface that trees can grow, and grains can be cultivated and livestock reared. Oases can sometimes even support small lakes.

The inhabitants of the desert are mainly Arabs, who cultivate and trade, and Tuaregs, who engage in caravan transportation. The deserts are also important for their mineral locations, for example, the iron ore deposits of Mauritania, and the tin and uranium of Niger Republic. Oil has also been traced in Niger.

Summary

The vegetation of West Africa grows progressively less dense from thick forests in the south through grasslands in the interior to the desert in the north. This is mainly the result of the corresponding decrease in rainfall, but factors like soil and altitude account for local variations from this broad pattern. The forest and grassland regions are economically the most important, the deserts and mountains the least, apart, of course, from certain mineral resources found in them.

Revision exercises

1. a) On the map of West Africa which you have prepared, insert and name the major vegetational belts.
   b) Describe in particular the nature and seasonal changes of the plant cover in the belt in which your home district is located.
2. a) With the aid of a sketch map locate the main areas of savanna in West Africa.
   b) Describe and account for the nature of the savanna areas marked in your sketch-map.
   c) Explain briefly how these savanna areas are utilised for farming.
   (*WASC/GCE November, 1972*)
3. With the aid of an annotated diagram, describe and account for the changes in climate and vegetation encountered on a north-south traverse through West Africa.
   (*London GCE January, 1974*)

PART TWO

West Africa – a country by country study

6 Nigeria (1)

Preparation

1. Build up a small album of Nigerian postage stamps, pictures and relevant newspaper and poster cuttings of Nigerian scenes. What can you learn from these of life in the country?
2. Trace two blank maps of Nigeria, inserting in each the courses of the Niger, Benue, Cross, Sokoto, Gongola, Kaduna and Hadejia Rivers.

You must have heard a great deal about Nigeria in current West African news. But do you know much about the geography of this country? The following three chapters will attempt to introduce you to it, and to provide you with the background for appreciating the current affairs of the country.

Nigeria has an area of 923 300 square kilometres. The 1973 census result was not accepted by the Government of the country, but in 1976 the population was estimated at 79.5 million. It may well be that by the next census the population will have grown beyond this figure. Compared with the other countries of West Africa, Nigeria is fourth in area, but has a population more than that of all of them put together.

Figure 6.1 shows the nineteen states of Nigeria as created in 1976, and their capitals. It also shows the new federal capital, Abuja.

Independent in 1960 after approximately 60 years of British rule, the country became a republic within the Commonwealth three years later. It came under military rule in 1966. Between July 1967 and January 1970 it passed through thirty dark months of civil war, which obviously retarded progress in many sectors. The military rule ended in 1979 when the government was once more handed back to the civilians under a new constitution where the country is ruled by an executive president, with a governor at the head of government in each of the states.

During this period, 1960 to 1979, the federal composition of the country underwent a number of changes. It started from a three region structure which it carried over from the pre-independence years, to a twelve-state structure created in May 1967. In February 1976 it was further divided into nineteen states. Lagos remained the federal capital until February 1979 when a more central location, Abuja, was officially declared the capital of Nigeria. Capital institutions have started to move to Abuja but it will not be until the early 1990's when all the capital offices and institutions will be completely transferred to the new capital. Figure 6.1 shows this latest political set-up.

The peoples and their settlement

The population census of 1963 recorded thirty-five language groups in Nigeria, each with a population of 116 000 or over. The most important are the Hausas, Yorubas, Igbos, Fulanis, Kanuris, Ibibios, Tivs and Ijaws, but there could very well be as many as one hundred or more lumped together under the heading 'Other Nigerians', who totalled over 3.6 million in that year.

The *Hausa* people are pure negroes who live in northern Nigeria. They are dark-skinned, tall and elegant in stature. They live a sedentary life, are famous groundnut and grain farmers, shrewd traders and clever craftsmen. Recently they have started to establish modern businesses and have shown remarkable success at it.

Their settlement patterns reflect the physical environment as well as their history. Thus in the past they built walled cities like Kano, Zaria and Katsina to protect themselves against the Fulani invaders who harassed them so much. Both the walls and roofs of their traditional city houses are made of baked clay, which keeps the interior relatively cool.

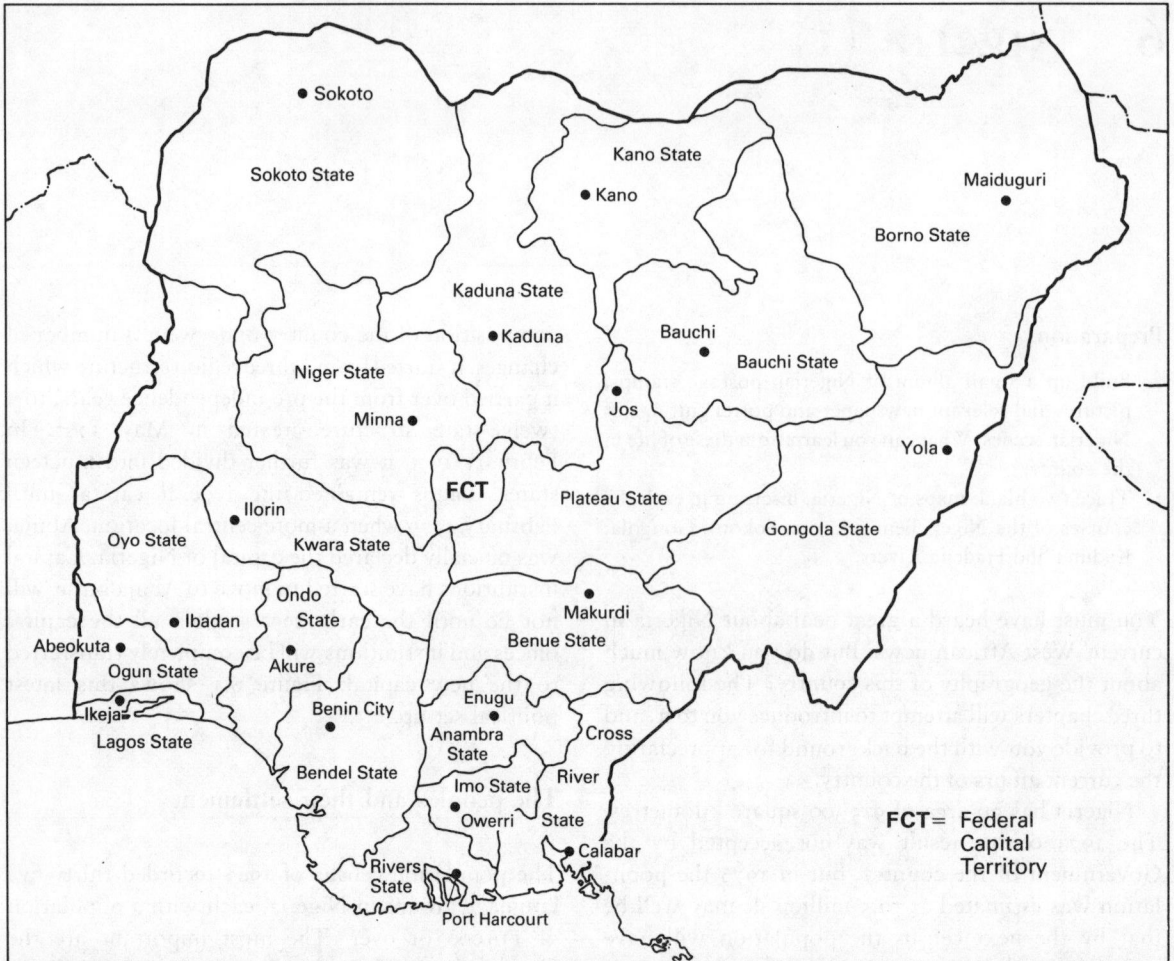

6.1 The states of Nigeria.

In the villages, clay is used for the walls, but thatch is used for the roofs, since the Hausas live in a grassland region. Here the settlements are either located at the bases of inselbergs, for defensive purposes (see Figure 6.2) or are on the plains, where they are fenced round with stones for the same reason.

The *Fulani* people are nomadic herdsmen who are believed to have come to Nigeria from the north as invaders at different periods from the 13th century to the 19th. Some are still nomadic. These are the 'cow' Fulani who still retain their tall, slim features and light complexion. Others, called the 'town' Fulani, have since learnt to live together and even inter-marry with their Hausa neighbours. They speak the Hausa language as well and it is now difficult to say who is a Hausa and who is a 'town' Fulani merely by looking at them. The 'town' Fulani, however, form the ruling and aristocratic class of the north in the tradition of their great warrior, Othman dan Fodio. Most emirs in northern Nigeria today belong to this class.

Their settlement types depend on whether they are the 'town' or the 'cow' Fulani. The former, as we have seen, live with the Hausa people, but the 'cow' Fulani live in temporary tents made of cow hides or grass – easy to set up and equally easy to dismantle. This is practical in view of the fact that they are nomadic pastoralists who are always on the move.

Living mostly in Borno State are the *Kanuri* people. They are also negroes, have a language of their own, but also speak the Hausa tongue and live very much like the Hausa people. Some, however, make their living by fishing on the shores of Lake Chad.

The major negro group in the Lagos and three

6.2 A village settlement in northern Nigeria. Describe the siting of the village. Why is it located at the valley between two hills? See the farmland. What crops would be growing there? Describe the vegetation and rocks around.

6.3 Ijaw housing type in the Delta region of Nigeria. Describe the houses, the mode of transport and the occupation of the people as you can see or deduce from the picture.

western states are the *Yoruba* people. They have a long tradition, mostly based on facts but sometimes on legends. They trace their ancestry to one Oduduwa who is believed to have led them from across Sudan to Ife. From here they spread to other parts of Yorubaland, and built cities and kingdoms ruled by influential chiefs called Obas.

Today the Yoruba people are good cocoa and root crop farmers, traders and craftsmen. They have responded well to western culture with which they were the first in Nigeria to come into close contact.

Many Yorubas lead an urban life. As many as 35–40% of them live in towns. They walled their traditional cities as the Hausas did, and for the same reason. But most of these walls have now collapsed because of the wetter conditions in the south. The mosque is the core of the Hausa city; with the Yorubas it is the *afin* or the chief's compound where they assemble for social occasions and for receiving directives from 'Obas'. They live in forest clearings.

The *Igbo* people live principally in Anambra, Imo and parts of the Rivers and Bendel States. They are negroes, renowned for their industry and resourcefulness. They did not, however, learn to build traditional cities or kingdoms as did their Yoruba counterparts. The village, therefore, is the traditional unit of settlement in Igboland.

They are good farmers and keen businessmen, and have readily absorbed western education and culture.

The dispersed type of village settlement is traditional among the Igbos. Each homestead is made up of houses arranged in an oblong fashion around a compound. At the gate or in the middle of a compound is a shrine for the gods. Traditional houses are built of local materials – clay for the walls, and mat or thatch for the roofs. Modern houses are, however, making successful inroads into the villages as a demonstration of increasing prosperity.

The *Ijaw* people live in the Rivers State and part of Bendel State. Because of the marshy delta conditions of their homeland, they build houses raised on piles to keep them above the flood water.

Since there are so many creeks where they live, fishing, net-making and boat building have become their main occupations. They have few roads, so travel, even to buy things from the market and visit friends, is by canoe. For the same reason traditional settlements are few and far between, usually by the sides of creeks so that they are easily accessible.

Of the other peoples of Nigeria we must mention the *Ibibio* and *Efik* peoples of the Cross River State, the *Nupe* and *Tiv* (or *Munshi*) peoples of Kwara and Benue State respectively, and the *Edo* and *Urhobo* peoples who, with some Ijaws, live in the southern part of the Bendel State. These and the many smaller groups, too numerous to list here, are the people who make up the estimated 79.5 million Nigerians.

Try these review exercises:
1. When did Nigeria become independent? How many States has the country and when were these States created?
2. Name the major language groups in Nigeria.
3. Describe the traditional settlements of the Hausas, Fulanis, Igbos, Yorubas and Ijaws. How are the settlement types related to the history and environment of the people?

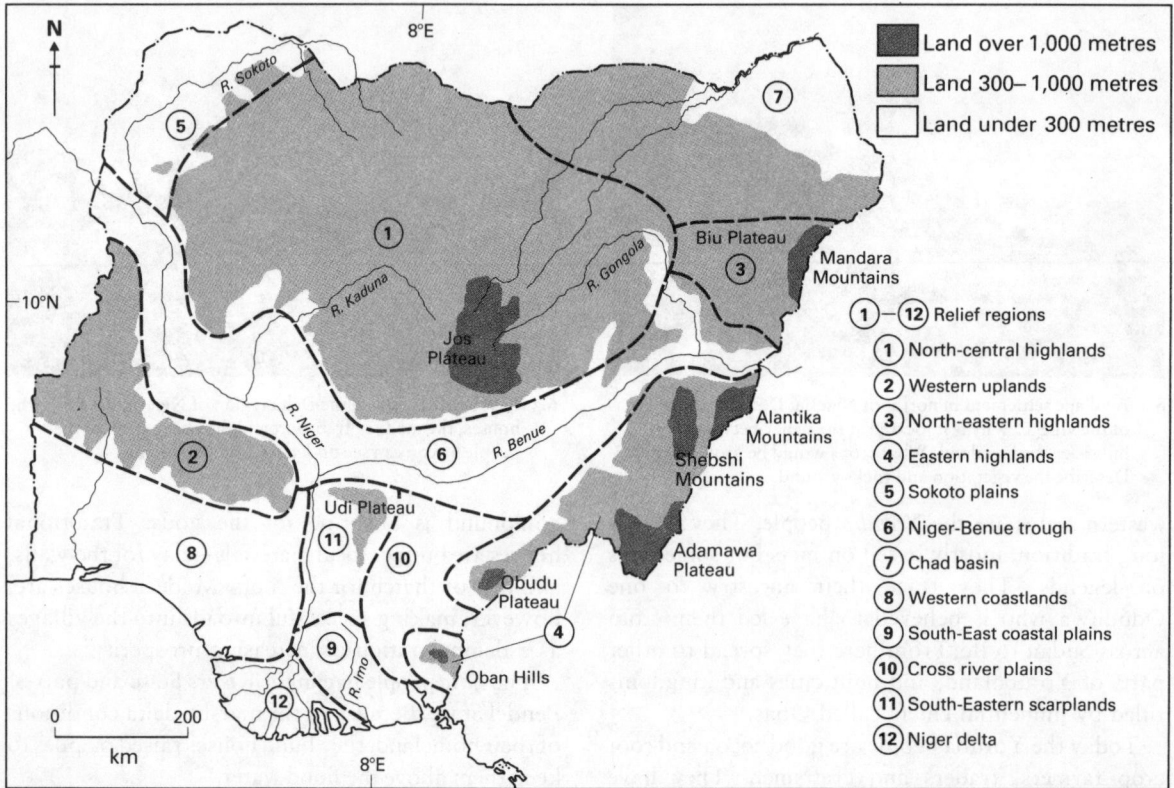

6.4 Nigeria: relief and relief regions.

Physical environment

The physical landscape of Nigeria

Dominating the physical landscape of Nigeria are four highland areas, one in the north, one in the west and two on the eastern borders. Flanking the highlands are eight lowlands. The highlands are separated from the lowlands roughly by the 300 metre contour line. Together, they constitute the twelve relief regions in Nigeria shown in Figure 6.4.

  1. The *north-central highlands* are made up of granite rocks with some volcanic rocks among them. They rise in two distinct steps – the first is the 800 metre High Plain area of Hausaland and the second the 1200 to 1500 metre Jos Plateau. They are separated from each other by a steep 600 metre scarp. The Zaria inselbergs, the Zuma rock and the Kano inselbergs, are examples of the granite hill remnants which are dotted among these highlands. Rivers like the Kaduna, Sokoto, Gongola, and Hadejia, which rise from

the Jos Plateau, flow by many routes down the highlands, carving deep and impressive valleys in them.

  2. The *western uplands* are also made of granite. They too contain some inselbergs, like the Idanre and Aseke hills, and the Amoye and Akure inselbergs. Several rivers also rise from them. One group flows to the Niger in the north and the other to the Atlantic in the south. They differ, however, from the north-central highlands in that they are much lower 300 to 600 metres and are clad with denser vegetation, particularly on their wetter southern approaches.

  3. The *north-east highlands* lie north of the Benue Valley. They consist of the 1500 metre granite Mandara Mountains from which rivers like the Gana and others rise and flow northwards to Lake Chad, and the 1000 metre Biu Plateau which is made up of volcanic rocks.

  4. South of the Benue Valley are the *eastern highlands*. Five granite massifs, or great blocks of highlands, may be noted here. These are the

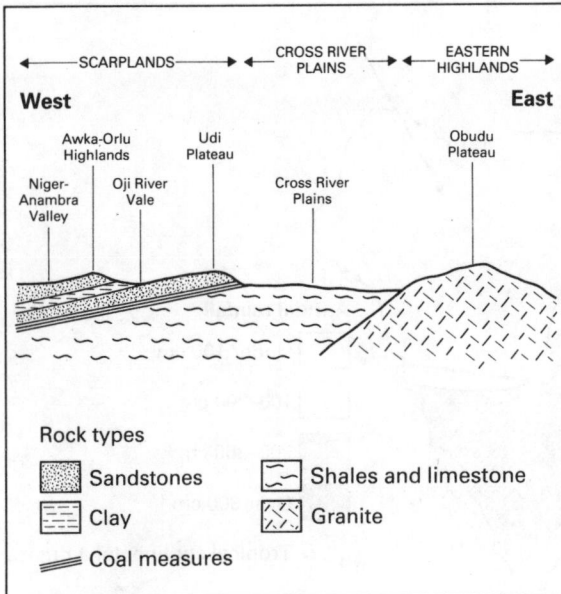

6.5 East-West section from the South-east scarplands to the Eastern Highlands.

Alantika, Shebshi and Adamawa massifs, all of which lie at between 2 000 and 2 500 metres above sea level, and the Obudu Plateau and Oban Hills, 1 500 metres and 1 200 metres high respectively.

5. Of the lowlands, the *Sokoto Plains* flank the north-central highlands in the northwest. They consist of younger sedimentary rocks, are generally below 300 metres, have a flat relief and are drained by the Sokoto, Zamfara and Rima Rivers.

6. The *Niger-Benue trough* lies south of the north-central highlands. The theory that it is a rift valley has been put forward by some writers, but so far no one has conclusively proved it. We know, though, that at one time in the geological history of Nigeria it was an arm of the Atlantic Ocean and older sedimentary rocks were deposited in it. Today it is drained by the lower Niger and Benue rivers which, at high levels, have cut the area into tabular blocks and, at lower ones, have deposited thousands of tonnes of alluvium.

7. The *Chad Basin* in the north-east, like the Sokoto Plains, has a foundation of young sedimentary rocks. But it is a structural basin once occupied by a large inland lake. Now only a shallow survival of this original body of water remains (Lake Chad), and the area is drained by the rivers whose characteristics were outlined in chapter 4. The Chad Basin is one of the main areas of inland drainage in Africa into which drain the Hadejia, Gana, Yobe and other Rivers.

8. South of the western uplands we descend to the *western coastlands*, built of young sedimentary rocks. The coast itself is lined with sand bars, lagoons and marshes; the interior is a low plain of between 100 and 160 metres and chopped into sections by north-south parallel rivers including the Ogun and Oshun Rivers.

9. Linked with this plain by a narrow corridor across the Niger are the *southeast coastal plains*. They slope gently from an elevation of 160 to 200 metres at their northern margin to near sea level at their coastal terminus. Rivers like the Imo and Qua Iboe drain the area.

10. Stretching from the longitude of Enugu to the foot-hills of the Oban and Obudu highlands are the undulating *Cross River Plains*. They occupy the basin of this river and represent an unroofed anticline – that is an upfold whose top has been eroded away. As a result, the older sedimentary rocks beneath, as well as some granite intrusions have been exposed on the floor of the plains.

11. West of these plains is the unique *south-eastern scarpland*. The rocks here are made up of alternating sandstones and clays which slope gently westwards. They give rise respectively to dry scrubby low plateaus with east-facing escarpments and wet vales in between as shown and named in Figure 6.5. This is the best example of a scarpland area in West Africa and it is drained by the Anambra, Imo and Oji Rivers.

12. Finally, we have the fan-shaped, mangrove-covered *Niger Delta* in the very south of the country. It is a monotonously level area over which there has been considerable deposition of sand, clay, mud and silt. It has been built up by the inter-communicating distributaries of the Niger and constitutes a classic example of a delta.

By now it should have been clear to you that the landscape of Nigeria is varied. So too are its climate and vegetation which we shall next turn our attention to.

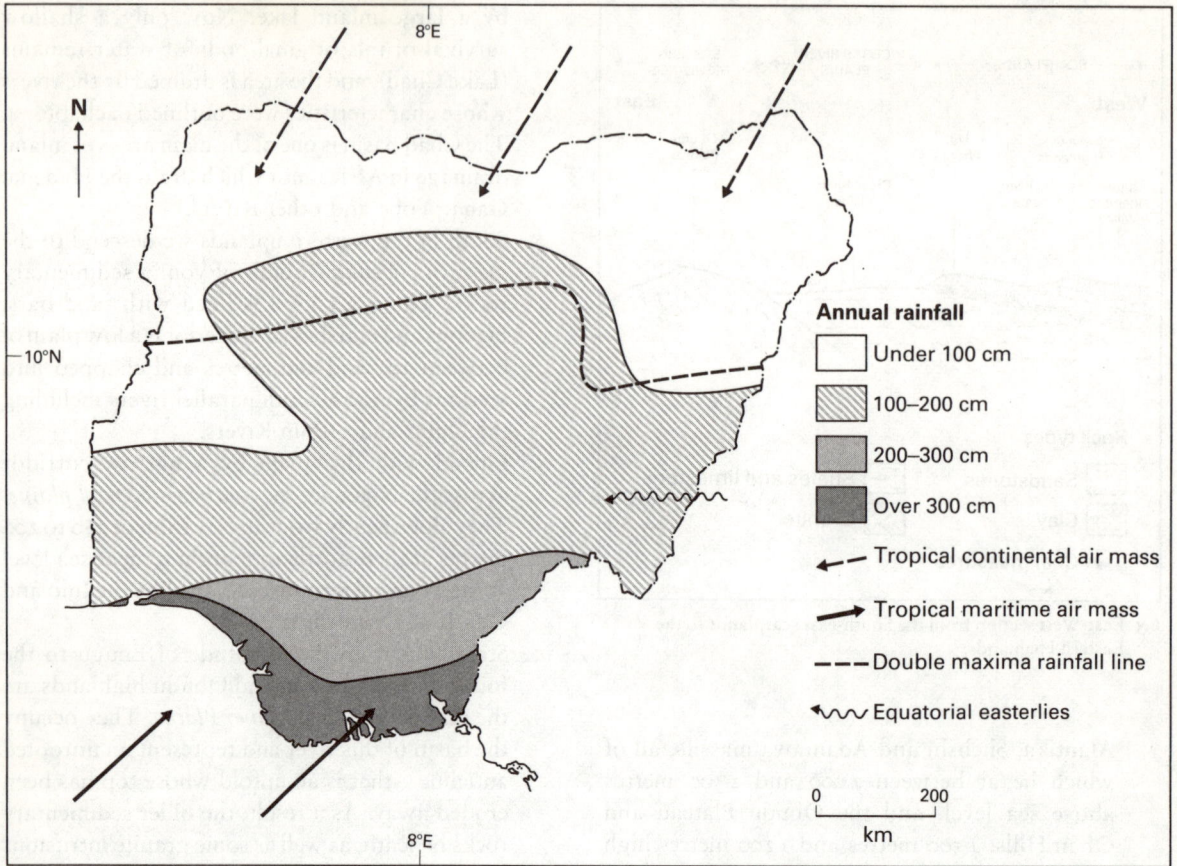

6.6 Nigeria: rainfall and air masses.

Climate and vegetation

The climate and vegetation of Nigeria are more varied than those of any other country in West Africa. This is because the distance from the south to the north of the country is very great and it therefore covers many of the climatic and vegetational belts of West Africa. A full description of each type has already been made in chapters 3 and 5, and need not be repeated here.

However, you should study Figure 6.6 which provides a summary of the air masses and rainfall of Nigeria. See also Figure 3.8 and notice that all but three of the climatic regions of West Africa are found in Nigeria. Name those that are included.

If you then turn to Figure 5.1, you will observe that the desert belt is the only vegetational zone in West

Africa not represented in Nigeria. This means that the country's vegetation includes the forest zone and the swamps, the whole range of savannas and the montane vegetation.

Now review the characteristics of these air masses, climatic types and vegetational belts which are represented in Nigeria.

Revision exercises

1. Describe and comment on the ways of life of the major language groups in Nigeria.
2. Insert the twelve physical regions of Nigeria on one of the maps you have drawn. Describe each of them.
3. Use your second map to indicate the main vegetational belts. Describe and account for the nature of their plant cover.

7 Nigeria (2)

Preparation

1. List the food and export crops which farmers grow in your district.
2. Study the illustrations in this chapter. Are there any crops shown in them that are also grown in your district?
3. What forest products are obtained in your district?

We shall continue our study of the geography of Nigeria in this chapter by looking at its primary industries. These are agriculture, fishing, forestry and mining. They are called primary industries because the major activities in them involve obtaining the primary products of nature before they are processed for use. Secondary industries deal with processing these products or using them as raw materials in manufacturing.

Agriculture

Agriculture (or farming) is a vital pursuit in Nigeria – it provides food for the country's estimated 79.5 million people and occupies some 70% of its working population. It accounts for 25% of the country's gross domestic wealth, although it contributes only

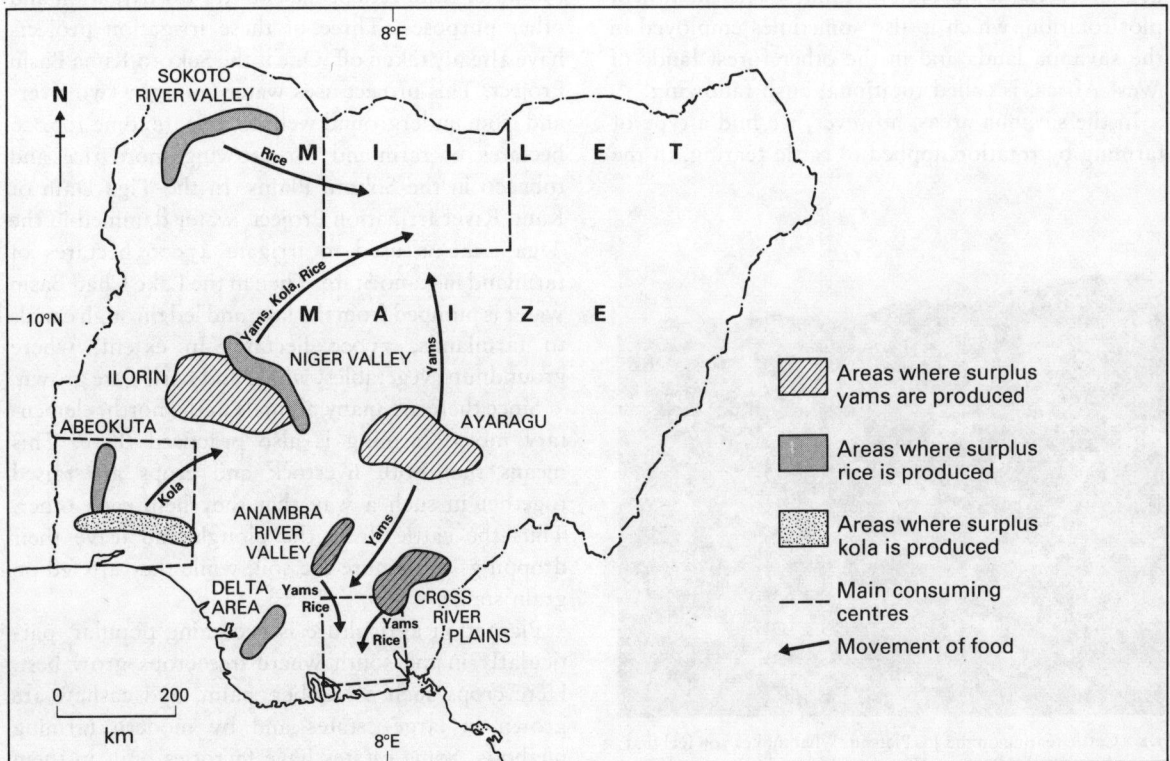

7.1 Nigeria – Some food crops.

4–5% of the value of the country's exports. This low export figure is because much of the produce from agriculture is utilized or consumed locally, and mineral oil assumes a dominant position in the country's exports.

Farm methods and ownership

Farm methods vary widely over Nigeria. This is because the physical environment on which farming mainly depends also varies. Also the cultures of people who do the actual farming vary widely over the country.

Thus in the forested southern belt, where humid and forest conditions prevail, the simple hoe is the traditional farm implement used by the farmer to cultivate his one or two hectares for a year or two. He then leaves this plot for another, and after a further year or two for yet another, and so on. This allows the previous plots to lie fallow, overgrow with vegetation and regain their fertility by natural means. He finally returns to the original plot after about six to twelve years, depending on how much land he has available. And so the cycle continues. This method of plot rotation, which is also sometimes employed in the savanna lands and in the other forest lands of West Africa, is called rotational bush fallowing.

In the savanna areas, however, we find a type of farming by rotation applied to cattle rearing. In the

7.2   Cattle rearing on the Jos Plateau. What makes you feel that this is the Jos Plateau? What breed of cattle are reared here? Why is the Jos Plateau suitable for cattle rearing?

dry season the grass on the upper plains is scorched and water is unavailable except in the streams, in Lake Chad, and in the pools left behind in the flood plains of rivers as the floods recede. So the Fulani herdsmen drive their cattle down to these places for water and pasture (see Figure 7.3). But with the onset of the first rains, the valleys become swampy, tsetse-fly infested and therefore unhealthy. So the herdsmen migrate with their cattle back to the higher plains which now have fresh and succulent grass. This annual cycle of movement in cattle rearing is a type of *transhumance*.

The north also uses some crop raising methods which are peculiar to its dry and savanna conditions. Water from the rivers is used to irrigate the thirsty lands so that crops can grow better. The low-lying flat lands adjacent to the river valleys in the north are flooded in the wet season. Thus naturally irrigated, the lands are planted with rice and cane sugar. When the floods recede, tobacco is grown.

More recently, however, the River Basin Development Authorities, 11 of which were created in the country in 1976, have set out plans for utilizing the water resources of the country for irrigation and other purposes. Three of these irrigation projects have already taken off. One is the Sokoto-Rima Basin Project. This project uses water from the two rivers and from underground wells to irrigate some 100 000 hectares of farmland for growing more rice and tobacco in the Sokoto Plains. In the Tiga Dam or Kano River Irrigation Project, water dammed in the Tiga Lake is used to irrigate 45 000 hectares of farmland in Kano State. Then in the Lake Chad Basin water is pumped from the lake and led through canals to farmlands, 75 000 hectares in extent, where groundnuts, vegetables, wheat and barley are grown.

Since there are many animals in the north, elementary mixed farming is also practised there. This means that both livestock and crops are raised together in such a way that they help each other. Thus the cattle draw the plough and leave their droppings to manure the soil, while they are fed on grain stalks.

Plantation agriculture is becoming popular, particularly in the south where tree crops grow best. Here crops such as rubber, palm, and cashew are grown in large estates and by modern farming methods. Some estates have factories built in them where the crops are initially processed. Many of these

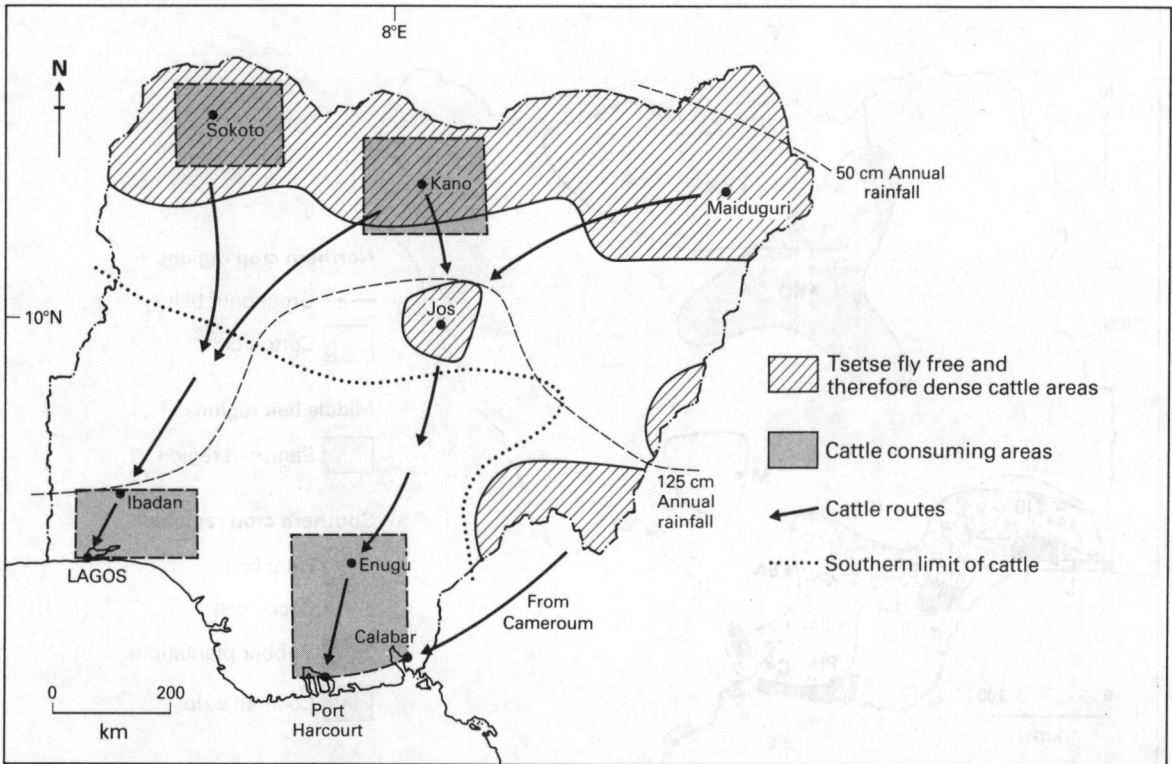

7.3 Cattle areas and movement in Nigeria.

plantations were established between 1952 and 1962, but the Federal Government has recent plans for establishing more commercial planatations over the country.

The ownership of farmland in Nigeria can be traced to three categories of people and organizations – private individuals, the co-operative societies and government. Private farmers run traditional farms and a few estates. Individuals may form co-operative societies, own and cultivate their farms collectively and later share the proceeds in common. Government owns and runs farm projects directly, or through government bodies like agricultural development corporations.

Food crop production

Cocoyams, cassava, fruits, plantains, maize, millet and guinea corn form the basic subsistence crops in Nigeria. These are so widespread that they are not shown specifically on Figure 7.1. In southern Nigeria, where there are two rainy seasons separated by the August break, it is possible to grow crops like maize

and vegetables twice a year. But in the north, only one growing season is possible.

There are also market garden crops like vegetables, tomatoes, onions and potatoes. These are either intercropped with the basic food crops, or grown around large urban areas like Kano, Ibadan, Lagos and Enugu where the market is readily available, or raised in specially favoured cool, high altitude areas like the Obudu and Jos Plateaus.

Yams, rice, tobacco and kola form the principal internal exchange crops. These are crops grown for extensive sale within the country. Cotton and ben-iseed are now more for internal exchange than export since their exports virtually ceased in 1974 and 1975 although limited export of cotton started again in 1977.

The middle belt, and the Cross and Anambra Rivers Basins are famous for yams. Swamp rice grows well in these two plains and also in the flooded *fadamas* of the Sokoto and Niger valleys. Upland rice thrives better in Abeokuta and Benin areas. Tobacco grows around Zaria, while kola is essentially a crop of the Yorubaland, though it is consumed chiefly in

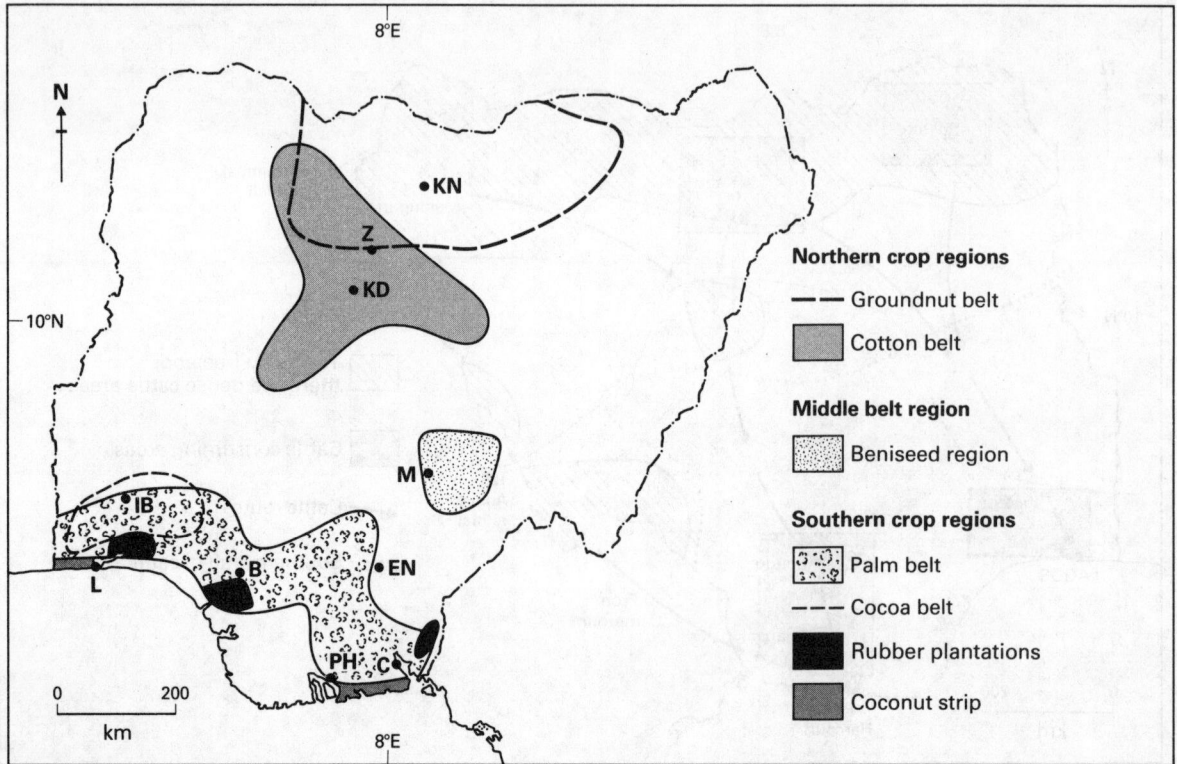

7.4 Nigeria: export crop regions.

Kano and the northern states. The chief areas where the crops are grown are shown in Figure 7.1.

Livestock raising

This embraces the rearing of cattle, sheep, goats, pigs, horses and poultry. Cattle rearing is the most important, and Figure 7.3 shows the main areas where it is carried on.

This map shows that a rainfall of 500 mm to 1250 mm per annum and freedom from the tsetse-fly are the vital factors determining where cattle are reared. These areas also coincide with the wide open high plains of northern Nigeria which have luxuriant grass cover, low relative humidities, a cool, invigorating climate and wide ranges of temperature. Cattle are moved from Niger and Cameroun into Nigeria; the methods used by the Fulani herdsmen in rearing them have already been described.

The meat and milk yielded by the cattle are locally consumed, but hides are exported. The country earned ₦10.6 million from sales of cattle hides, sheep and goat skins in 1974 and ₦6.8 millions in 1975.

Export crop production

In Figure 7.4 name the crops grown in the north and those grown in the south. Notice that the middle belt is relatively poor in export crops. Even the beniseed shown there is no longer exported in any appreciable quantities.

Cotton was first grown in the Oyo State but the centre of production has now shifted north-wards, for a number of reasons. Among these are the introduction of the high yielding variety of cotton which thrives particularly on the black loams and the 750 to 1250 mm annual rainfall of Zaria area, the extension of the railways to the north, and the stiff competition given to cotton in the west by tree crops like cocoa and kola. However, a variety of the crop is grown on the Ishan Plateau of Bendel State and in Kwara State south of the Niger.

The Hausa farmer, who is the chief cultivator of the crop, plants it in June or July, leaves it to grow during the three to four months of the rainy season and harvests the lint in November. He then sells the

7.5 Cotton production in Nigeria. In this picture the cotton, harvested and dried is put in bales ready for sale.

7.6 Cotton. In this picture the cotton is bought by buying agents from the cotton markets and carried to towns or railway stations for use or transportation to factories.

lint to buying agents, who in turn carry it to the cotton ginneries where the seeds are extracted. The seedless lint is then packed in bales and either sent to the country's cotton mills or sent by rail from collecting points like Funtua and Kaduna to Lagos for export. Overseas sales of cotton have decreased from some 25 000 tonnes worth ₦6.8 million in 1969, to 8 230 tonnes worth ₦4.7 million in 1973, because of the increased use of raw cotton in Nigeria's local textile mills. In 1974 exportation of the crop virtually ended only to revive a little in 1977.

The groundnut belt overlaps the cotton-growing areas but extends further north, as Figure 7.7 shows. This is because the crop enjoys drier climates (500 mm to 1 000 mm annual rainfall), finishes its life cycle within a shorter growing period (three months) and develops better on the loose, sandy soils nearer the desert margin. Nigeria is, after Senegal, the largest producer in West Africa.

Planted about June, it is harvested about September. The nuts are then shelled, and put into sacks which are assembled in huge pyramids at

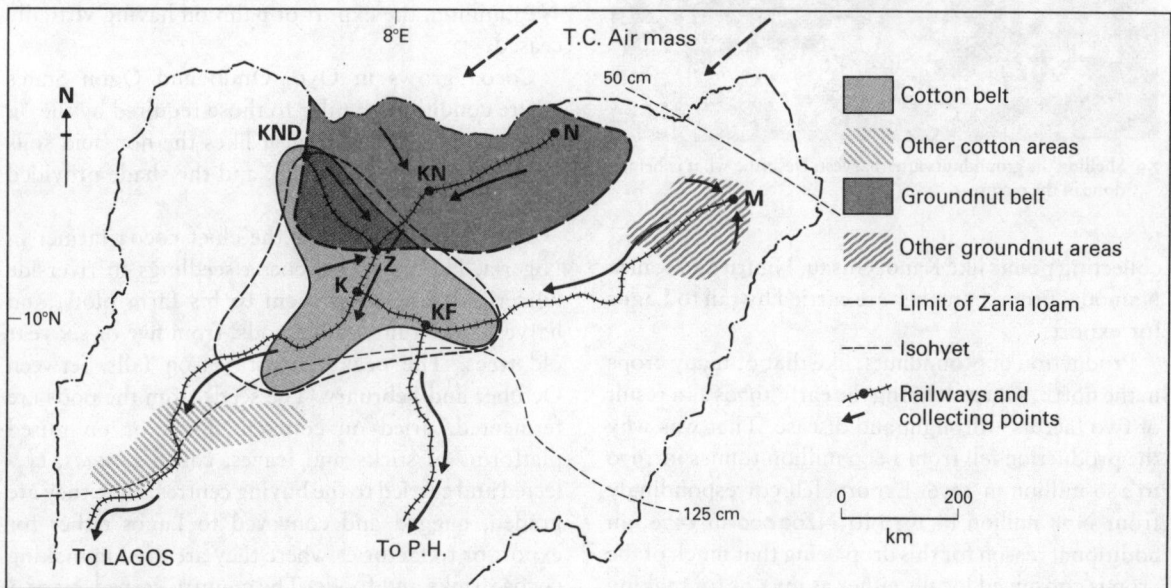

7.7 The map of cotton and groundnut production in Nigeria.

7.8 Groundnut production in Nigeria. Planting the groundnuts.

7.9 Shelling the groundnuts after harvest. Describe what is being done in the picture.

collecting points like Kano, Gusau, Nguru and Kaura Namoda. From there they are carried by rail to Lagos for export.

Production of groundnuts, like that of many crops in the north, suffered during the early 1970s as a result of two factors – drought and disease. That was why the production fell from 1 600 million tonnes in 1970 to 280 million in 1976. Exports fell correspondingly from ₦78 million in 1970 to ₦200 000 in 1976, an additional reason for this drop being that much of the crop is consumed locally either as nuts or for making groundnut oil and poultry feeds.

Beniseeds and soya beans are two oil seeds grown by the Tiv (Munshi) population of the Benue Valley. They thrive under guinea savanna conditions, and as we noted above, export of these items virtually ceased in 1974.

Of the export crops from the south, palm produce is the most widespread. The palm belt, shown in Figure 7.10, yields more palm produce than all the other parts of West Africa put together. The high annual rainfall of over 1 500 mm, the brilliant sunshine necessary for ripening the fruits, the forest soils and the rolling, well-drained surface account for the importance of this area for palm production.

Over 90% of the produce is obtained from tall, semi-wild trees which are grown on private farms and mature in eight to ten years. The peak harvest season is November to April. The oil is extracted from the nuts either by manual methods, with a hand press operated by two men, or in pioneer oil mills. The last is the most efficient.

Kernels and palm oil are consumed at home or in the soap and vegetable oil factories at Aba, Lagos and elsewhere. Some quantities of palm kernels are hauled by rail, road and river from collecting points in the interior to the ports from where they are exported. Lagos principally ships kernels. In 1966, just before the outbreak of the civil war, 536 700 tonnes of palm produce worth ₦66.8 million were exported. In 1976 exports of palm kernels stood at ₦27 million, the export of palm oil having virtually ceased.

Cocoa grows in Oyo, Ondo and Ogun States where conditions similar to those required by the oil palm prevail. In addition, it likes the non-acid soils weathered from the granite and the shade provided by the forests of the area.

The Yoruba farmer is the chief cocoa farmer in Nigeria. He grows his cocoa seedlings in riverside nurseries, transplants them to his farm plots, and harvests the fruits, called pods, from five or six year old trees. The peak harvest season falls between October and February. The seeds from the pods are fermented, dried on concrete floors or on raised platforms of sticks and leaves, called taragas, collected and carried to the buying centres. Here they are graded, bagged and conveyed to Lagos either for export or to factories where they are used in making cocoa drinks and foods. The country earned ₦105.2 million from 170 900 tonnes of cocoa sold overseas in

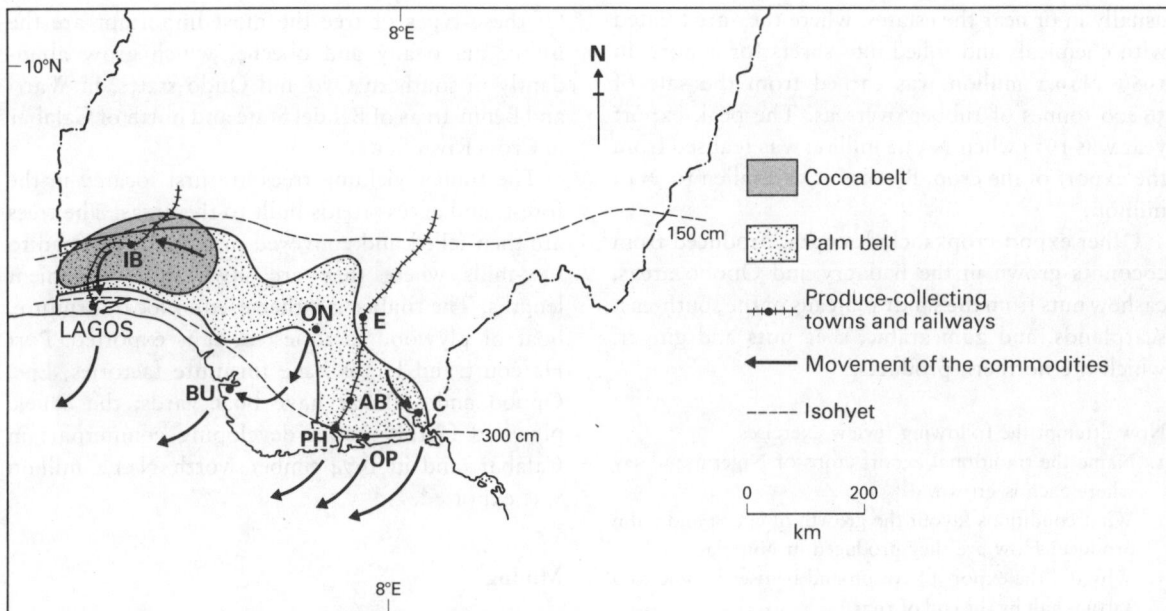

7.10 The map of cocoa and palm production in Nigeria.

7.11 Harvesting palm produce.

7.12 Potted cocoa seedlings ready for transplanting. What is each person in the picture doing? Why was it necessary to build a shed over the young seedlings?

1969. Exports in 1976 rose to ₦233 million.

Rubber grows under similar forest conditions as palm trees and cocoa, but it is usually grown in plantations in Benin, Sapele, Ijebu Ode and Calabar areas.

The plantation trees mature after about six years. The juice (called *latex*) is tapped and sent to factories usually in or near the estates, where they are treated with chemicals and rolled into sheets for export. In 1969 ₦19.2 million was earned from the sale of 56 400 tonnes of rubber overseas. The peak export year was 1974 when ₦33.2 million was realised from the export of the crop. By 1976 it had fallen to ₦14 million.

Other export crops include copra, produced from coconuts grown in the Badagry and Opobo areas, cashew nuts from the sandy plateaus of the south-east scarplands, and gum arabic, shea nuts and ginger, which are northern products.

Now attempt the following review exercises:
1. Name the traditional export crops of Nigeria and say where each is grown.
2. What conditions favour the growth of cocoa and palm produce? How are they produced in Nigeria?
3. Why did the export of cotton and beniseed come to a virtual halt by the end of 1975?
4. How are cotton, palm produce and groundnuts utilized other than for export?

Fishing, forestry and mining

Fishing

Fishing in Nigeria is associated with four main areas – the main rivers, Lakes Chad and Kainji, the coastal creeks and lagoons, and the open sea.

Fishing in rivers and on the lakes is of considerable importance; the Ijaw and Sobo peoples are famous creek and lagoon fishermen, while both the Nigerian government and fishing companies engage in open sea fishing, fish preservation and distribution.

It is not easy to say what the total Nigerian catch is, because large quantities are consumed locally and are never weighed. But recent estimates run to 4 000 tonnes or more per annum. Dried mangala fish is traded from Lake Chad and the north, and frozen fish is transported from the coast to the interior, while a certain amount is exported to neighbouring countries.

Forestry

The most vital commodity produced in the forests is timber. As many as thirty out of three hundred species of trees yield commercial timber in Nigeria.

Of these types of tree the most important are the iroko, mahogany and obeche, which grow abundantly in southern Oyo and Ondo states, in Warri and Benin areas of Bendel State and north of Calabar in Cross River State.

The timber yielding trees are first located in the forest, and access roads built to the areas. The trees are then felled and conveyed principally by road to saw-mills where they are sawn into convenient lengths. The timber is either used in local furniture, boat or plywood factories, or it is exported. Port Harcourt and Lagos have furniture factories; Epe, Opobo and Calabar have boat yards; the Sapele plywood factory has a developing counterpart in Calabar, and in 1974 timber worth ₦11.2 million was exported.

Mining

Mining in Nigeria has become increasingly important in recent years; many more people are now engaged in it. In 1966 minerals accounted for one-third of the value of the country's exports, but in 1976 the contribution went up to over 95%. We can classify the minerals obtained in the country according to the types of rocks in which they are found. Thus we have basement complex and sedimentary rock minerals.

Basement complex minerals

The chief of these are tin, columbite and gold.

Tin is mined in the Jos Plateau, principally from the surface so that there is no need for underground pits. The mineral is washed, smelted at Bukuru, near Jos and sent down by rail to Port Harcourt for export. The 12 000 tonnes produced in 1969 constituted only 5% of the world's output but over 95% of West Africa's and were worth some ₦28 million. However production fell to just over 4 650 tonnes in 1975 when it yielded only ₦19.7 million from its exports.

Columbite is extracted from tin ore. It is a rare and valuable mineral. That is why the small amount of 1 500 tonnes recovered in 1969 formed 80% of the world's supply. Nearly all of it was bought by the United Kingdom and the United States of America. Production however fell to negligible quantities by 1976.

Gold, of the alluvial type, is locally produced and used in Ilesha in the Oyo State.

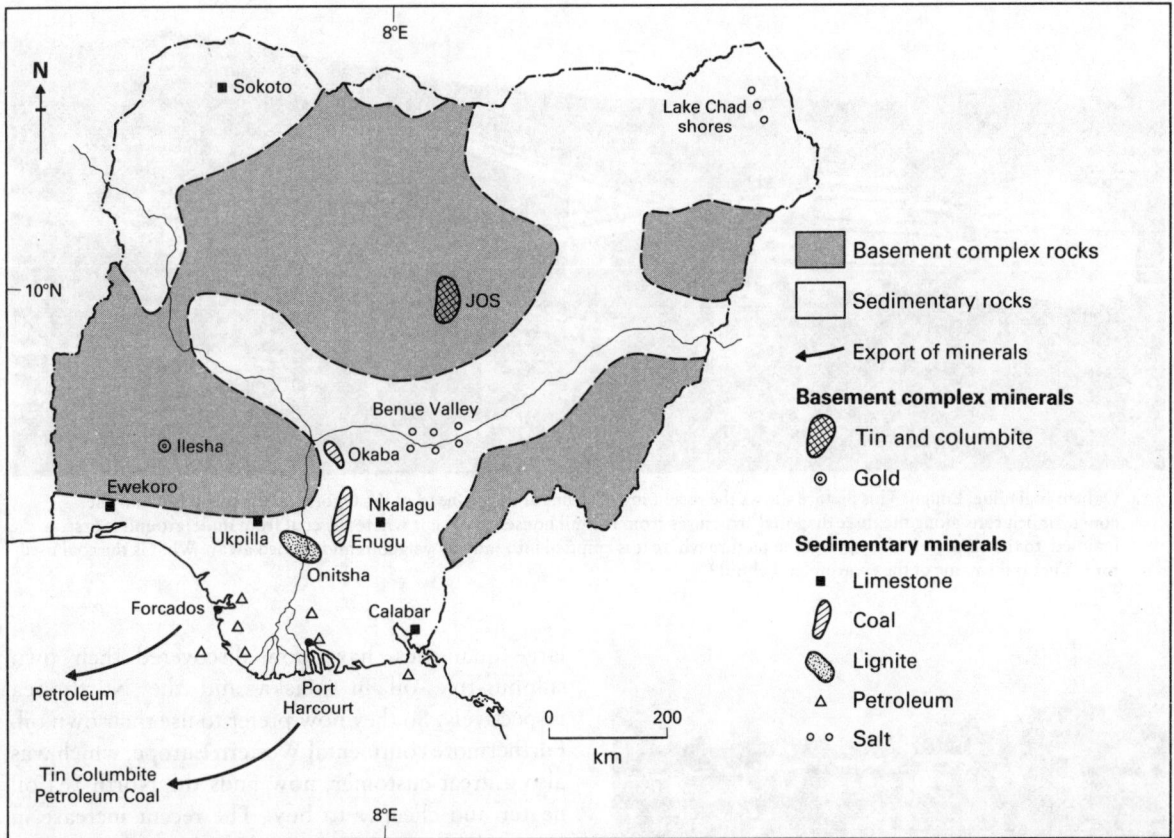

7.13 The chief rocks and minerals in Nigeria.

Sedimentary minerals

Fuel and rock minerals are the most important of these.

Coal, of the sub-bituminous type, was first obtained from an adit mine (that is, a mine with horizontal tunnels) near Enugu in 1915. From that year on the number of mines and the production of coal rose to a peak output of 910 000 tonnes in 1958/59. But since that year, as exports diminished and the Railway Corporation bought and used more diesel engines instead of engines powered by coal, many of the Enugu mines closed down and production slumped to 630 000 tonnes in 1966.

Since the war the industry has not yet fully returned to life. In 1970 80% of the miners were declared redundant leaving a skeleton staff of only 500 who in June 1970 produced less than 350 tonnes of coal! In 1972 production rose to 341 000 tonnes, but in 1975 it fell again to 237 000 tonnes.

Coal is also found in Kwara State and production

started there in 1969 at the Okaba field near Ankpa, some 100 kilometres north of Enugu. Although reserves are high there, production is still relatively small.

The Enugu coal is used in the Oji River power station, in the industries in and around the city and for domestic purposes.

Although it is a relatively late addition to the list of the country's mineral resources, mineral oil has grown to be the most important single mineral and export commodity in Nigeria. First struck at Oloibiri in the Rivers State in 1956, there are now many productive oilfields, including those at Owaza, Afam and Egbema in Imo State, Bormu and Akatta in the Rivers State, and Ughelli and others in Bendel State. There is also an off-shore well near Escravos, which was discovered in 1965.

There are now over ten companies, including British, Dutch, Italian, French and American concerns, engaged in the 'oil rush'. But the most

7.14 Ogbete coal mine, Enugu. This picture shows the recent installations at the pit-head of the Ogbete coal mine in Enugu. The conveyor belt runs along the three diagonal structures from the tall houses to the left where the coal from underground is first handled, to the bunkers in the right of the picture where it is emptied into railway waggons and carried away. What is the coal used for? What is the name of the escarpment behind?

7.15 Extracting mineral oil in Nigeria. This is a system of pipes and valves which regulate the flow of oil from the wells to the storage tanks. What do you think the people are doing?

important is the Shell-BP Company – an Anglo-Dutch Company. In April 1977 the government formed the Nigerian National Petroleum Corporation with wide powers to prospect, mine and refine mineral oil and sell petroleum products.

Production of oil has fluctuated in recent years. From a post war recovery level of 50 million tonnes in 1970, it rose to a peak of 111.6 million tonnes in 1974. In 1975 it slumped to 88.4 million tonnes and showed a slight recovery thereafter to 105.3 million tonnes in 1977. The slump is due to many factors most important of which is that the U.S.A. and Britain, which formerly bought Nigeria's sulphur-free oil in large quantities, have now discovered their own sulphur-free oil in Alaska and the North Sea respectively. So they now prefer to use their own oil. Furthermore continental Western Europe, which was also a great customer, now finds the North Sea oil nearer and cheaper to buy. The recent increase in production is due to increased local use of petroleum products in the country. These fluctuations notwithstanding, Nigeria still remains the largest producer of petroleum in Africa; its closest rivals being Libya and Algeria.

Nigeria's oil is either exported crude or refined locally. The off-shore oil is piped straight into the tankers for export. From the oil fields, pipelines lead to oil terminals, formerly Bonny alone, but now Forcados, from where it is shipped in bulk overseas. Two refineries now exist in the country – the Port Harcourt refinery opened in 1965 and the larger Warri refinery was commissioned in 1978. By the early 1980s the Kaduna refinery, now being built, will go into operation. Together all three will be handling 260 000 barrels of crude oil a day brought in by long distance pipelines from the oil fields.

The future of oil in the country is however not very certain. Production is likely to depend largely on external factors, and current estimates indicate that the oil may not last beyond 25 years!

Associated with mineral oil is natural gas. There are large reserves, but currently only some 660

7.16 The limestone quarry at Ewekoro, Ogun State of Nigeria. Describe the quarry site. What are the vehicles used for?

million cubic metres of gas are being produced and this represents 3% of potential production. Gas is used at the NEPA power station in Sapele and it is compressed and liquified in a factory at Warri, where it is then stored in huge metal cylinders for local use or in bulk for export.

High quality limestone is quarried at Nkalagu in Anambra State, 40 kilometres north of Calabar in Cross River State, at Ewekoro (Figure 7.16) south of Abeokuta in Ogun State, at Ukpilla in Bendel State and near Sokoto in Sokoto State. The limestone beds here are either horizontal or slightly inclined, and therefore easy to quarry. It is used in the cement factories in these areas.

Other minor minerals include the lead and zinc intruded into the sedimentary rocks south of Abakaliki; iron ore located near Enugu and at Itakpe Hills near Ajaokuta but not yet mined; lignite found in the lower Niger Basin, and salt and clays widely scattered throughout the country.

The importance of minerals

Minerals are important to Nigeria in a number of ways. They provide the raw materials for various processing industries; they are major sources of energy in the country; they have led to the growth of towns like Enugu and Jos, and have enhanced the importance of others like Port Harcourt and Warri; they offer employment opportunities to many, and

contribute over 93% of the country's revenue from exports. The oil business, in particular, earns the country high royalities and at the same time trains a core of skilled workers who form one of Nigeria's major assets. Warri has a petroleum institute and the workers also learn on the job.

Summary

Agriculture, fishing, forestry and mining are the four primary industries we have discussed in this chapter. Agriculture is fundamental to the country's economy, but mining has gained ground on it because of its increased contribution to the national wealth.

Revision exercises

1. Find out from the text the values of the chief crops exported from Nigeria in 1975 or 1976, and arrange them in the form of a table. Then draw bars whose lengths are proportional to the values of the commodities, as in Figure 23.3, to show the values of the crops in order of importance.
2. Show on a sketch map the distribution of minerals in Nigeria. Describe their distribution and comment on their production. Account for the importance of minerals generally to the country.
3. Describe and account for the recent trends in the petroleum industry in Nigeria.

8 Nigeria (3)

Preparation

1. List the things made by local craftsmen in your home area. Visit one or two craftsmen and discuss with them the raw materials they use, the people they employ, the goods they make and how they dispose of them.
2. Trace a map of Nigeria and mark the country's railways on it. Show also the Niger and Benue Rivers.

In this last chapter on Nigeria, we shall first discuss the country's manufacturing industries, then go on to study its towns, population and means of transport, and finally make a survey of its internal and external trade.

Manufacturing industries

Local crafts

Widely scattered throughout Nigeria are raffia works, wood and metal craft industries, potteries, and cloth and leather industries. They rely mainly on local raw materials and simple implements to operate; few people are engaged in each industry; the products vary in quality, and many people patronise them now, principally because they want to keep and admire their products as souvenirs.

Modern factory industries

These are of more geographical significance. They grow at such a fast rate that, whereas twenty years ago they were only found in a handful of towns in the country, today it is possible to define some industrial zones (see Figure 8.1), each with a cluster of towns engaged in manufacturing industries.

Apart from the large internal market and the resources in the country which have led to the rapid overall growth of industries in recent years, there are many other specific reasons for the growth of industry in these zones. The areas correspond with the densely populated parts of the country where labour is abundant; they have raw materials near at hand, and they are well served by roads, railways and banking and advertising facilities. Also it is the government which finally determines where a factory is to be sited, so the zones and the industries in them have grown up also as a result of government policy.

1. The *western industrial axis* contains well over half of the industries in Nigeria. Lagos alone has more than three-quarters of these for the reasons mentioned above, and because of the ease with which it assembles raw materials and attracts technicians both from overseas and from the hinterland. There also exist extensive areas in Apapa, Ilupeju, Ikeja and Maryland for industrial development. Building materials like metal frames, asbestos-cement goods, aluminium products and paints are made in these areas. Some factories make foods and drinks like margarine, beer and soft drinks; others manufacture chemical products like soap, cosmetics and pharmaceuticals.

   There are also factories for the production of canvas shoes, singlets, cotton and other textiles, and engineering works which include vehicle and battery assembly plants and railway engine and ship repair depots. The Ijora stand-by power plant chiefly produces and supplies power to the city. There are scores of others but mention must be made of the Volkswagen car assembly plant which was opened in 1972 along the Badagry road.

   In the Abeokuta area, cement is made at Ewekoro from the local limestone, and some of this is used in the manufacture of concrete poles. Fruits are canned and soft drinks bottled and sold locally. Cement is also manufactured at Shagamu.

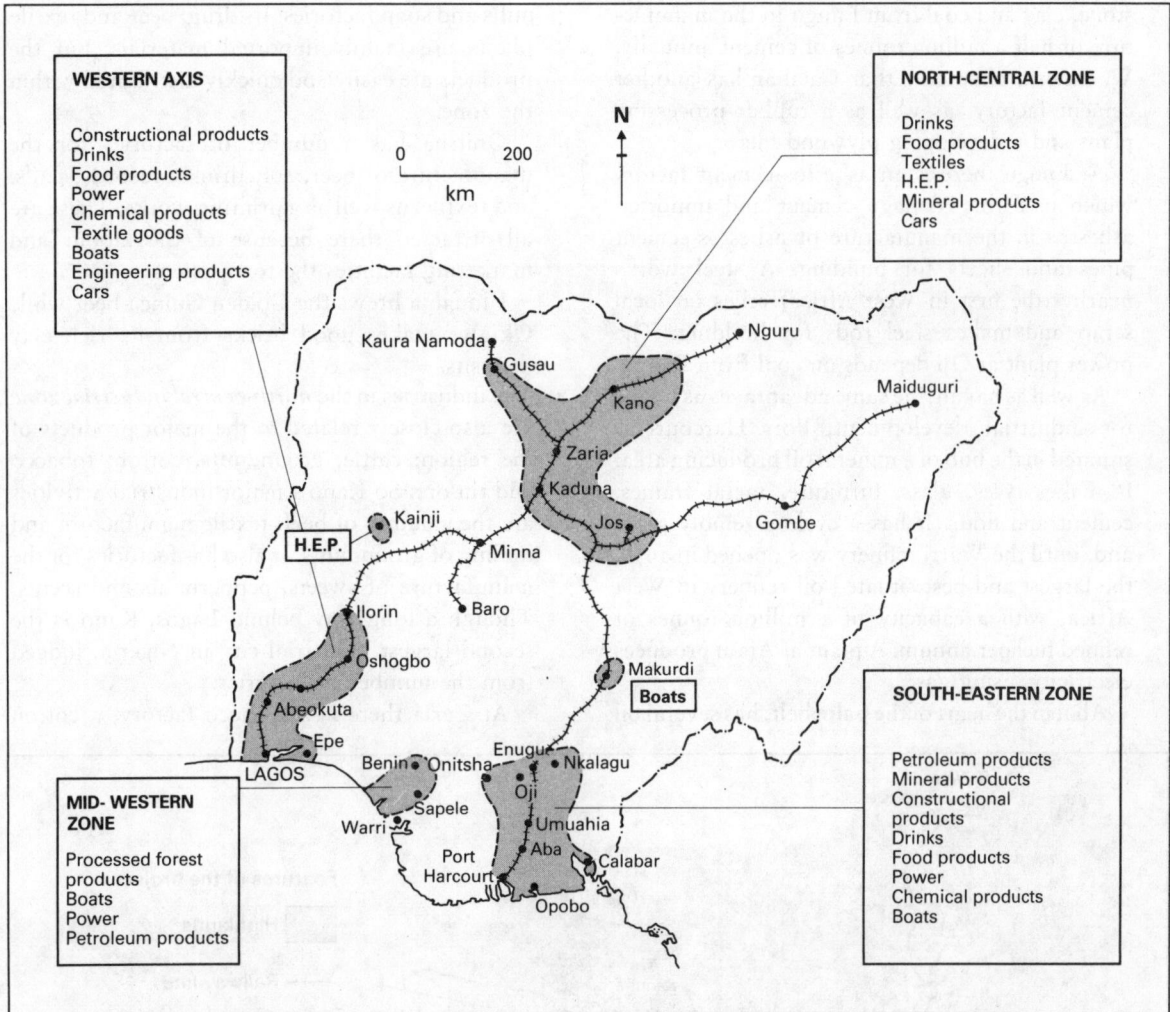

WESTERN AXIS

Constructional products
Drinks
Food products
Power
Chemical products
Textile goods
Boats
Engineering products
Cars

NORTH-CENTRAL ZONE

Drinks
Food products
Textiles
H.E.P.
Mineral products
Cars

MID- WESTERN ZONE

Processed forest products
Boats
Power
Petroleum products

SOUTH-EASTERN ZONE

Petroleum products
Mineral products
Constructional products
Drinks
Food products
Power
Chemical products
Boats

8.1 The industrial zones of Nigeria.

At Ibadan, bags and tubes are made out of artificial fibres; plastic containers, cigarettes and tinned food are manufactured; tyres are retreaded, and books are printed at the Caxton Press located in the city.

2. The less extensive *mid-western industrial zone* has a number of active and new industries which depend on the timber, palm, rubber and mineral oil produced in the area. The plywood factory in Sapele uses timber from the nearby forests. It is by far the largest in West Africa, employing 3 000 men. Veneers, plywood, planks and flush doors are made there. Both Sapele and Benin have crêpe rubber factories. Sapele makes canvas shoes and has a gas power plant. There are oil and saw mills

scattered throughout the zone. Warri is a rapidly growing industrial and commercial city which owes its recent growth to the mineral oil produced in the area. Thus it has a big oil refinery, a petrochemical complex and a fertilizer plant; an iron smelting plant is scheduled to go into operation in the city in 1981.

3. The *south-eastern industrial zone* lies in the area of rubber and palm production, and of vital minerals like coal, limestone, clay and mineral oil. It is therefore not surprising that most of the industries here are connected with their processing.

Thus at Nkalagu there is a cement works which employs some 1 500 people and uses local limestone, clay and coal from Enugu in the manufacture of half a million tonnes of cement annually. We saw in chapter 7 that Calabar has another cement factory, as well as a rubber processing plant and a developing plywood factory.

At Enugu there is an asbestos-cement factory which uses the Nkalagu cement and imported asbestos in the manufacture of asbestos-cement pipes and sheets for building. A steel works nearby (the first in West Africa) relies on local scrap and makes steel rods for building. The power plant at Oji depends on coal from Enugu.

As well as having the same advantages as Lagos for industrial development, Port Harcourt is situated in the hub of a mineral oil producing area. It makes tyres, glass, furniture, metal frames, cement and flour. It has a cycle assembly plant and, until the Warri refinery was opened in 1978, the largest and best situated oil refinery in West Africa, with a capacity of 2 million tonnes of refined fuel per annum. A plant at Afam produces electricity, using gas.

Aba, in the heart of the palm belt, has several oil

mills and soap factories. Its drug, beer and textile plants use mainly imported materials, but the products are easily and quickly distributed within the zone.

Onitsha has a number of factories for the manufacture of beer, soft drinks, records, nails, and textile, as well as a printing works. These are all attracted there because of the labour and marketing facilities the town offers.

Umuahia brews the Golden Guinea beer while Okigwe makes good bricks from its rich clay deposits.

4. The industries in the *north-central industrial zone* are also closely related to the major products of the region: cattle, groundnuts, cotton, tobacco and tin ore. So Kano's major industrial activities are the canning of beef, textile manufacture and milling of groundnuts. It also has factories for the manufacture of sweets, peppermints and scents. Though a long way behind Lagos, Kano is the second largest industrial city in Nigeria, judged from the number of factories.

At Zaria there is a tobacco factory, a cotton

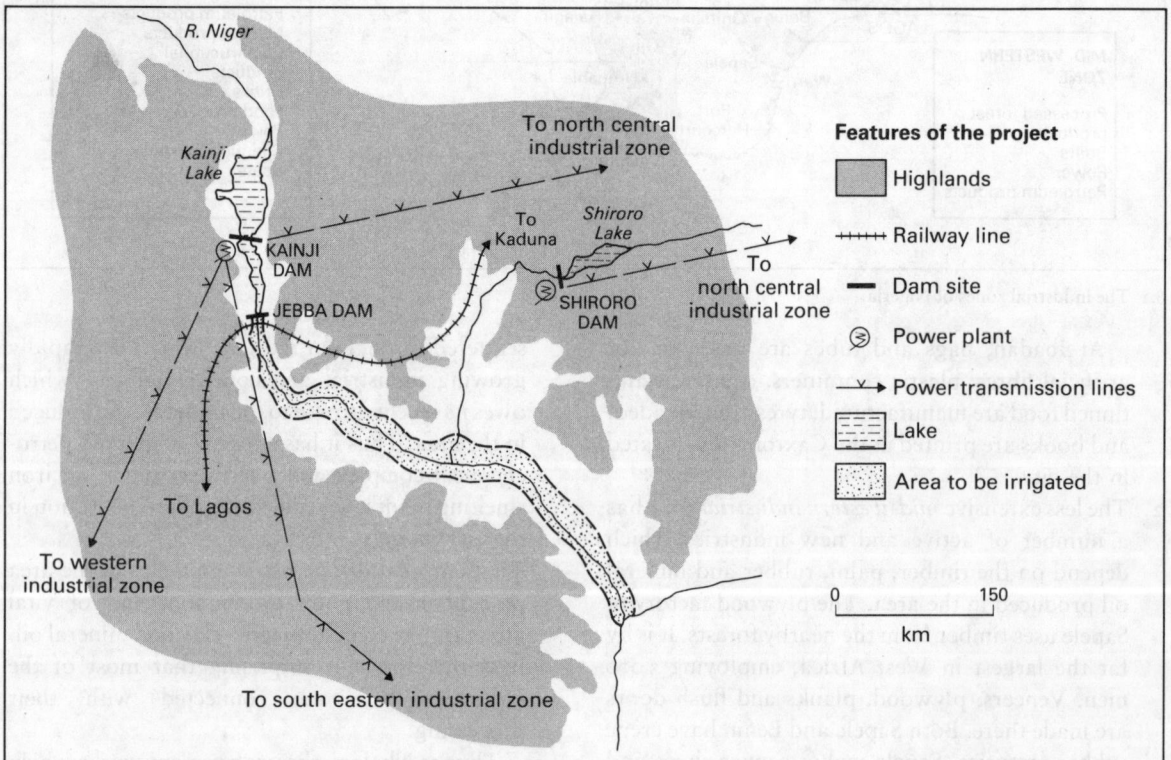

8.2 The Kainji and Niger Dam sites.

ginnery, a cycle assembly plant and a press which prints Arabic and other books.

Kaduna operates three large cotton textile mills and has a mineral water factory, a Peugeot car assembly plant commissioned in 1974 and a new refinery due to go into production by 1981.

The tin smelter near Jos has been noted. Vom makes butter, cheese, clarified fat and powdered milk, and power is produced at Kurra Falls south of Jos.

5. Finally, we must mention two industrial outliers in Kwara State – the *Kainji power project* and the *Ajaokuta iron and steel works*.

Kainji is one of the most important industrial projects undertaken during the 1962–68 Development Plan at a total cost of ₦175.4 million. Aspects of the project are shown in Figure 8.2. The entire Niger Dams project involves damming the Niger at Jebba and Kainji, and its tributary, the Kaduna, at Shiroro. The Kainji Dam has been completed, having been commissioned in 1968. It has a power plant with six generating units and six turbines at the site. Six more will have to be built by 1980. Nigeria is now gaining benefit from this major undertaking.

The electricity generated by this major plant is distributed to the northern, south-eastern and western industrial zones as shown in Figure 8.2. Major sub-stations for power distribution have been built at Jebba, Oshogbo, Lagos, Benin and Kaduna. A sixth has been constructed at Onitsha and a transformer was completed at Asaba in 1971. In addition, the Kainji Lake, which is held up behind the dam, makes water available for the irrigation of the Niger Valley below the dam and

8.3 The Kainji Dam. This is a photograph of the dam itself and the River Niger below the dam. What is the dam made of? Compare it with the Volta Dam in chapter 11.

for fishing. It also creates facilities for transport and tourism. The flourishing Kainji Hotel, for instance, caters for tourists and business representatives to the site, and the Niger is now navigable all the year round up to the border with the Niger Republic. Finally, it has led to the erection of well over 100 modern villages to settle some 42 000 people whose villages were drowned by Lake Kainji.

A one billion naira iron and steel complex is being built at Ajaokuta to use the medium grade iron ore deposits at Itakpe, nearby, and high grade ore imported from Guinea and Liberia if necessary. It is expected to go into operation in 1983 with a production capacity of 3 million tonnes of iron and steel goods per annum, rising to 5 million tonnes by 1990.

Towns

The previous section dealt with the industrial importance of many Nigerians towns. We shall now select the chief ones and examine the other aspects of their geographical importance.

Lagos

Lagos (over 1 million in 1975) is the federal capital of Nigeria and in February 1979 the new capital – Abuja – was officially named. Different parts of Lagos are located on Victoria, Ikoyi, Lagos and Iddo Islands, and on the mainland. Bridges and fly-overs connect them, the most recent being the Eko and Carter bridges and the ring road fly-overs.

Lagos is a focus of land, sea and air routes. In 1970 its international airport at Ikeja admitted over 3 500 planes carrying some 3 500 tonnes of cargo. The new Murtala Mohammed Airport, opened in March 1979 has two runways, one 3 900 metres long by 60 metres wide, the other 2 740 metres long by 40 metres wide, and a gigantic airport terminal building covering an area of 1 500 hectares. You can also see for yourself in Figure 8.10 the proportion of Nigeria's import and export trades that comes and goes through Lagos compared with other ports.

The port of Lagos suffered from serious congestion in 1975–76 when each day as many as 200–300 ships could be counted in the open seas waiting to come in.

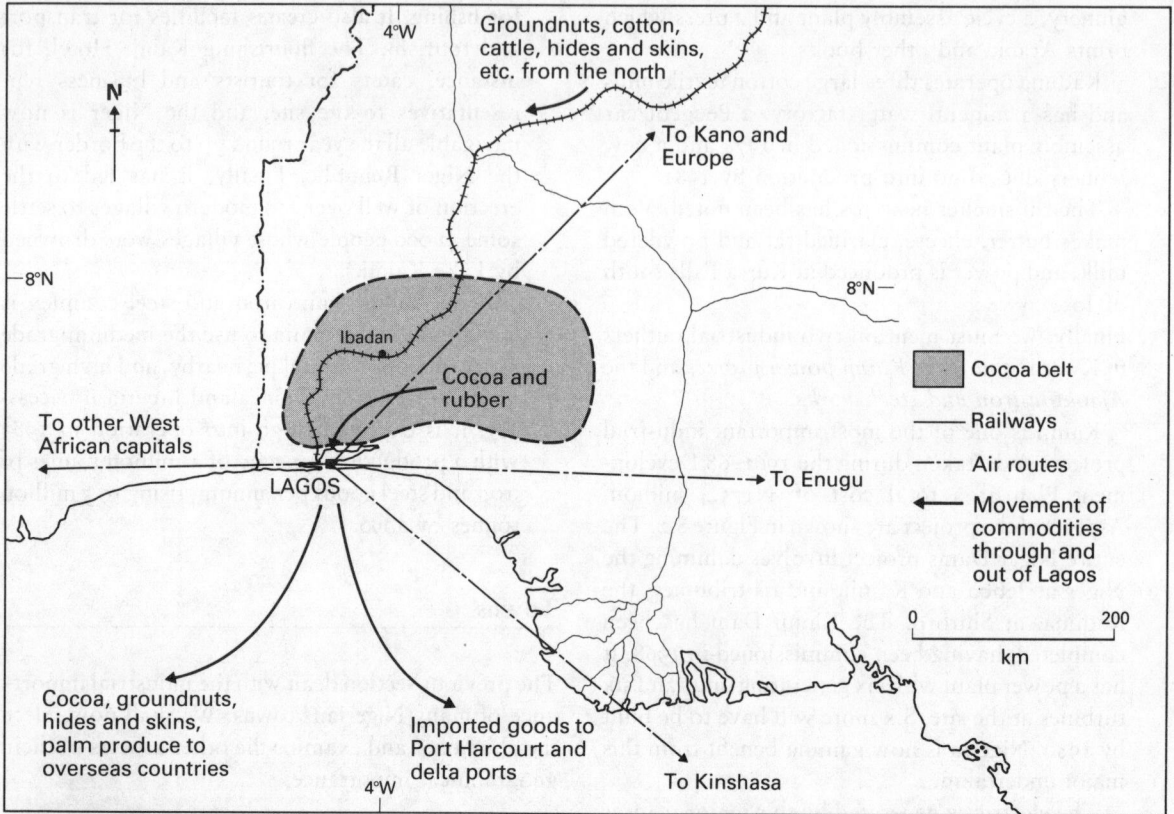

8.4 Lagos and part of its hinterland.

8.5 The new Murtala Muhammed airport. This photograph shows the airport terminal building with the tower. It was commissioned in March 1979.

This congestion of course was caused by a number of factors including massive importation of cement, FESTAC materials and other goods ordered without realising that the port facilities in Lagos were grossly inadequate to handle all of them fast enough. To decongest the habour, government stopped other ships from coming in immediately, diverted some to Lomé, Cotonou and Tema and started immediately to build the Tin Can Island Port as a stop gap port to ease the congestion in the main Lagos port. Five new berths were also added to the existing ones in Lagos. By the end of 1977 the congestion was all over and Lagos Port once more started to operate normally.

Because of its transport and other facilities, Lagos has grown to be the premier banking and commercial city in Nigeria, and to its dominant position as the economic capital of the country can be added its institutes of learning, its churches, its public parks and its giant new skyscrapers.

Port Harcourt

Port Harcourt (212 000 in 1975) is located on the Bonny River some 65 kilometres from the open sea. It also has rail, road and air routes converging on it. Its out-port, Bonny, used to be the only crude oil port of Nigeria.

Until Warri came into prominence it was the main centre of the oil business in Nigeria. For around it are rich fields, east of it is the oil refinery mentioned

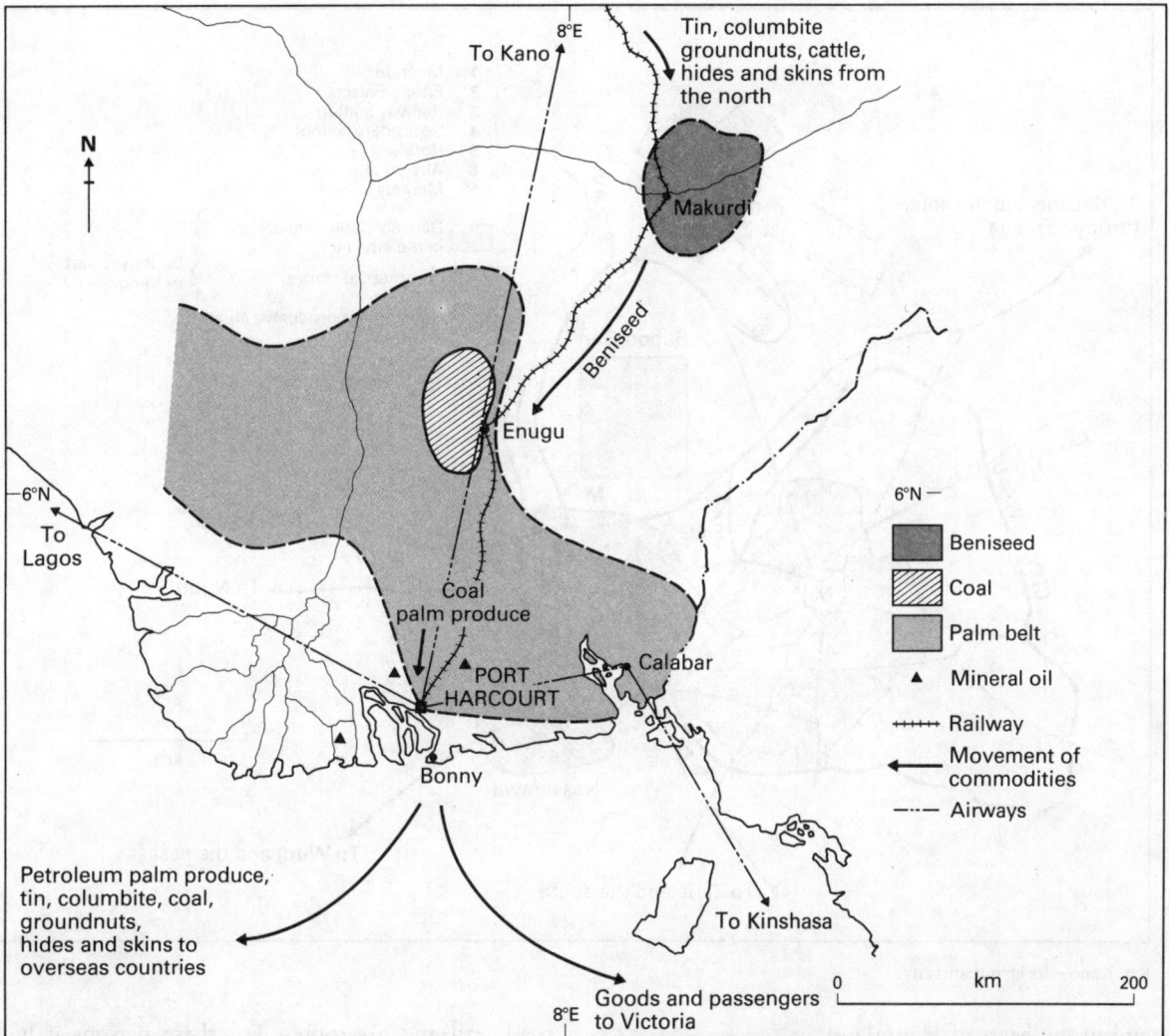

8.6 Port Harcourt and part of its hinterland.

above, south of it is the Bonny oil terminal and within the city are the offices and residential areas of famous oil firms.

But now that the head offices of these major oil companies have moved to Warri and Lagos, it has lost this position. Though the second largest port in Nigeria, it has a hinterland as wide as that of Lagos, the premier port.

Port Harcourt's exports were normally more than those of Lagos by weight because of the heavy palm oil, tin and petroleum which it handles. On the other hand, Lagos, being the capital port and nearer Western Europe and North America than Port Harcourt, takes a greater share of the imports into

the country, among which are raw materials and technical equipment destined for the many industries in the city.

Kano

Kano, a 1 000 year old Hausa city, had a population of 399 000 in 1975. It is a typical northern Nigerian town with an old walled city and a modern urban development outside it.

It owes its importance to its location at the southern approaches of the Sahara, and at a focus of road, rail, international air and caravan routes. It is also in the middle of the groundnut and cattle belts,

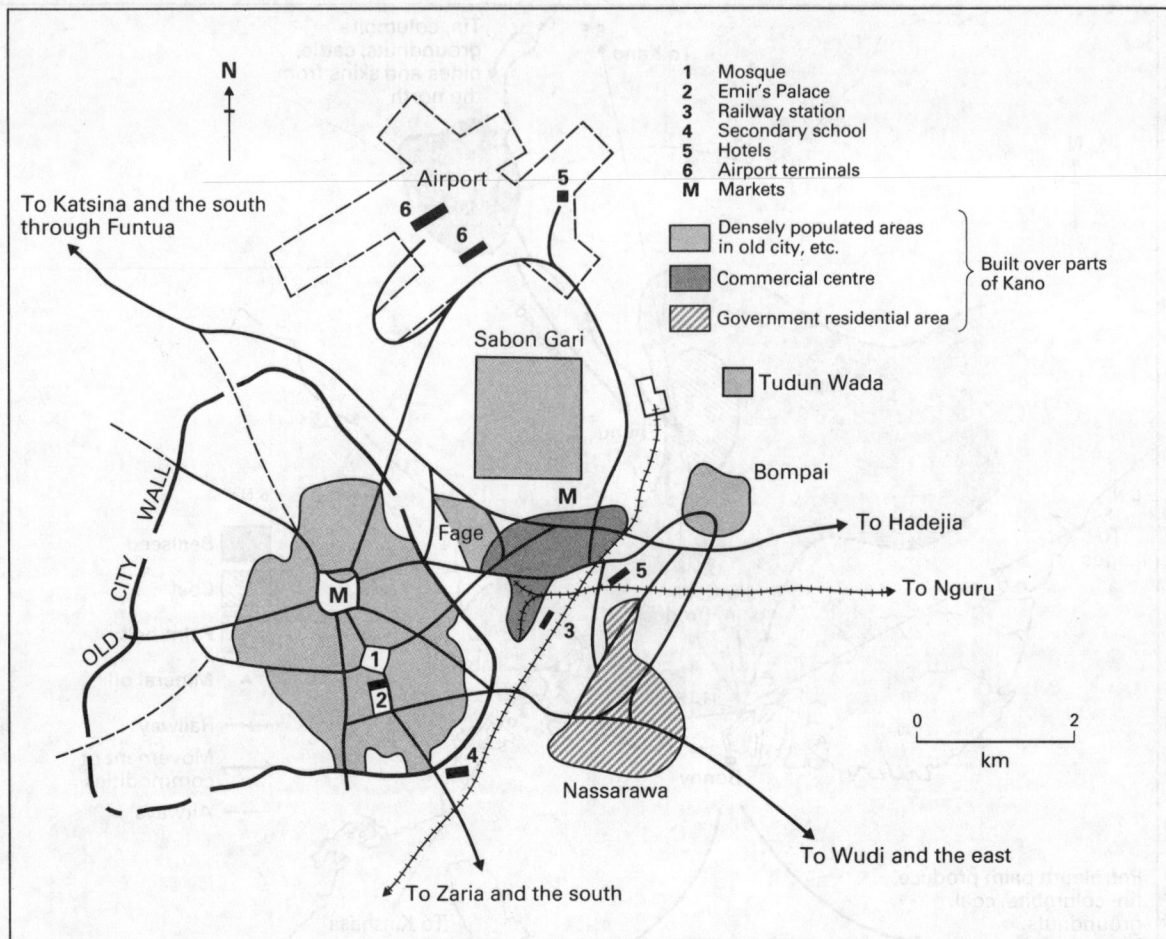

N

To Katsina and the south through Funtua

Airport

1 Mosque
2 Emir's Palace
3 Railway station
4 Secondary school
5 Hotels
6 Airport terminals
M Markets

Densely populated areas in old city, etc.
Commercial centre
Government residential area
} Built over parts of Kano

Tudun Wada

Sabon Gari

Bompai

To Hadejia

Fage

To Nguru

OLD CITY WALL

Nassarawa

To Wudi and the east

0   2
km

To Zaria and the south

8.7 Kano – Its layout and city.

and in the heart of Hausaland.

For these reasons Hausa, southern Nigerian and European cultures in turn have followed the routes to the city. It has therefore become a major industrial and commercial town and it is the principal collection and distribution centre for products to and from the north.

Ibadan

Ibadan is important for a number of reasons apart from its industrial activities. It is the second largest city in tropical Africa, the largest traditional negro city in the world and the capital of Oyo State with a population of 847 000 in 1975.

It is located in the heart of the cocoa and kola belts of Nigeria, well inside Yorubaland and served by

road, rail and air routes. For these reasons it has become an important Yoruba town, a collecting and distributing centre for cocoa, kola and some palm products, and a commercial city with many shops, banks and one of the largest markets in West Africa.

Finally, it is a city of learning, with the oldest university in Nigeria, as well as many research institutes and colleges.

Enugu

Enugu, with a present population of over 187 000, owes its origin to two chief factors – the discovery of coal near the town in 1915 and the choice of the city as the headquarters of the southern Provinces of Nigeria in 1939.

Thus a railway line was extended from Port

8.8 Kano, a Hausa metropolis. Describe the houses in this picture. What is peculiar about their roofs? Why are they built like that?

· 8.9 Enugu, the capital city of Anambra State. This picture shows the location of Enugu on the Cross River Plains and at the foot of the Udi Cuesta. The hill at the background is the scarp face of this cuesta. Describe the houses. The settlement in the distance is Coal Camp. Why do you think this part of Enugu is located nearest the hills?

Harcourt to the town to enable the coal to be transported to the coast for export, and roads were built to provide easy access to its area of authority.

Sections of the city were planned and constructed to house coal miners and civil servants. Coal attracted a number of the industries mentioned earlier, and the political importance which the city acquired has been maintained; it is now the capital of Anambra State of Nigeria.

The cultural institutions in Enugu include a branch of the University of Nigeria, an institute of management and technology, a zoo and a public library.

Now do the following:
1. Name four major industrial zones of Nigeria. Identify the manufacturing activities in each of them.
2. Where are the following located in Nigeria?
   a) Car assembly plants.
   b) Petroleum refineries.
   c) Textile goods and manufactures.
   d) Breweries.
   e) Cement manufacturing plants.
3. For each of the above, state two reasons why the industry is located where it is.
4. Apart from industries, what factors make the following towns important?
   a) Lagos.
   b) Ibadan.
   c) Enugu.
   d) Port Harcourt.
   e) Kano.

Population distribution

We have learnt about the peoples of Nigeria, their ways of life and their occupations; we must now find out how they are distributed over the country and account for the many variations in the pattern.

Three areas in Nigeria have very high population densities – western Nigeria, north-central Nigeria and south-eastern Nigeria. The first area corresponds with greater Lagos and the fertile, highly urbanized, cocoa land of Yorubaland. The second is in the heart of Hausaland which is rich in cotton and groundnuts, and where the Hausa and Fulani people have had a stable government and prosperous economy in the past. The third falls within the palm belt of Igboland and Ibibioland, which many believe was more fertile in the past than it is now, but where people have

stayed on because of their traditional attachment to the land. This factor is sometimes known as human inertia. We should also notice that these three areas are well served with industries and networks of good roads (refer to your atlas).

That leaves us, on the map, with three other areas where few people live. The first is Borno State, which is the driest part of the country. Then there is the middle belt area where slave raiding in the past, the laterite soils, tsetse flies and the rugged highlands in the east all discourage settlement. Finally, there is the Niger Delta which is inhospitable because of its hot and humid atmosphere, and its swamp and mangrove vegetation.

Transport

Waterways

The most frequently used of the 6 500 kilometres of navigable inland waterways in Nigeria are shown in Figure 8.10. Notice the importance of the River Niger, the Benue, the Cross River, the creeks and Kainji Lake.

In addition to these waterways, coastal sea routes link the ten chief Nigerian ports of Lagos, Burutu, Warri, Sapele, Koko, Degema, Abonema, Port Harcourt, Bonny and Calabar. International sea routes connect these ports with overseas countries.

Railways

The railways of Nigeria shown in Figure 8.1 total over 3 500 kilometres. The oldest is the Lagos to Abeokuta line opened in 1898, and the most recent, the Kuru to Maiduguri extension, commissioned in 1964. Most of the others were constructed within the first three decades of the century.

These railways were not built at random – they were constructed principally to help collect agricultural products and minerals, distribute imported goods, link up towns and facilitate the flow of people, industrial commodities and ideas.

Roads

Currently, there are over 96 000 kilometres of roads in Nigeria. But not all of them are of the same quality. There are well-surfaced 'A' trunk federal roads, surfaced 'B' trunk state roads, good laterite dry season roads, and many roads which are usable but of very poor quality. The 1930's and the post-independence years are the periods of the most active highway construction in Nigeria. The areas with the densest road networks correspond with the industrial zones shown in Figure 8.1.

The construction of the roads, however, like that of the railways, was often hindered by the many rivers which flow through Nigeria. Therefore it often became necessary to spend huge sums of money on bridging the rivers or ferrying traffic across them. Some notable bridges in the country are the Jebba and Onitsha–Asaba bridges across the Niger, the two

Makurdi bridges across the Benue, the Carter and Eko Bridges across the Lagos Lagoon, the Sapele Bridge across the Ethiope and the Oron–Calabar Bridge across the Cross River.

The most recent developments in road construction in Nigeria are directed along three lines:
(i) rehabilitating and widening township and inter-urban roads;
(ii) construction of inter-city expressways, and
(iii) building ring-roads to avoid the traffic jams in cities.
All these are aspects of the 1975–80 Development Plan in road construction in the country which were vigorously pursued by the ex-military regime.

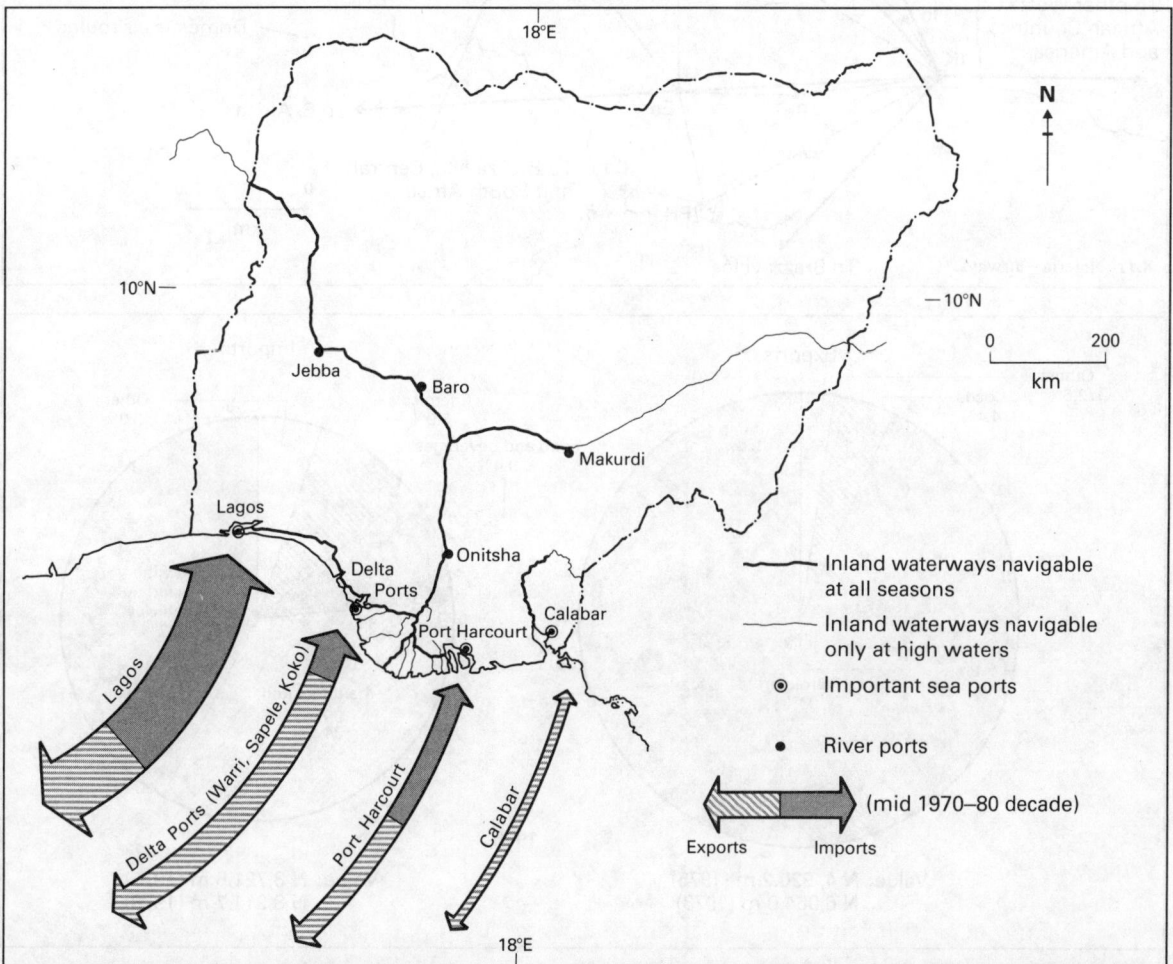

8.10 Navigable waterways and trade through sea ports. Name the major seaports shown in the map above. The size of the arrows indicates relatively the volume of export and import cargo handled at each port. Which of the ports handles the largest volume of cargo? Why does Lagos handle more import cargo than export cargo? What commodities account for the higher volume of export cargo handled by the Delta ports and Calabar? Name the river ports shown in the map. Are there any more you know of? Locate them on the map.

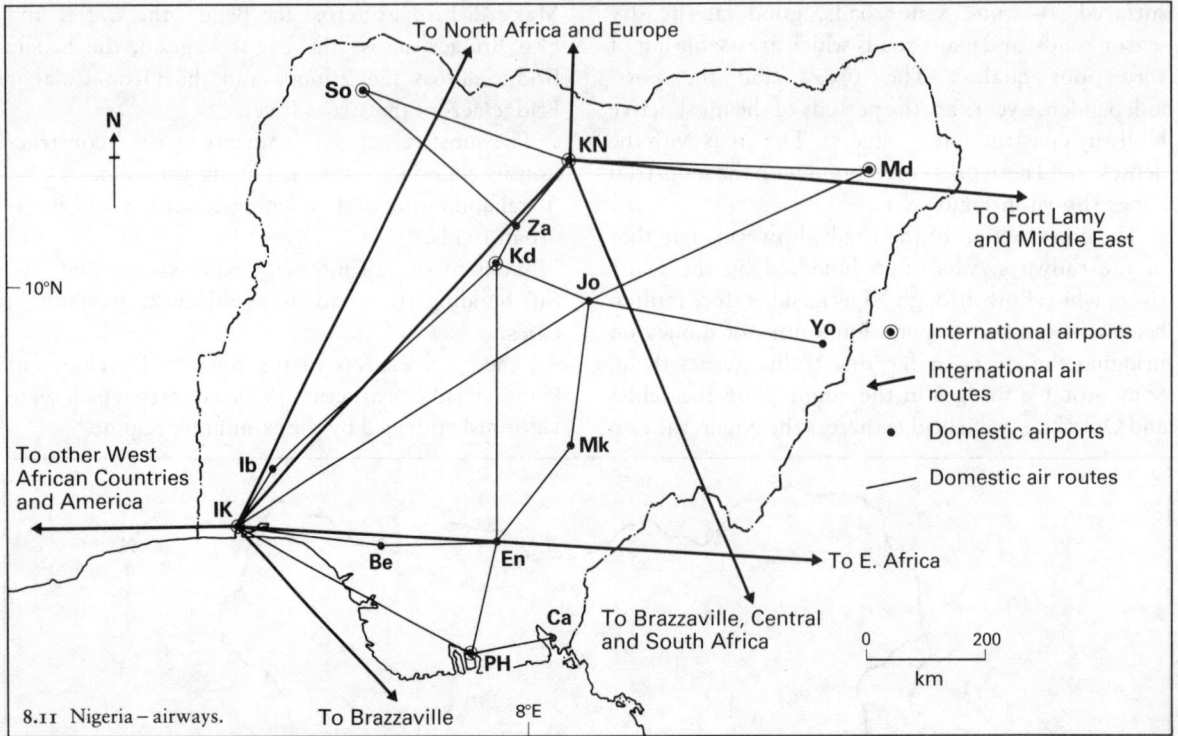

8.11 Nigeria – airways.

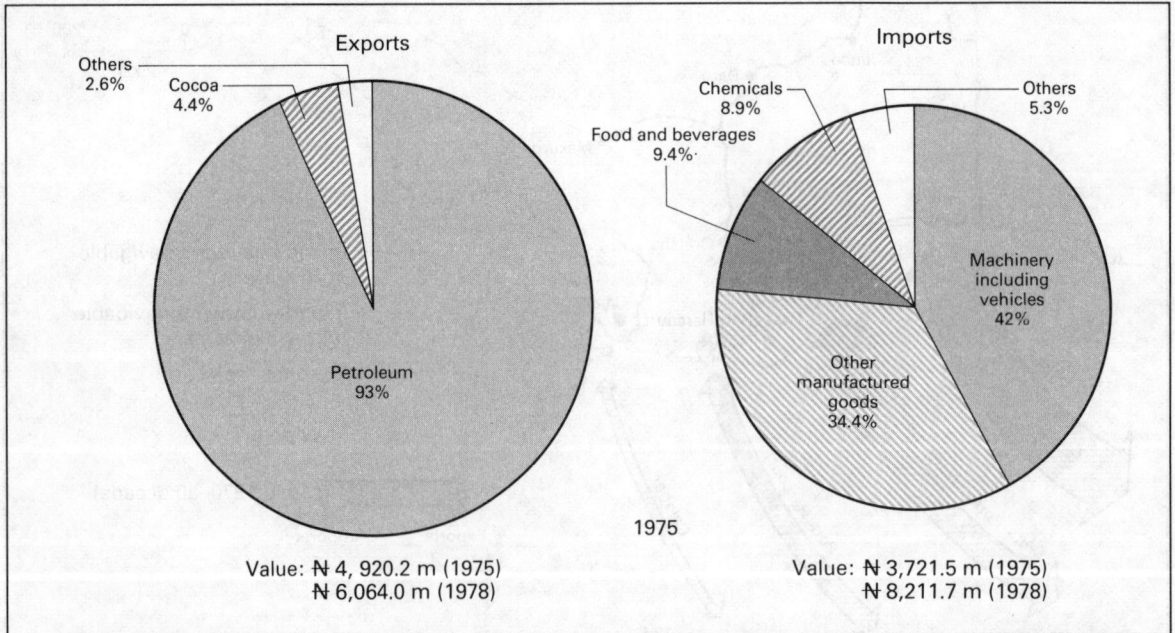

Exports

Others
2.6%
Cocoa
4.4%

Petroleum
93%

Value: ₦ 4, 920.2 m (1975)
₦ 6,064.0 m (1978)

Imports

Chemicals
8.9%
Food and beverages
9.4%

Others
5.3%

Machinery
including
vehicles
42%

Other
manufactured
goods
34.4%

1975

Value: ₦ 3,721.5 m (1975)
₦ 8,211.7 m (1978)

8.12 Nigeria's foreign trade in mid 1970–80 decade. Note the over-riding dominance of petroleum in the country's export earnings. How much was realised from that commodity in 1975? Comment on the relative importance of the import commodities. To draw the pie diagrams above, we first of all found the square roots of ₦ 4 920.2 and ₦ 3 721.5 which are approximately 70 and 61. Then we drew two circles with radii proportional to these square roots. Finally we divided up each circle into sectors each proportional to the % value of the export or import commodity. Now if you drew such circles for 1978, which will be the larger? Why? Draw the circles to prove your answer right or wrong.

Air routes

Of the commercial air routes in Nigeria the first to be operated was the Lagos (Apapa) to Kano Line. That was in 1935. The years of the second world war saw a prolific growth of airfields. But as soon as the war emergency was over there came a period when many airfields were closed down and only the most economically viable were left. The Apapa field was closed and the Ikeja and Kano airports grew to be the largest and most important in the country. They were the only international airports, until recently when Sokoto, Maiduguri, Kaduna, Ilorin and Port Harcourt were up-graded to international status.

Two types of services are operated – foreign and domestic. Trace both routes in Figure 8.11 and name the airports. Both Nigerian and foreign airlines operate the foreign services while Nigeria Airways alone run the domestic services. Can you name some of the cargo carried by these lines? In which ways is transportation by air superior to that of rail or road?

Trade

Commodities are exchanged within the country and also between Nigeria and other countries. The first is domestic trade, the other foreign trade.

Domestic trade

Items of internal trade include foodstuffs, raw materials, and imported and locally manufactured goods. Foodstuffs move across the country from south to north and vice versa, but there is a more restricted movement, particularly of perishable items, from the villages to the nearby towns. Manufactured goods are distributed from the ports of entry, or the towns where they are manufactured, to all parts of the country.

The market is the focus of internal trade. Every town in Nigeria has at least one. Some are held daily, others – especially those in the villages – less frequently. But the market place is not the only centre for the internal exchange of goods. Shops, stores, road-side stalls and even pavements are filled with articles for sale.

Foreign trade

The pattern of Nigeria's foreign trade is shown in Figure 8.12. Name the exports and imports in order of importance. Through which ports do the goods pass? Until recently Nigeria sold more than she bought and therefore registered a favourable trade balance. What commodity was chiefly responsible for this? Find out when the balance of trade changed. Why was this?

Nigeria's most active customers are the United Kingdom, the West European countries, and the African countries. She buys livestock from Niger and Mali and sells manufactured goods like plywood, cigarettes and textile goods to her West African neighbours.

Summary

In this chapter we have discussed Nigeria's industries, the growth of her towns, her population, the transport system and trade. The link between all these is the transport system, for it promotes the growth of industries and towns, makes the population mobile and encourages the flow of trade. Now go through this important chapter again, noting carefully the most relevant points.

Revision exercises

1. This section contains the population figures of five major towns in Nigeria. Draw five bars, proportional in length to the population figures to show the size of the towns. Assuming that the ratio of male to female is 51%:49%, divide each bar to show the male and female population. Shade them differently. This diagram, which is like the one you constructed for Question 1 in the Revision Exercises at the end of Chapter 7, is called a bar chart or graph. Use it to describe the population of the major towns in Nigeria.
2. On the map of Nigeria you have prepared, insert and name:
   a) twelve major towns on the railways;
   b) the industrial zones, and
   c) the navigable waterways.
   Account for the importance of communication lines in the development of industries in the country. Give specific examples.
3. Discuss the importance of Kano, Enugu and Port Harcourt.
4. Describe the Kainji Dam project and say how useful it is to the people of Nigeria.

9 Togo and Benin

Preparation

1. Which is the major language group found in western Nigeria?
2. What are the main cash and food crops in the region?
3. Where else in West Africa would you find a house like the one shown in Figure 9.1?
4. See Figure 9.2. Which is larger – Togo or Benin.
5. Draw a full page map of Togo and Benin.

Togo and Benin are alike in many respects, but they also offer interesting points of contrast. Both are small West African countries, French speaking and formerly under French rule immediately before 1960 when both became independent. They also belong to the West African Monetary Union and other unions of West African States. However, whereas Benin (formerly called Dahomey until 1976) immediately became a French territory when the European powers shared Africa among themselves in late 19th Century, Togo was then given to Germany, and only came under French rule as a mandated territory after the first world war, 1914–1918.

Both countries, with Senegal, had the highest standard of education among the colonial French speaking West Africa countries. They therefore supplied much of the manpower who occupied top and middle level civil service posts in these other countries. But Togo had, and still has, more varied and richer resources than Benin. Consequently, when these other countries became independent and adopted a policy that forced the Togolese and Beninians back to their homes, Togo could absorb her returnees into ready jobs, whereas Benin could not. To make matters worse, Benin's educational system was meanwhile producing even more educated people. As a result there grew in the country a class of educated

9.1 A typical Fon house in southern Benin. Describe this house. What makes it curious? Why is it built the way it is? Answer the other questions on it in the text.

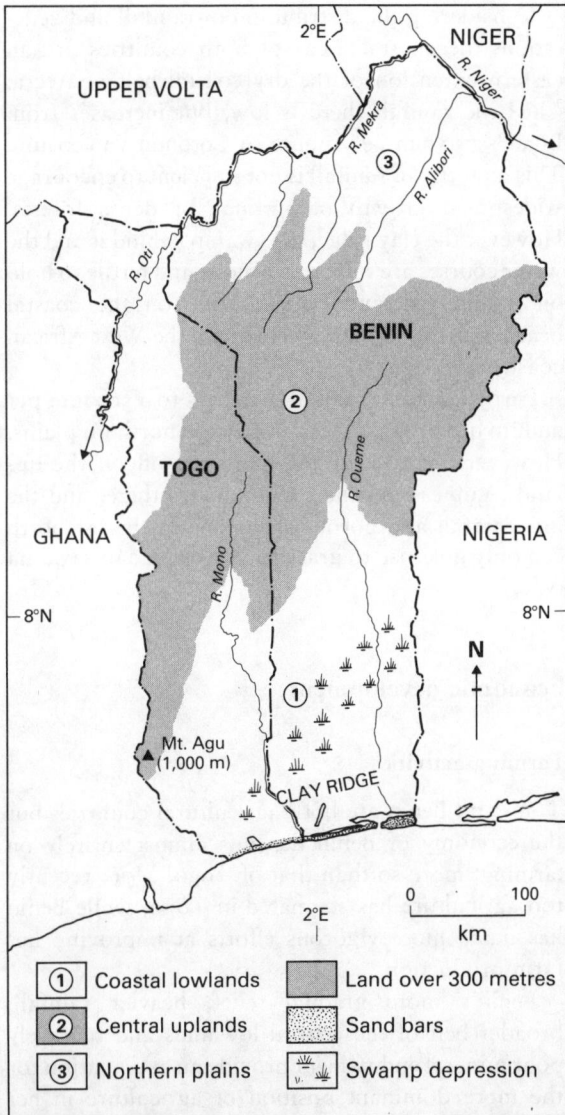

9.2 Togo and Benin – relief.

①	Coastal lowlands		Land over 300 metres
②	Central uplands		Sand bars
③	Northern plains		Swamp depression

Table 4

Togo and Benin: area and population

Country	Area in sq. km.	Pop in millions (1977)	Pop per sq. km.
Benin	115 760	3 112	26.9
Togo	56 000	2.312	41.3

Areas

Togo and Benin are two narrow territories sandwiched between Nigeria in the east and Ghana in the west. But as you can see from the table above, Benin is more than twice as large as Togo and has nearly one and a half times the population of the latter. However, Togo has a higher population density – in fact it has the highest density of all French speaking West African countries. How many times greater is the density of Togo than that of Benin?

Peoples

The dominant groups of people in the two countries are the Ewes of southern Togo and the Fons in southern Benin. They are basically farmers and also constitute the educated élite in their respective countries. The Ewes belong to the same group as the Ewes of Ghana, whereas the Fons live with some Yoruba people in Benin. You will of course remember that the bulk of the Yoruba people live in western Nigeria. A number of the Fons also live and fish in the coastal areas under conditions similar to those of the Ijaw people of the delta area of Nigeria.

See Figure 9.1 and answer the following questions:
i) What is the house built of?
ii) Why is it raised on stilts? What would it be like living in them?
iii) What do you think is the major occupation of the people here? Why?
iv) What is the easiest way of going to places here? Why are the other means of transport difficult to use?
v) Compare this figure with Figure 6.3 showing houses in Ijaw land in Nigeria – in which ways are they alike?

In northern Togo the Kabres are the major farmers

élite who had no jobs. Since 'a hungry man is always an angry man', this class of jobless but educated people became a source of trouble in Benin which has given rise to the country's political instability, resulting in over 6 bloodless coups and changes of government which the country has had since it became independent in 1960.

In studying these two countries, therefore, we shall bear the above historical and social background in mind while comparing in turn the sizes and peoples, physical environments and economies of both countries.

who terrace the hillsides and cultivate them intensively. In Benin the major farmers in the north are the Sombas. In both countries the Fulanis constitute the main pastoralists who live in the north. Also both countries have shed much of the European population they had before independence, although they are now being replaced by technical assistance personnel from overseas.

Physical environment

Physical regions

Although, as shown in the map above, the two countries are divided into three physical regions, each of which runs from one country to the other, the surface of Togo is generally more varied than that of Benin. The *coastal plains* are however wider in Benin than in Togo, as you can see. They are made up of a line of coastal sand bars, a chain of lagoons behind it, an elevated ridge made up of clay, a depressed zone of marshlands and an interior coastal lowland.

This last zone rises to the *central uplands* which reach heights of over 1 000 metres. They are narrow and high in Togo where they are a continuation of the Akwapim – Togo Ranges of Ghana. In Benin they swing to the east, broaden and flatten out, and continue eastwards beyond the frontier to the uplands of western Nigeria. See in Figure 9.2 how two sets of rivers rise from these highlands – one set flowing southwards to the Atlantic and the other heading northwards to the Oti and Niger. Name these rivers. What special name do we give to a highland from where rivers take their rise and flow in opposite directions?

North of the uplands, the land drops to the northern sandstone plains which, in Benin, are drained by the Mekra and Alibani sloping gently to the Niger Valley, but in Togo drop quite steeply to the valley of the River Oti.

Climate and vegetation

The climate of both countries is dominated by the three principal air masses in West Africa. Can you name these air masses? Which of them is associated with the wet season, which with the dry and which with the change-over of seasons?

Considering the distribution of rainfall and vegetation, the coastal areas of both countries are an eastern extension of the dry coastal belt of Accra. Thus the rainfall there is low, but increases from Lomé's 750 mm per annum to Cotonou's 1 300 mm. This quantity of rainfall is not sufficient to encourage widespread growth of swamps or dense forests. However the clay ridge, the swamp behind it and the water courses are sufficiently moist and fertile to hold oil palms. Coconut palms thrive on the coastal beaches as they do elsewhere along the West African coast.

Further inland, rainfall increases to 1 500 mm per annum but drops to 1 000 mm in the northern plains. However, because of the rapid run-off on the uplands, guinea savanna predominates there, and the low rainfall and porous sandstone of the far north can only give rise to grassland of the sudan savanna type.

Economic development

Farming activities

Togo and Benin are both agricultural countries but the economy of Benin depends almost entirely on farming, more so than that of Togo. More recently too agriculture has stagnated in Togo, while Benin has made more vigorous efforts at improving her farm production.

Benin's more gradual relief, heavier rainfall, broader belt of the coastal lowlands and relatively poor mineral endowment provide an explanation for the more dominant position of agriculture in her economy.

Palm production is the major pursuit in Benin. To the 400 000 or more hectares of natural palm groves have been added over 20 000 hectares of industrial palm plantations – mainly situated in the south. Production in 1976 rose to over 80 000 tonnes of palm kernel and 50 000 of palm oil. Benin is the chief producer and exporter of palm produce in French-speaking West Africa. The fastest expanding crop is however cotton, cultivated in the southern interior and exported together with palm produce through the port of Cotonou.

In Togo the principal crops are cocoa and coffee. The former thrives on lighter soils than the oil palm

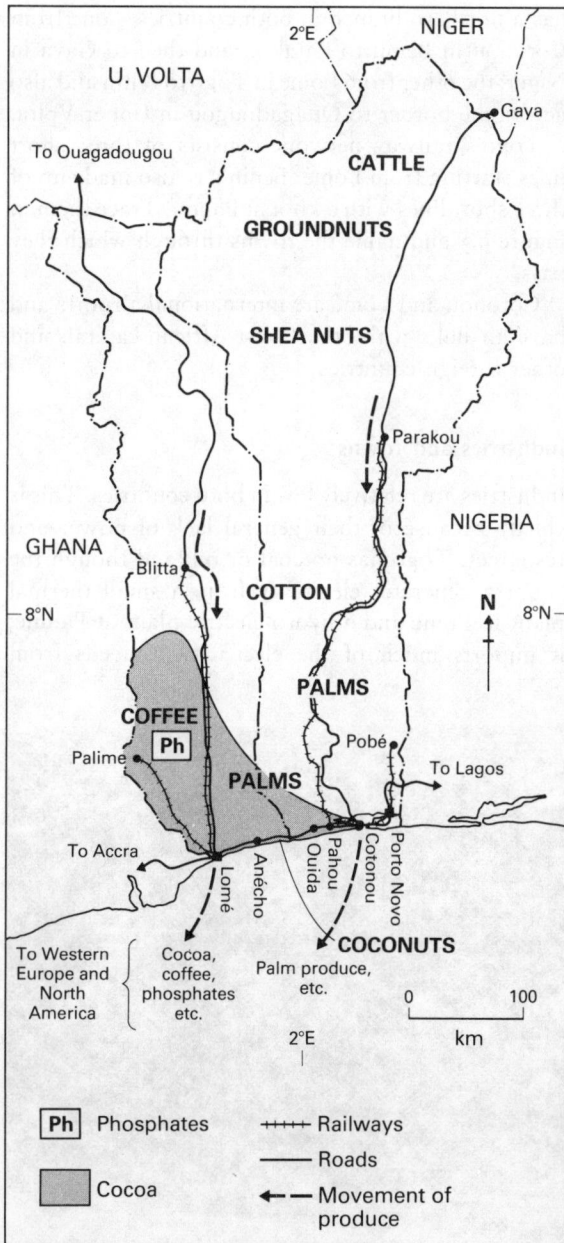

9.3 The economy of Togo and Benin.

while little cotton and shea nuts are grown in the north for export.

Mining

Mining in Benin is only rudimentary. The only mineral so far located and exploited is limestone.

Togo, on the other hand, produces large quantities of phosphates. The quarrying of this mineral started in 1960 at the reserves in Akoupame near Palimé. Production rose steadily to over 1 million tonnes in 1975 and to a peak of 2.55 million tonnes in 1974. Prices in the world market of phosphates fell in 1975 and that caused a drastic fall in the production for that year to 1.13 million tonnes. Faced with this crisis Togo held a number of meetings with other producers to regulate the prices, and this brought about a revival in production in 1976 and subsequent years.

See the graph which tells the recent story in the production of this mineral and answer the questions below:

i) In which year was the highest production recorded? What was the figure for the year?

ii) How would you describe the production from 1971–1974?
- steadily falling,
- steadily rising, or
- constant.

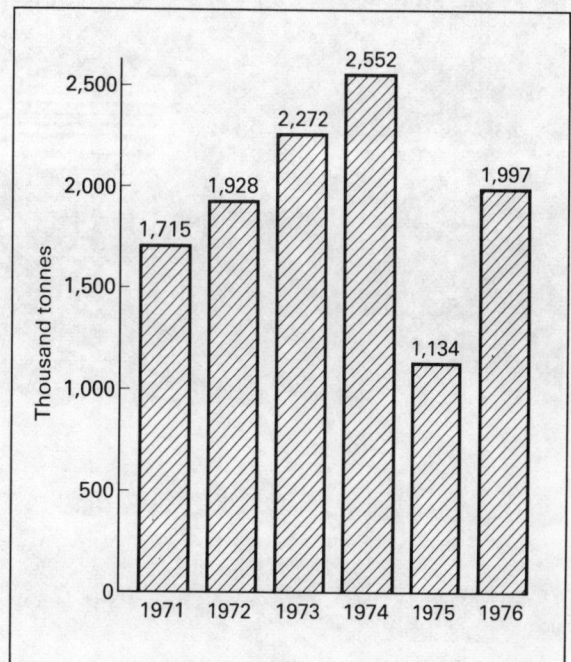

9.4 Togo: the production of phosphates in recent years.

and the latter is grown on the southern slopes of the Togo Ranges. Production remained stagnant between 1970 and 1976, and, in fact, showed a slump in some years due to the greater attention paid by the country to mineral production. The lighter rainfall in the south permits the growing of groundnuts. Copra is produced from the coconut groves in the south

iii) How much was produced in 1975? Why was there a drop in the production for that year?

iv) What made it possible for the production to rise again in 1976?

v) Judging from the trend after 1975, is the production for 1977 likely to be more or less than 1 997 000 tonnes?

Near the same area as phosphates there are extensive deposits of limestone. This mineral is being quarried for the manufacture of cement clinkers.

Communications

The geography of both countries, is perhaps most alike in this respect. The maze of lagoons provides continuous coastal transport from Togo to Benin and even to Lagos in Nigeria. Cotonou and Lomé are sea as well as lagoon ports.

The principal road transport systems in both countries consist of a lovely coastal drive which forms part of the Lagos–Accra highway. This drive has a northern branch in both countries – one from Cotonou in Benin to Parakou and then to Gaya in Niger, the other from Lomé in Togo to Blitta and also across the border to Ouagadougou in Upper Volta.

Togo's railway network consists of three short lines starting from Lomé. Benin's is also made up of three short lines with a knot at Pahou. Trace them in Figure 9.3 and name the towns through which they pass.

Cotonou and Lomé are international airports and have air links with other West African capitals and other foreign countries.

Industries and towns

Industries are relatively few in both countries. This is chiefly because of their general lack of power and resources. Togo has no coal or oil, and though the country generates electricity from a small thermal plant in Lomé and a hydro-electric plant at Palimé, it imports much of the electricity it needs from

9.5 Lomé, the capital of Togo. The big building in the centre is the 'Hotel du Benin' and the one to the left is the National Assembly. At the background is the city itself. Describe the sea near the shoreline.

Akosombo in Ghana. Similarly, Benin has neither coal nor oil and imports electricity from Akosombo in Ghana and also from Kainji in Nigeria.

In both countries we have industries built to process agricultural products for export; industries established to produce some basic consumer goods which otherwise would have to be imported, and one or two isolated large factories which represent more recent serious efforts at industrialization. Thus in Benin we have palm oil and kernel processing plants, cotton ginneries and groundnut oil and shelling factories. Togo has, in addition to the above, coffee roasting plants. These process the agricultural products for export. Both countries have footwear, soft drinks, beer making, confectionery, paint, cycle and motor vehicle tyre factories – all located in the major cities. Three of the large recently established factories in Togo are the 1 million tonne capacity oil refinery in Lomé which went into production in 1977 using crude oil from Gabon and Nigeria, the 2.4 million tonne clinker cement factory near Palimé owned by

CIMACO a combined Togo, Ghana and Ivory Coast company which started in 1979, and the phosphate fertilizer factory near the same town which was opened in 1978. In Benin, a textile factory was opened at Parakou in 1975, and a 300 000 tonne capacity cement factory, a sugar mill and an oil refinery, are billed to be established in the country by 1980.

Lomè, the capital and largest town and port in Togo had a population of 200 000 in 1977 and is situated in the south-western corner of the country. It is the chief industrial and commercial city of Togo, having corn, flour and cassava mills and several other factories. Its port handles over 750 000 tonnes of merchandise including transit goods from Upper Volta and Niger, and is being improved by installing a quay capable of handling a million tonnes of ore.

Porto Novo and *Cotonou* are the joint capitals of Benin, the latter being the outport of the former. Porto Novo has a population of 104 000, is situated by a lagoon that goes by its name and has rail and road connections with Cotonou, and lagoon connec-

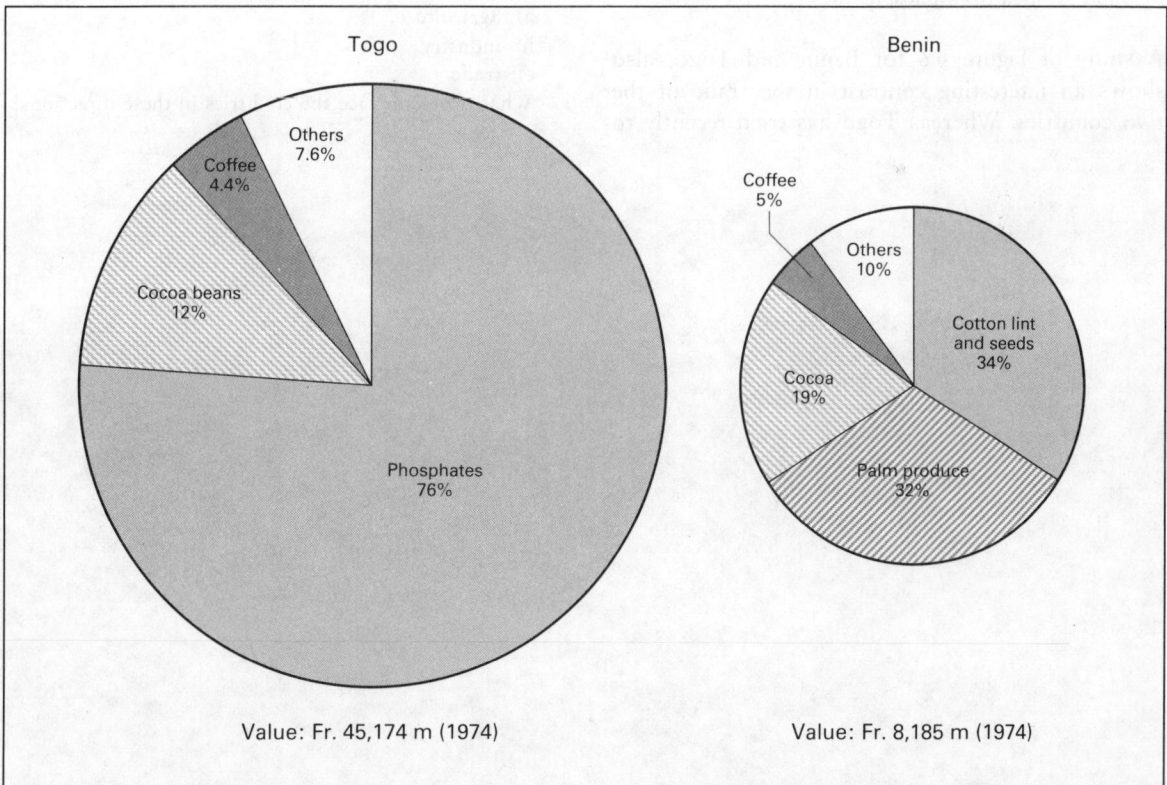

9.6 The export trade of Togo and Benin (mid 1970–80 decade). How many times is the value of Togo's export that of Benin's? Which is the dominating export commodity in each case? Which country has a more balanced export trade – Togo or Benin?

tion with Lagos in Nigeria. Cotonou's population of over 178 000 people makes it the largest town in Benin. It is the chief port and commercial centre, handling the external trade of not only Benin but land-locked Niger in the north.

Trade

The overseas trade of Togo is dominated by the export of a single mineral – phosphates. Cocoa and coffee follow in that order of importance.

Benin, on the other hand, depends principally on the exportation of agricultural produce of which cotton has recently taken the first place from palm produce.

Study the pie diagrams which show the export trade of Togo and Benin and then do the following exercises:
i)   Which country has the higher export earnings?
ii) Which country has a more balanced export trade? Give reasons for your answer.
iii) Approximately what percentage of Togo's export is the value realised from phosphates?

A study of Figure 9.6 for Benin and Togo, also shows an interesting contrast in the trade of the two countries. Whereas Togo has tried recently to make her exports yield more money than she spends on imports, Benin, a relatively poorer country, has regularly recorded trade deficit over the years, the value of her exports being consistently lower than that of her imports. Togo therefore has a better trading position than Benin. Both countries trade principally with France, the Netherlands and Western Germany, the three overseas countries which account for over 75% of the trade of both countries.

Revision exercises

1. On the map of Togo and Benin which you have prepared, insert and name the following:
   a) the cocoa belt;
   b) important areas for coffee, phosphates, oil palm, cotton, limestone and coffee;
   c) Lomé, Palimé, Cotonou and Porto Novo.
   What effects has relief on the agriculture of both countries.
2. Compare the recent efforts made by both countries towards improving:
   a) agriculture;
   b) industry;
   c) trade.
   What problems face the countries in these directions?

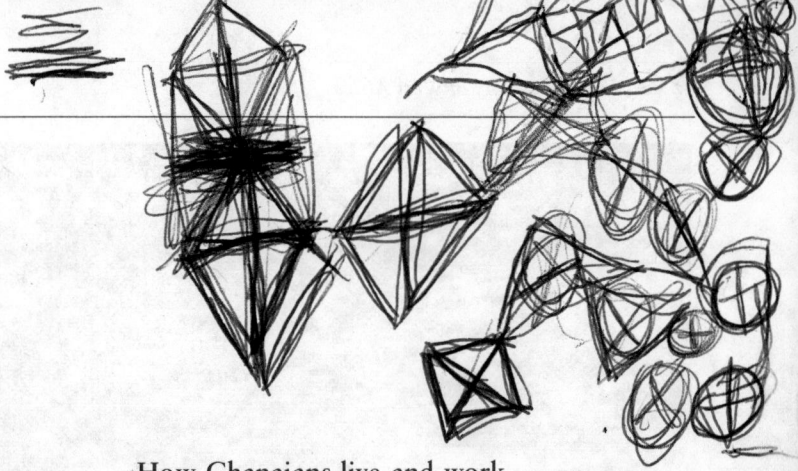

10 Ghana (1)

Preparation

1. Name six of the ancient empires in West Africa. (Figure 1.2)
2. Name three forest crops and three savanna crops grown in Nigeria. Where are cattle reared in Nigeria? Give two reasons why they are found there.
3. Prepare two blank maps of Ghana, and insert the River Volta and its tributaries on one of them.

On attaining independence from Britain in 1957, the then Gold Coast re-christened itself Ghana after the ancient West African empire of that name. (See Figure 10.1.) We will now see how the 9.9 million Ghanaians who inhabit their country, 238 500 square kilometres in area, live and work.

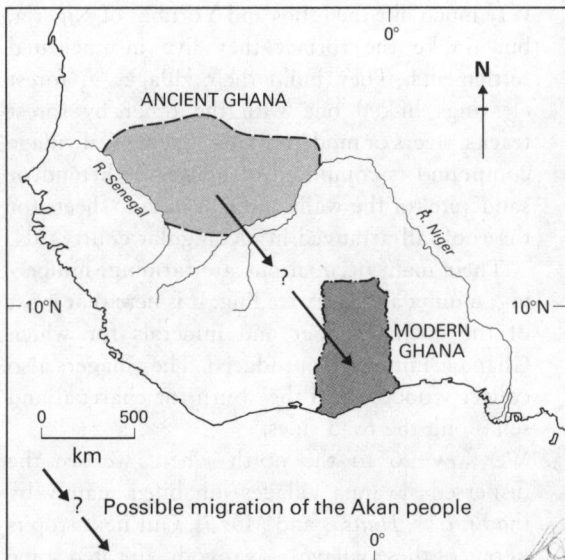

10.1 Ghana: ancient and modern.

How Ghanaians live and work

Ghanaians live and work both in towns and in villages as people do in other parts of West Africa.

Town life

Town life is very popular in Ghana – what with the employment opportunities, recreational facilities, club houses and other social amenities which attract people from the villages around. Most of the urban centres are found in the southern one-third of the country. Turn to your atlas map of Ghana and locate the following towns – Accra, Tema, Takoradi, Sekondi, Tarkwa, Winneba, Cape Coast, Mpraeso, Kumasi and Akosombo. Locate also the few northern towns like Tamale and Bolgatanga. About one-third of the population of Ghana live in these and other towns. They live close together as they do elsewhere in other West African towns, and engage in mining, manufacturing, transporting and other service industries.

We shall study more about the individual towns in the next chapter. Meanwhile let us find out how Ghanaians live and work in the villages. In doing so we shall make a journey from the coast to the very northern part of the country, stopping at convenient places and seeing things for ourselves.

Life in the villages

1. There are over 60 fishing villages found along the coast. Our first stop will be at Mouri, one of them, located near Cape Coast almost midway between Winneba and Takoradi. The people who live here are *Fantes* who speak the Fanti language.

   The village settlement itself is sited on elevated land. Its sea front is lined with coconut palms which grow on the low sandy sea beach, and

10.2 A coastal fishing scene in Ghana.

behind it is a broad tidal marsh which has to be crossed to reach the village from the mainland.

The houses are built of mud for the walls, and either raffia or zinc sheets for the roofs. Scattered everywhere among them are fish ovens indicative of the main occupation of the people.

They also make nets for fishing, and rear pigs which forage from the fish refuse and garbage lying around in the poorly drained marshes. The men also brew *akpateshie* – a type of gin distilled from raffia palm wine which is drunk locally or sold to the Ghana distilleries for making more refined drinks.

Fish from Mouri and other similar fishing villages are landed and sold in fish markets along the coast like the one shown.

2. The interior forest villages are found in the forest belt and inhabited by the *Akans* who constitute over 44% of the population of Ghana. They live very much like the Igbos and Yorubas of Nigeria, but unlike the former they live in nucleated settlements. They build their villages in forest clearings linked one with the other by forest tracks, rivers or modern roads. The typical village compound is composed of houses with mud or sandcrete for the walls and mat or zinc sheets for the roof, all arranged in rectangular courtyards.

Their main occupations are farming, lumbering, mining and petty trading. It is here that most of the cocoa, timber and minerals for which Ghana is famous are produced. The villagers also collect wood, which they burn for charcoal and sell along the road sides.

3. We now go to the north where we see the dispersed savanna villages inhabited mainly by the *Frafras*, *Hausas* and *Mossis*. Our next stop is in one of these villages – Nangodi – located some 25 kilometres east of Bolgatanga on the road to

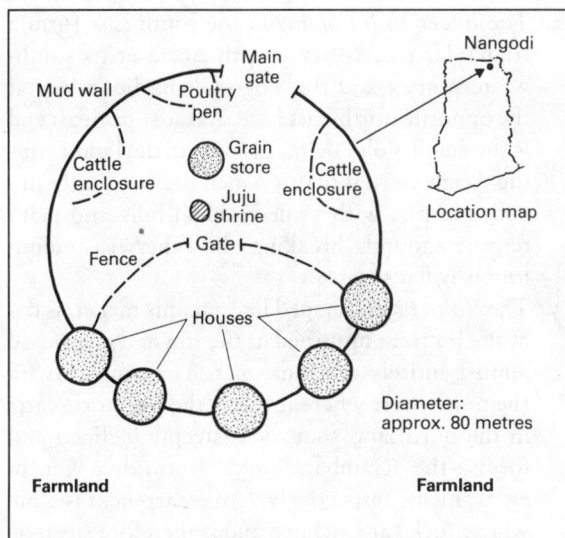

10.3 A compound in Nangodi, Ghana.

10.4 The modern resettlement village of Makongo, Ghana. This is one of the modern villages built by the Volta River Authority to resettle those whose homes were drowned by the Volta Lake or who were otherwise displaced by the project. Can you name one other such village?

Bawku. (See where it is in Figure 10.3.)

Over 4000 people live in Nangodi in round houses arranged in circular compounds which are scattered over the landscape with farmlands in between. Describe the layout of one such compound shown in Figure 10.3. The compound is more than an ordinary family home with houses only for the family inmates. It also contains a grain store, a poultry pen, enclosures where cattle are kept for the night and, like most traditional compounds in West Africa, a juju shrine symbolizing the co-habitation of the family's ancestors with the present generation. In short, from the compound, we learn much about the economy, culture and religion of the people of Nangodi.

Some of the houses have conical, thatched roofs. Others have roofs which are flat and, like the walls, are made of mud reinforced with the soaked and beaten bark of the baobab tree. Grains are dried on the flat roof, but the people sleep on it all night during the hot season!

Farming in Nangodi is intensive and mixed. The villagers use cow dung and poultry droppings to manure their farms, and they practise crop rotation, irrigation and terracing where necessary. Two main crops grown are grains and groundnuts, but with the recent introduction of market gardening the villagers grow vegetables including large quantities of tomatoes for sale. Their livestock include cattle, sheep, goats and guinea fowls – these last being traditionally important in the performance of marriage rites.

The Nangodi area is one of the most densely peopled in Ghana, and there are other settlements here like Navrongo and Zuarungu where life is very similar to that in Nangodi which we have just described.

4. Our journey leads us to a modern resettlement village – Makongo – located 80 kilometres north of Yeji on the Kumasi Tamale road. See in Figure 10.4 how the houses in this village are made of concrete and aluminium sheets and are arranged in rows – very different from the houses in Nangodi. The streets are paved with tar or concrete. The village has co-operative shops, parks, schools, a clinic and a market. The 2 500 people who live here engage in market gardening, crop farming, commercial poultry keeping and running provision stores.

Makongo is one of over 52 resettlement villages all over Ghana, built by the Volta River Authority, to resettle people whose original homes were drowned as the Volta Lake was formed in 1964/65. We shall learn more about the Volta River scheme in the next chapter.

Physical environment

Relief

In Figure 10.5, we see how the relief of Ghana can be divided clearly into six regions – three lowlands and three highlands. Can you, by comparing this figure with an atlas relief map of Ghana, identify which of the regions are lowlands and which are highlands?

1. The *south-west coastal lowlands* rise from a low cliffed coastline, through undulating terrain, 50–70 metres high, to the interior forested low Akan Plateau, 150–200 metres above sea level. It is dissected by the Ankobra, Pra and other rivers, and dotted here and there by low residual hills.

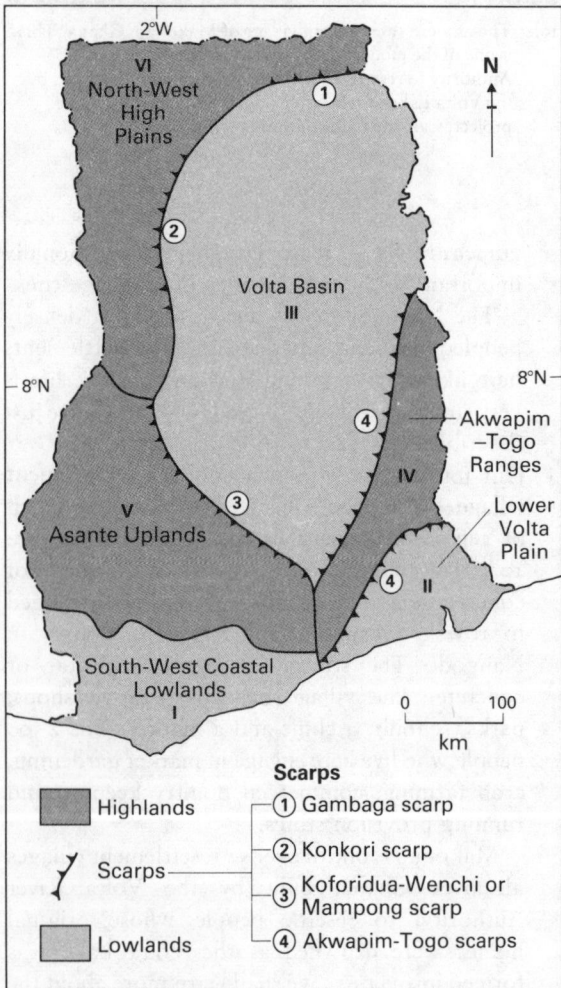

10.5 Relief regions of Ghana.

2. The *lower Volta plains* in the south-east form a triangular piece of land with Accra at its south-western apex and the Togo-Ghana boundary at the opposite north-east base. At the south-east end is the small Volta delta. Elsewhere the land forms the Accra coastal plains which are peculiarly dry and infertile, with some residual hills and giant termite mounds breaking the otherwise monotonously flat surface.

3. The *Volta basin*, shaped like a tennis racket, is flat at the bottom, upturned at the rim and composed almost entirely of sandstones. The rim is low in the north-west where it forms the Konkori scarp. In the north and south it is steeply inclined and forms the Gambaga and Koforidua-Wenchi escarpments respectively. (An escarpment is a hill whose rocks are inclined and is therefore steep on one side and gently sloping on the other.)

4. The *Akwapim-Togo ranges*, east and south-east of the Volta Basin, are made up of old folded and twisted rocks set in north-north-east to south-south-west parallel ridges. They are the highest mountains in Ghana – well over 700 metres in places – and are cut through by the Volta River gorge. The highest point here, and in Ghana, is the Afajato Peak – 870 metres above sea level.

5. The *Asante uplands* extend northwards from the south-west coastal lowlands and terminate with the Koforidua-Wenchi Scarp (see Figure 10.5). They lie between 150 and 600 metres and are heavily forested.

6. Finally, the *north-west high plains* rise gently from the 150 metre high Konkori Scarp to heights of 300 metres. They have open undulating surface, dotted here and there with granite round topped inselbergs.

Climate and vegetation

Figure 10.6 shows the rainfall distribution in Ghana. The country is wettest in the south west, and surprisingly driest in the coastal southeast. Can you say why? How much rainfall is received in these places? See also how the highlands receive heavy rainfall while the Volta basin, in the rain shadow of the Asante uplands, is comparatively dry. The rainiest parts of Ghana are also the most thickly forested. Why is this?

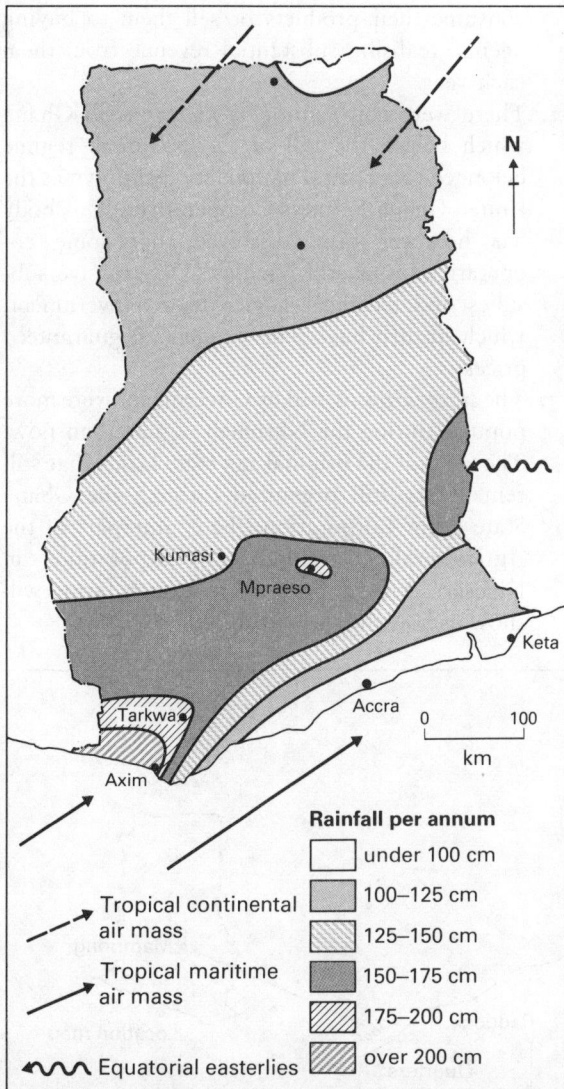

10.6 Ghana: total annual rainfall and prevailing winds.

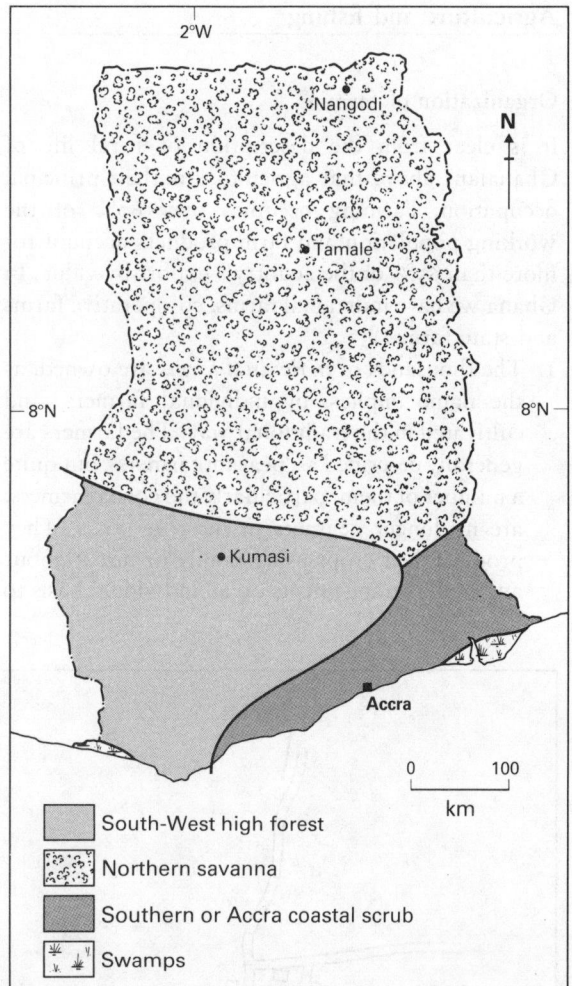

10.7 Ghana: vegetational belts.

Ghana has three main climatic types – the wet sub-equatorial type, the dry Accra coastal plains type and the dry tropical continental type. Corresponding roughly with these three, are also three vegetational types – the high forest, the Accra coastal scrubs and the northern savanna respectively. There is, in addition, a fourth vegetational type – the mangrove swamp located at the south-west corner of Ghana and in the Volta delta.

These climatic and vegetational types have been described in Chapters 3 and 5, and by way of revising them and what

we have so far learnt in this chapter, do the following exercises:

i)   When did Ghana attain independence?
ii) What work do Ghanaians do in towns?
iii) Describe two village settlement types in Ghana. How are the houses and life there similar to, or different from, those in your home area?
iv) Show on the first map of Ghana you prepared three lowland and three highland regions. Describe the surface features of each.
v)   Name three prevailing winds in Ghana and describe the type of weather each brings to the country.
vi) Describe the features of the continental type of climate and savanna vegetation in Ghana.

Agriculture and fishing

Organization of farming

It is clear from the description of rural life of Ghanaians above that agriculture is their principal occupation. Farming occupies over 60% of the working population and farm products account for more than 65% of the country's export by value. In Ghana we have individual farms, co-operative farms and state farms.

1. The thousands of *individual farms* are owned, as the name implies, by individual farmers, and cultivated in the traditional way. The farmers are generally described as 'peasant farmers', but quite a number of them, particularly the cocoa farmers, are no longer peasants in the true sense. They produce their crops using family or hired labour and make arrangements on an individual basis to consume their products or sell them to buying agents, realising substantial revenue from them each year.

2. There were many *co-operative farms* in Ghana which before the fall of the Nkrumah regime belonged to a central national body known as the United Ghana Farmers Co-operatives. This body has however been dissolved, but some co-operative farms still remains. They receive subsidies and technical advice from Government, which in turn buys their produce at guaranteed prices.

3. The *state farms* owned by Government were more popular during the Nkrumah regime than now. The 40% of the original 125 state farms that still remain are still organized through the Ghana State Farm Corporation (the counterpart of the Agricultural Development Corporation in Nigeria). A description of two such farms will show us how they are organized.

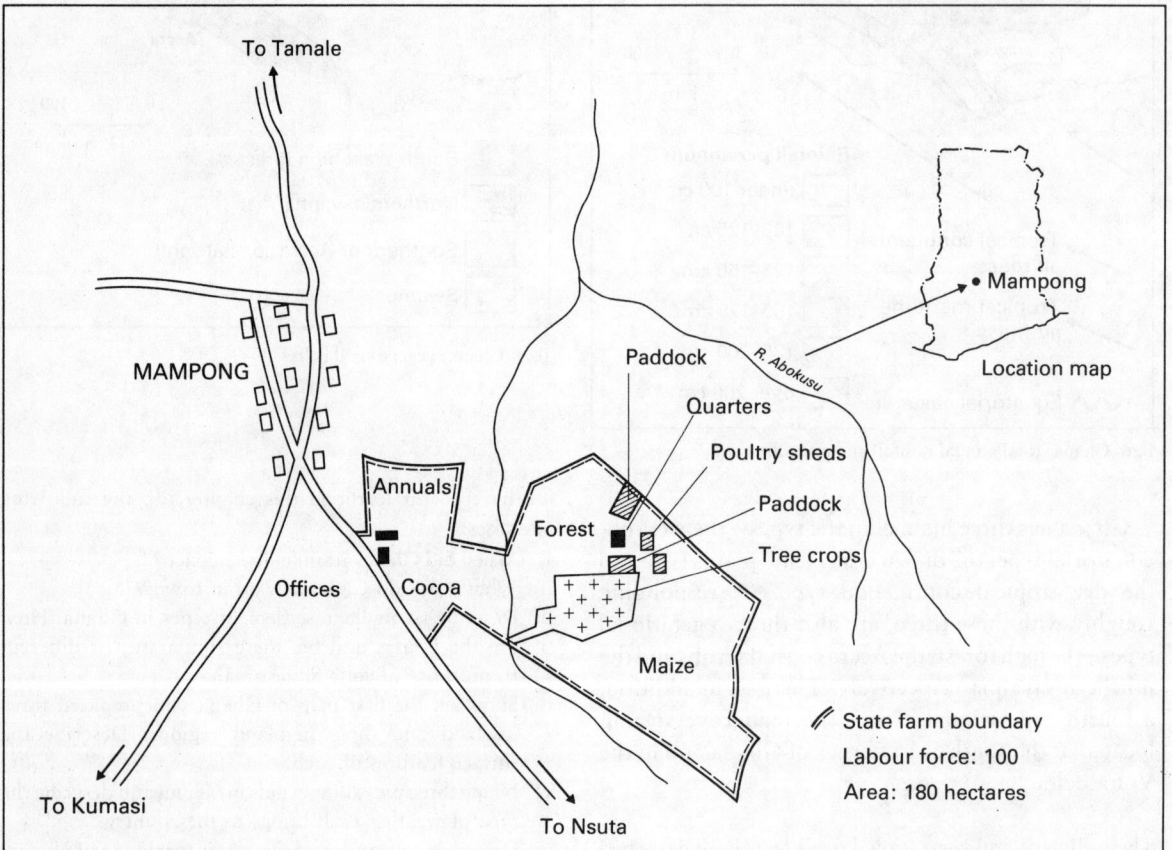

10.8 The Mampong state farm, Ghana.

The Okubeyeye state farm is located near Nsawam. This 250 hectare farm was surveyed and demarcated, and the land allocated mainly to pineapples. There are also staff quarters and offices. Over 500 farmers work here and get paid for doing so. Some 12 000 tonnes of pineapples are produced annually from the farm and taken to the Nsawam cannery where they are canned both for domestic and foreign consumption.

At Mampong in the forest region (Figure 10.8) is another state farm. It occupies a 180 hectare piece of surveyed land, employs some 200 men and produces cocoa, maize, tree crops and some poultry. Describe other uses to which the land is put as shown in the figure.

Let us now look at the crops that are generally produced in the country.

Crops

Cocoa is the main cash crop in the forest belt.

Introduced by one Tetteh Quarshie from Fernando Po in 1879, the crop is now grown all over the forest belt. (Compare Figures 10.13 and 10.9.)

Certain conditions in this belt favour the growth of the crop. The atmosphere is humid (over 80%), temperatures are sufficiently high at the crucial time of year and annual rainfall adequate (1250 to 2000 mm). The forest trees provide the necessary shade and serve as wind breaks for the young cocoa plants. Furthermore, the undulating, and therefore well drained, surface and the loamy virgin soils of the forest belt provide ideal growing conditions. Finally, the brilliant sunshine of this region helps in ripening the cocoa pods and in drying the seeds after harvest.

The way the crop is grown in Ghana is typical of most other cocoa growing areas of West Africa. Let us therefore choose one cocoa farmer here and study in detail how he grows his crop.

Near the Mampong state farm (Figure 10.8) lives the family of Opanin Kwaku Kyeame – the chief

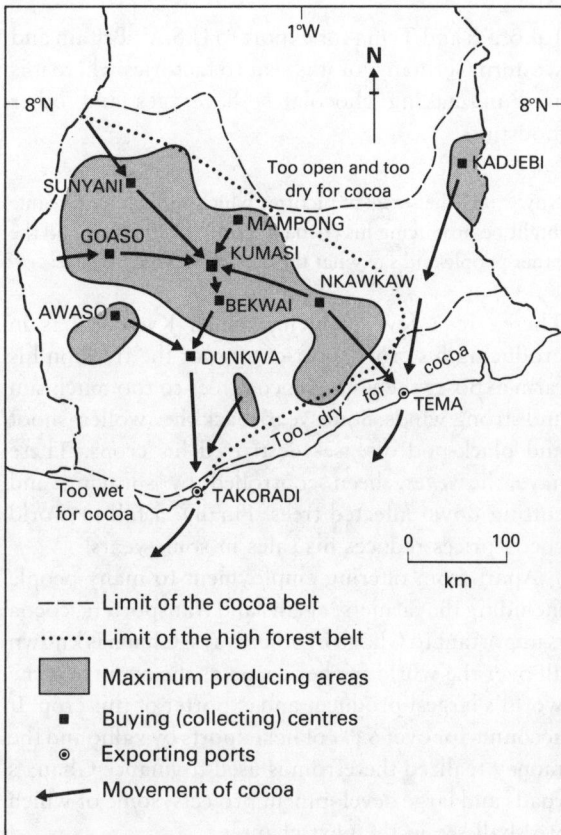

10.9 Cocoa producing areas in Ghana.

10.10 Cocoa production in Ghana. The pods grow out of the stem and branches of the cocoa plant.

10.11 This picture shows how the cocoa beans are spread out to dry.

10.12 This picture shows huge cocoa silos built to store the cocoa at the ports before it is exported.

cocoa farmer in Mampong. Mampong itself is in the heart of the cocoa belt. Kyeame selects his plots in January, hires labour to clear them, and first of all (about February or March) plants food crops like cassava, vegetables, cocoyams, plantains and bananas. All over the forest belt the last two are planted both as food crops and to provide shades for the young cocoa plants. While these crops are growing, Kyeame makes cocoa nurseries at the riverside of a nearby river and plants the cocoa seeds. About May to June he transplants the cocoa seedlings to his plots, weeds them as the need arises and waits for five years to harvest the first cocoa fruits from the trees.

During harvest (October to February and August of each year) his workers cut the pods, remove the beans, leave them to ferment over a period of one to two weeks and later spread them out to dry. During this period the seeds acquire their good colour and taste.

To sell his crop, he bags them and sends them to the Mampong branch of the Cocoa Marketing Board. Here the agents of the Board select, grade and buy his cocoa, paying him cash according to the grade of cocoa.

From Mampong and other buying centres throughout the cocoa growing belt, Ghana's cocoa is assembled and transported by road and rail to Takoradi and Tema for export to U.S.A., Britain and Western Germany, or it is sent to factories where it is used in making chocolates, beverages and other foodstuffs.

Now study the series of pictures which show how Kyeame might be producing his cocoa. Identify the farmers and the other people and say what they are doing in each case.

There are a few problems which Kyeame has in producing his crop. Over-cutting of the trees on his farm exposes the young cocoa trees to too much sun and strong winds. Some years back the swollen-shoot and black-pod diseases destroyed his crops. These have, however, been controlled by spraying and cutting down affected trees. Finally, a fall in world cocoa prices reduces his sales in some years.

Apart from offering employment to many people including the farmers, agents and transporters, cocoa is important to Ghana in other ways. Ghana is known all over the world for her cocoa as the country is the world's largest producer and exporter of this crop. It accounts for over 64% of her exports by value and the money realized therefrom is used to finance Ghana's roads and large development projects, some of which we shall see in the next chapter.

But cocoa and the food crops named above are not

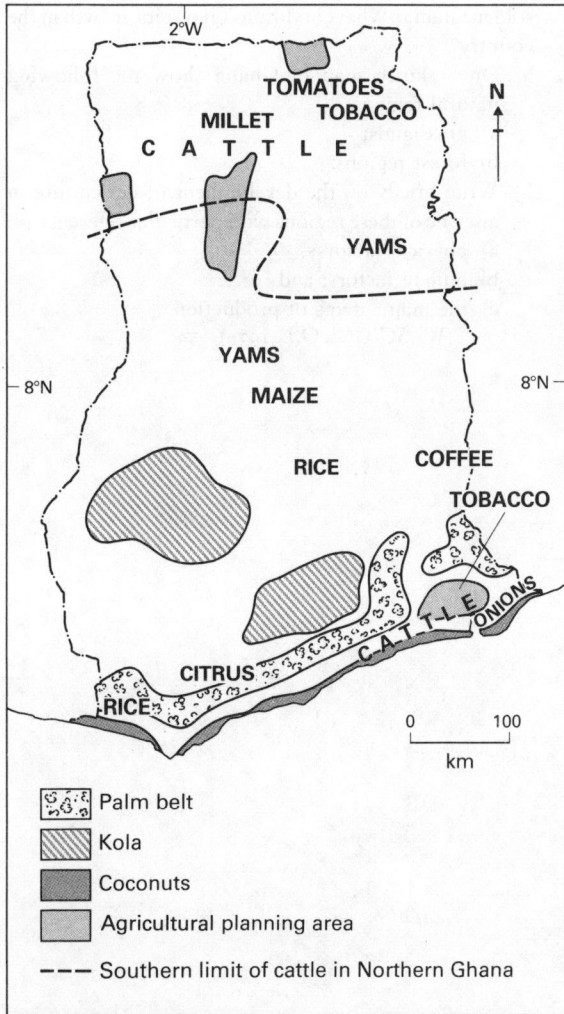

10.13 Other crops and cattle in Ghana.

are common to both, the grain in the south-east being chiefly maize, while those in the north are principally millet and guinea corn. Yams are however peculiar to the northern guinea savanna belt from where they are sent in lorries principally to the south for consumption. The broad flooded valleys of the Volta basin form excellent *rice* fields.

Special crops are grown in market gardens or special areas over the country. These include *tomatoes* grown in market gardens around Nangodi and elsewhere, *onions* cultivated chiefly in the lower Volta plain behind the Keta lagoon and *tobacco* cultivated in the north-east as well as in the Wenchi, Koforidua and Tamale areas.

Fishing

Fishing is a vital occupation for the Ghanaians – vital in the sense that the product, fish, is an important source of food. It is particularly practised, as we saw in Mouri village, by the coastal village settlers who fish in the lagoons and open sea. Fishing is also done along the river banks and in the inland lakes, notably the Bosumtwi and Volta Lakes. The rivers and lakes are the main sources of fresh water fish.

Lagoon fishing is most active at low tide and at the beginning of the dry season. During these times the tide and flood water which bring in the fish have respectively receded leaving large quantities of fish stranded in the shallow waters of the lagoons. The Keta lagoon is famous for its fish.

Open sea fishing is most active fom July to November. Tema, Takoradi and Axim have special harbours for handling fish where it is treated for preservation before being sent inland for sale.

As for the quantities caught, 42 000 tonnes of inland fresh water fish and 213 000 tonnes of open sea fish were landed in 1975.

Summary

Ghana is a medium-sized West African country with an area of 238 500 square kilometres and an estimated population of 9.9 million. It has three areas of highland and three of lowland, three climate types and four vegetational belts.

There are four main types of rural settlements in the country. In three of them farming is the principal

the only crops grown in the forest belt, or, for that matter in Ghana. There are others as Figure 10.13 shows.

Oil palm is grown in the south but away from the coastal scrub-land; *rice* is cultivated in the wet south-west, while *kola* and *rubber* are obviously forest crops. *Citrus* plantations cover many hectares behind Winneba and Cape Coast, and *pineapple* estates are located in state farms in the south. The well-drained slopes of the Akwapim-Togo ranges provide suitable conditions for *coffee*, while the coastal beaches form veritable havens for *coconut* groves, as they do in Togo and Benin.

The products of the savanna belts of the north and south-east are almost identical. *Grains* and *livestock*

occupation while in the coastal settlements fishing is predominant. Of the cash crops grown, cocoa is the most important, cattle are reared in the grasslands of the north and south-east Accra coastal plains, while yams, plantains, maize and other grains constitute the main food crops.

Revision exercises

1. On the second blank map you have prepared, locate the cocoa growing areas. How is the crop produced and sold in Ghana? What conditions favour its growth in the country?

2. a) On a sketch map of Ghana show the following natural regions:
   a) grasslands;
   b) forest regions.

   b) Write briefly on the development of agriculture in any one of these regions with particular reference to:
   a) physical factors;
   b) human factors; and
   c) the major items of production.
   (*WASC/GCE O.L. 1976*)

11 Ghana (2)

Preparation

Go through the maps and photographs in this chapter. Without reading the text say what they tell you about the geography of Ghana.

We shall continue our study of the geography of Ghana in this chapter with a survey of the rest of the country's economic activities. These include forestry, mining, the production of power, manufacturing industries and trade. We shall also look at the towns and population distribution.

Forestry

Timber, charcoal, firewood and building materials are the forest products of Ghana, but timber is the most important.

11.1 Transportation of logs, Ghana. Timber is one of Ghana's major products and exports. What is it used for?

The largest amount of timber in Ghana is obtained from the 25 000 square kilometres of forests in Asante and the south-west. (See Figure 10.7.) Felling is regulated, and restricted to areas which would in any case be cleared for cocoa planting. As in Nigeria, the principal species are the mahogany, obeche, iroko and sapele. The industry is in the hands of private companies. These companies fell the trees and transport them by road to Awaso and Kumasi railheads, and from there by rail to either Takoradi for export or the various sawmills in the forest belt. Alternatively, they are taken by road straight to the sawmills or Takoradi.

Originally most of the timber was exported as logs. Today over fifty saw-mills are scattered all over the forest belt where the timber is sawn into planks for local building and other constructional works. There are also plywood and veneer factories at Samreboi, Sefwi and Wiawso, and a most recent 10 million cedi wood processing plant opened in 1978 at Akim Apapatia in the Eastern Region. The products from these factories are either sold locally or exported.

From the logs and sawn timber exported in 1974, Ghana earned 98 million cedis, that is 12% of the total amount realized from exports.

Mining, railways and roads

Mining

There has been a recent decline in the production of minerals in Ghana. This is due to three main factors:
i) fall in world market prices;
ii) competition from better placed countries which produce similar minerals, and
iii) loss of labour since the Government drove away many non-nationals (including miners) out of the country in the early 1970's.

This decline notwithstanding, mining is still important in the country and is second to agriculture in the money it fetches from exports. Agriculture (mainly cocoa farming) accounts for just over 65%, mining 15% and forestry 12%. Mining also employs directly some 25 000 people and has led to the construction of the many railways in the country. It has also given rise to mineral processing industries.

Having seen the recent trend and the importance of mining in Ghana above, we will continue our study of this occupation by visiting a typical mining community. We can go by either rail or road from Takoradi, 65 kilometres northwards, and stop at Tarkwa. Very close to Tarkwa are two other towns, Nsuta and Abontiakoon, all located in a dry tributary valley of the River Bonsa. Originally separate, the three towns have now grown together to form a large mining community where some 25 000 people live, 2 500 of whom are directly engaged in mining. Look up the towns in an atlas map of Ghana, and see also their location in Figure 11.2. Gold and manganese are the two chief minerals obtained in this community.

Modern mining in Abontiakoon started in 1880. There were many gold mines here before, but now only two large productive mines remain.

To obtain the gold, the miners sink vertical or inclined underground holes (called *shafts*), some 1 000 to 1 500 metres deep, until they reach the rock layer(s) where the gold is. Here they construct horizontal tunnels as they mine the gold using explosives or power drills. The gold bearing rocks are then brought up in cages to the surface through the tunnels and shafts, using a system of pulleys operated by the head gear. The rocks are crushed in the factory, waste rocks removed, and the clean gold sent to Tarkwa. Here it is refined further and made into bars in which form it is sent to Takoradi for export.

Originally the miners lived in old shacks which they built for themselves. Now the State Mining Corporation has erected quarters for them nearby. Amenities like schools, hospitals, markets and canteens have been provided, but these are grossly inadequate. The streets are narrow and sanitation poor as in many mining communities.

At Nsuta there is an open cast manganese mine – the largest single manganese mine in the world. The ore is exposed in two parallel ridges from where it is cut away in terraces. This operation in one such ridge is shown in Figure 11.3.

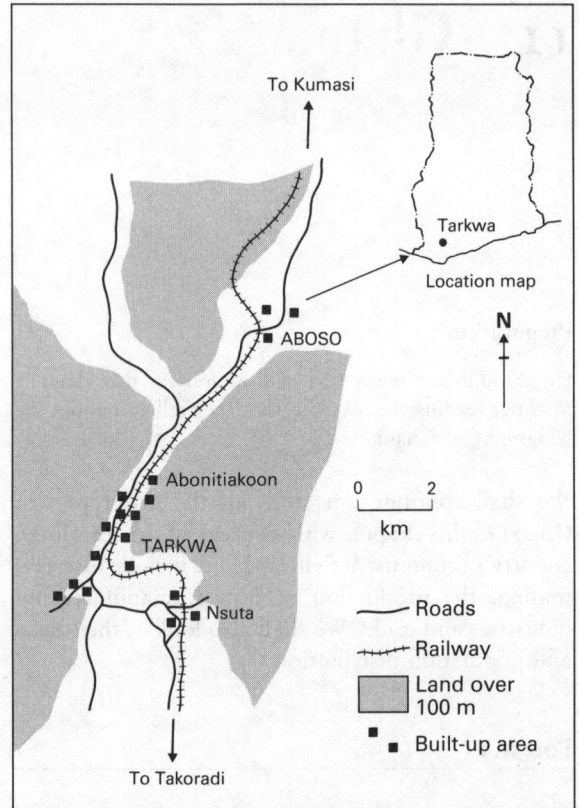

11.2 Abontiakoon-Tarkwa-Nsuta mining community, Ghana.

It is then carried away in trucks to a local plant for crushing and washing before it is sent by rail to Takoradi for export. Ghana used to be the third largest world producer of manganese – after the U.S.S.R. and India – when it was producing half a million tonnes of this mineral per annum. Now production has fallen to an average of 250 000 tonnes per annum and it has stepped down in the list.

There are many more mining communities in Ghana like the Abontiakoon – Tarkwa – Nsuta community just described. See Figure 11.4 and locate Prestea, Konongo and Obuasi. They are gold mining towns too. The Obuasi mine is the largest in Ghana and the richest in the world. Elsewhere along the Ankobra River valley gold is dredged from the river sands.

The total output of gold in Ghana has fallen in recent years, from 920 000 fine ounces in 1965 to 480 880 in 1977. Can you give three reasons for this decline?

Diamonds are found in the sands of old river beds,

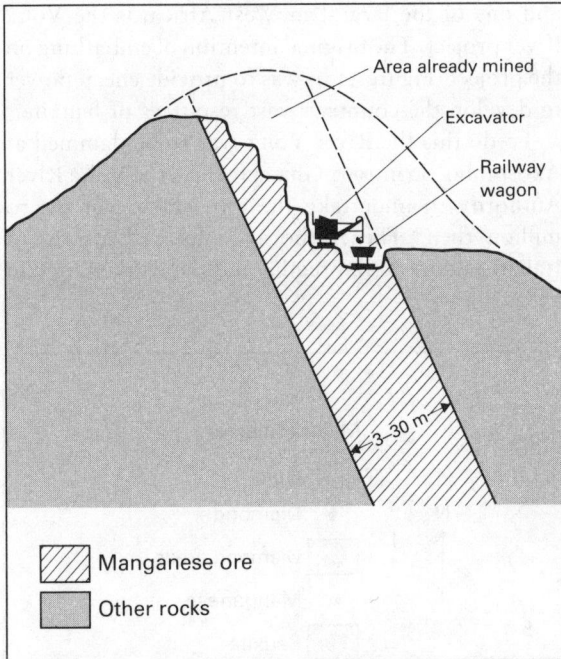

11.3 A section of the Nsuta manganese mine.

notably along the valley of the River Birim where Kade and Oda are important mining centres. To obtain the diamonds, the top soil is removed and the diamond bearing gravels are found, usually within 2 metres of the surface. The gravels are then recovered and washed to obtain the gem. Both large companies and individual prospectors are engaged in diamond mining, but the government officially controls the sale from Accra.

Just as in the case of gold and manganese, production of diamonds has fallen. Formerly 3 273 000 carats in 1960, it dropped to 2 408 000 carats in 1974.

Bauxite is mined at Kibi, Mpraeso and Awaso mainly by open cast methods. The extensive reserves in the Asante uplands, west of Kumasi, are however yet to be developed.

Apart from the four major minerals of Ghana mentioned above, there are deposits of limestone, chromite, iron ore and asbestos, elsewhere. Salt is recovered from the coastal lagoons and there is a modern salt-making plant at Weija. Various building stones are quarried and used locally.

Mineral oil has been located off the coast of Ghana near Saltpond. Three wells have been drilled by 1978 by the prospecting firms which proved that each is capable of producing 1 000 barrels a day. Production however is yet to start.

Railways

Figure 11.5 shows how the railway lines connect the principal mining towns. The western lines were specifically constructed to bring in the heavy mining equipment and, of course, to transport the minerals to the coast for export. Thus the line was extended from Takoradi northwards to Tarkwa, Dunkwa and Obuasi with a branch to Prestea, chiefly to serve these gold-mining areas. The offshoots to Awaso and Kade connect these bauxite and diamond mining towns respectively. Accra-Tema and Takoradi are the coastal termini of the Ghana Railways, while Kumasi is at the northern apex.

Thus the 1 260 kilometres of railways in Ghana are concentrated entirely south of Kumasi and serve principally the mining towns. Contrast this pattern with that in Nigeria where the railways run to the very extremities of the country and connect the chief agricultural zones.

Roads

The densest road network in Ghana is also found south of Kumasi. The roads connect the main towns and compete with the railways for speed. Kumasi is the principal inland road junction, and from here the great north road strikes off to Tamale, crossing the Volta Lake at Yeji by a ferry (Figure 11.6).

Now attempt the following questions, referring to the text only where necessary:
i) Where is timber produced in Ghana? How is it recovered and to what use is it put?
ii) Describe the Abontiakoon-Tarkwa-Nsuta mining community in Ghana.
iii) Name the six main minerals in Ghana. Describe where, and how, each of four of them is produced.
iv) Why are minerals important to Ghana?
v) Study Figure 11.5 once more. Describe the rail and road systems shown there. Why are they mostly concentrated south of Kumasi?

Power, manufacturing and towns

The Volta Scheme provides over 99% of Ghana's

power; her industries are located, as shown in the map, in two zones – the Akosombo-Accra-Tema triangle and the Kumasi-Sekondi-Takoradi zone; while most of her towns are either associated with power production and manufacturing industries, or with mining, governmental or commercial activities.

The Volta River project

The most important industrial undertaking in Ghana

and one of the largest in West Africa, is the Volta River project. The original intention of embarking on the project (Figure 11.6) was to provide cheap power to develop the country's vast resources of bauxite.

To do this the River Volta was to be dammed at Akosombo. So in 1961 Ghana formed the Volta River Authority to undertake the job which cost it £70 million then. The Authority employed a firm of Italian engineers (Impregilo) and the work started in 1962.

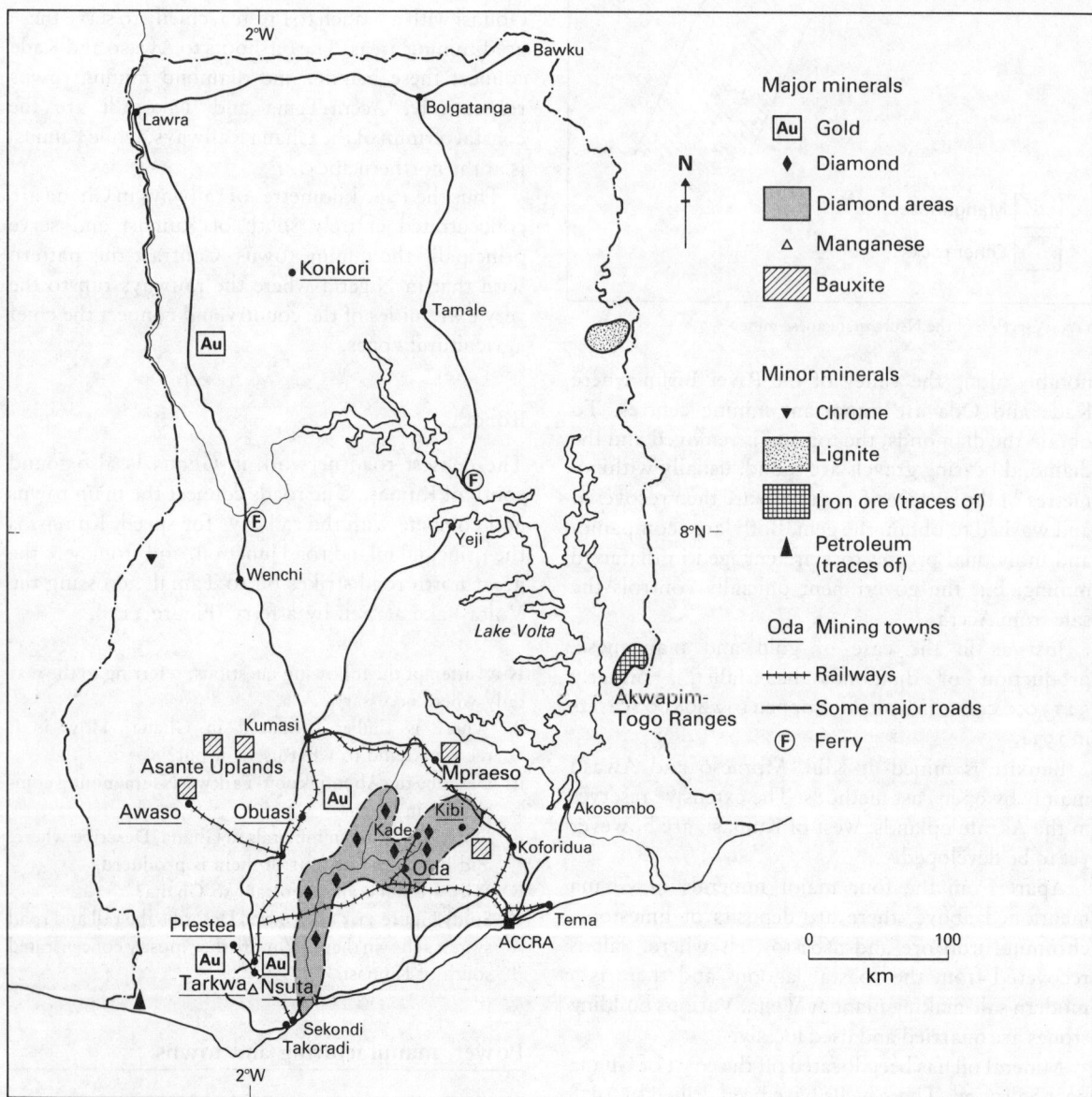

11.4 Distribution of minerals, railways and roads in Ghana.

11.5 A ferry across the River Volta near Yeji.

By January, 1966 when the site was opened, up to 4 500 men were working at Akosombo and the following tasks had been completed:

1. The main dam, with dimensions as shown in Figure 11.8 had been built. Surprisingly, this dam is not of concrete as the Kainji Dam, but of local rock fill and clay. There are two reasons for this. It is cheaper to use rock fill, and, whereas concrete can be cracked by the earth tremors which this part of Ghana is often subjected to, rock fill will not. Behind this dam, the Volta Lake, 400 kilometres long and 8 400 square kilometres in area – the largest artificial lake in Africa and the fourth largest in the world – was formed.

2. An auxilliary dam, half as long as the main dam, had been built to close up a gap in the nearby hills.

3. A power plant with four turbines and four generators had been erected (two more of each were added by 1972).

4. Akosombo town had been greatly expanded to provide housing for the workers, and hotel accommodation for tourists.

5. The aluminium smelter had also been built at Tema to use the power from Akosombo.

Now Ghana derives considerable benefits from this project, far in excess of the original intention, just as Nigeria does from her Kainji project. The Volta project supplies most of the power needed by Ghana for her industries, notably the VALCO aluminium smelter at Tema, and for domestic and other uses. The smelter at Tema does not handle the local bauxite as originally intended, but uses imported alumina to produce aluminium bars.

In addition Ghana now exports power to other

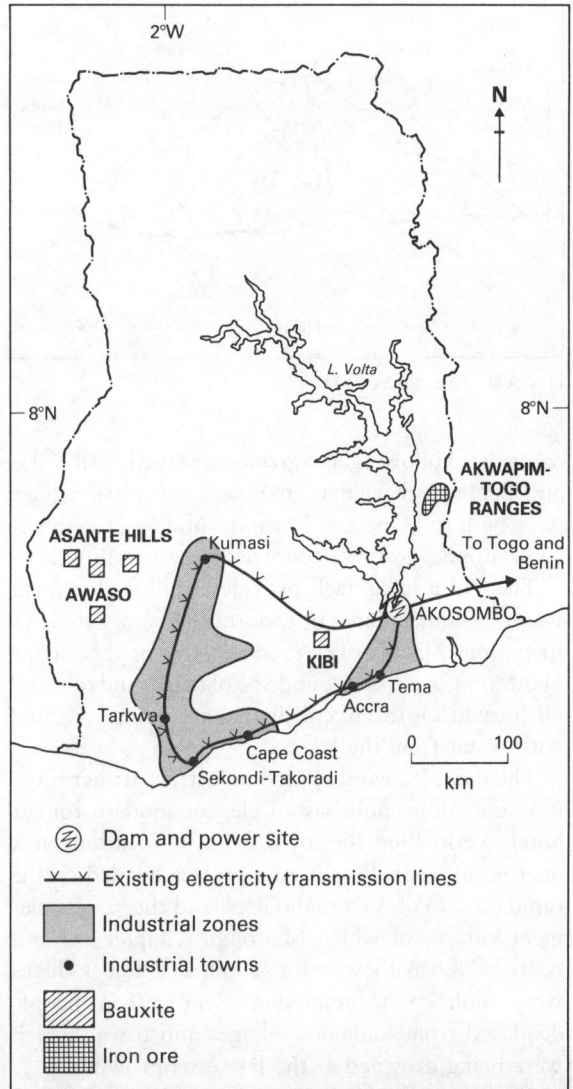

11.6 The Volta River project and industrial zones of Ghana.

11.7 The Volta Dam site. Identify the dam in the picture. Can you see the dammed lake behind the dam? See the overflow through shine gates at the right of the picture. Compare it with the Kainji Dam in Figure 8.3. How beneficial is this dam to Ghana?

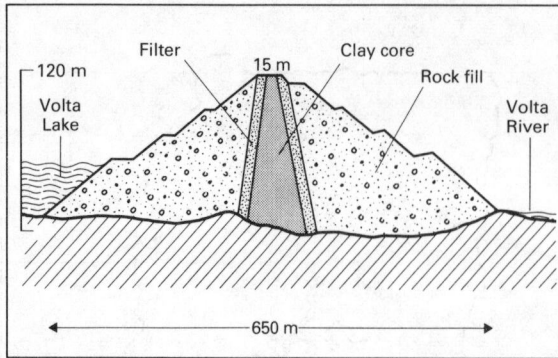

11.8 A sketch of the Volta Dam.

11.9 The Conference Hall, Accra.

countries. Following an agreement signed with Togo and Benin to that effect in 1969, transmission lines were built to Lomé and Cotonou, and by December, 1972 supplies to these countries began to flow.

The Volta Lake itself provides facilities for fresh water fishing, inland transportation and extensive irrigation. Already over 3 200 hectares of cane sugar plantation, 4 400 of rice and 800 of maize and tobacco all located on the Accra plains, are being irrigated with water from the lake.

The dam, lake and related industries attract tourists, and Akosombo has an elegant modern tourist hotel overlooking the town from its location on a nearby hill spur. Finally, the project has led to the rapid growth of Akosombo itself and the 52 resettlement villages of which Makongo (chapter 10) and nearby Nkwakubew are examples. These villages were built to accommodate over 77 000 people displaced from some 600 villages and towns which were being drowned as the lake was growing!

The Accra/Tema industrial complex

Accra and Tema, once separate towns, have now grown together to form a growing industrial conurbation, with a population of 738 000 in 1970 and nearly 900 000 in 1975.

Accra itself, with a population of 750 000, is the capital and largest city of Ghana, though it suffers from some natural disadvantages. It is often subjected to earth tremors, its coasts are surf beaten and its immediate hinterland is the infertile and dry scrubland of the Accra coastal plains.

In its favour, however, is its dry, crisp and healthy climate which was probably why the Europeans built the Ussher, James and Christianburg Castles there in the 17th century, and later chose it to be the capital of the then Gold Coast in 1877.

Today its beautiful residential areas, its elegantly designed and attractively constructed public buildings, the many commercial and business houses, as well as the University at Legon combine to make Accra a lively, charming and modern city.

Accra's industries are comparatively few and modest in size. They include furniture factories, printing works, breweries, soft drinks and food processing factories.

The town is also a route centre with roads, railways and the Kotoka international airport.

Tema was formerly a fishing village 28 kilometres east of Accra. But when Ghana needed to develop a port to serve Accra and relieve Takoradi of its congestion, Tema was chosen as the site because of the following locational advantages which it has:
i)   it is near enough to Accra and the Volta River Project site;
ii) the rocks from the nearby Shai Hills are available for constructional works at the harbour, and
iii) the land behind is flat and allows for extensive development while the sea in front is deep thus making dredging relatively unnecessary.

To develop the port, the government of Ghana set up the Tema Development Corporation and charged it with the responsibility of planning and constructing the city and port. The Corporation started work in 1952 and by 1977 it had built a number of facilities including those outlined below.
1. A 175 hectare artificial harbour (twice the size of

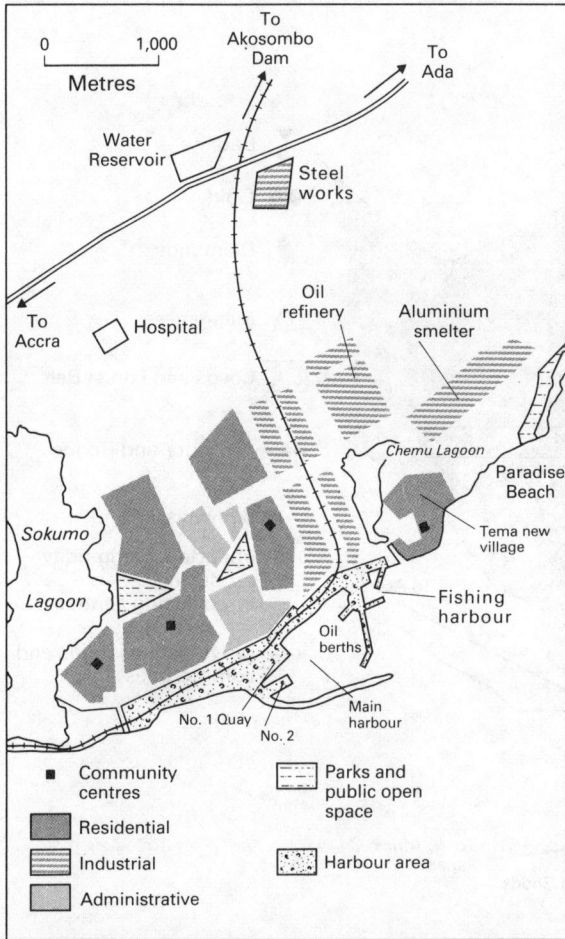

11.10 A plan of Tema, Ghana.

Takoradi's) and a 12 hectare one meant to handle only fish had been constructed.

2. Several harbour facilities including a dry dock, over 2 400 metres of quays, goods sheds and loading cranes had been provided.

3. Six well planned residential areas to house the people who work in the harbour and industries had been built.

4. Several factories had been established. These include an oil refinery using imported crude oil, a factory which uses local cocoa in the manufacture of cocoa products, a steel works which makes steel from scrap, pharmaceutical industries, cotton textile and truck assembly plants and the giant VALCO aluminium smelter. This smelter was opened in 1967, produces aluminium ignots from imported alumina, employs well over 1 000 work-

ers and now has the capacity of handling 200 000 tonnes of alumina per annum.

Today Tema continues to grow; roads have been extended to it from Accra and Akosombo and a transmitting station has been erected to the northeast of the city. It has also grown to be the premier port of Ghana. Can you name some of its exports and imports?

Other industrial towns and ports

Takoradi (161 000 with Sekondi in 1975) has an 88 hectare artificial harbour built in 1928. This harbour was handling over 80% of Ghana's trade until Tema started to absorb some of its Accra traffic and it has now been finally displaced as the premier port of the country.

However, it still has a productive hinterland which includes the forest belt, as Figure 11.11 shows. It therefore exports much of the cocoa and almost all the minerals and timber for which this belt is famous. In return it imports foods, manufactured goods and industrial raw materials.

Industrially, Takoradi is important for its tobacco factory, cocoa processing plants, a paper factory, furniture factories, a car assembly plant and several saw-mills.

It is a port of call for cargo and passenger vessels which sail between Liverpool and Lagos, and has air and road connections with Accra and Kumasi, and a direct rail link with the latter.

The table below compares the importance of Tema and Takoradi in the recent export and import trade of Ghana:

Exports	Tema	Takoradi
Cocoa	51%	49%
All Exports	28%	72%
Imports		
Petroleum	99%	1%
Cement	69%	31%
Foodstuffs	70%	30%
All Imports	75%	25%
All Trade	54%	46%

Can you account for the relative percentages in the trade handled by both ports as shown above?

The neat residential town of *Sekondi* is sited on a healthy promontory some seven kilometres east of Takoradi (A promontory is a narrow piece of land

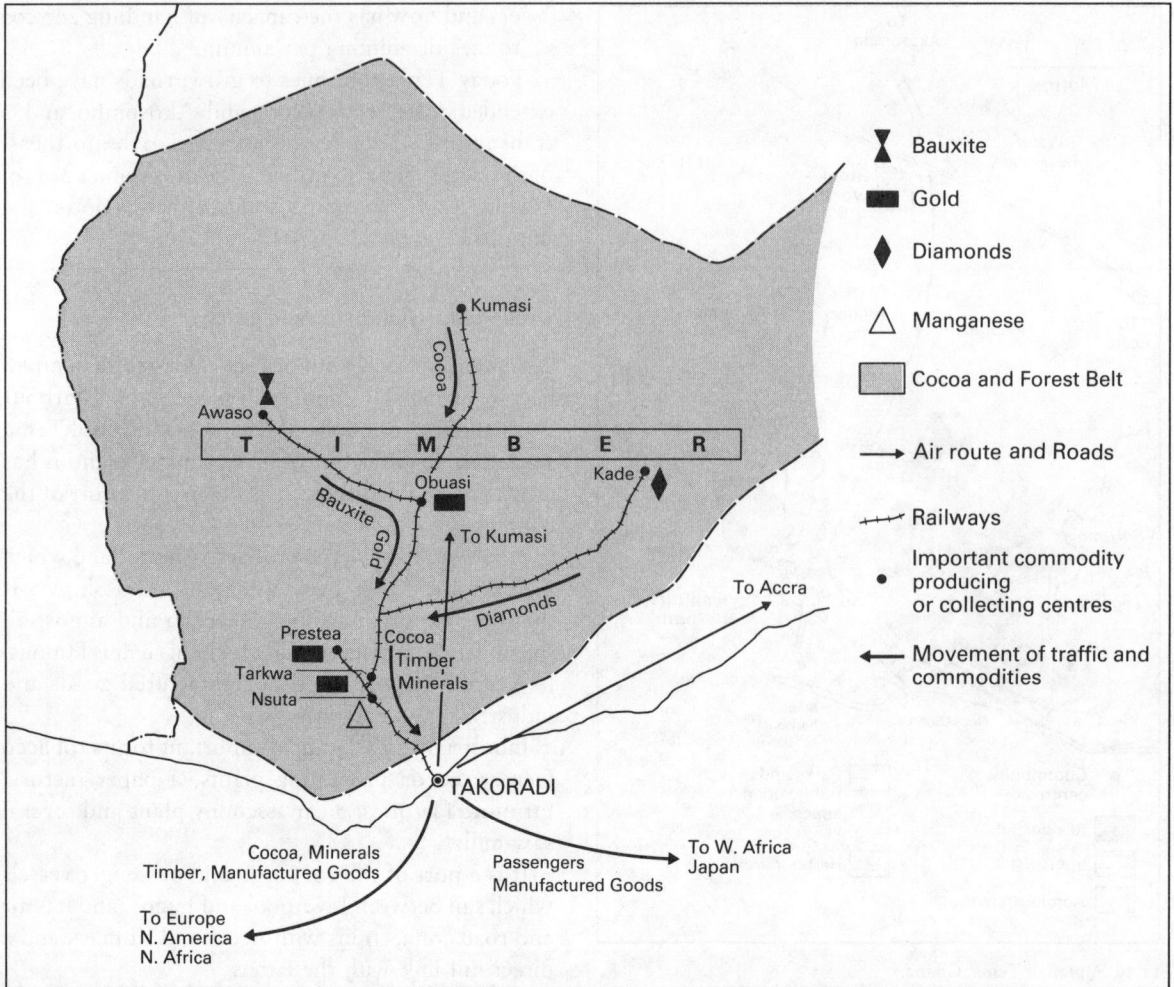

11.11   Takoradi and part of its hinterland.

which juts out into the sea). Many people who work in Takoradi actually live in Sekondi and go to work from there. That is why it is called a residential town.

Kumasi (343 000), is the second largest city in Ghana. It is the chief inland city and the capital of Asante, with substantial historical connections.

Its location at a route centre in the heart of the cocoa belt makes it the collecting centre for not only cocoa but also other products of this belt.

The industries of Kumasi include a fibre bag factory, which makes the bags used in packing the cocoa, a biscuit factory, cocoa processing factories, a brewery and a furniture factory. It is the seat of the University of Science and Technology, Ghana.

The other industrial towns are mainly located along the railway between Takoradi and Kumasi,

and are connected with processing minerals and forest products as earlier described.

In the north of the country are *Tamale* and *Bolgatanga*, which have some local industries. They are, as well, regional capitals.

Population distribution

Ghana had, by the latest population census of 1970, a population of 8.6 million. By 1975 it had grown to 9.9 million. As shown in Figure 11.13, these people are not evenly distributed over the country. The coastal district, forest region and north-east Ghana, where in fact most of the major towns in Ghana are located, are the most densely peopled. On the other hand, the

11.12 Takoradi and its harbour. How do you tell that the harbour is artificial? When was it built? How is it like the Tema harbour? Point to the ships, the floating logs, the warehouses and the oil storage tanks. What is the coastal town at the extreme right of the picture?

interior Volta basin is relatively empty. See the map and note the densities in each case. There are reasons for these differences in densities.

1. The dry crisp climate of the coastal district, its level topography and water availability, and the early European contact with the district which generated trade, and lately learning and employment, have attracted many people there. The district too has most of the industries in Ghana and the densest network of communication systems in the country.

2. In the forest region we find an abundant water supply, over 90% of the wealth of Ghana – the cocoa, timber and minerals – some industries and a dense network of roads and railways, all of them factors which promote high population densities.

3. North-east Ghana, in fact the southern extension of the Mossi territory of Upper Volta, had a strong and politically well organized group of people who not only resisted aggression but also received refugees from weaker groups around. Today they are industrious and practise mixed and intensive farming as described of the Nangodis in Chapter 10.

4. Conversely, the Volta basin has many factors which repel population. It is infertile, dry in the harmattan season, but wet, water-logged and pest-infested in the rainy season. It has few cash crops and little industrial activity of note. Furthermore, past inter-tribal wars and slave

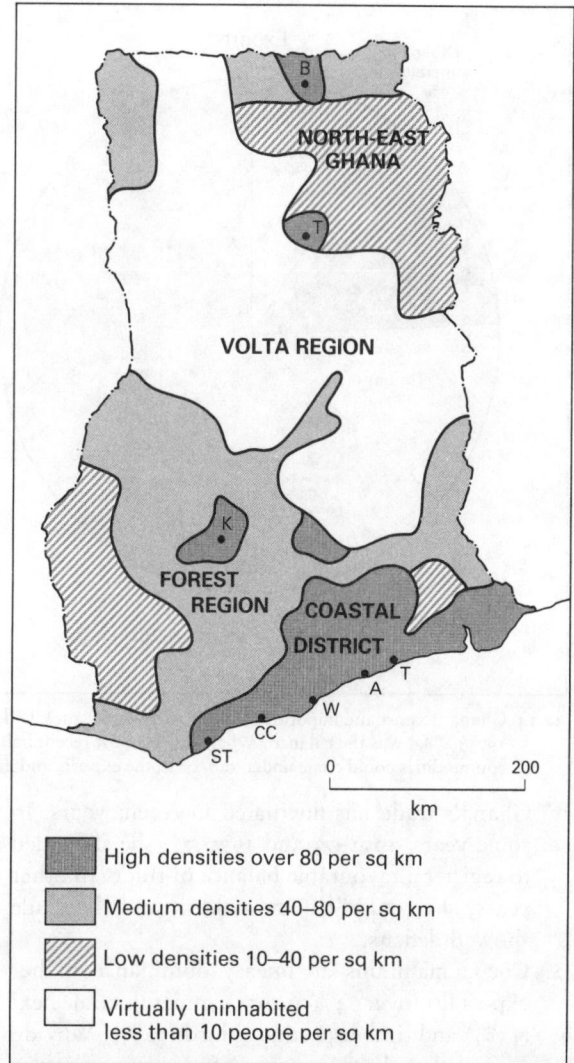

11.13 The distribution of population in Ghana.

raiding heavily depopulated this middle belt of Ghana as was the case in Nigeria too.

Now can you compare the population distribution in Ghana with that in Nigeria (Chapter 8). Compare also factors which account for the differences noted in each case.

Foreign trade

Ghana's trading position can be found from Figure 11.14 and Figure 25.5. Three points stand out clearly from the illustrations and a fourth one from studying the country's trading partners:

Exports

Other
minerals
4%

Others
9%

Gold
11%

Timber
12%

Cocoa
64%

Value: ₵ 943.5 m (1975)

Imports

Others
7.6%

Manufactured
goods
23.3%

Chemicals
13%

Mineral fuels
16.6%

Machinery and
vehicles
22.5%

Food and
beverages
17%

Value: ₵ 922.0 m (1975)

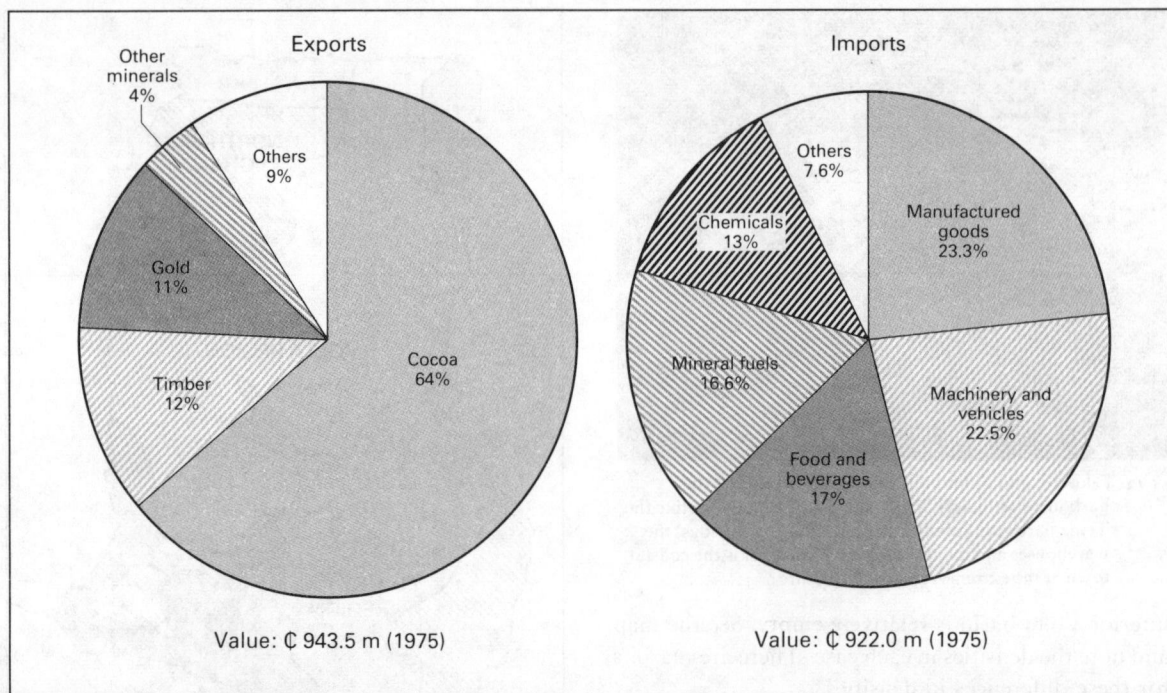

11.14 Ghana: Export and import trade (mid 1970–80 decade). Did the country record a favourable or unfavourable balance of trade in 1975? What was the balance? What was the most recent balance? Which commodity dominates the export trade? What commodities could come under 'others' in the exports and imports?

1. Ghana's trade has fluctuated in recent years. In some years, 1972–73 and 1975–77, she struggled to register a favourable balance of trade. In other years, she couldn't quite make it and the trade showed deficits.

2. Cocoa maintains an uneasy dominance in her export list (over 64% in 1975), minerals come next (15%) and timber products third (12%). Why do we say that the dominance of cocoa is uneasy?

3. Of her imports, manufactured products come first (some 23.3%), machinery next (22.5%) followed by foods and beverages (over 17%). For an agricultural country like Ghana, importation of such large quantities of foods is an unsatisfactory situation. Why is this so?

4. Ghana has a wide range of trading partners, and these include the United Kingdom, communist countries, Western Germany and U.S.A. in that order. Less trade is with fellow African countries.

Summary

Let us now briefly summarise what we have learnt in this chapter. Mining is next in importance to farming among the occupations of Ghanaians. Gold, diamonds, manganese and bauxite are the chief minerals. Timber is third in the list of Ghana's revenue yielders, Takoradi being the main port of export of these products.

The Volta River project is the key to Ghana's recent industrial growth and supplies over 99% of the power needed in the country. The southern one-third of Ghana and the north-east are the most densely peopled. Little wonder then that it is in these regions that most of the towns of note – Accra, Tema, Takoradi, Kumasi, Tamale and Bolgatanga – are located. Ghana's trade has fluctuated in recent years and cocoa is still the chief export crop, while machinery and manufactured goods continue to be the principal imports.

Revision exercises

1. On a map of Ghana, insert the railways, their main termini, the chief minerals and the mining towns. Write a concise geographical account of mining and railways in Ghana.

2. With the aid of a sketch map describe and account for the distribution of population in Ghana.

   (London G.C.E. O.L. 1974)

12   Ivory Coast

Preparation

1. See the introductory figures in Chapter 1. Name Ivory Coast's neighbours. What are the area and population of Ivory Coast? How many other countries of West Africa are larger in area, and more heavily populated than Ivory Coast?
2. Study the photographs and maps in this chapter. Where in Ivory Coast do you find the following: lowlands, highlands, rain forests, grasslands, cocoa, oil palm, timber, cotton, bananas, Virdi Canal and Abidjan?
3. See the map of the cocoa belt of Ghana (Figure 10.9). In which part of Ghana is cocoa grown – the south or north? Why?
4. Trace two full-page maps of Ivory Coast for use in the revision exercises.

A visitor to Ivory Coast will not fail to observe many striking features which will make him ask a number of questions about the country.

i)   There are many Frenchmen still living in Ivory Coast – in fact over 50 000 of them. What are they doing in an African country which has been independent for nearly 20 years?
ii)   There are also nearly 1 million immigrant Africans in the country. What brought these people here?
iii) Why is the country so obviously prosperous with the glittering multi-storeyed buildings in Abidjan, smart restaurants, clean streets and bustling economic activity?
iv) Ivory Coast is one of the few countries in West Africa which has never seen a coup d'etat since independence. How has the country been able to achieve such political stability?

Possibly by the time we finish this chapter, you will be able to find answers to these questions yourself.

Ivory Coast is a country of 322 500 square kilometres with a 1975 population of 6.7 million. These people are made up of many language groups, principally the *Senoufos* and *Ebriès* who are farmers in the south, and the *Dioulas* who are itinerant traders and farmers like the Hausas of Nigeria, and who live in the north central part of the country. The one million or more immigrants in the country are all foreigners – principally the *Mossis* from Upper Volta and *Malians* from Mali and a few others from adjoining West African countries who have come to work in the plantations and cities. In 1975 foreign Africans in Ivory Coast constituted one third of the total wage earners in the country. There are also over 50 000 *Frenchmen*, who not only offer technical assistance to the country but also manage industries, run cafés and own plantations.

French contacts with the country started in the 17th century and her influence was consolidated when Africa was partitioned by the European powers in Berlin and Ivory Coast carved out and given to France. The country passed through colonial tutelage for over 70 years and became independent in 1960. Since then, its president, Felix Houphouet-Boingy, has run a policy which encourages foreign investors – the major reason why there are so many Frenchmen in the country. Now are you able to find answers to two of the questions asked above?

Physical environment

Relief regions

Ivory Coast has a generally uniform relief. But three relief regions, as shown in Figure 12.1, can be clearly distinguished. Name them and say approximately how much of the area of Ivory Coast each covers.

The *coastal plains*, 150 to 250 kilometres wide, are a continuation of the coastal plains of Ghana. They are likewise undulating, generally below 150 metres high but are interrupted in places by low hills. East of Fresco the coastline is backed with lagoons and sand

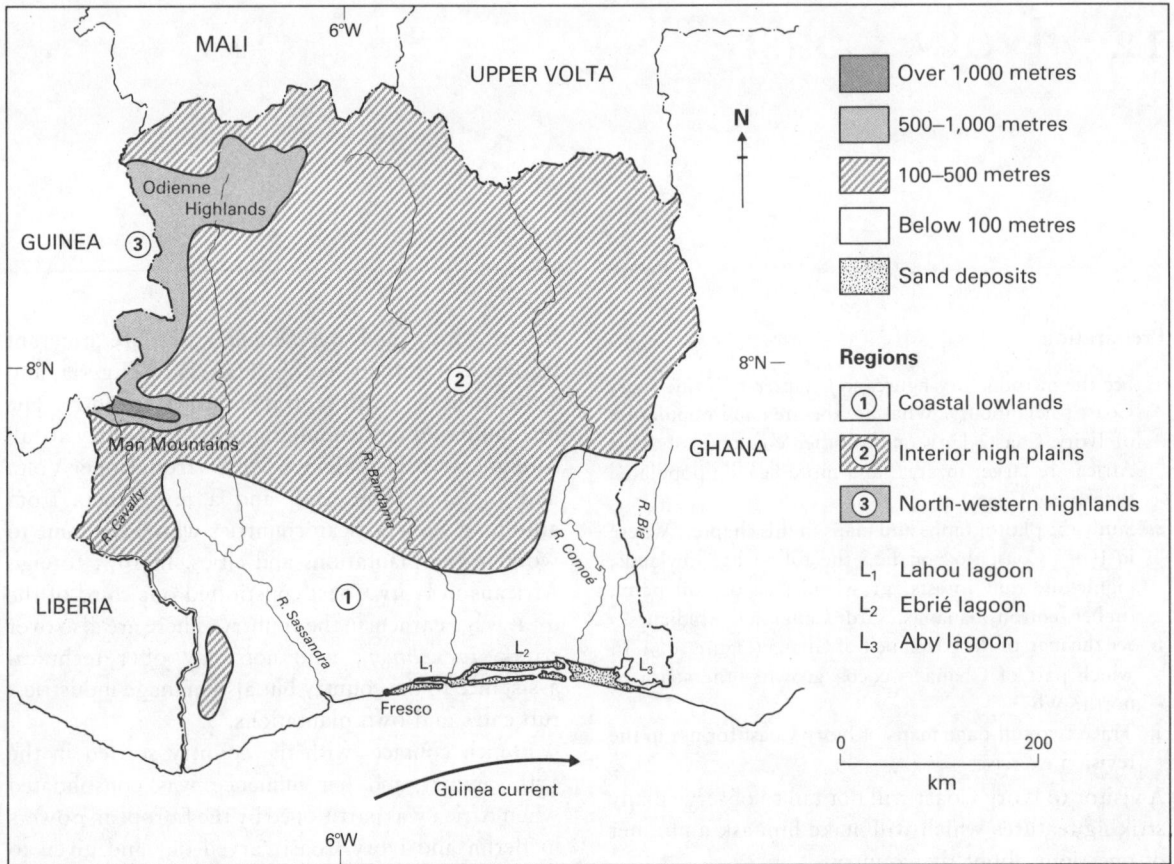

12.1 Ivory Coast: relief and relief regions.

bars, but west of it the view from the sea is dominated by low coastal cliffs like those of Sekondi in Ghana.

The *interior high plains* resemble the coastal plains in their gentle relief, and are equally traversed by north-south fast flowing rivers as shown in the figure. They are however more open, higher in elevation (150 to 450 metres) and are dominated in places by many more granite inselbergs.

Further inland we ascend the granite *north-western highlands* which represent the eastern spurs of the Guinea highlands of Guinea, surmounted here by the 1 200 metre Man Mountains and the 960 metre Odienne highlands.

Climatic and vegetational types

i)   Study the climatic map of Ivory Coast in Figure 12.2
ii) Name the climatic types shown and one town typical of each. Try to recall what we said about each climatic type in Chapter 3.

iii) Which of them have single maximum rainfall, and which double maxima?
iv) Name the three air masses which blow over the country. During which months of the year do they prevail?
v)   What relevance has the ocean current got to the climate of Ivory Coast?
vi) Which town do you think would have lower temperatures – Man or Abidjan. Why?

Apart from what you might have discovered of the climate of Ivory Coast from answering the questions above, the climate of the country has some other distinguishing features worthy of note.

1. Much of the rain that would have fallen in the country is cut off by the Guinea highlands and the coast north-west of Cape Palmas. Generally therefore it has less rainfall than the adjacent south-west Ghana.

2. Its gentle relief and compactness ensure that the rain it receives is evenly spread over its surface,

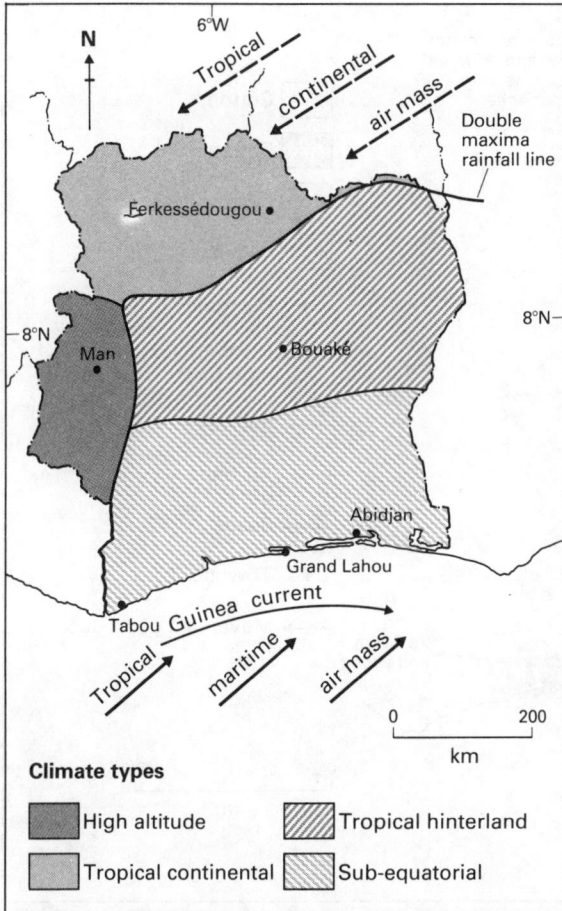

12.2 Ivory Coast: climatic types.

Climate types

- High altitude
- Tropical continental
- Tropical hinterland
- Sub-equatorial

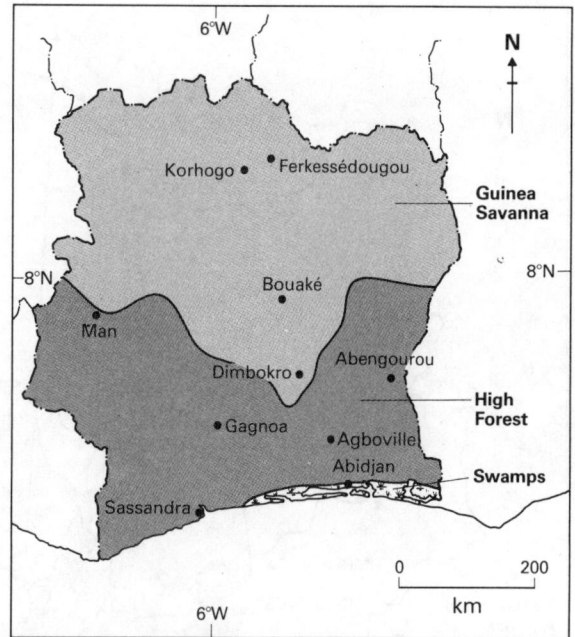

12.3 Ivory Coast: vegetational belts.

more so than that of Ghana or Nigeria. For example, rainfall varies from 2 000 mm in the south to about 1 500 mm in the north. Compare this relatively small range with Ghana's 2 000 mm in the south which falls to 1 000 in the north, or Nigeria's 3 000 mm in the south and less than 500 mm in the north-east.

Because of the relatively even spread of rainfall vegetational contrasts in Ivory Coast are not great. Only three belts – swamps along the coast, high forest inland and guinea savanna in the interior are represented in the country, as shown in Figure 12.3. See also how the guinea savanna extends rather curiously southwards in the region of Dimbokro. This is a result of forest clearing for cultivation. Like Ghana, Ivory Coast derives much of its wealth from the forest belt as we will see below. Before then

however, can you suggest two products derived from the forest belt here?

Economic development

Recall the third question we asked about the country at the beginning of this chapter. The economic prosperity of Ivory Coast can be attributed to five principal factors:
i) well planned and diversified commercial agriculture;
ii) large scale timber extraction;
iii) development of industries;
iv) well calculated encouragement of foreign investors; and
v) protected and diversified trade with a long standing favourable balance of trade.

We will now examine these aspects of the country's economy.

Commercial agriculture

Four commodities feature prominently in the commercial agriculture of the country – coffee, cocoa, bananas and pineapples. Palm production and cotton

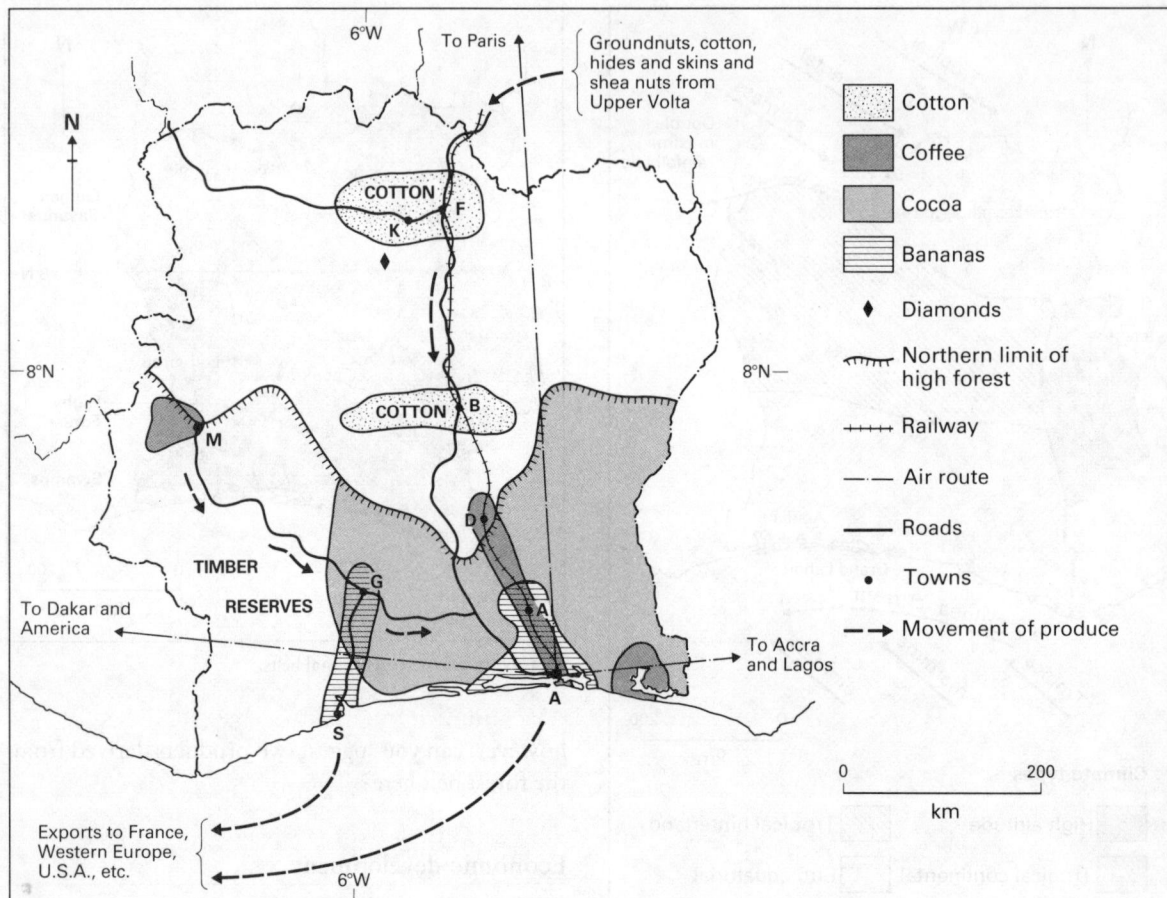

12.4 Ivory Coast: economy.

growing are however being vigorously encouraged in order to further diversify the agriculture.

There are many coffee farms in Ivory Coast numbering over 280 000 in the whole of the country. Two varieties of coffee are grown – the *Cafèa Liberica* found principally in the southeast, and the *Cafèa Arabica* located in Man Mountain region and grown on the mountain slopes.

The total annual production of the crop started with some 100 000 tonnes at the turn of the century immediately after the crop was introduced, and rose to 200 000 in 1960 and 280 000 tonnes in 1975. This makes Ivory Coast Africa's largest coffee producer and exporter and third in the world after Brazil and Colombia. Formerly all was exported raw, but coffee is now also processed locally before export. France and Western Europe, being great coffee drinkers, take over 50% of her product, and U.S.A. 30%.

Cocoa is the next important crop. It was introduced from Ghana in 1895 and is planted in a belt, which, as you can see from comparing Figure 12.4 in this chapter with Figure 16.9, is a continuation of the cocoa belt of Ghana. Similar conditions as in Ghana therefore prevail.

As in coffee, it is raised in small farm lots scattered all over the growing belt. In the 1960's Ivory Coast ranked third among West African cocoa producers – next to Ghana and Nigeria. Then the production in the country was 135 000 tonnes in 1964 and 150 000 in 1968. In 1975, however, its production rose to 225 000 tonnes and thus the country clinched the second position from Nigeria which in that year had a production of only 220 000 tonnes. Ivory Coast hopes by the end of her 1976–80 Development Plan to increase production to 335 000 tonnes per annum and even to replace Ghana as the World's leading pro-

12.5 Drying cocoa beans in Ivory Coast. How are the seeds dried? What are the girls doing?

12.6 Harvesting palm produce in Ivory Coast. Are these wild palms or plantation palms? How do you tell? How are the palm fruits carried home?

ducer by the mid-1980's. This is really an ambitious programme. Do you think she can achieve it? Why? Again France, Western Europe and the U.S.A. are her best buyers of this crop.

Cocoa and coffee are admirable twin crops in Ivory Coast because in wet years more cocoa than coffee is produced, but in dry years the reverse is the case. Nature thus helps conscious planning to maintain a balance in the production of both crops.

Bananas are almost exclusively grown by Europeans who employ local and immigrant labour. Can you say where the immigrant labour comes from? See the map in Figure 12.4. Why are the banana estates located almost entirely along the rail line from Abidjan to Agboville and along the road from Sassandra to Gagnoa – each with an opening to the sea? Ivory Coast and Guinea are West Africa's largest producers and exporters of bananas. The former enjoys an equable climate, a flat topography and an even monthly production – more so than Guinea. Its annual production of 205 000 tonnes is therefore higher than that of Guinea. France again takes the lion's share of this crop.

Pineapples and *oil palm* have recently grown in importance. Ivory Coast produced 245 000 tonnes of the pineapples in 1975 and its export of 70 000 tonnes of raw pineapples for that year made her the leading world exporter of that commodity. It also tins the fruits before export. It has recently made huge investments in *oil palm* production which should make the country the World's second largest producer of this commodity by 1980.

Timber and mineral production

Timber production is the chief extractive industry in Ivory Coast. Timber and allied products account for nearly 35% of her export trade. Logs are felled mainly along the principal rivers, roads and railways in the forest belt as these provide routes for transport to the Coast or to plywood factories. Over 2 million tonnes of timber were exported in 1975.

The only mineral in Ivory Coast worthy of note is the Bangolo iron ore deposit. It is hoped that this ore, when mined, will be carried by rail to the new port of San Pedro where it will be part-processed and turned into small balls, called pellets, before it is exported.

Manufacturing industries and towns

There are two classes of manufacturing industries in Ivory Coast.

1. There are those which process local materials either for local consumption or for export. These include oil and saw-mills, fruit canneries, cocoa, coffee and butter processing factories, and also the textile mills. The textile mill at Bouaké was built in 1922 and was the first, and for a long time the only one, in West Africa. A larger more modern one costing Fr 17 000 million, was opened at Dimbokro in 1975 with an initial production capacity of 8 million tonnes of cotton materials.

By 1980 it will be capable of producing 12 million tonnes, 60% of which will be designated for export to other African countries, 30% to Western Europe and 10% for local use.

2. The second set of industries depend on imported raw materials and are therefore more logically located along the coast – Abidjan having the largest share of these. They include a number of breweries, chemical and plastic works, electronics and vehicle assembly plants and the giant oil refinery of Abidjan opened in 1965. The refinery uses crude petroleum from Nigeria and Gabon and now refines more than 1 million tonnes of oil per annum.

Particularly encouraging to her industries is the fact that Ivory Coast opens her doors to foreign investors. Her resources are varied and, of course, she has taken steps recently to harness her electrical power. Two dams, one at Kossu completed in 1972 and another at Taabo commissioned in 1974 and due to go into full service in 1979, and both located on the River Bandama, will together supply Ivory Coast's industrial power needs.

Like Lagos in Nigeria, *Abidjan* is the capital, major port and chief manufacturing town in Ivory Coast. Like Lagos too, it is situated beside a lagoon and covers an island and part of the mainland.

i)   Study Figure 12.4 carefully.
ii) What products are found in Abidjan's hinterland?
iii) How far does the hinterland extend?
iv) Which countries does Abidjan export the goods to?
v)   Which other countries of West Africa export their goods through the port?
vi) Trace the routes that converge on the city.

In 1975 the port allowed in 2 600 vessels loading and off-loading over 6.6 million tonnes of cargo. The cutting of the 2.8 kilometre long Vridi Canal in 1950 has greatly enhanced sea going traffic to and from Abidjan. Its international airport has connections with other West African capitals and a straight flight to Paris.

Abidjan is also the leading commercial city of Ivory Coast with many banks, hotels and commercial houses.

Like Lagos also its population has grown tremendously in recent years, reflecting the high degree of urbanization in the country. It was only 300 000 in 1965. Ten years later in 1975 its population tripled to 900 000! However, unlike Lagos, Abidjan has a more European population. It is also a better planned and more pleasant city with numerous cafés, parks, wide and well-kept streets lined with ornamental trees and modern multi-storeyed offices and apartment buildings.

Overseas trade

From a study of the pie diagrams which show the export and import trade of Ivory Coast for 1976, the following features of this trade emerge:

1. Ivory Coast's exports are higher in value than her imports, and have been consistently so for many years. This means that she has been enjoying a favourable balance of trade and has been able to accumulate surplus. No wonder she is able to develop her schools, telephone system, roads, hospitals and other services which make a visitor obviously see the prosperity of the country.

2. Her export trade is diversified – no one item dominates all the others put together. Coffee was the most important export crop in the 1960's. Now, even though the export value of this item has multiplied three times, the export value of timber and timber products has surpassed that of coffee. This shows how the country has been anxious to diversify and increase her exports.

3. Unlike other countries of West Africa where minerals account for the favourable trade balance, here it is agricultural and forest products all the way.

4. Finally, though not shown in Figure 12.8, France and Western Europe have, for many years, been Ivory Coast's best customers. They give her preferential treatment, charging very little or no duties on her products. In 1976, France, Western Germany and the Benelux countries of Western Europe bought 47.5% of her exports and sold to her 51.7% of her imports.

Summary

The environment and resources of Ivory Coast are comparable to those of Ghana, except that Ivory Coast is not rich in minerals. Her prosperity is based on her agricultural and forest products found prin-

12.7 Abidjan from the air. This picture shows its beautiful buildings, avenues and fly-overs. Compare it with other pictures which show other capital cities in West Africa.

cipally in the forest belt, conscious diversification of her Development Plan efforts and substantial assistance with capital from France and her other West European friends. The country also enjoys a protected market in those countries. Abidjan is the capital and has a number of the country's industries. It is like Lagos in many respects but it is a better planned city and only some 100 000 smaller in population.

Within living memory of most Ivorians they have seen their country transformed from a poor agricul-

tural country to a rich country with a balanced economy and steady favourable trade. This is through the progressive policy of their president, Houphouet Boigny. As a result, social amenities are reasonably adequately provided, the roads are in good condition, telephone services in towns are efficient, parents easily find places for their children in schools and health facilities are within easy reach of the population. Why shouldn't the people therefore be happy? And if they are happy why should anyone think about a coup d'etat? However, Ivory Coast

Exports

Others
24%

Timber and
timber products
34.7%

Cocoa and cocoa
products 17.5%

Coffee and coffee
products 23.8%

Value: Fr. 392,500 m (1976)

Imports

Others
25.7%

Other manufactured
goods 30.7%

Fuels 5.6%

Foods
9.5%

Machinery and
vehicles 28.5%

Value: Fr. 311,500 m (1976)

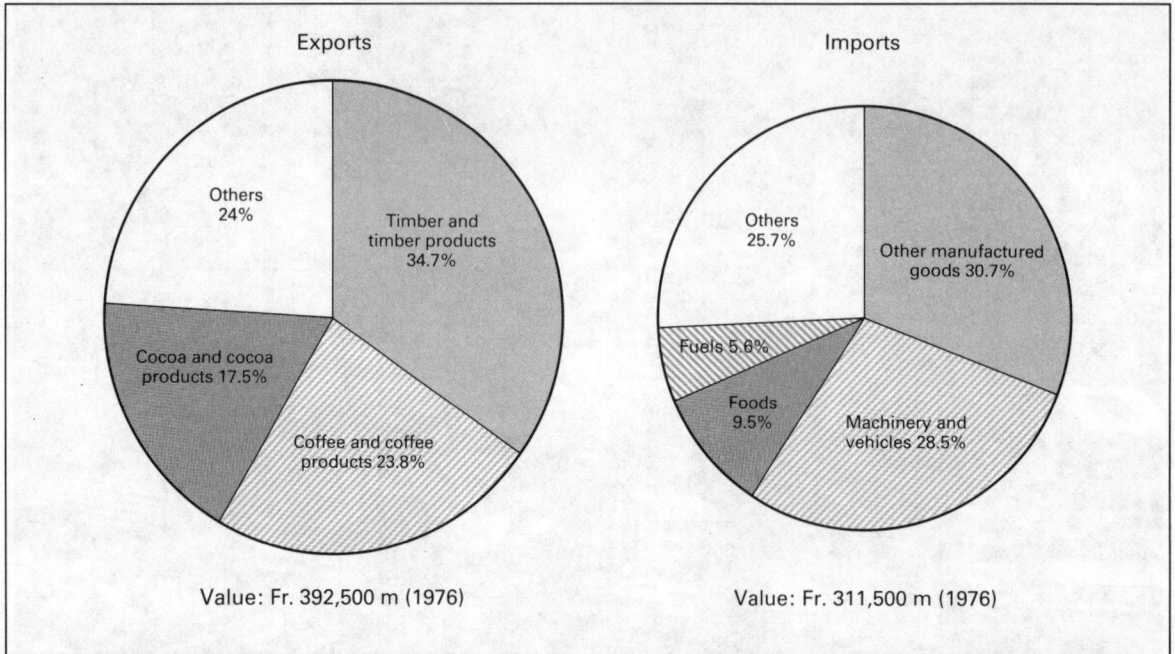

12.8 Ivory Coast: trade (mid 1970–80 decade). Which is higher in value – the export or import trade? Which commodity or set of commodities fetches most money for the country? Approximately how much did the set of commodities fetch in 1976%? Which set of commodities does Ivory Coast spend most money in buying? Approximately how much was thus spent in 1976%. Compare the export trade figure above with that of Ghana in Fig. 11.14. What are the main differences?

must watch her recently rising level of unemployment and keep it down if she hopes to continue to enjoy her political stability for long.

Now can you, after reading the text above answer all the questions we asked about the country at the beginning of this chapter? Attempt them now and then do the following exercises.

Revision exercises

1. On one of the maps of Ivory Coast you have prepared, insert and name the following:
   a) Man mountains,
   b) the July air masses,

c) the double maxima rainfall line.
How do relief and winds influence the climate of the country?

2. On the other map, insert:
   a) the main communication lines,
   b) Abidjan, San Pedro, and two inland towns.
   Compare the location, hinterland and functions of Abidjan and Lagos. Which town would you prefer to live in? Why?

3. Explain and give reasons for the following about Ivory Coast:
   a) the country has a large foreign population;
   b) the country is one of the most economically prosperous in Africa.

13 Liberia

Preparation

1. We studied Ivory Coast in the previous chapter. Name the three relief regions in the country. Describe them.
2. Revise the main features of the monsoon type of climate. Name two countries in West Africa (as shown in Figure 3.8) which experience this type of climate.
3. Which of the regions in Figure 5.1 shows the tropical rain forest? Describe it. In which countries in West Africa is this type of vegetation found?
4. Do you remember from your history when the slaves in America were freed?

Liberia was the first modern State in West Africa,

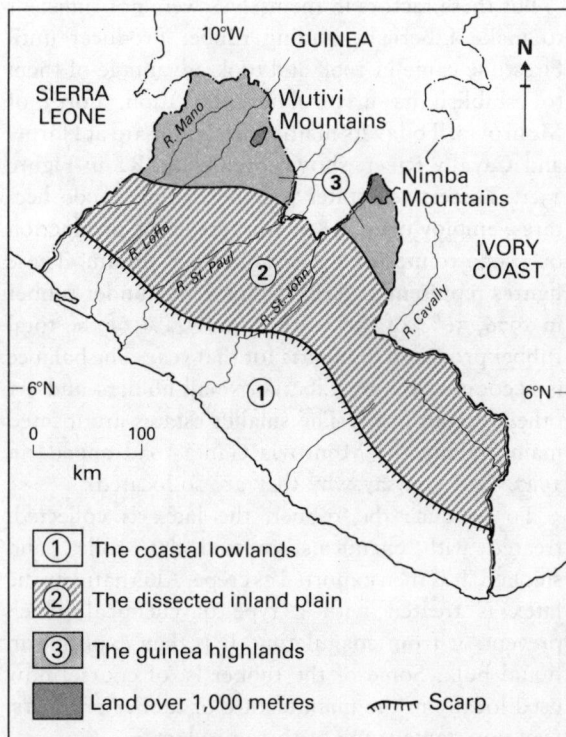

13.1 Liberia: relief regions and drainage.

founded in 1847 by liberated slaves from America – hence the name 'Liberia'. But the country was then made up of few coastal settlements including Monrovia, Sinoe and Marshall-Edine. It was only years later that the area behind the coast was added and the boundary eventually extended to the hinterland. Today the country covers an area of 113 370 square kilometres which, in mid-1976, 1.6 million people inhabited.

Peoples

Apart from the descendants of the original settlers, known as *Americo-Liberians*, and who live principally in the coastal towns and villages, the bulk of the Liberians are indigenous people. These include the *Kpelles, Bassas, Gios, Grebos, Kissis* and *Mandigoes* who live in the mainland and principally engage in agriculture. Foreigners, mainly Americans and Lebanese, live in the cities and numbered 31 000 in 1976.

Physical environment

Relief

Which country lies to the east of Liberia? Do you recall the three relief regions in that country? Name them. These three regions continue westwards to Liberia, as you can see in Figure 13.1. The regions comprise the coastal lowlands, the inland plain and the Guinea highlands:

1. The *coastal lowlands*, some 50 to 100 kilometres wide, are bordered along the coast by low cliffs and promontories. They lie generally below 200 metres. The surface is rolling, and is punctuated with occasional marshlands.

2. Behind the coastal lowlands is a fairly steep rise which leads on to the *dissected inland plain*. This region is about as wide as the coastal lowlands, but it is higher, lying generally between 300 and 700 metres above sea level. It is maturely dissected by rivers and has several isolated granite hills.

3. The last region is the *Guinea highlands*, cut in two sections as shown in Figure 13.1 by the southern extension of Guinea, though they are topographically continuous. The highest parts of these highlands are the Wutivi Mountains to the west and the Nimba Mountains to the east, the summits which rise above 1 200 metres.

As would be expected, the major rivers of Liberia rise in these mountains, cascade down their slopes, dissect the plains and lowland below and flow into the Atlantic. Name the rivers from Figure 13.1. Do you expect them to be sluggish or fast flowing? Why? Name two ways the rivers can be of use to Liberia.

Climate, vegetation and soils

Of the countries treated so far, Liberia is unique in its climate. It has a monsoon type of climate, with high temperatures (26°C to 32°C), and over 80% of its very high monsoon rainfall of 2 500 mm – 5 000 mm per annum falls between April and October, with a peak in August. The tropical maritime air mass (sometimes called the monsoon winds) hits the coast and highlands squarely, giving rise to heavy precipitation and making the country one of the wettest in West Africa. The dry season is, of course, short and lasts from November to March. Which winds do you think prevail over the country then?

The heavy rainfall makes the soils of Liberia some of the most heavily leached in West Africa. It also encourages erosion and laterite formation. For this reason plants with shallow roots do not do well in the country. Only tree crops with deep firm roots, like rubber and oil palms, can grow very well. The uncultivated vegetation similarly consists of dense forests, except for the highlands where grasslands occur.

Now before we go further, see how much you have mastered of what we have studied so far by answering these questions. Try not to refer to your text.

i) When was Liberia founded and by which people?
ii) About how many people now live in the country?

iii) Name the three major groups who live there.
iv) How would you divide Liberia into relief regions?
v) What type of climate has the country?
vi) Why are Liberia's soils mostly leached?

Economic development

The economic development of Liberia is tied up with two key commodities – rubber and iron ore. For just as the establishment of rubber plantations led to the extension of roads to the plantations, so the recovery of the Bomi Hills and Nimba Range iron ore deposits instigated the construction of the railways to the mining regions. The roads and railways in turn helped to open up the interior, introduce modern facilities and stimulate settlement.

Agriculture and roads

Rubber is the crop for which Liberia has been known for so many years. It grows well on the undulating and drained sections of the coastal plains with high rainfall, high tropical temperatures and virgin soils.

But these factors in themselves were not sufficient to make Liberia a leading rubber producer until Firestone came in 1908 and took advantage of them to establish its first rubber plantation, north of Monrovia. Today its major plantations are at Harbel and Cavally River, shown by R1 and R2 in Figure 13.2. These two estates together, some 40 000 hectares, employ over 14 800 workers in the production of 33 000 tonnes of sheet rubber per annum. These figures represent 31% of the total area under rubber in 1976, 36% of the workers and 40% of the total rubber produced in Liberia for that year. The balance is accounted for by Liberian small-holders and six other foreign firms. The smaller estates are located mainly along the Monrovia Ganta road opened in 1947. Can you say why they are so located?

To produce the rubber, the latex is collected, treated with chemicals, pressed flat, rolled and smoked. It is then exported as crêpe. Alternatively the latex is treated with a type of chemical which prevents it from coagulating. It is then exported in liquid bulk. Some of the rubber is, of course, now used locally in the manufacture of rubber products. Can you name some of these products?

See the graph in Figure 13.3 and trace how the

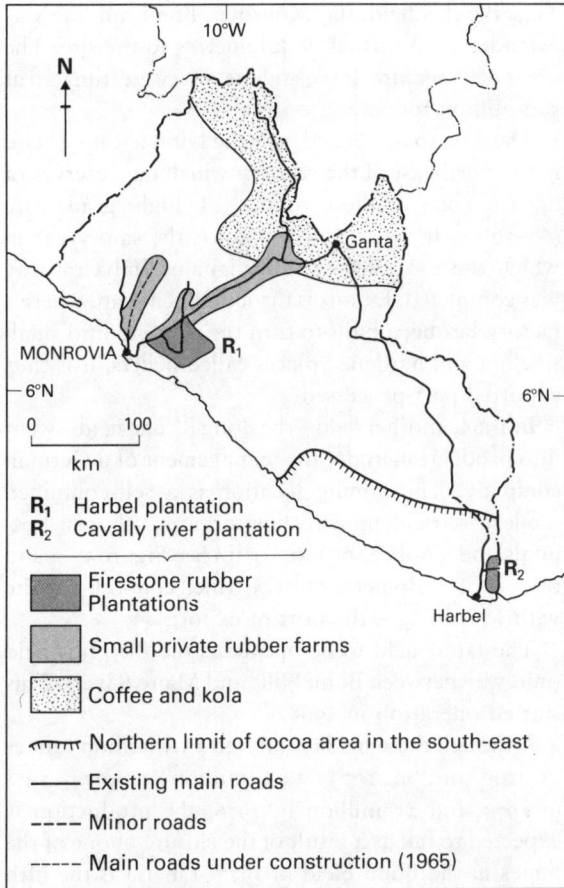

13.2 Liberia: farm products and roads.

production of rubber in Liberia has grown in recent years. The drop in 1973 is as a result of a fall in the world price of the commodity. However Liberia continues to be the leading West African exporter of rubber.

Coffee and *cocoa* are the country's other cash crops. The former, together with some *kola*, is cultivated on the slopes of the Guinea highlands, while the latter is grown in the southeast.

Rice is the major food crop. The country, at one time, imported a lot of rice, but government initiated many programmes aimed at reducing the quantity imported. This yielded good fruits and Liberia today produces over 200 000 tonnes of rice paddy per annum and has thus reduced drastically its import of this item.

Other food crops include cassava, bananas, sweet potatoes, yams and beans.

To give an idea of how poorly developed the roads in Liberia are, in 1925, there were only 5 vehicles and one 40-kilometre road in the whole country! In 1968, the figures had risen to 12 000 vehicles and 3 600 kilometres of roads, and in 1975 to 21 850 vehicles and 6 700 kilometres out of which only 370 were tarred! Liberia, therefore, has fewer cars than many West African capital cities – in fact there are more than three times as many cars in Lagos as there are in the whole of Liberia!

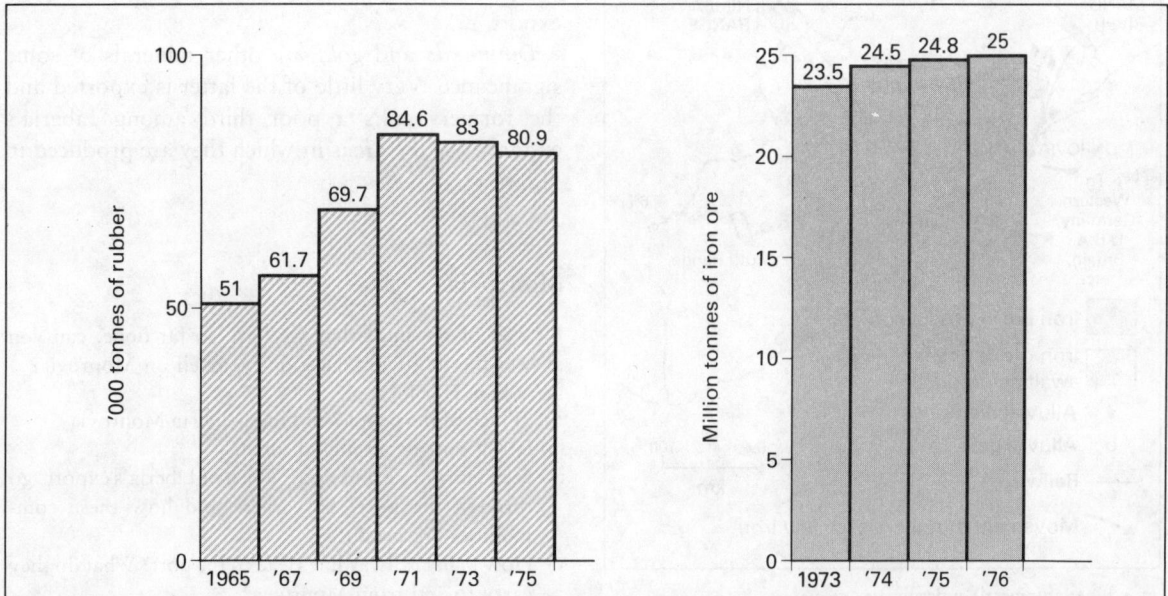

13.3 Liberia: production of two key commodities: iron ore and rubber.

Minerals and railways

Extensive prospecting for minerals has uncovered the presence of many minerals in Liberia, chief of which is iron ore. Financial aid was obtained from abroad to exploit the minerals, and in order to reach the mining regions, railways – only three of them in Liberia – were built to take machinery, equipment and men to the sites and evacuate the ore to the coast. As you can see in Figure 13.4 they start from coastal towns, run across the country, head towards the mining regions and terminate at the mining towns. Can you name these coastal towns and the termini?

Iron Ore is of course the most significant mineral carried by these railways. The ore mining industry fetches three times as much money to the country as all the other industries put together. Five iron ore fields have so far been developed. The Bomi field, opened in 1951, is operated by the Liberia Mining Company. It is connected with Monrovia, through which the ore is exported, by a 68 kilometre mineral railway. The reserves are estimated at 20 million tonnes and the ore content 60%.

The Mamo River field started production in 1961.

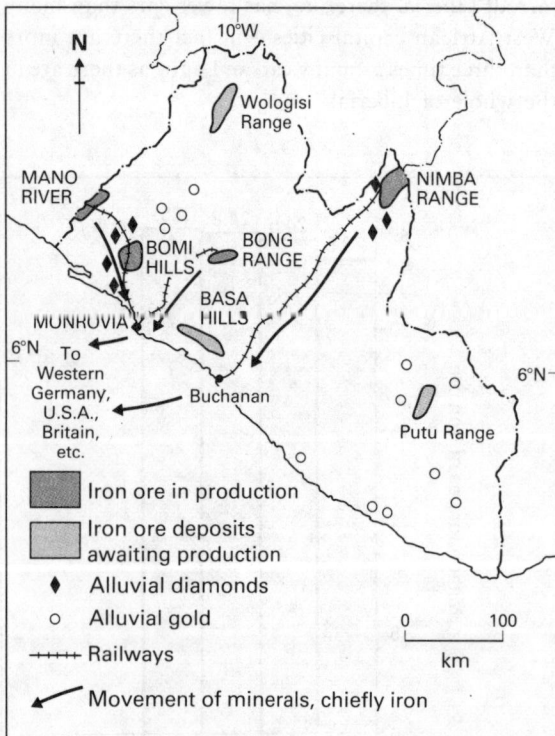

13.4 Liberia: minerals and railways.

To serve this field, the Monrovia-Bomi rail line was extended by a further 78 kilometres to the site. The ore is of a medium grade and the reserves estimated at 500 million tonnes.

The next to be opened, was the Nimba Range field, in the northeast of the country which has reserves of up to 1000 million tonnes of high grade ore (60–70%). It was opened in 1963, the same year in which the 270 kilometre Buchanan-Nimba railway was completed. Export is through Buchanan, where a factory has been built to turn the iron ore into small smelted and hardened pieces called pellets. It is thus exported part-processed.

In 1965, another field – the Bong Range field – went into production under the management of a German company. The mining location is a self-contained modern settlement with bus services, schools, hospitals and a police station. Again See Figure 13.4 and trace the 80 kilometre railway which connects the site with Monrovia – the port of export.

The latest field to be opened is the Bie Hills field (mid way between Bomi Hills and Mano River). This started operation in 1968.

Although these fields produced 23.5 million tonnes of iron ore in 1973, 24.5 million in 1974, 24.8 in 1975 and 25 million in 1976, the production is expected to fall as a result of the closure of one of the mines in the Bomi Field in 1977. Liberia is the fifth largest iron ore exporter in the world and the commodity accounts for nearly 75% of the country's export.

Diamonds and *gold* are other minerals of some significance. Very little of the latter is exported and the former ranks a poor third among Liberia's exports. See the areas in which they are produced in Figure 13.4.

Monrovia

By way of revising what we have so far done, can you answer the following questions yourself on Monrovia?
i)   Where is it located?
ii) Which of the peoples of Liberia live in Monrovia?
iii) Is it a port or an inland town?
iv) See Figures 13.2 and 13.4. Which of Liberia's exports go through the port? Say where and how these commodities are produced.
v)   How many railway lines lead to the port? What do they carry to and from Monrovia?

13.5 Monrovia. Describe the plan of this city – the arrangement of the streets, houses and open spaces (if any).

Now study carefully Figure 13.6 which shows the recent traffic through the port of Monrovia and then answer these short questions:

i) How much cargo recently entered the port?
ii) Is the cargo handled on the increase or decrease?
iii) Which is the most important cargo handled? Can you say why?

There is more you need to know about the town. It is the capital and the largest town in Liberia. It has an artificial harbour like Tema and Takoradi, but its importance and popularity lie in the fact that it is the only port in West Africa where ships can offload, store and onload cargo free of duty. Monrovia handles some 53% of Liberia cargo, Buchanan 45% while other smaller ports take the balance.

Apart from the iron ore plant at Buchanan and the smelters at the various ore fields, most of the other industries in Liberia are in and around Monrovia. Here we find Coca Cola and other bottling plants built in 1961, a chemical explosive factory established near Robertsville in 1964 and a 12 million dollar petroleum refinery opened in 1968 with a total annual production capacity of 650 000 tonnes of refined oil. It also has a $2.5 million cement factory commissioned in the same year and capable of producing 125 000 tonnes of clinker cement per annum. During the 1970's over six more industries have been opened and located in and around Monrovia.

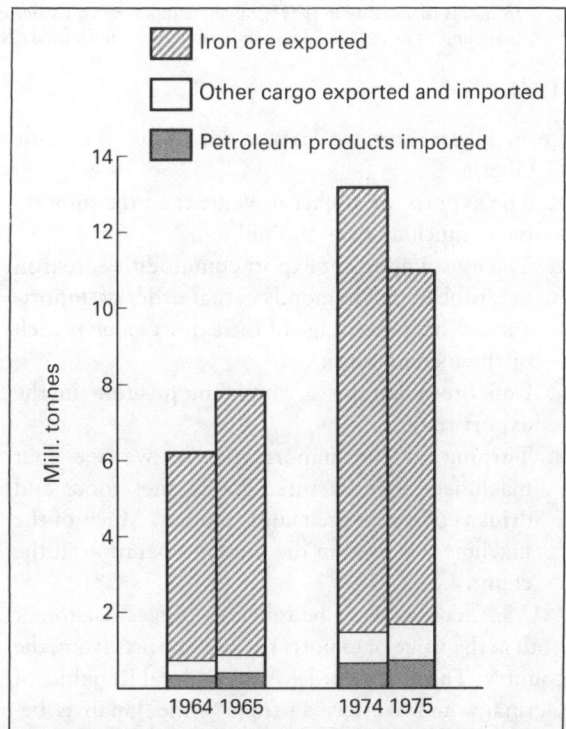

13.6 Traffic through the port of Monrovia 1964/65 and ten years later. Has the total cargo increased or decreased during the decade? Which item has consistently dominated the cargo? Can you suggest reasons why there was a drop in the iron ore exported in 1975? Approximately how much cargo was handled in each of the four years?

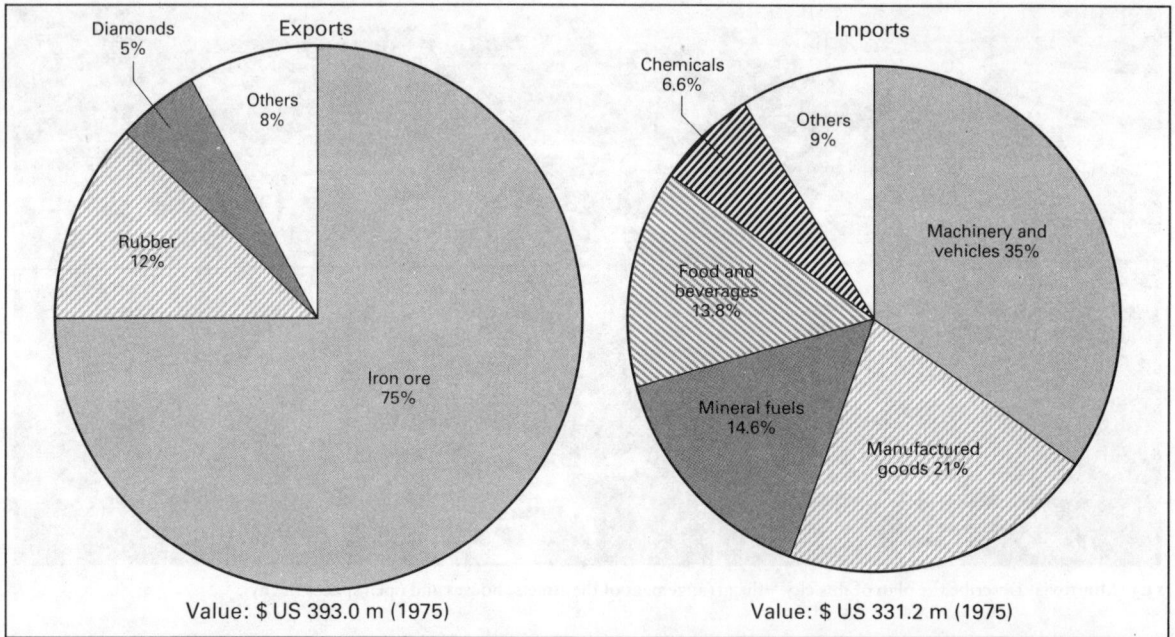

13.7 Liberia: trade (mid 1970–80 decade). Which item dominates the export trade of Liberia? Approximately how much was realised from this commodity in 1975%? By how much was the value of export greater than that of imports for the year 1975? Name the main import items. Why does Liberia export so much food? Name some food items it imports.

Trade

From Figure 13.7 we learn a lot about the trade of Liberia.

1. The exports are higher in value than the imports by as much as over $60 million.
2. The most important export commodities are iron ore, rubber and diamonds in that order of importance. What percentage of the export value is each of these commodities?
3. Iron ore maintains a dominant position in the export trade.
4. Turning to the import picture we see that machinery, manufactured goods, fuel, foods and drinks constitute the major imports. Much of the machinery is used in the mining operation in the country.

U.S.A. continues to be Liberia's biggest customer both in the value of exports to, and imports from, the country. The next in order is the Federal Republic of Germany and Western Europe, while Japan is becoming an interested trade partner from the far east.

Summary

Liberia is a typical tropical West African country though its climate is unique in being monsoonal. The economy of the country revolves around two key products – iron ore and rubber. Together, they account for over 86% of Liberia's exports and they have stimulated the extension of roads and railways with all their economic benefits, led to the establishment of many processing industries, and they dominate the export trade of Monrovia and Buchanan.

Revision exercises

1. Draw two maps of Liberia. On one insert the areas important for rubber, coffee and cocoa production, and the main roads. On the other insert and name the iron ore and diamond mining areas, the main railways and the coastal termini. Describe the roads and railways and show how they have helped farming and mining in the country.
2. Account for the importance of:
   a) Monrovia;
   b) foreign investment in the economy of Liberia;
   c) iron ore mining in Liberia.
3. For either Liberia or Sierra Leone, write a description of:
   a) the relief and drainage;
   b) the climate;
   c) the communications.
      (WASC/GCE 1974)

14 Sierra Leone

Preparation

1. Name the three relief regions of Liberia which we studied in chapter 13.
2. Which are the main language groups who live in Liberia?
3. What is Liberia's main food crop?
4. Draw a map of Sierra Leone from your atlas map. Insert her two neighbouring countries and Freetown, Bo, Yengema and Pendembu.

Sierra Leone, 71 740 square kilometres in area with a population of 3 million by the 1974 census, became independent from British rule in 1961. In April, 1970 a bill was passed declaring the country a republic.

The peoples of Sierra Leone

As in Liberia, there are three main language groups in Sierra Leone – the Creoles, the indigenous peoples and some foreigners.

The *Creoles*, like the Americo-Liberians, are descendants of freed slaves who arrived here in shiploads from North America and the West Indies in late 18th and early 19th centuries. They live mostly in the Peninsula. In towns, they occupy many of the office and professional jobs, while in the hillside villages they grow fruits and market garden crops, keep poultry and livestock which are sold to the coastal towns like Freetown and Wellington.

i) Study Figure 14.1 which shows where the Creoles and other indigenous peoples of Sierra Leone live, with sketches of their housing types.
ii) Of what are the walls and roofs of a Creole house built?
iii) How many floors has it?
iv) How is it different from the other houses in the picture?
v) What is the difference in shape between the *Mende* house in the south and the *Temne* and other housing types in the north?
vi) What are the walls and roofs made of?
vii) See in particular the Temne house – it has low eves to keep off as much rain as possible, and two concentric walls built to keep the inner bedroom cool and naturally 'air-conditioned'.
viii) Which of the houses would you like to live in and why?
ix) Do you find houses like these in your home area?
x) Now can you name the main indigenous groups in Sierra Leone? These groups are mainly farmers, but a number also prospect for diamonds.

The *foreigners* who live in Sierra Leone include the British and Lebanese who live in the cities as they do in most English-speaking West African countries.

Physical environment

Relief Regions

The three relief regions of Liberia extend north-westwards into Sierra Leone to form respectively the *coastal lowlands*, the *dissected inland plain* and the *eastern highlands*. But there is a fourth one – the *Sierra Leone peninsula* – which is unique to the country. Compare Figure 14.2 with Figure 13.1, and identify the corresponding regions.

The three regions in Sierra Leone have similar features to their counterparts in Liberia. But there are a number of differences

1. Cliffs are found along the Liberian coast, but *rias* indent Sierra Leone's coastline north of Shebro Island, and to the south it is lined by sand bars.
2. The highlands of Liberia are made up of two segments of the granite Guinea highlands. Those of Sierra Leone are more extensive and cover almost the eastern one half of the country.
3. The Lomar and Tingi Hills of Sierra Leone rise to over 2 000 metres. They are therefore higher than their Liberian counterparts – the Wutivi and the Nimba.

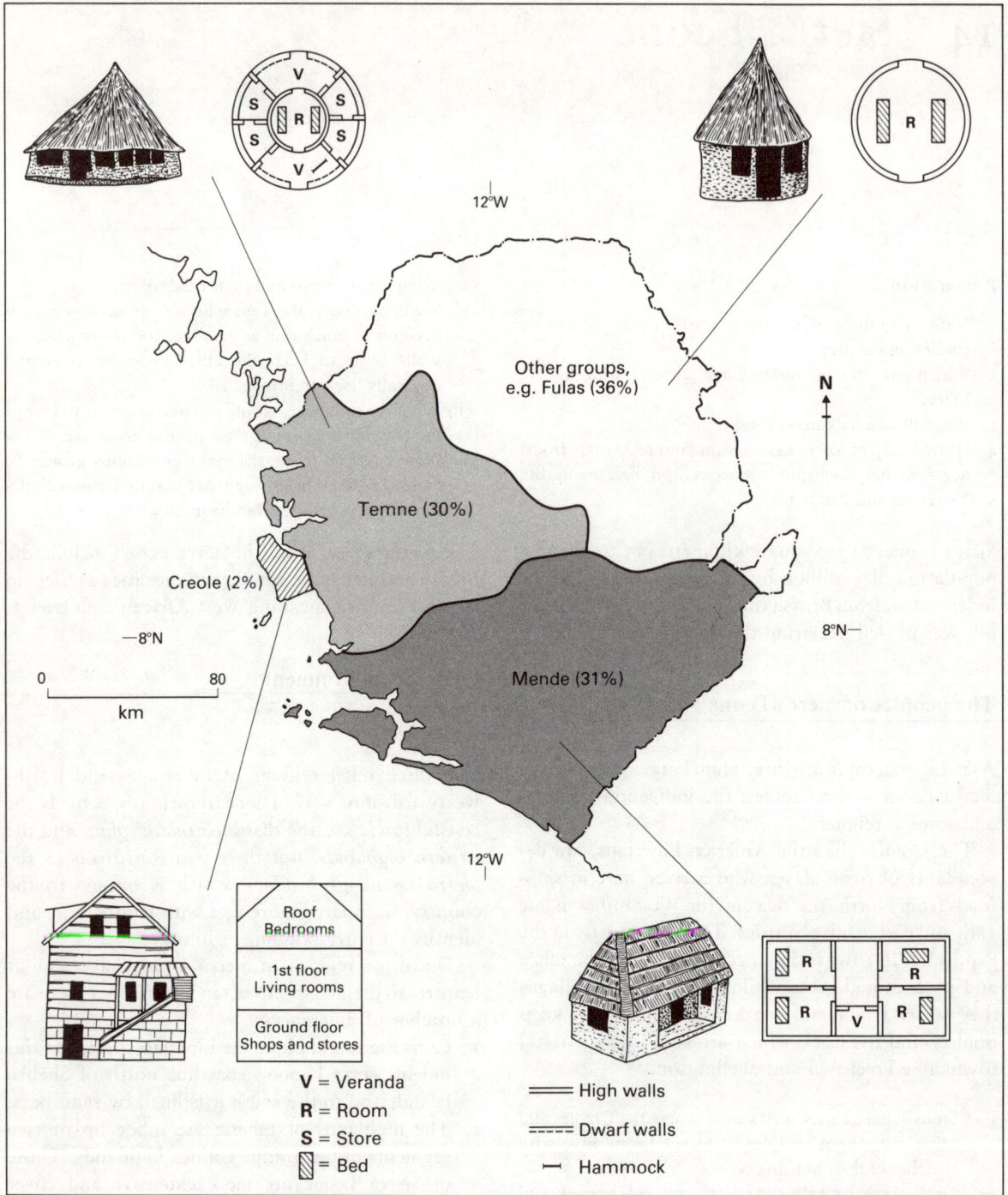

14.1 The peoples of Sierra Leone and their housing types.

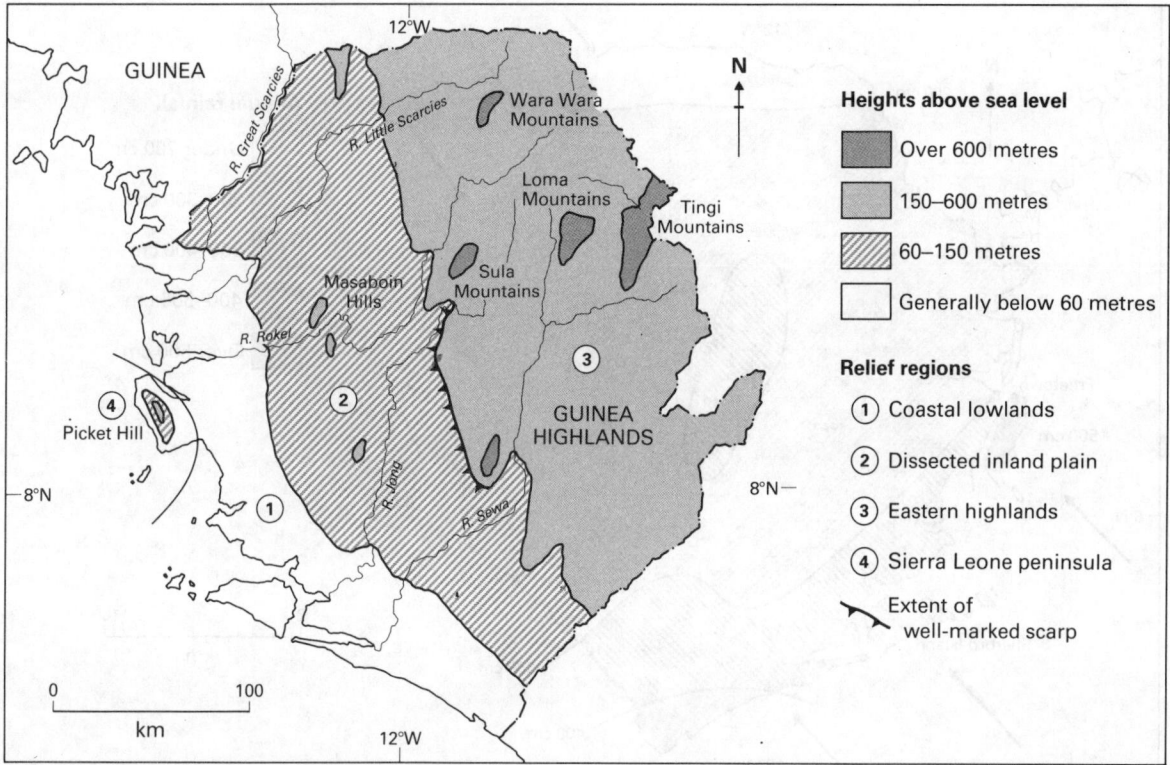

14.2 Sierra Leone: relief and relief regions.

The Sierra Leone Peninsula is a mass of intrusive rocks extending for 40 kilometres south-east from Freetown (see Figures 14.2 and 14.7). It is steep on all sides and dominated by several peaks, the highest of which is the Picket Hill, 940 metres above sea level.

Climate and vegetation:

The monsoonal climate and tropical vegetation of Liberia are repeated here in Sierra Leone. High temperatures are recorded and rainfall is everywhere heavy (2 000 mm – 5 000 mm per annum) being very much enhanced by the presence of the highlands. The country has a typical monsoon type of climate, with a peak in July as the following figures for Freetown clearly show

Total annual rainfall	Total rainfall May to October	July peak
3 500 mm (100%)	3 250 mm (92.8%)	965 mm (27.6%)

The high temperature and torrential downpours promote soil erosion, leaching and the formation of poor laterite soils. Mangrove swamps flourish along

the rias, and forests thrive on the slopes of the Sierra Leone peninsula. Palm bush and secondary forest cover much of the interior while grassland of the guinea savanna type is found in the drier north.

Economic development

Agriculture

Of the food crops grown in Sierra Leone, *rice* is the most important, occupying the largest area under cultivation and accounting for 500 000 tonnes out of 950 000 tonnes of food crops produced by the country in 1975.

Two principal varieties are grown – the upland and swamp types. The former thrives over much of the country since rainfall is abundant everywhere. The swamp variety however prefers the coastal swamps and frequently flooded lower river valleys, particularly that of the Great Scarcies. Here fresh water, silt, clay and organic materials are constantly

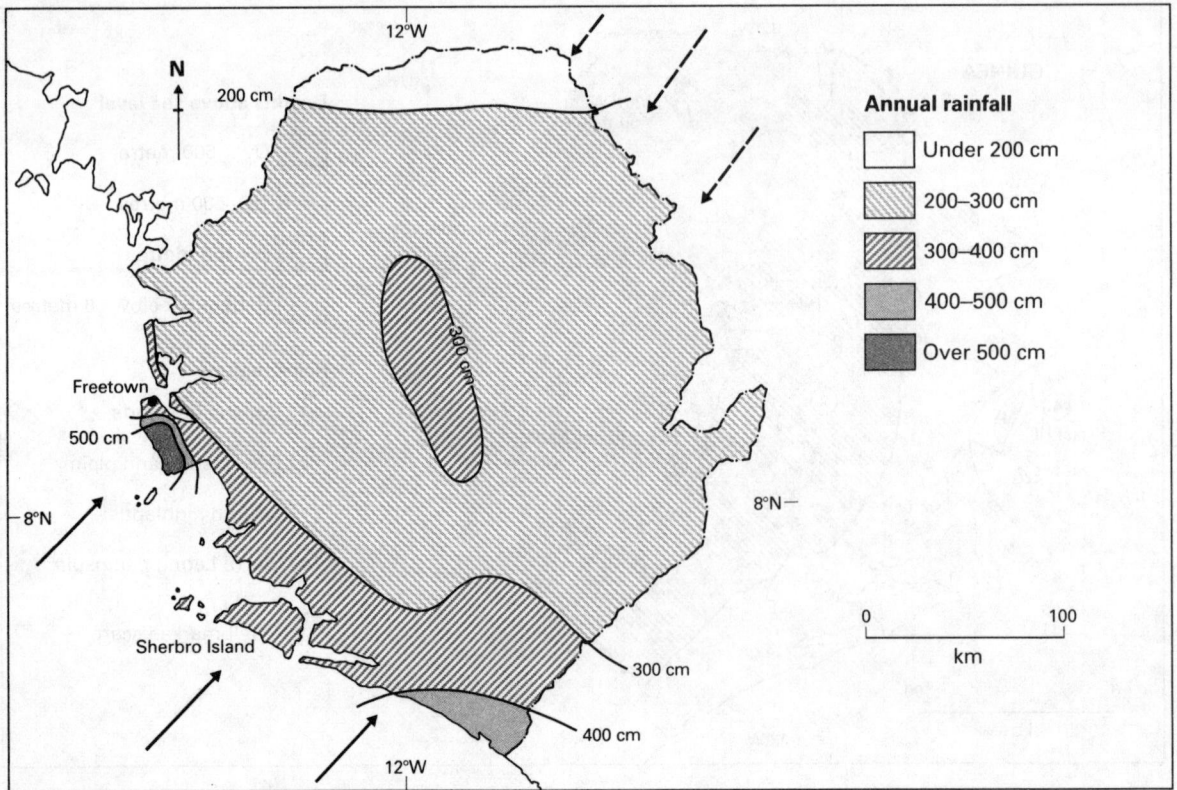

14.3 Sierra Leone: annual rainfall and air masses.

brought down by the rivers to enrich the soil. Two crops a year are grown thus making the annual yield per hectare very high. Conscious of the importance of rice in the farming economy of the country, the government has set up a rice research station and mills in the growing areas, reclaimed more swamp for cultivation and introduced quick ripening varieties. As a result the ½ million tonne production mark reached in 1975 has now been exceeded and in 1977 550 000 were produced.

Cassava, citrus fruits and *sweet potatoes* are widely cultivated, while *millet* and *beniseed* constitute the main food crops grown in the north.

Cash crops, principally palm produce, cocoa, coffee, groundnuts, kola and ginger, constitute over 10% of the value of the country's exports. The *oil palm* grows well on the dissected inland plain, away from the coastal marshes on the one hand and the highland areas on the other.

Cocoa and *coffee* are distributed as shown in Figure 14.5, the heaviest concentration being in the region of Pendembu and Kenema. The production of

coffee, cocoa, oil palm and other cash crops is being vigorously encouraged now that minerals are becoming increasingly less dominant in the economy of the country. In fact, by 1980, it is expected that the agricultural sector will have completely overtaken the mineral sector in the export trade of Sierra Leone.

The Ndama cattle are the livestock kept on the dry rolling grassland plateau of the north. The Fulas and Mandigoes who rear them come down from Guinea to make use of the better veterinary services which Sierra Leone offers. There is an estimated 300 000 head of cattle in Sierra Leone, and poultry keeping too is becoming increasingly important.

Mining

Sierra Leone used to be an important producer of *iron ore* in West Africa, constituting, as it did in the 1960's, some 12.5% of the country's exports. The ore was found at Marampa, recovered there and transported via a mineral line, to Pepel at the coast and then overseas. Production however began to fall in

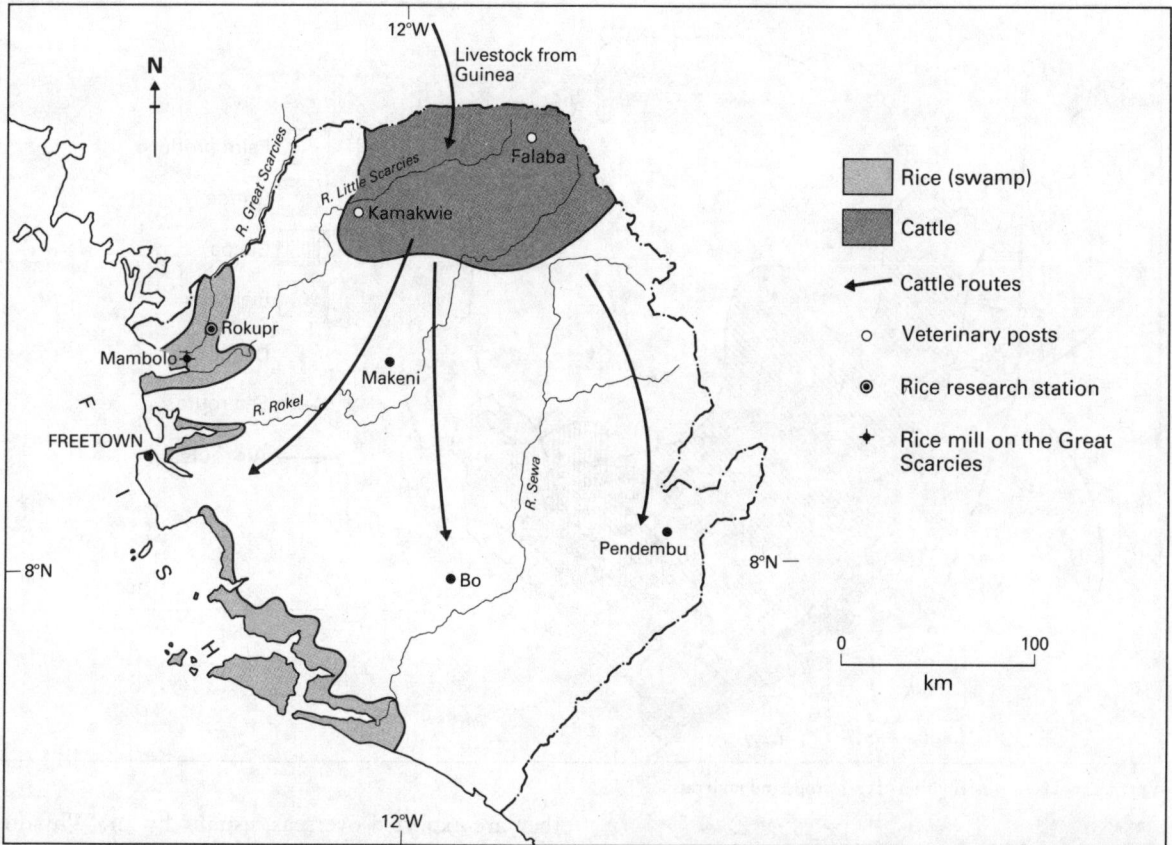

14.4 Sierra Leone: distribution of rice and livestock.

the late 1960's and only an agreement signed with Japan in 1968 to sell ore to it, kept the industry alive for a few more years. But it was destined to die because the mining company (called DELCO) was increasingly operating at a loss in the face of competition from better ores of Liberia and Mauritania. Production thus fell from 3 million tonnes in 1968 to 2.5 million tonnes in 1972 and 1.98 million in 1974. By 1975 the Company could no longer stand it and in October of that year it went into voluntary liquidation. Sierra Leone then ceased to exist on the iron ore map of West Africa.

Rutile is another mineral which Sierra Leone used to produce. Mining and export from Shebro Island began in 1967 but lasted for only 4 years, for the mining company suspended operations in April 1971.

Diamond dredging is however still active in Sierra Leone and *alluvial diamonds* continue to be Sierra Leone's chief mineral. The gem is recovered from Yengema, Tongo and parts of the Sewa Valley, though the recovery is scattered all over the country.

Serious diamond mining was started in 1934 by a British-based firm called Sierra Leone Selection Trust. This firm, now known as the National Diamond Mining Company, accounted for 50% of the 1.5 million carats officially mined in 1975.

We say 'officially', because illicit mining of diamonds, and smuggling them out of the country are the order of the day in Sierra Leone. So it is difficult to know exactly how much is produced in the country and sold out. To try and reduce this practice, government extended mining licences to other companies and even to private individuals. But the practice still goes on unabated.

Production continues to fluctuate over the years. However a significant drop was noticed in the late 1970's, a drop which should be of some concern to Sierra Leone.

See Figure 14.6 and describe how the mineral is recovered. From such locations as this the mineral is sent to a factory in Freetown where the diamonds are washed, graded, cut into shapes and polished before

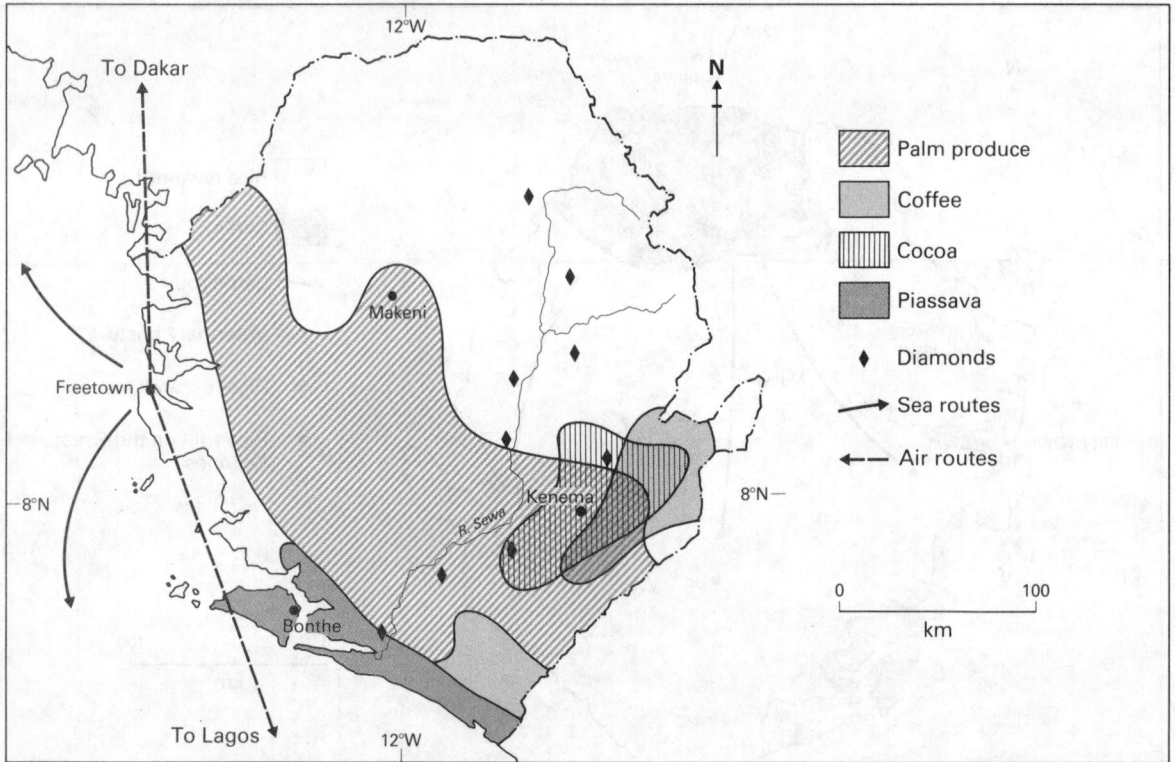

14.5 Sierra Leone: distribution of cash crops and minerals.

14.6 Dredging alluvial diamonds in Sierra Leone. Describe the location and the machines used. What suggests that the diamonds recovered here are alluvial?

they are exported overseas, usually by air. Why do you think it is not considered too expensive to export this mineral by air?

The other vital mineral in Sierra Leone is *bauxite*, found in the south-west. Mining started in 1964 with a production of 127 000 tonnes. In 1975, 672 000 tonnes of this mineral was recovered. Production continues today.

Transportation

Sierra Leone used to have two railway systems – a one-metre gauge private DELCO mineral line which ran from Marampa to Pepel, and a 0.83 metre gauge public line which linked Freetown with the hinterland. With iron ore mining ceasing in 1975, the mineral line of course fell out of use. But even before then, the public line was running at a loss. The trains were light, slow and antiquated, the line narrow and tortuous and it was costing government over 2 million leones annually to subsidize. So in 1971, when government could bear the cost no longer, the line was forced to close down.

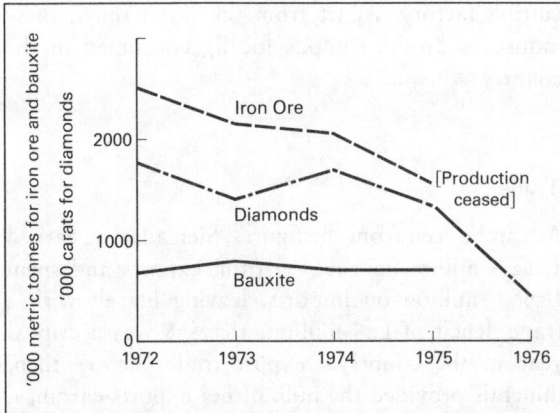

14.7 Recent production of key minerals in Sierra Leone.

Roads now constitute the most useful means of transport in Sierra Leone. They carry practically 100% of the traffic in the country. Even then there are only 8 000 kilometres of road in the whole country and less than 10% of it is tarred! Travelling on the roads is considerably slowed down by the numerous ferries across the many rivers and the bad surface on the untarred sections. However, government is making efforts to improve the road system and a direct link from Freetown to Monrovia (capital of Liberia) has been planned.

The Lungi airport which serves Freetown has modern and international facilities, and links Freetown with other West African capitals.

Freetown

Freetown is the capital, chief port and the principal commercial and industrial centre of Sierra Leone. It is also the largest town with a population of 274 000 by the latest census of 1974.

i) See the view of the town in Figure 14.8.
ii) Describe its location.
iii) Can you identify the hill slopes behind the foot of the hills where the town is located, and the harbour in the fore-ground?
iv) See the ships and the warehouses at the harbor. What products do you think the ships are carrying out of or bringing in to the country?

The hills behind are those of the Sierra Leone peninsula. The harbour is the deep, calm water entrance of the Sierra Leone River which enables cargo, passenger and mail boats to enter the port undisturbed. Thus Freetown is able to handle over 80% of the trade of Sierra Leone.

Three factors however have restricted the growth

14.8 Freetown. Answer the questions on this picture asked in the text.

of the port despite its natural advantages of a deep and sheltered harbour. Its hinterland, Sierra Leone itself, is a small and not particularly wealthy country. Secondly, the railway that led to the port was a narrow gauge line which could not carry heavy traffic. Now the railway is no more and only limited traffic can be carried by road. Finally, even when the country was exporting iron ore, it all went out through Pepel, rather than through Freetown. So the ore handling facilities were all installed at Pepel rather than at Freetown.

Among West African ports, Freetown has a character all its own. Though old-fashioned in places, with the oldest University in West Africa, narrow winding streets and half wooden and half stone storeyed buildings, there are modern developments as well in the city. Ultra-modern buildings are replacing the old ones at the University, the new Kissy residential area has grown up to add a new look to the town, and it has a developing industrial suburb.

More than 75% of the industries in the country are located in Freetown and its suburbs. These include a paint works, a nail factory, breweries, a cigarette factory and an oil refinery. There are also plastics, textiles and cement works and the new diamond cutting factory. Apart from the last named, these industries produce goods locally consumed in the country.

Trade

As can be seen from the figures, Sierra Leone earned L162.6 million in 1976–77 from exports and spent L190.6 million on imports, leaving herself with a trade deficit of L28 million. 1977–78 was a critical year in the country's export trade. Before then, minerals provided the bulk of her exports earnings. But with the cessation of iron ore exports after 1976 and rutile earlier on, a steady decline in the official exports of diamonds, and galloping increase in that of cocoa and coffee, agriculture displaced mining as the largest export revenue earner. Cocoa exports nearly quadrupled between 1974–75 and 1977–78, and coffee exports multiplied nearly 8 times! This is unprecedented.

Of the import items, manufactured goods come first, foods second and machinery third. Why does the country import a lot of food items? What should the country do to import less of these items?

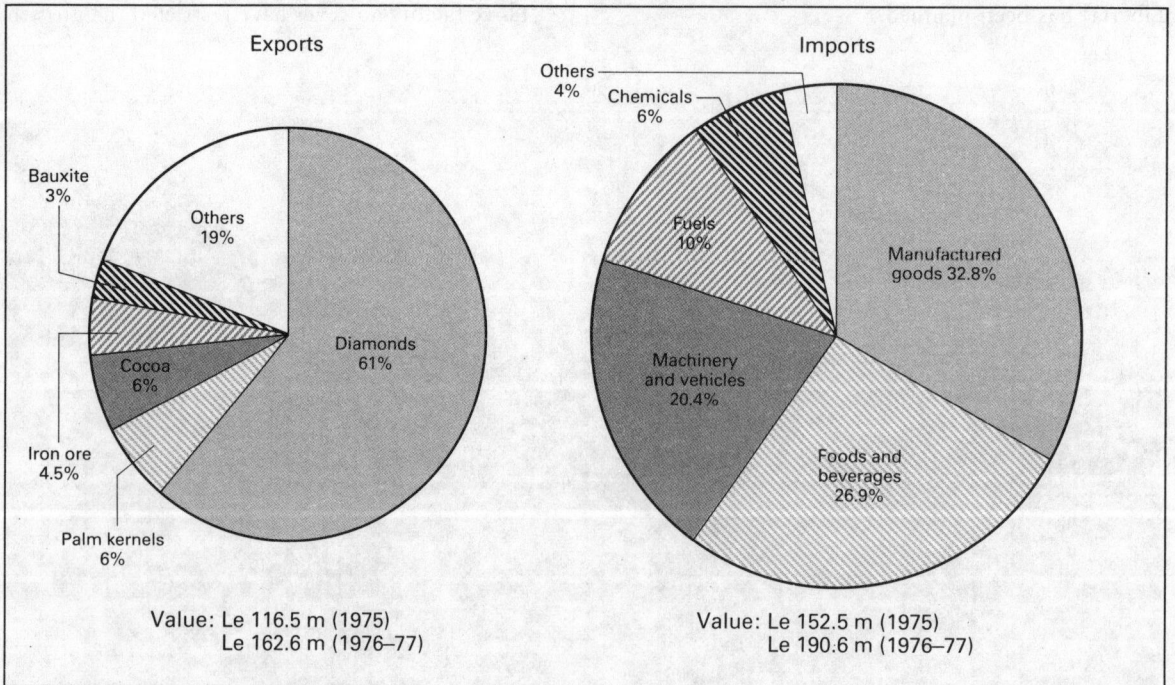

14.9 Sierra Leone: recent external trade.

Britain, Western Europe, U.S.A., Venezuela and Japan are Sierra Leone's main overseas customers.

Summary

You should leave this chapter by remembering the most important aspects in the geography of Sierra Leone. These are:
i)   a similarity in environment and economy to Liberia;
ii) the former over-riding but now diminishing importance of minerals in her economy;
iii) the vital nature of rice production in her food production programme;
iv) the low state of her industrial and general economic development owing to poor transportation facilities and lack of power, and finally
v)   a chronic unfavourable trade balance.

Revision exercises

1. On the map of Sierra Leone you have prepared, mark and name the following, using distinguishing symbols: Sierra Leone peninsula, Sula mountains, the Great Scarcies, Rockel and Sewa Rivers, areas important for diamond, cocoa and cattle.
2. With the aid of a sketch map compare the coastal lowlands with the interior hill and plateau areas of Sierra Leone under the following headings:
   a) relief
   b) climate
   c) soils
      (*WASC/GCE, 1977*)
3. Compare the environments, peoples and economic activities in Sierra Leone with those of Liberia.

15   The Guineas

Preparation

1. Name two food crops, two cash crops and two minerals found in Sierra Leone.
2. Turn to your atlas map of the Guineas. Trace the map of the Republic of Guinea and Guinea Bissau. Look for the following places and insert them on your map – Bissau, Conakry, Los Islands, Fria, Boké, Kindia, Mamou, Kankan and Siguiri.
3. Practise drawing the outline map of the Guineas several times until you can draw it really well.

The Guineas comprise two countries – the Republic of Guinea or simply Guinea which is French speaking, and Guinea Bissau whose official language is Portuguese. Guinea, 245.860 square kilometres in area with a 1972 estimated population of 5.14 million, became independent in 1958 when it opted completely out of the French union. Normal relations with France were broken until 1975 when the two countries gradually came together once more as friends.

Guinea Bissau, only 36 125 square kilometres with 800 000 people, declared itself independent in September, 1973, but was recognized as such by Portugal only in September, 1974.

The peoples of the Guineas

The Guineas are noted for the rich and bewildering variety of their peoples, physical environment, resources and economy. Of the peoples the largest group who live in Guinea are the over 1 million *Fulas* who moved into and settled in this area about the 18th century. Unlike the Fulani people in other parts of West Africa, the Fulas of Guinea are not nomadic. They combine crop cultivation with rearing the dwarf Ndama cattle on the Futa Jalon Plateau, and

also produce beautiful works of art. They also live in large numbers in Conakry and other cities.

Next to the Fulas are the farming *Susus* and *Kissis*. Common among the Susus is the traditional Guinea house shown in Figure 15.1. It is similar to the Temne house in Sierra Leone. Do you remember how the house is built and why it is built the way it is? The *Malinkes* live mainly on the upper Niger plains (see Figure 15.2), while the *Bagas* inhabit low lying Guinea Bissau and the adjacent areas of Guinea. There are over 10 other groups, fragmented by the difficult relief of the Guinea highlands and who therefore live in little pockets in the highland valleys.

The physical environment

Physical regions

Four relief regions, as shown in Figure 15.2, can be identified – the Coastal plains, Futa Jalon plateau, the upper Niger plains and the Guinea highlands. Each of these has its unique relief, climate and vegetation – all contributing to the variety of landscape for which Guinea is noted.

The *coastal plains*, with an average width of 60 kilometres, are narrow in Guinea but wide in Guinea Bissau where they cover practically the whole country. The coastline has shallow drowned river estuaries and mangrove swamps. Alluvial deposits carpet the floor of the valleys, and elsewhere laterite soils occur. Only at two places – Cape Verga and Conakry – do ancient rocks abut at the coast. At Conakry they provide firm ground which has made the development of the capital and routes to the interior easy. Weathering of the rocks has produced bauxite which is being quarried off-shore at Los Islands.

The sandstone *Futa Jalon plateau*, 1 000 to 1 500

15.1 A traditional homestead in Guinea. Describe the shape of the houses. Look closely inside the second house to the left. Can you see the inner round wall with a door to it? Which of the housing types in Sierra Leone (fig. 14.1) is it most similar to? Why is it built this way? What crop is being spread to dry in the foreground?

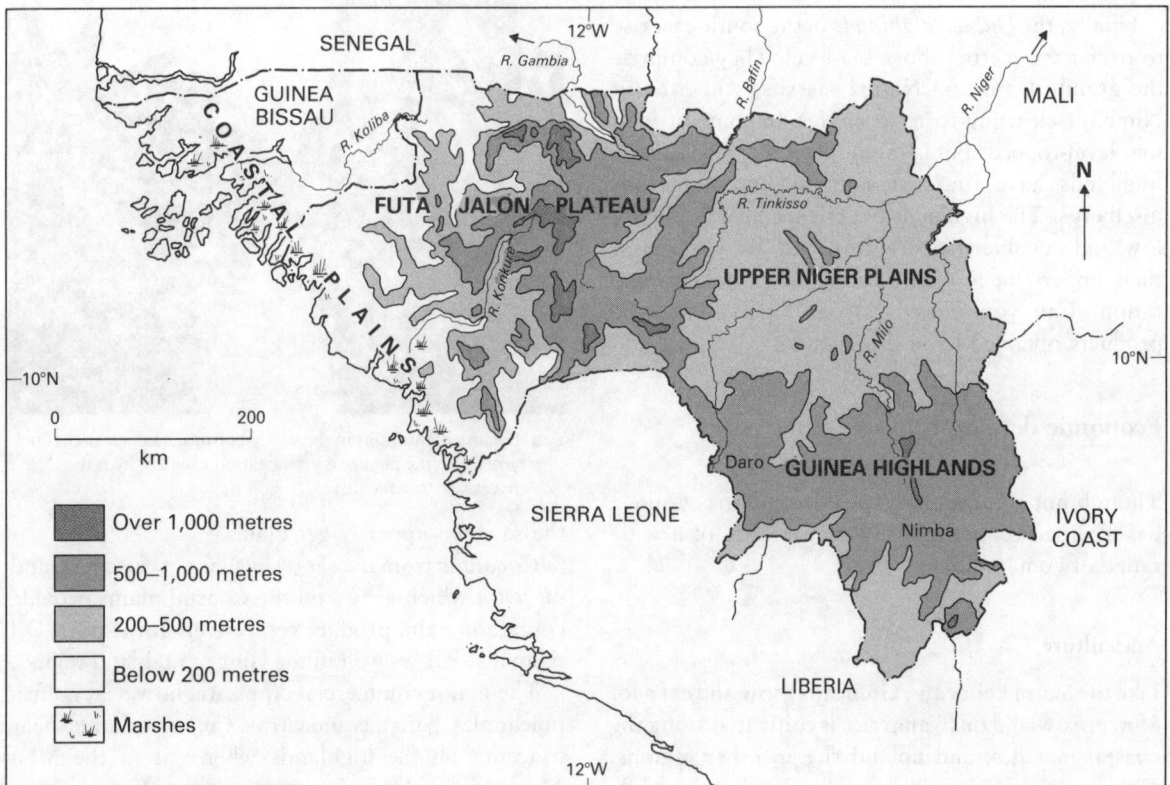

15.2 Relief and relief regions of the Guineas.

metres high, is perhaps the most impressive plateau in West Africa after the Jos plateau of Nigeria. With level tops, but a steep and almost sheer vertical drop at the edges, it occupies the west-centre of the country.

Rainfall here is very heavy. Can you say why? But the vegetation is made of sedges and herbs because the sandstone cover is porous, the laterite on the surface is not fertile, temperatures are fairly low and the area has been cultivated and grazed for centuries. Much of the rain drains into the numerous deeply incised West African rivers that rise from the plateau. Can you name some of these rivers?

The rolling *upper Niger plains* east of the Futa Jalon plateau, are made up of precambrian rocks. They are about 350–500 metres high and slope gently eastwards to the Malian border. They are drained by many tributaries of the Niger, chief of which are the Milo and Tinkisso. Exposed to the harmattan winds from the north-east for a greater part of the year, they have the tropical continental type of climate and are covered by the guinea savanna vegetation of the type described in chapter 5.

Finally, the *Guinea highlands* in the south-east rise to over 1200 metres above sea level. They comprise the granite Daro and Nimba massifs, with Mount Nimba itself rising to 1752 metres. In contrast with the level-topped Futa Jalon plateau, the Guinea highlands have rounded summits and numerous inselbergs. The highlands experience heavy rainfall, low and equable temperatures, and are covered at their upper slopes with the montane type of vegetation. Can you identify, from Figure 15.6, the products obtained from this region?

Economic development of Guinea

Though not a particularly wealthy country, Guinea has a varied economy, producing a little of a wide range of commodities.

Agriculture

Like the Sierra Leoneans, Guineans grow and eat a lot of *rice*. Lowland or swamp rice is cultivated along the coastal marshes, and upland rice in other regions. *Cassava* is another widely grown food crop, while *maize* and *millet*, as would be expected, grow well on

15.3 Banana plantations at the foot of the Plateau. The mountain you see at the background of the picture is the Kakoulima Mountain, part of the Futa Jalon Plateau. Why is the banana plantation at the foot of the plateau not at the slopes?

15.4 Banana plantations in the valley bottom. The water channel you see in the picture is an irrigation canal. Why is it necessary to have this?

the savanna upper Niger Plains.

Coconuts from the sandy beaches of the coast, and *oil palm* which grows on the Coastal plains provide copra and palm produce respectively for export. Oil palm also grows well in the Guinea highland region.

The major commercial crops are, however, coffee, pineapples, bananas and citrus. *Coffee* is planted near Macenta on the highlands where, as in the Man Mountains of Ivory Coast, the slopes offer adequate drainage, low temperatures and early morning mist which are ideal for the crop. Coffee is Guinea's most important export crop, second in value only to alumina (processed bauxite).

Pineapples, bananas and *citrus* constitute the country's major fruits. They are grown in plantations on the Coastal plains. But as indicated in Figure 15.6, banana estates are most common along the Conakry-Mamou railway which provides quick transportation to the coast. Previously owned by French farmers but now reverted to state ownership, these estates are ideally located in valley bottoms or at the foot-hills of the Futa Jalon plateau as Figures 15.3 and 15.4 above clearly show. Such valleys and foot-hills have deep soils and provide warmth and shelter for the banana plants. These photographs were taken in April. What season of the year is this in Guinea? The mountain in Figure 15.3 is the Kakoulima Mountains, part of the Futa Jalon Mountains. Bananas used to be Guinea's chief export crop by value, but since the French abandoned the estates in 1958, and disease attacked the crops soon after, both production and export fell. Now coffee is first among the crops; pineapples second and banana third.

Mining

This is Guinea's most dynamic economic pursuit and the most important earner of foreign currency. The country's most vital minerals are bauxite, iron ore, diamonds and gold.

The *bauxite* deposits in Guinea are the third largest in the world, accounting for 25% of the world's known reserves of this mineral. The mineral is currently obtained from four places – Los Islands, Fria, Boké and Debele (near Kindia).

The Los Island deposits, west of Conakry are locally mined by open cast method, crushed, smelted into alumina and exported via the island's port of Kassa. The Fria ore is crushed and smelted at the Fria alumina works – the largest factory in the country and the largest alumina works in West Africa (Figure 15.5). It uses electricity from the Konkouré hydro-electric power station and turns out 650 000 tonnes of alumina a year. This is transported via the 145 kilometre railway to Conakry for export. The Boké mine, opened in 1965, is the largest and produces just over 6 million tonnes of bauxite annually. The bauxite is transported by rail to a new port at Kamsar, 136 kilometres from Boké. The newest mine

15.5 Fria alumina works. In this factory, bauxite is turned to alumina – the form in which this mineral is exported from Guinea. Find Fria on your map of Guinea. Trace the route and port of export. Name other bauxite mining areas of Guinea. To which countries does Guinea export alumina?

is the Soviet financed and operated Debele mine near Kindia. This was opened in 1972 and has capacity of 2 million tonnes a year. The deposits near Dabola with a reserve of 425 million tonnes are yet to be mined.

From all the four operating mines above, Guinea produced over 7 million tonnes of bauxite in 1975 and 9 million in 1976. Alumina alone accounts for over 60% of Guinea's export by value. By the early 1980's when the Dabola mine will have been commissioned and a 300 000 tonne capacity alumina plant located there, the country hopes to produce a total of 13 million tonnes of bauxite and some 1 million tonnes of alumina a year.

The former *iron ore* mine at Kaloum was closed down in 1967 because it became uneconomic to continue it. But in 1973 Guinea entered into an agreement with Nigeria, Liberia, Libya, Algeria and other countries including Japan and France to explore her richer iron ore deposits at Nimba Mountains. It is expected that production from this location will reach 30–40 million tonnes annually and a 1200 kilometre railway built from Nimba to Conakry to carry the ore to the coast.

Alluvial diamonds are dredged at the headwaters of the Milo at Kissidougou and near Beyla on the Highlands. As in Sierra Leone, illicit recovery is rife, so the official production figures of 80 000 carats per annum can only be regarded as a very conservative estimate.

Gold, the last of the important minerals, is mined from underground by the local people at Siguiri on the upper Niger plains.

Now let us pause a little and answer the following review questions:

i)　Name the major peoples of Guinea. In which parts of the country do they live?

ii)　When did Guinea Bissau become independent? When did the Republic of Guinea obtain her independence?

iii)　Name the four relief regions of Guinea. Which of them is the highest? Describe each briefly.

iv)　Where are the following grown in Guinea – bananas, palm trees, pineapples, coffee and rice? Why are they grown in those places? Which of them is the most vital export crop?

v)　Name four places where bauxite is mined in Guinea. What is the mineral used for? How is it mined, processed and exported?

vi)　Locate Fria on your map of Guinea. What is it noted for?

vii)　What plans has Guinea for further developing her minerals?

Towns, industry and transportation

Conakry, the capital of Guinea, is a city of 526 000 people. It is located at the western terminus of the Guinea railway and has a number of industries including fruit canneries, furniture factories, a printing press, a cigarette factory and a textile mill located in and around the city. Can you say more about the town from what we have already studied above?

Study the transportation system in Figure 15.6 and the towns connected by the railways. *Kindia* and *Mamou* guard the approaches to the holiday resorts

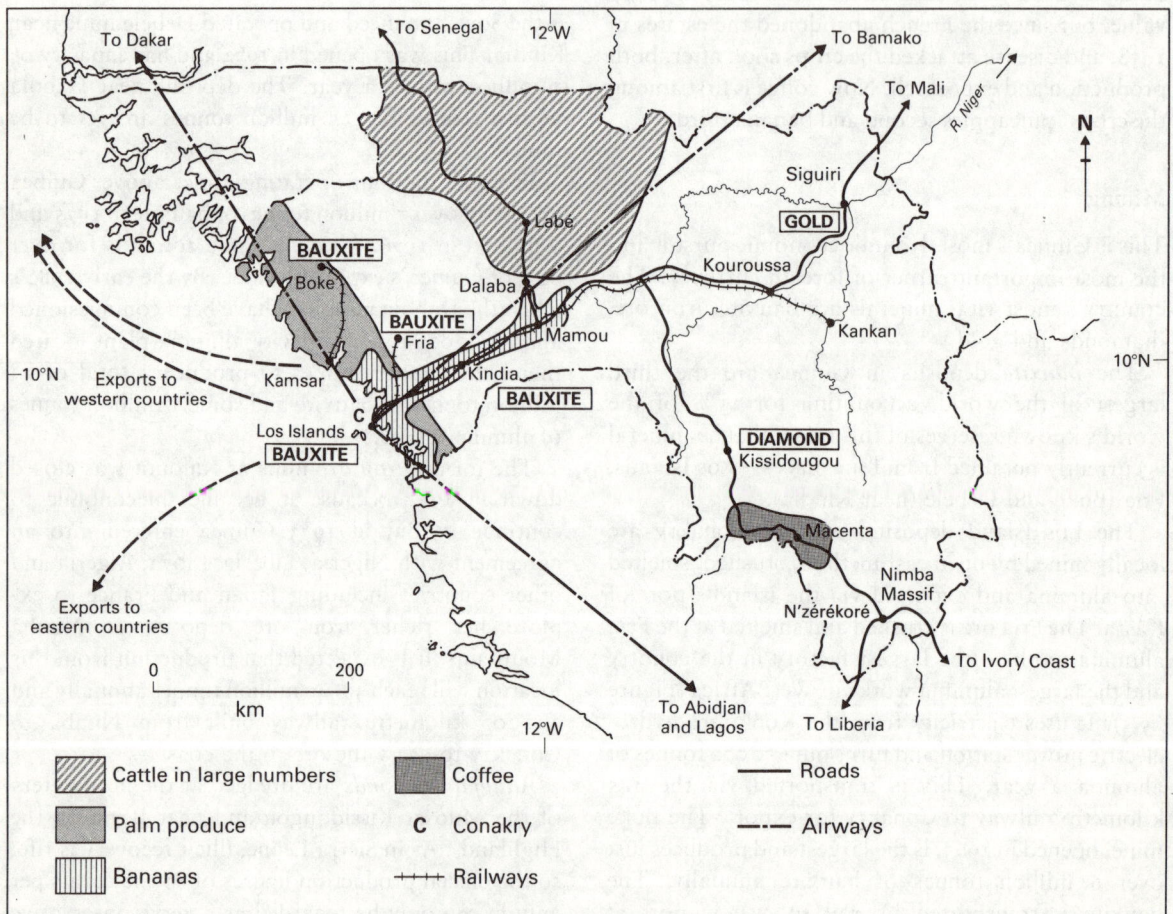

15.6 Guinea: economy.

of *Dalaba* and *Labé* on the Futa Jalon plateau.

Kankan is the eastern terminus of the 640 kilometre narrow gauge railway from Conakry, while a 135 kilometre heavier gauge links *Boké* with the port of *Kamsar*. Do you remember what major commodity this line carries? The gold mining town of *Siguiri* is a river port located at the confluence of the Milo and Tinkisso and commands the gateway to Mali.

On the whole, transportation presents a great problem in Guinea. Of the 28 400 kilometres of roads the country has, only 520 kilometres are tarred. Fuel is very expensive and vehicles look generally worn down for lack of spare parts to repair them.

Overseas trade

Since 1958 when France suddenly withdrew all aid to the country including preferential treatment to Guinean exports, the country has had a chronic trade deficit. Recently however with the opening up of trade partnerships with China, U.S.A. and East European countries, the return to friendship with France, and the increased production of bauxite which is locally processed to alumina before export, the country has shown trade surpluses with exports being higher than imports in value. The main imports are machinery, food items, fuel and textiles. Can you name the exports?

The economy of Guinea-Bissau

Before independence Guinea-Bissau produced little more than groundnuts, coffee and cotton (grown and harvested from the elevated interior), coconuts and palm produce (obtained from the lower coastal plains) and rice from the coastal marshes. Portugal exploited these products and did very little else to develop the country.

The 10 years fight for national liberation (1963–1973) set the economy of the country back even further. For since most people took to arms, agriculture was neglected, timber, coconut and oil palms were devastated by a decade of continuous air bombardments by Portugal and road links were completely disrupted.

Since independence however, the government of Guinea-Bissau has given priority to increased production of rice, diversification of the range of crops produced, expansion of the fishing industry and the reconstruction of roads and other facilities. In the long term, the country hopes to unify with Cape Verde Islands and has been gradually working towards this, although it is not too clear what obvious economic advantage this unification may bring to Guinea-Bissau.

Summary

Guinea has similar relief and climate to Sierra Leone and Liberia, though it is more economically developed than the former. Her resources are also more varied than both. Though not as rich as either Senegal or Ivory Coast, she has, until late, received comparatively little assistance from the Western countries since her independence. Recently bauxite mining and the export of alumina have brought an economic boom to the country.

Revision exercises

1. On a map of Guinea show the distribution of four major farm crops, four minerals, two main railway lines and at least two towns on each. Comment briefly on:
   a) mining in Guinea;
   b) the importance of Conakry.
2. Compare farming in Guinea with that of either Sierra Leone or Ivory Coast.

16 Senegambia

Preparation

1. Revise the characteristics of the tropical continental type of climate (Chapter 3) and the features of the three types of savanna vegetation (Chapter 5).
2. Review how groundnuts are produced and sold in Nigeria and the factors favouring their production (Chapter 7).
3. Look at the pictures and maps in this chapter, in particular those of Dakar. Locate the main rivers and towns in Senegal and The Gambia.

Senegambia is the name given to Senegal and The Gambia together. The former, 196 200 square kilometres in area had a population of 5.1 million in 1976. Like most West African countries, it became independent in 1960, but it retained its three-century old link with France through its continued membership in the French Community.

The Gambia, 460 kilometres long by 25–30 kilometres wide, is a narrow snake-like enclave thrust into the belly of Senegal, following closely the winding Gambia River. One of Africa's smallest states, it is only just over 10 500 square kilometres in area and had, in 1973, a population of 494 000 – that is less than half the population of Lagos! It became independent from British rule in 1965 and a republic in 1970.

The peoples

The largest and the most progressive indigenous group of people in Senegambia are the *Wolofs*. They live in the cities where they constitute the educated working class. In the hinterland they farm groundnuts and grains. The *Sérères* and *Dioulas* live mainly in the villages and are good farmers. The *Mandigoes* inhabit The Gambia and the Casamance district of southern Senegal. They too are farmers. The *Fulas* and *Moors* are the nomadic herdsmen of Senegal who live in the interior and along the valley of River Senegal.

Like Ivory Coast, Senegal maintains an open door policy to European immigration, so it has a substantial European population, mostly Frenchmen who remained after Senegal became independent or who have come into the country since then. They are attracted also by the cool climate of Dakar, its city life and the country's relative nearness to France.

Physical environment

In contrast to Guinea, Senegambia is remarkably flat, uniform in relief, and arid in climate. Its low-lying nature ensures that the four rivers that drain the area flow sluggishly (Figure 16.1). It also provides little incentive to precipitation and so it combines with the presence of the cool Canary current and proximity to desert latitudes to place Senegambia in the semi-arid continental climatic zone. Off-shore condensation over the current which gives rise to fog however helps to temper the climate along the shoreline.

As shown in the map, four air masses influence the region. The *trade wind* (called l'alizé in Senegal) blows from the Azores high pressure belt in the north between the months of November and March and brings the fog mentioned above. The *tropical continental airmass* takes over in March, lasts till June and brings dry and dusty weather from the Sahara. The *tropical maritime airmass* which brings rains from the Atlantic predominates from July to September and tails off in October and November, while the *equatorial easterlies* which, as usual are associated with turbulent weather, mark the change-over of seasons.

Grassland vegetation predominates and this thins

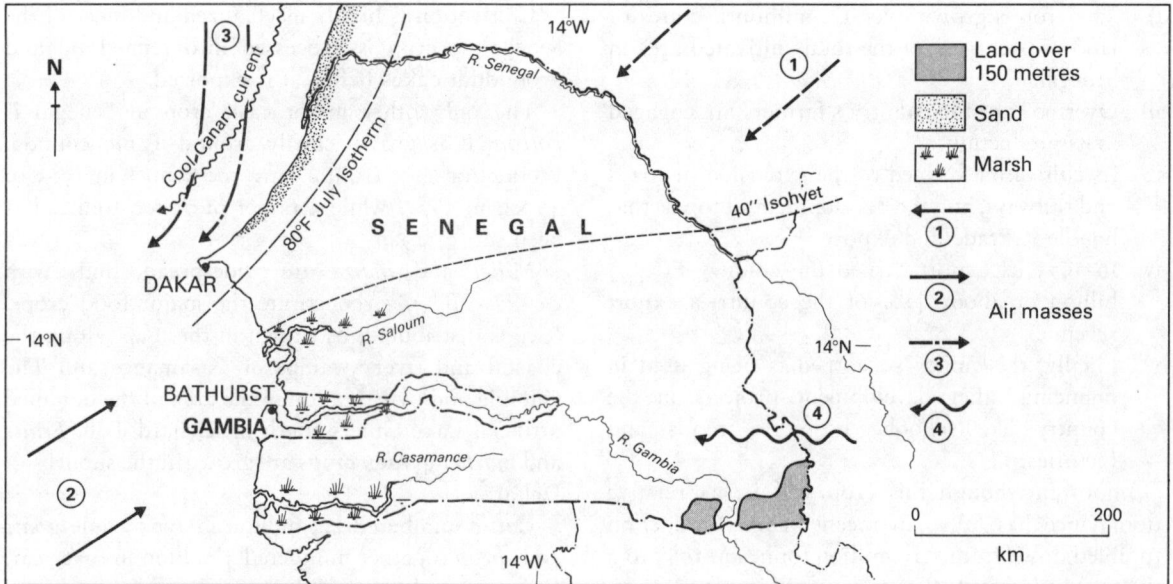

16.1 Some aspects of the physical environment of Senegambia.

from the guinea savanna in the wetter south, where rainfall approximates 1 000 mm per annum, to the sahel savanna in the drier north where precipitation diminishes to 500 mm per annum. Along the water courses where the soil is moist, marshes and fringing forests are found. Forest vegetation is also found in Casamance in the southwest.

Economic development of Senegal

Agriculture and fishing

Senegal gets over one-third of its wealth from agriculture, and by far the most important farm crop is *groundnuts*. There are a number of reasons for this.

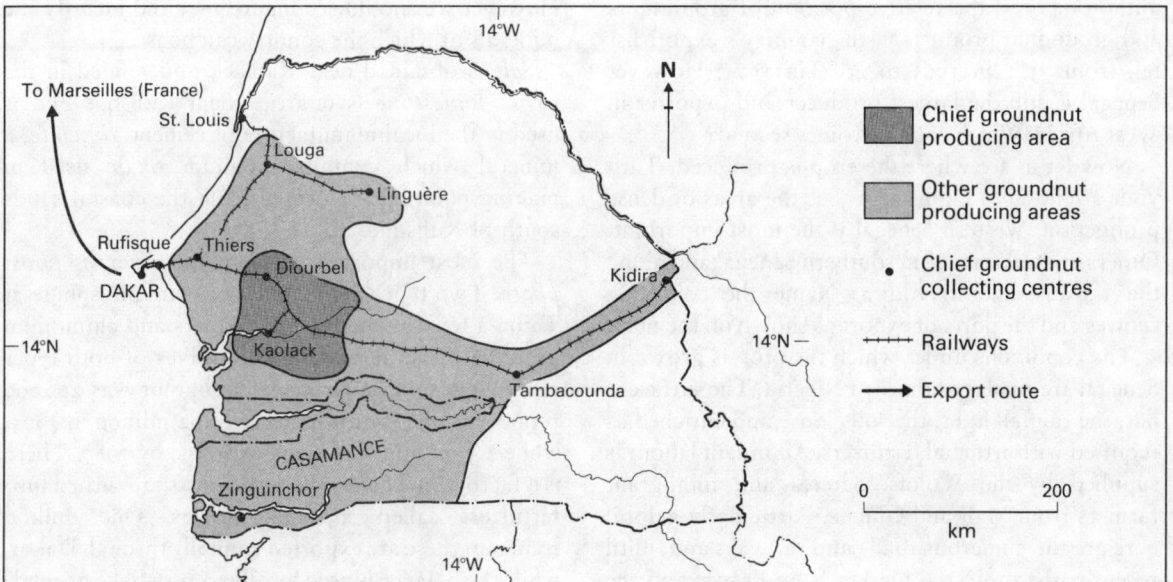

16.2 Senegambia: distribution of groundnuts and railways.

i)   The crop is grown over 1.2 million hectares of land or over 45% of the total cultivated area in Senegal.

ii) Over 90% of the country's farmers are engaged in its production.

iii) Its cultivation has led to the extension of roads and railways, and the development of towns that handle its trade and export.

iv) In 1975 its export earned the country Fr. 40.3 billion or about 40% of the country's export revenue.

v)   Finally, the money so earned is being used in financing other development projects in the country like schools, hospitals, roads and factories.

Important though this crop still is, its relative dominance has fallen in recent years. Production tumbled down from 1.17 million tonnes in 1965 to a disaster level of 587 000 in 1972. This drop can be attributed to three major factors:

i)   the abolition in 1968 by the main buyer, France of the subsidy she used to give to Senegalese groundnuts in her markets;

ii) the drought of 1972–74 which devastated much of the crop; and

iii) the conscious efforts being made by the country to grow other crops and develop her fisheries to reduce her over-dependence on this one crop.

As a result, even though production revived to 1.48 million in 1975, the relative position of groundnuts and groundnut products in the country's export list fell from 75% in 1965 to 40% in 1975. However Senegal is still the largest producer and exporter in West Africa. Which country comes second?

Now let us see where the crop is produced. Turn your attention to Figure 16.2. See the areas of dense production. Western Senegal is the most important. Others are Casamance in southern Senegal and along the railway line to Kidira. Name the collecting centres and the ports of export as shown on the map.

The conditions under which the crop is grown in Senegal are similar to those in Nigeria. The surface is flat, the rainfall light, the soils loose and enriched as required with artificial fertilizers. Abundant labour is supplied by the Wolofs, Sérères and immigrant farmers from Mali and Guinea. Particularly helpful here are the numerous roads and railways and, until recently, the protected market from France and the European Economic Community.

Cultivation is highly mechanized and most of the Senegalese crop is processed into refined oil and groundnut cakes before it is exported.

The only other major cash crop in Senegal is *cotton*. It is grown chiefly around Tambacounda. Production rose from a bare 700 tonnes in 1965 to 42 000 in 1975, while a target of 75 000 tonnes has been set for 1980.

Millet and *maize* are widespread, and, with *cassava* and *rice*, constitute the major food crops. Rice is distributed, as shown in the map, along the coastal and river swamps of Casamance and The Gambia and by irrigation in the area of the dammed artificial Lake Guiers south of Richard Toll. *Fruits* and *market garden crops* are grown at the suburbs of Dakar.

Cattle numbered 2.4 million in 1975 while *goats* and *sheep* together numbered 3 million in that year. *Fish* are caught from the rivers, along the coast, and off-shore in the open waters. The catch is landed, refrigerated or canned at Dakar and other ports. Sizeable quantities are exported, while the balance is consumed locally.

Mining

Unlike Guinea and Liberia, but like Ivory Coast, mining is relatively unimportant in Senegal. It contributes less than 2% of the wealth of the country. However we should see Figure 16.3 and identify the minerals of which the country can boast.

Salt is obtained near Kaolack and refined in the town. *Limestone* is quarried near Rufisque and is used in the local manufacture of cement. *Ilmenite*, a mineral which contains titanium oxide used in making paints, is recovered from the coastal sands south of Rufisque.

The most important mineral, however, is *phosphate*. Two types are mined – calcium phosphate at Taiba a few kilometres from Thiès and aluminium phosphate also near Thiès. Reserves of both types run to 130 million tonnes. The output was 200 000 tonnes in 1960, but it increased to 2 million in 1975, while 2.5 million was being expected by 1980. There is a factory in Thiès where the rocks are turned into fertilizers called super-phosphates. One million tonnes of these are exported annually through Dakar, while the balance is used locally to enrich the ground-nut and other farms.

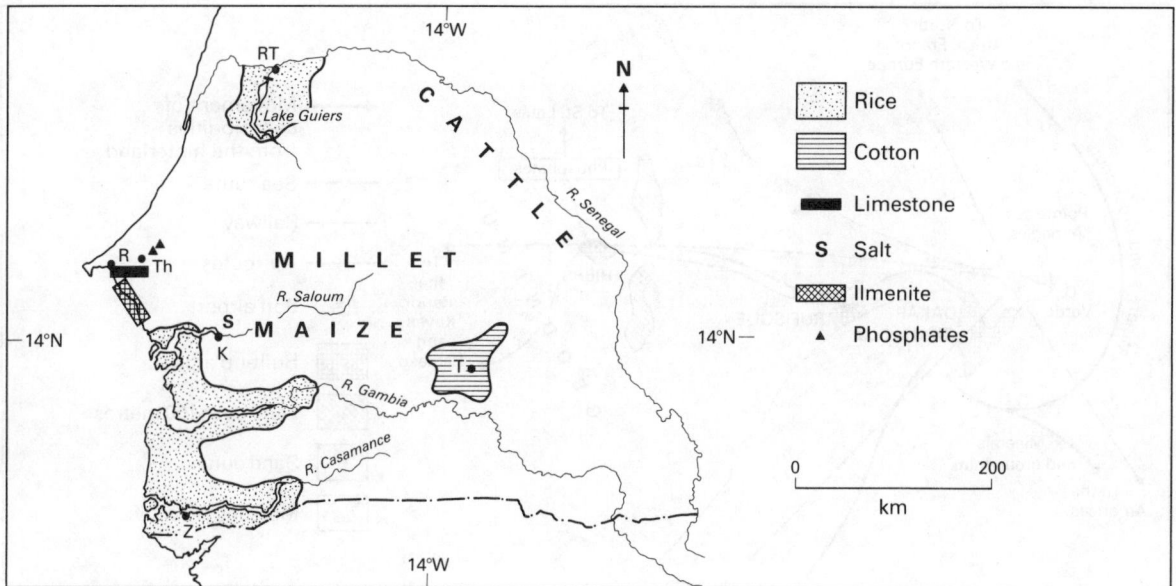

16.3 Senegambia: other crops and minerals.

Now read the foregoing text once over and then try your hand at the following review questions.

1. Name five indigenous peoples who live in Senegambia. In which parts of the countries do they live? What are their main occupations?
2. Why do so many Frenchmen live in Senegal? In which other country in West Africa do they live in such large numbers?
3. Name four airmasses which blow to Senegambia. In which months do they blow? Where do they blow from and what type of weather does each bring? What is the effect of the Canary current on the climate of Senegal?
4. Where is groundnut produced in large quantities in Senegal? Which condition favours the production there? How much of it is produced annually? Why is the crop very important in the economic life of Senegal? Give three reasons why the relative importance of the crop in Senegal has fallen in recent years.
5. Name other crop and animal products raised in Senegal.
6. Apart from salt, limestone and ilmenite what other important mineral is recovered in Senegal? Where is it mined and how much of it is produced annually?

Manufacturing industries

Manufacturing industries contribute one-third of the wealth of the country. There are two types – the older industries principally set up in the pre-independence era to serve all French speaking West Africa, and the newer ones set up to manufacture some commodities which were otherwise being imported from abroad.

Of the older ones, groundnut oil processing is the most important. Six groundnut oil mills exist in Dakar and other towns in the growing belt, and they produce altogether 1 million tonnes of groundnut oil annually. Tambacounda has a large textile mill and we have of course seen the cement and fertilizer plants. Where are these latter located?

The two largest of the second type of industries are the petroleum refinery and the petrochemical plant, both located at Caya at the outskirts of Dakar. The oil refinery was opened in 1964, now employs over 1 000 men and handles 6 million tonnes of crude oil annually. The petrochemical plant uses by-products of the refinery to produce plastics, pomade, insecticides and other petrochemical products.

Other industries include cigarette, shoe, soap, chocolate and soft drink factories, breweries and flour mills.

Population and towns

Figure 16.5 shows clearly two main areas of population concentration in Senegal and a third outlier where more people live than in the surrounding areas. Name them and say from the map, the average densities in each of the areas. The map also shows that the interior and southeast Senegal are thinly

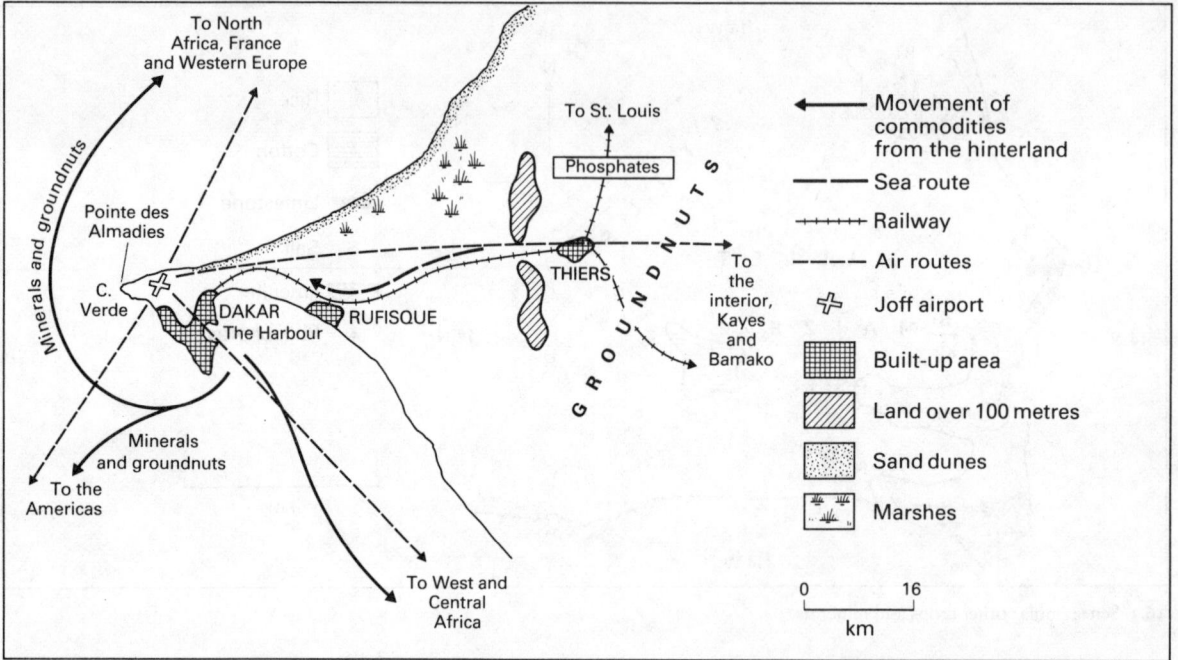

16.4 The geography of Dakar.

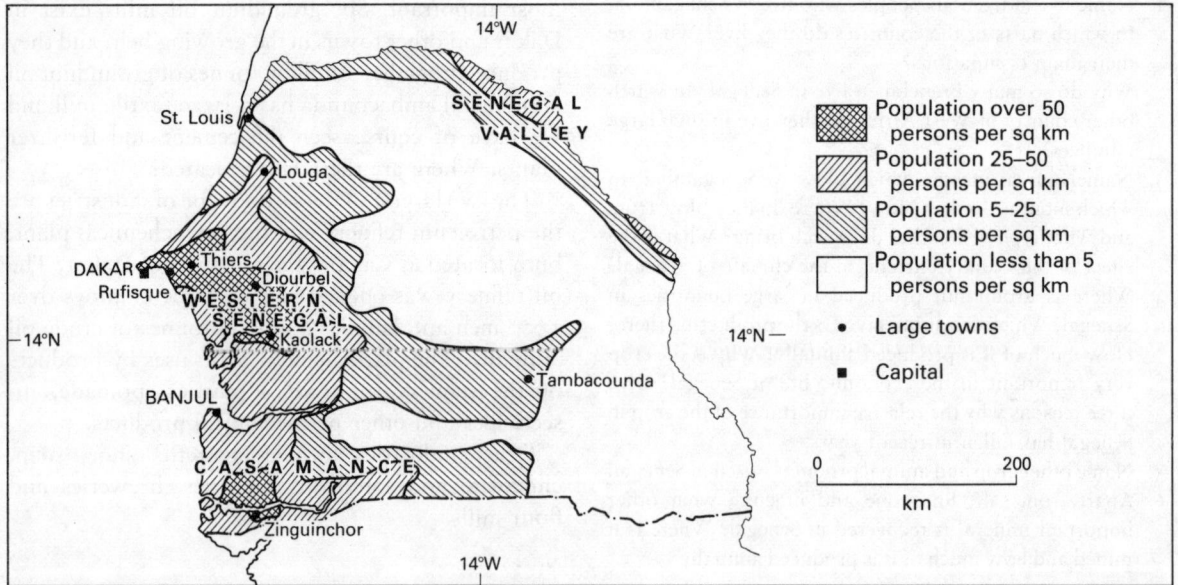

16.5 Population distribution and towns in Senegambia.

peopled. What is the average density in these areas? Several factors account for the distribution just noted.

1. Western Senegal and Casamance are flat, have a mild climate, and most of the commercial crops,

minerals and industries in Senegal. It is well served with roads and railways, has the very dynamic and industrious Wolof population, and had the earliest contact with Europe which has generated trade, education, jobs and therefore employment.

16.6 The port of Dakar. Can you see the harbour? What is the name of the sea at the background? Can you identify the ships, oil storage tanks and warehouses to the left of the picture? How is it similar to the port of Tema in figure 11.10?

In fact western Senegal is one of the most densely peopled and highly urbanized districts in West Africa.

2. The Senegal Valley has possibilities of irrigated farming, livestock raising and underground water supply, and therefore offers attraction to the population from the surrounding areas.

3. The interior and southeast, on the other hand, are dry, have a harsh climate, are remotely located and are economically under-developed. Few people live there as a result.

Of the towns of Senegal, *Dakar* (600 000), is the largest. It is the capital and chief port of the country.

The city itself, part of which is shown on Figure 16.6, is the most beautiful of its kind in West Africa. It is a masterpiece of French town planning and architecture, with well sited residential areas, magnificent apartment buildings and hotels, beautiful avenues and neatly planned recreational parks. Like every city, however, it has its slum areas.

Dakar owes its importance as well to a number of other factors. As you can see from Figure 16.4 it is the focal point of many land, sea and air routes. Trace these routes and their destinations. It is located in a well sheltered deep water bay protected by Cape Manuel. Its location at the most western point in Africa and its well equipped port make it a convenient last port of call for aircraft and sea vessels before they start on their long trans-Atlantic journey. It is therefore an important bunkering port i.e. where ships and aircraft call to take on fresh supplies of fuel food and water.

Dakar is also an important commercial port. In 1975, its airport located at Yoff admitted 13 650 flights carrying 407 500 passengers and 12 700 tonnes of cargo. The same year its sea port handled 30 000 vessels carrying 9 000 passengers and 3 750 000 tonnes of cargo. Compare these figures with those of other large commercial ports in West Africa.

Dakar's hinterland, once extended to practically the whole of French speaking West Africa, has now shrunk to Senegal itself, southern Mauritania and western Mali. Even then it is one of the most extensive in West Africa. Can you name the export commodities that are obtained from this hinterland, and the imported items distributed to the area?

Much commercial activity also goes on within the city itself, with its many banks and trading houses.

As a naval base, Dakar has a number of military installations located at strategic points. Its industries have already been dealt with. Can you name some of them?

Trade

The trade items and partners of Senegal are clear

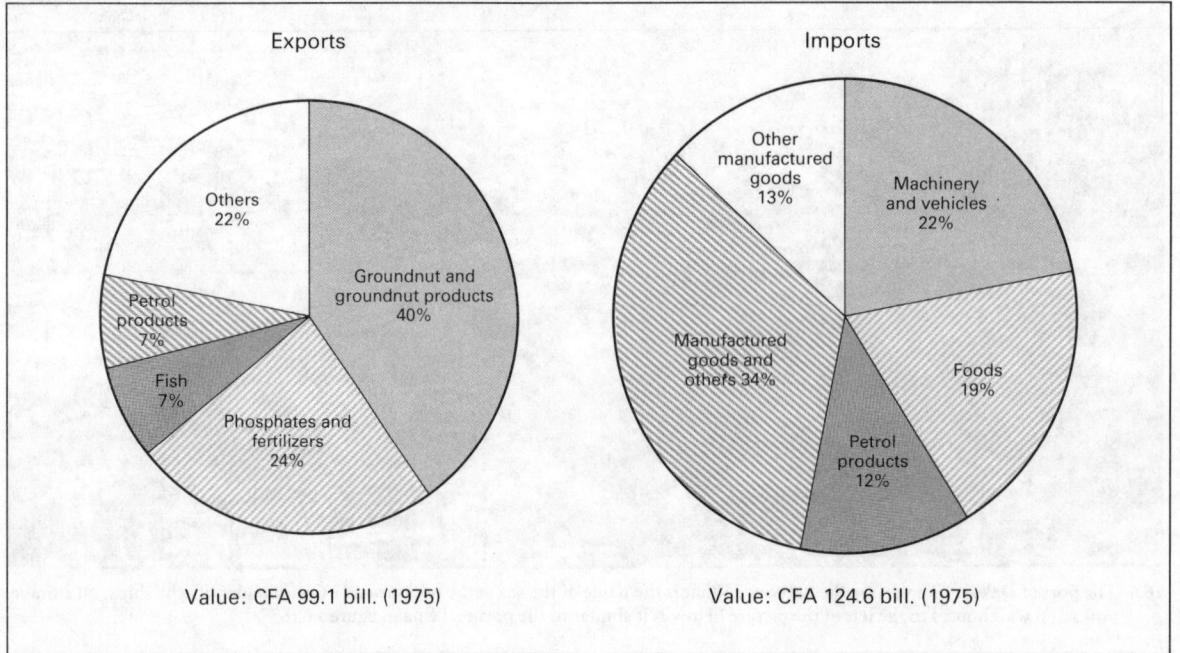

Exports — Value: CFA 99.1 bill. (1975)

Groundnut and groundnut products 40%
Phosphates and fertilizers 24%
Others 22%
Petrol products 7%
Fish 7%

Imports — Value: CFA 124.6 bill. (1975)

Machinery and vehicles 22%
Foods 19%
Manufactured goods and others 34%
Other manufactured goods 13%
Petrol products 12%

16.7 Mid 1970–80 trade of Senegal. Draw an elongated rectangle, 9.9 cm long to represent the value of the exports for 1975. Draw another rectangle of the same width and to scale to represent the value of imports. Divide both rectangles in the proportion of the export and import items. Shade the sections as appropriate and label them. The diagram you have drawn is another way of showing the trade of the country. Then use either the pie diagram above or your own diagram to answer the questions in the text on Senegal's trade.

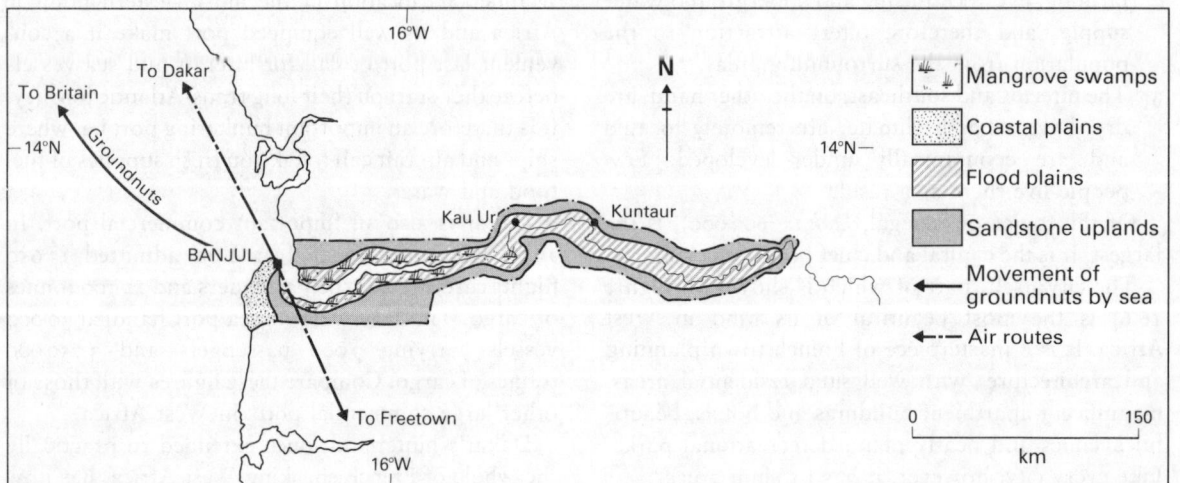

16.8 The geographical regions of The Gambia.

from the foregoing description.

What are the export and import values for 1975? Which is higher – the export or the import value – and by how much? Name the items in order of importance. Her most dominant overseas partner is France which accounts for over 40% of her imports and 48% of her exports.

You will notice that Senegal has been registering a chronic trade deficit over the years. What was the deficit in 1975? What do you think is responsible for this?

The economy of The Gambia

Small as it is, The Gambia is divided into three geographical regions and its economy and land use neatly fit into these regions.

1. The *coastal plains* are covered with marine sands and clay. They extend south of Banjul, and are famous for coconuts and palm produce, sizeable quantities of which are exported.
2. The *flood plains* are covered with salt water mangrove for 90 kilometres upstream. Beyond this point they form good rice lands. The River Gambia itself is navigable for launches for 460 kilometres upstream but only 240 kilometres for ocean liners.
3. On either side of the flood plains are the well drained *sandstone uplands* – a region best known for groundnuts. This crop, and its products constitute 95% of the value of The Gambia's exports. The crop is collected by road to the river ports from where it is moved downstream to Banjul for export.

A study of the economy of The Gambia is incomplete without looking at the country's growing tourist industry. In recent years, tourism assumed increasing importance in the country, particularly for Scandinavians who leave their countries in winter to enjoy the sunny, dry and crisp weather, and the sandy beaches of The Gambia. Over 250 000 tourists (that is more than half the population of the whole country) enter and leave the country annually and the revenue they bring to the country is second only to that from groundnuts. Previously the tourists paid their hotel and travel bills in their countries, but the government of The Gambia has ruled against it so that they now pay in the country.

Banjul, the capital, with a population of 39 200 in 1977, is located on St Mary's Island at the estuary of River Gambia. It is the largest town and the chief port. It has two groundnut oil mills and is served by an airport.

Its foreign trade is similar to that of Dakar, though it is considerably smaller. Also it does not export phosphates, and much of its trade is with Britain rather than with France.

Import duties are less in The Gambia than in Senegal, and Gambian goods are also cheaper at their points of origin (notably textiles from Britain and the Far East). Consequently, goods imported through Banjul are cheaper than similar items imported through Dakar. For this reason too, even though a merger of The Gambia and Senegal appears logical, The Gambia may not want it, and the Senegalese as a people are not too anxious about it either, since The Gambia's separate existence affords them a nearby source of smuggling cheap goods into their country!

Summary

Go through the whole chapter again. Note in particular what we said about the flat relief, the four air masses and the semi-arid climate of Senegambia. Groundnut production is vital to the economy of the two countries, but its dominance in the export trade of Senegal has decreased since 1965. Recall the importance of the Gambia and Senegal Rivers, and the functions of Dakar and Banjul. Then do the exercises that follow below.

Revision exercises

1. a) Draw a large sketch of Senegambia (The Gambia and Senegal) and on it:
    i)   show one area each of grassland and forest;
    ii) shade one area where groundnut cultivation is an important occupation;
    iii) mark and name *three* towns where extraction of groundnut oil is an important occupation;
    iv) write the words RICE and MILLET (one area for each) where these crops are extensively cultivated.
   b) Write *brief* notes on the importance to the economy of both countries (The Gambia and Senegal) of either rice or groundnuts.
        (*WASC/GCE, 1977*)

17 Mauritania and Mali

Preparation

1. Name five features found in arid lands.
2. Which is the largest desert in the world?
3. Give two reasons why the Sahara Desert extends westwards up to the North Atlantic coast of Africa.
4. Name two peoples you know live in the Sahara Desert.
5. Review the features of the River Niger in chapter 4. Through which countries in West Africa does it flow?
6. Trace an outline map of Mali for use in the revision exercise.

In this chapter we shall study two fascinating desert countries of West Africa – the coastal country of Mauritania and the land-locked country of Mali.

Mauritania

Environment and peoples

Mauritania has an area of 1 030 700 square kilometres (Note: In February, 1976 Mauritania took control of the former Western Sahara, re-named it Tiris-el-Gharbia with an additional area of 104 000 square kilometres although this annexation is still in dispute). Over 60 % of the country is made up of sand dunes, 35 % of arid rocks, and only 5 % is habitable. The arid and rocky areas are found in the interior where rainfall is far less than 120 mm per annum and

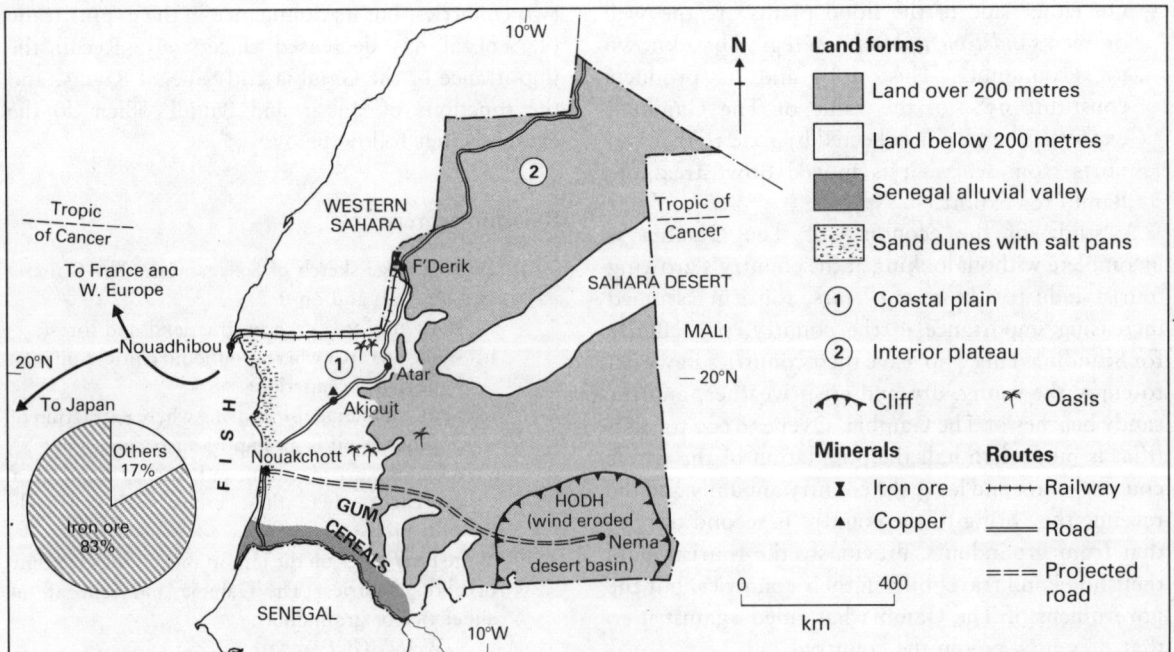

17.1 Mauritania – general.

temperatures at wide extremes. The habitable 5% is restricted to the southwest and along the coastal strip.

It is not surprising then that 80% of the 1.4 million people who live in Mauritania (1977 census) – predominantly a mixture of Berbers and Arabs – are nomads. The population is extremely scattered and mobile, the only permanent settlements being found in three areas:

i) along the Senegal Valley where water is available and some irrigated agriculture therefore possible;
ii) along the coastline where the relatively high coastal humidities and the cool Canary currents temper the otherwise harsh climate and some off-shore fishing practised, and
iii) in the mining towns of the interior where this economic pursuit has attracted a number of people.

Now study Figure 17.2 and explain the population distribution.

Agriculture and fishing

Mauritania's farming and fishing activities were formerly very rudimentary. These comprised the raising for export of camels, sheep, goats and dates from the Atar and other oases, grain crops and gum arabic from the Senegal Valley and fish from the seas. Since the 1970's however, the country has made efforts to improve this sector of its economy, realizing that it is a major source of livelihood for over 85% of its population. It has therefore invested much in agriculture, and lately, together with Senegal and Mali, formed the Senegal River Basin Development Organization which plans to build, by 1980, two dams across the Senegal River. One will be the Manantali Dam (to be located on Malian terri-tory but the benefits will be shared by the whole Organization) and the other the Diama Dam. Both are expected to irrigate respectively 100 000 and 10 000 hectares of land in Mauritania. The country's chief crops are *sorghum*, *millet*, *rice* and *dates*, but the dams will also substantially increase the total production of rice.

Vast resources of *fish* abound in Mauritania's territorial waters. Over 60 000 tonnes were caught and landed in 1976 and the figure is expected to reach the 100 000 tonne mark by 1980.

Mining and towns

Mauritania recovers some *salt* from the coastal marshes, *gypsum* for export to Senegal where it is used in cement manufacture, and *copper* from

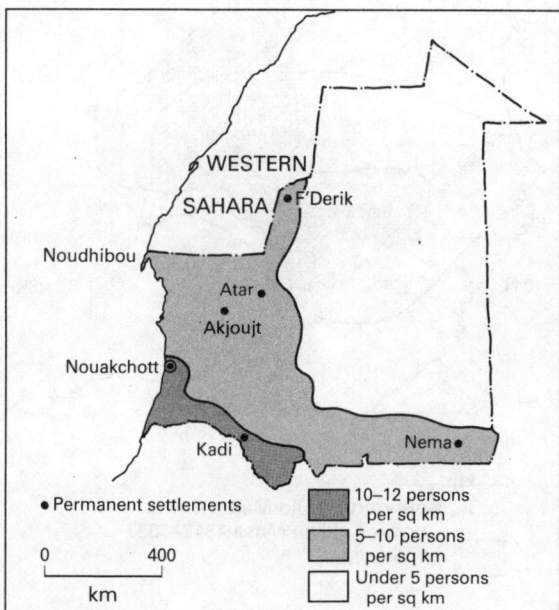

17.2 Mauritania – settlement and population density.

17.3 Iron ore mining in Mauritania. The picture shows the hills of F'derick where the ore is mined. You can also see the crushed iron ore dump, and the railway that carries it to the coast. Is the mining underground or by open cast? To which port would the railway be carrying the ore? Describe the landscape.

Akjoujt from where a road has been built to Nouakchott to convey the ore to the coast for export.

By far, however, the most important mineral in the country is *iron ore*. The economy of the country, formerly poor and primitive, took a new turn when this ore was discovered in 1963. Over 300 million tonnes of iron ore, with very high ore content (65%–75%), lie under the hills of F'derick, 360 kilometres from the coast in the wild arid lands of the Sahara.

Immediately the discovery was made, a company called MIFERMA (for short) was formed. It borrowed large sums of money from abroad to open three mines in the area – at F'derick, Tazadit and Rousessa. The miners live in the new township of Zouraté nearby, built for them by the mining company.

To serve this mining location, the company constructed the over 360 kilometre rail line from Nouadhibou to F'derick across the Sahara and under some of the most difficult and unique conditions in West Africa. See Figure 17.3 and describe the landscape.

Because the distance to be covered from F'derick to the port of export, Nouadhibou, is so long and the journey a difficult one, each train carrying the ore has to be as long as possible in order to take as much ore each time as possible. Thus MIFERMA ore trains are sometimes as long as 2 kilometres and are made up of up to 140 trucks carrying about 10 000 tonnes of ore and driven simultaneously by 3 or 4 diesel locomotive engines! These are certainly some of the longest trains in the world.

Just as in Liberia, the open cast method is used in the recovery of the mineral, and mining is highly mechanized. Production rose from 7.7 million tonnes in 1968 to 8 million in 1970, 9.3 in 1972, 11.1 in 1974 and over 12.5 million in 1976. The 15 million tonne mark was expected by 1978. The production in 1974 accounted for 6 200 million ouguiya (or 83%) out of the country's total export of 7 500 million ouguiya. The exports go mainly to Britain, France, Belgium, Western Germany, Italy, U.S.A. and Japan. This mineral is clearly of great importance to a hitherto poor country like Mauritania, which before its discovery could not even balance her budget and whose total exports in 1962 were worth barely 84 million ouguiya (£1 million)!

Hand in hand with the development of iron ore

mining in F'derick is the growth of the port of *Nouadhibou*. Located on a sheltered bay east of Cape Blanco, it was for many years a small fishing port, backed, as it was, by a hinterland whose economy was essentially based on oasis cultivation, caravan transportation and nomadic pastoralism.

But no sooner had iron ore been discovered and the rail line constructed from the port to the mining location as described above, than the town commenced an era of rapid growth, adding new services and facilities to its original functions. Thus the harbour was extended to handle cement and machinery required for developing the mining centre, and iron ore bound for export. MIFERMA also built a new sector of the town to house its staff at the port. Commercial firms were attracted to sell goods to people, and so the population grew – from 12 000 in 1970 to 23 000 in 1975. Nouadhibou is today the second largest town in the country, second only to the capital, Nouakchott. It is as well the main iron ore loading and commercial port in Mauritania.

Nouakchott, with a 1975 estimated population of 140 000, was chosen as the capital when the country became independent in 1960. Before then Mauritania had its capital at St Louis in another country!

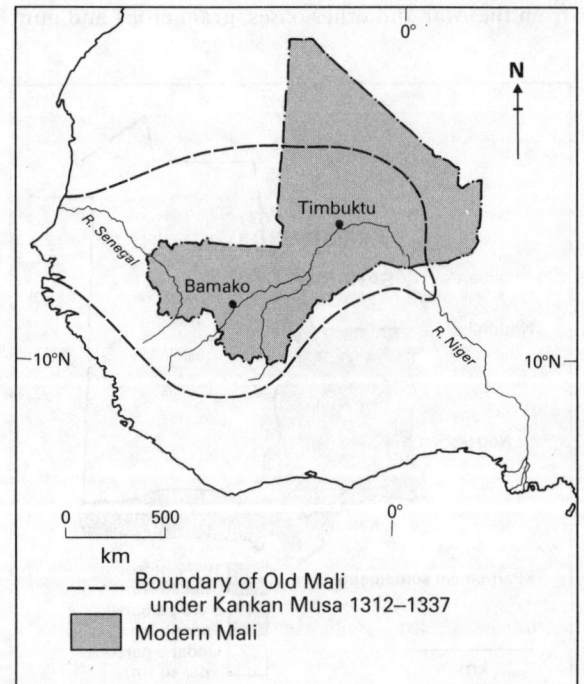

17.4 Mali: old and new.

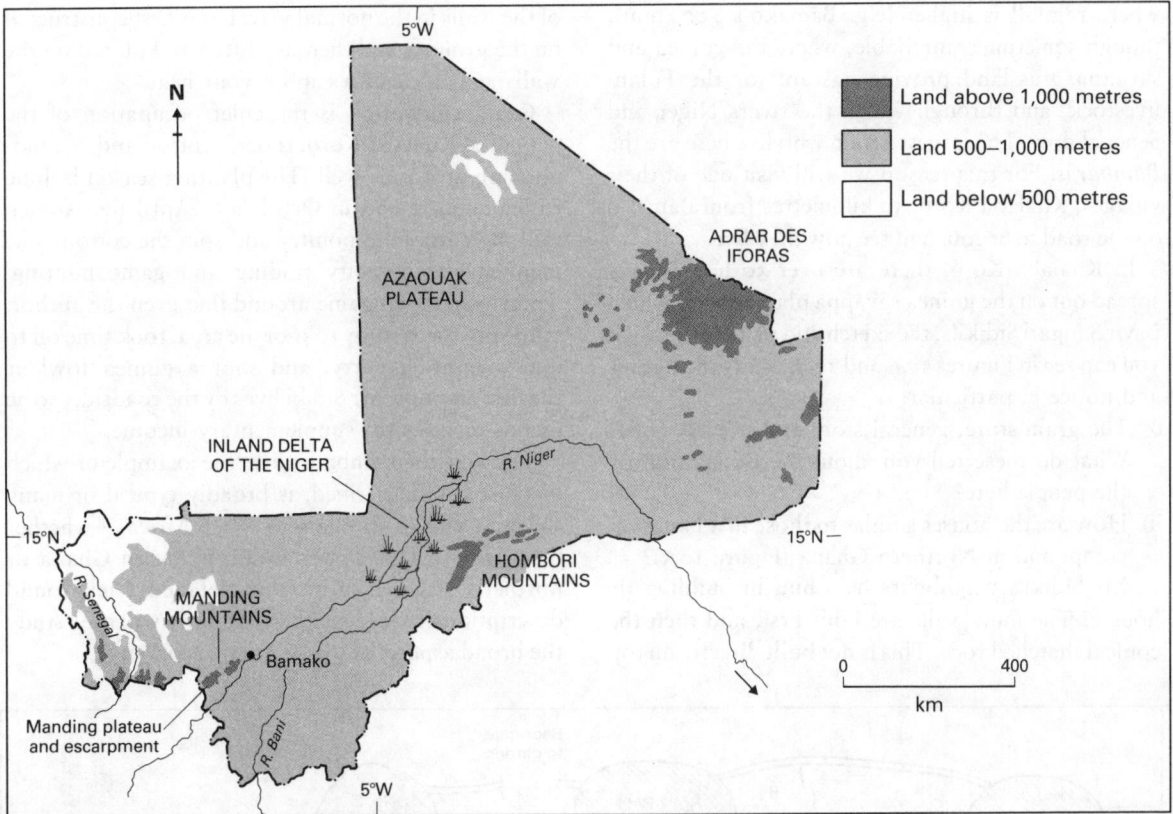

17.5 Mali: relief.

Located at the low sandy beaches north of St Louis, an artificial harbour was constructed there in 1970 to handle the copper brought down from Akjoujt. Another impetus is expected to be given to its growth when the 606 kilometre Nouakchott-Nema road to the interior is completed (see Figure 17.1). This road is being jointly financed by the four Arab countries of Saudi Arabia, Kuwait, Abu Dhabi and Fades, and is being built to link the port with the interior.

Now read through the section on Mauritania again and answer the following questions.
i)   How large is the country? Where do you find permanent settlements in Mauritania and why?
ii) How does Mauritania use the River Senegal?
iii) Describe the iron ore mining in Mauritania. Why are MIFERMA trains so long?
iv) How has the mining influenced the growth of Nouadhibou?
v)   Comment briefly on the importance of Nouadhibou and Nouakchott.

Mali

Environment and peoples

Mali, named after the ancient Mali Empire whose area overlaps that of present Mali (Figure 17.4) has an area of 1.24 million square kilometres and a population of 6.3 million (1976 census). It is thus the second most extensive country in West Africa. But just as with Mauritania, large tracts are dry, desolate and uninhabitable; as a result, it has a population density as low as 5.1 persons per square kilometre.

The northern half with the dry sandstone Azaouak plateau and the granite mountains of Adrar-des-Iforas (Figure 17.5) is the emptiest part of the country. Here wide ranges of temperature and very dry conditions prevail. Only the caravan driving *Tuaregs*, and the *Arabs* who rear camels and goats, and cultivate grains in the oases live in this region.

Most of the Malians, however, live in the south

where rainfall is higher (e.g. Bamako's 1000 mm), though sometimes unreliable, where the guinea and savanna grassland provide pasture for the Fulani livestock, and through which the rivers Niger and Senegal flow. The largest group who live here are the *Bambaras*. For this reason we will visit one of their villages, Kualaba Koro, 50 kilometres from Bamako on the road to Segou, and see how they live.

In Kualaba Koro, there are over 50 homesteads spread out on the guinea savanna plain, one of which is Mr Sangari Sidiki's, the sketch and picture of which you can see in Figures 17.6 and 17.7. Study the figures and notice in particular:

i) The grain store, general store and poultry shed. What do these tell you about the occupation of the people here?

ii) How are the houses similar to those in a Nangodi compound in Northern Ghana (Figure 10.3)?

Mr Sidiki's neighbours help him in building the houses. The mud walls are built first, and then the conical thatched roof. This is not built directly on top of the walls in the normal way, but is first constructed on the ground, and then it is lifted and placed on the walls as you place a cap on your head!

Grain cultivation is the chief occupation of the people of Kualaba Koro, though cotton and groundnuts are grown as well. The planting season is June to September, and in October to April the women mill the corn, tend poultry and spin the cotton. The men engage in petty trading and game hunting. There is so much game around that even the author, while on a field study tour of the area, took time off to join a hunting party, and shot a guinea fowl at the first attempt! Mr Sidiki lives by the roadside, so he mends bicycles for supplementary income.

The way the Bambaras live, the example of which has just been described, is broadly typical of many savanna village dwellers in West Africa – whether they are in Mali, Upper Volta, northern Ghana or northern Nigeria. With this detailed background description of life in southern Mali we will now study the broad aspects of the country's economy.

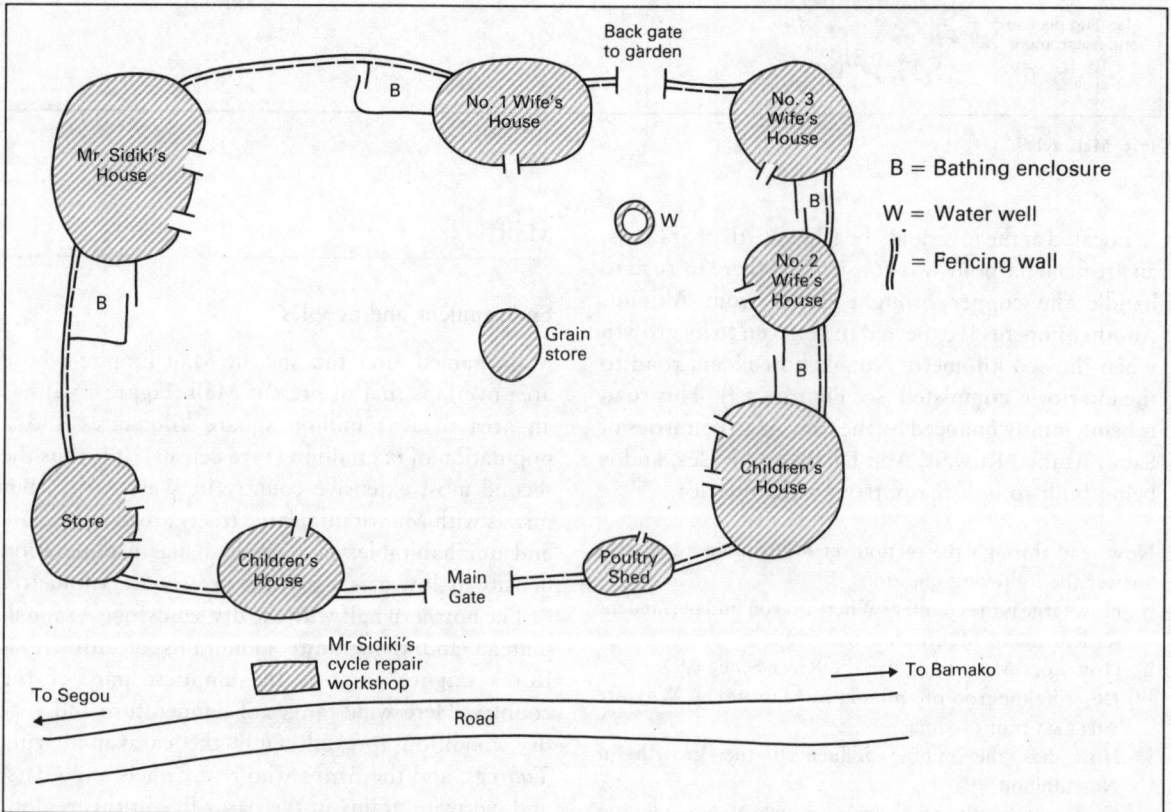

17.6 A Bambara homestead near Bamako, Mali.

17.7 The interior of a Bambara homestead. How is the hut in the centre different from the others? Can you identify it in the sketch? What is it used for?

Irrigation and crop production

Most vital and significant to the economy of Mali are the rivers Niger and Senegal, but more especially the Niger. They are important to the country because Mali itself is a dry country and anything that brings water to it must be economically vital. But the Niger is particularly important for the following reasons:

1. The river here flows through a broad flood plain making the cutting of irrigation canals relatively easy.
2. Between Segou and Timbuktu the river flows through its inland delta – a region fertilized by a mixture of the river's alluvium and the deposits at the floor of an ancient lake (called Lake Araouane).
3. The river is not seasonal and therefore can be used all the year round.
4. Finally, the gradient is gradual and it therefore has navigable stretches which can be used by river crafts.

Mali's livelihood – her irrigation programmes, much of her farming, transportation and settlement – depends greatly on this lone river, and of course to a lesser extent, on the Senegal. (See the colour photograph.)

The lands around these rivers are cultivated with

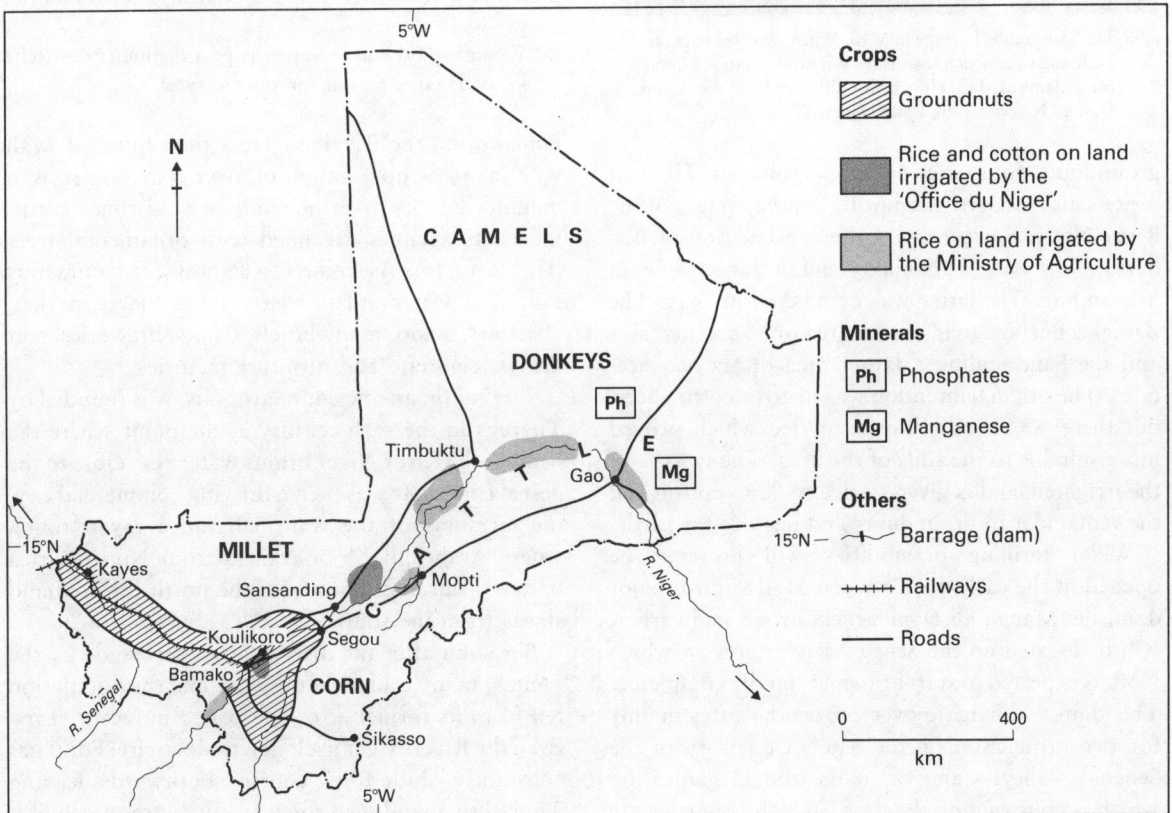

17.8 The economy of Mali.

17.9 The Sansanding barrage in Mali. When was this barrage built and over which river is it? Why was it built? Name other dams in Mali. How is this different from the Kainji Dam in Nigeria or the Volta Dam in Ghana?

Fishing and livestock raising

Fishing is a thriving occupation along the Niger and Senegal rivers, particularly around Mopti, Bamako, Segou and Kayes.

Mali is noted for its *livestock*, having well over 6 million cattle, 12 million sheep and goats and a large number of camels and donkeys. The cattle are concentrated along the Niger and Senegal valleys. The herders drive them nearer the river when the floods have receded so that they can drink from the pools left behind and feed from the fresh pastures. With the coming of the rains, the higher, healthier and drier grounds are preferred. Live cattle account for nearly 50% of the export trade of Mali and are sent to neighbouring countries, while Mopti, Gao and Bamako have large abattoirs where cattle are slaughtered for local and foreign consumption.

Towns and Industries

i) Study Figure 17.8 and name the major towns in Mali.
ii) On which two rivers are most of them located? Can you say why?
iii) Where would you therefore expect the industries to be located? Give reason for your answer.

Bamako, on the River Niger, is the capital of Mali with a 1976 population of over 350 000. It is a magnificent city, overlooked by a sandstone escarpment. Its avenues are lined with ornamental trees (Figure 17.10). As Figure 17.8 shows, it commands rail, road, water and air routes. It has a large market, abattoirs, a zoo, many hotels, banks, breweries, soft drinks, cigarette and furniture factories.

Timbuktu, an ancient metropolis, was founded by Tuaregs in the 12th century at the point where the bend of the River Niger brings water very close to the desert fringes. It was then a thriving commercial city, the terminus of the trans-Saharan caravan route, where Arab and Moor traders from North Africa bartered salt and dates from the north for gold and slaves from the south.

But soon after the disruption of this trade by the French, many traders left the city and the population fell from its former 40 000 to 10 000 in recent years. Even the River Niger itself deserted the city! For it has constantly shifted its course southwards leaving Timbuktu abandoned some 13 kilometres north of it high and dry in the lonely sands of the Sahara.

groundnuts, fruits, rice and some tobacco. The first serious and modern attempt to use the waters of the River Niger, however, was the construction of two barrages – one at Bamako and a larger one at Sansanding. The latter was completed in 1947. The Bamako Barrage irrigates an area of 10 000 hectares and the Sandsanding a larger area of 100 000 hectares. The original intention was to grow cotton here, but there was a switch-over to rice which proved more suitable to the soils of the area. Today 85% of the irrigated land is given to rice, 13% to cotton and the remainder to groundnuts and pasture for cattle.

Wider farming possibilities will however be opened in the early 1980's when Mali's third major dam, the Manantali Dam which, as we said earlier, will be located on the Senegal River, and on which work is expected to start in 1979, is finally completed. This dam will irrigate over 300 000 hectares mainly for rice production on the Malian territory of the Senegal Valley. Can you name the Organization which is constructing the dam? Which countries are in this organization?

17.10 View of Bamako. The photograph shows its planned streets lined with ornamental trees. Describe the layout of the streets and houses. Name other towns in Mali and in West Africa located by the River Niger.

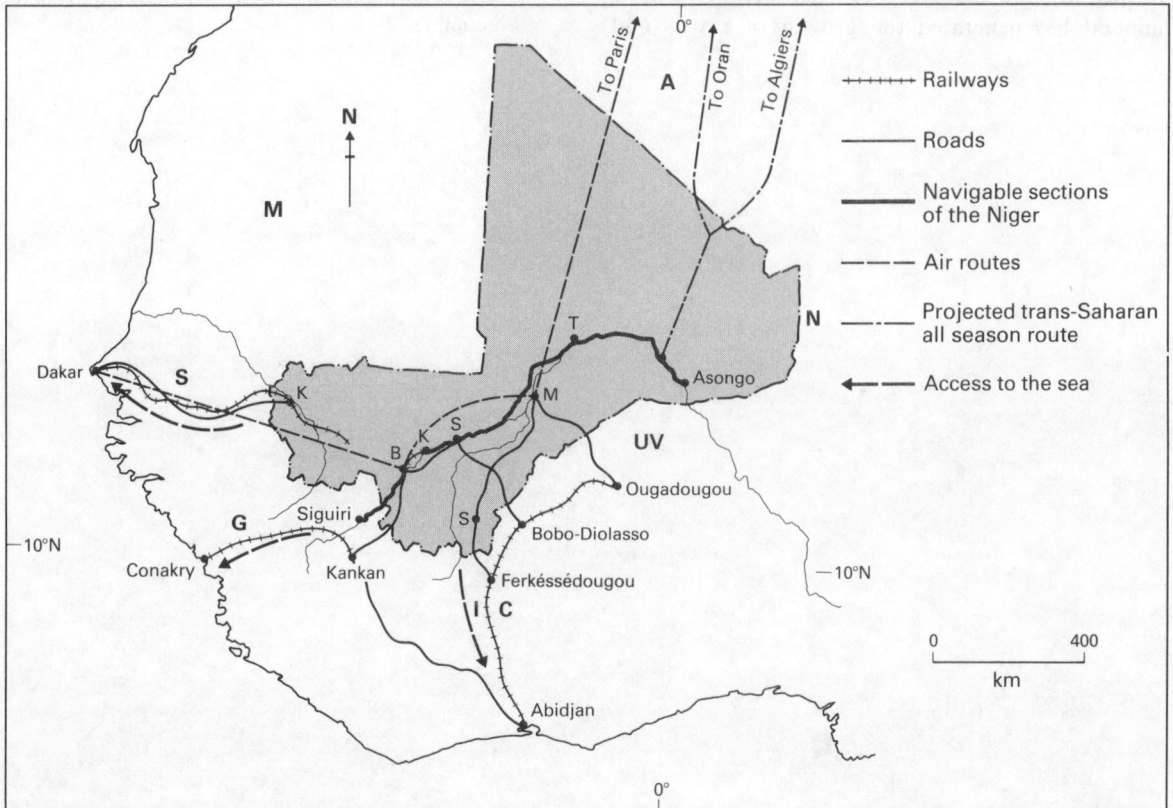

17.11 Mali: access to the exterior

Transportation and trade

Study Figure 17.11. The most striking feature is that Mali's location inland makes its access to the exterior difficult. Her exports have to travel long distances to Dakar, Conakry and Abidjan to get to the outside world. Some have to be flown out from Bamako, for example, meat to Paris. For this reason too, a large proportion of Mali's trade is with her immediate neighbours with whom she must maintain good relationships – not only to have markets for her goods but also to allow her goods going abroad to travel through their countries and go out through their ports.

Her overseas trade partners are France, U.S.S.R., China, Korea and the United States of America.

Summary

Mauritania is one of the poor desert countries in West Africa whose economy has only been recently transformed by the discovery of iron ore. This lone mineral has generated the growth of towns and settlements, led to the construction of the railway in the country and has brought substantial income to the country.

Location in the heart of the continent is a serious set-back to the economy of Mali, but her saving factor has been the presence of the Niger and Senegal rivers. On these rivers she depends for her agriculture, fisheries and transportation, and most of her settlements and industries are located by them.

Revision exercises

1. How does physical environment influence the life of the people in *either* Mali *or* Mauritania?
2. Describe the iron ore mining in Mauritania and irrigation agriculture in Mali. Show how these are vital to the economy of the country concerned.
3. On the map of Mali which you have prepared:
   i) draw the course of the Niger and Senegal Rivers;
   ii) insert five major towns;
   iii) insert the irrigated lands;
   iv) shade the areas important for cotton and groundnuts.
   v) Assess the importance of rivers in the economy of the country.

18   Upper Volta and Niger

Preparation

1. Review the principal features in the geography of Mali.
2. Study the positions of Upper Volta and Niger on a map of West Africa. Compare them with that of Mali. See how the countries are all land-locked.

This chapter will deal with the two remaining mainland countries of West Africa – Upper Volta and Niger.

Upper Volta

Environment and peoples

Though a land-locked country like Mali, Upper Volta has the advantages of compactness and a more southern location than Mali, and no part of its 274 000 square kilometres is really desert. That is why

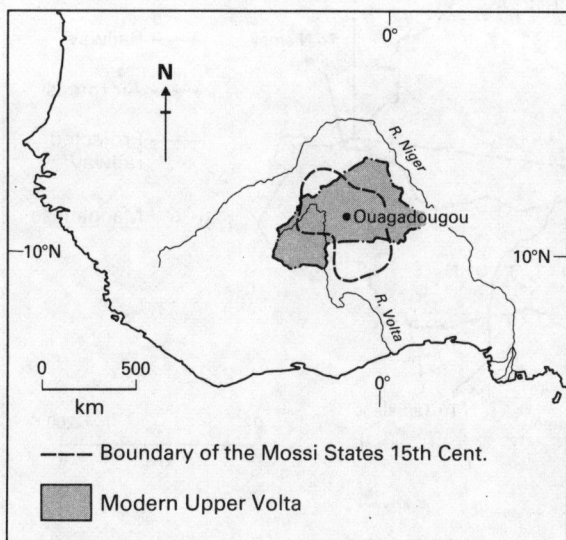

18.1 The Mossi State and modern Upper Volta.

its 1976 estimated population of 6.2 million gives it a density of 22.6 persons a square kilometre – nearly five times that of Mali. It also has a more concentrated river network, particularly in the south-west, and enjoys the additional advantage of direct and scarcely interrupted outlets to three sea ports – Lomé in Togo, Takoradi in Ghana and Abidjan in Ivory Coast.

See in Figure 18.1 how the modern state of Upper Volta overlaps the mediaeval Mossi States. Which town is common to both the modern and mediaeval states? Modern Upper Volta was created by the French in 1919 out of approximately the same area as the Mossi and surrounding states. In 1932 however, the country was shared among neighbouring Ivory Coast, Mali and Niger, and thus disappeared from the map of West Africa for a period of 16 years! In 1948, the pieces were re-assembled, and re-constituted into one country. Upper Volta followed the wave of nationalism in West Africa and became independent with many others in 1960.

More than half the population is made up of the *Mossi* people who live in the heart of the country, much the same way as the Bambaras live in Mali. The Mossis repeatedly resisted Islamic aggression and slave raids from the north and thus their territory remained one of the most densely peopled in West Africa. But because their soils are relatively poor and few industries exist in the country, they now emigrate to the factories and plantations of Ivory Coast and Ghana in search of employment. Of the estimated number of 460 000 that leave the country annually some 100 000 never come back. For this reason the population growth rate in the country is 2% per annum as against the average of 2.3% for West Africa.

Other smaller groups in Upper Volta include the *Serontos* and *Gourmas* who live and farm in the south-west and east respectively, and the *Fulas* and

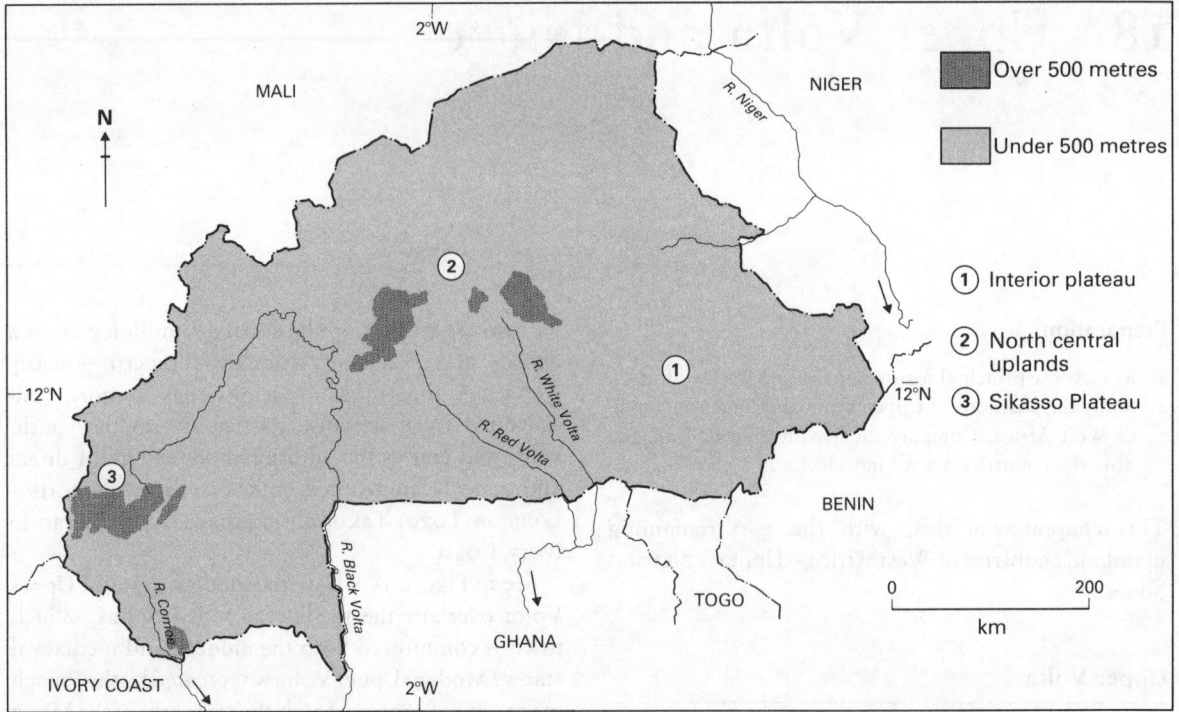

18.2 Upper Volta: relief and drainage.

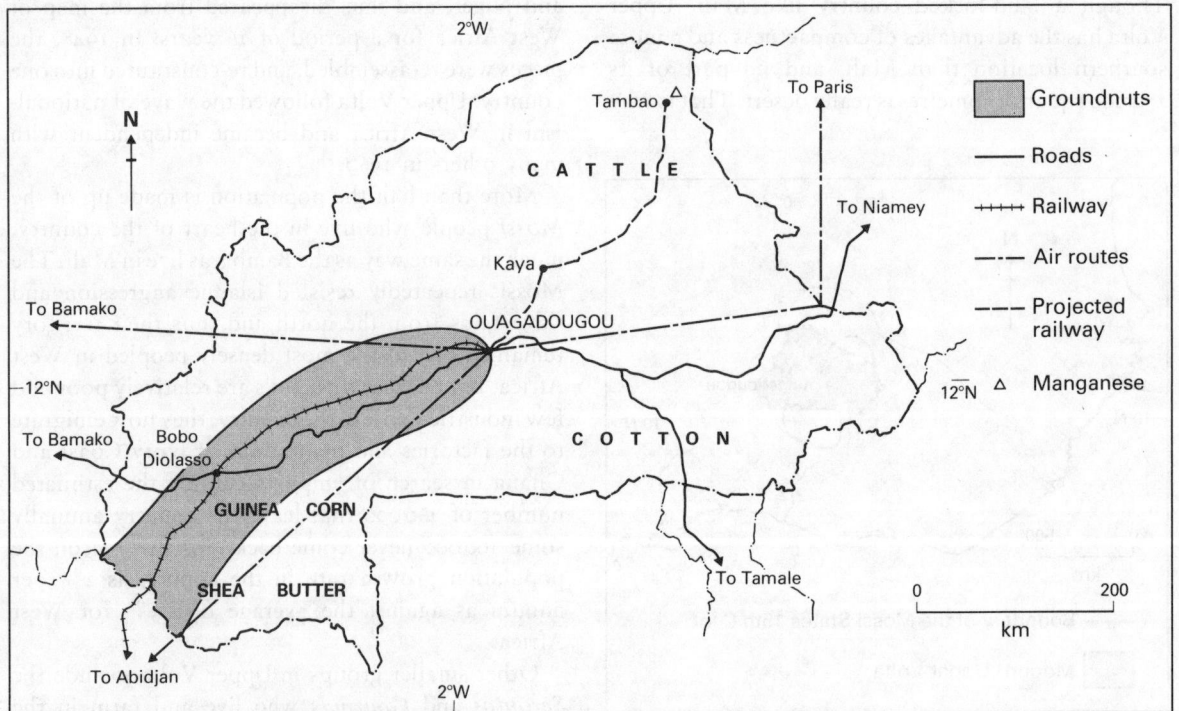

18.3 Upper Volta: economy and routes.

Tuaregs who are the nomadic herdsmen of the north.

The physical landscape of Upper Volta, as you can see from Figure 18.2, comprises three major regions – the granite *interior plateau*, the *north central uplands* and the sandstone *Sikasso plateau*. Like southern Mali, its climate is continental, and the vegetation of the guinea savanna type. Its rainfall, however, is higher and ranges from 1 250 mm per annum in the south to 600 in the north, even though it is also sporadic and sometimes unreliable. Except for the river valleys which are often flooded in the wet season, the country is remarkably well drained because when rain falls the flood water either runs off rapidly from the granite surface to the rivers, or if on the sandstone areas, it seeps underground rather fast. Name the rivers of Upper Volta.

Economic development

Figure 18.3 shows that the main products of Upper Volta are cotton, groundnuts, guinea corn, shea butter and cattle. These are similar to the products found in other savanna lands of West Africa.

The production of groundnuts, once dominant, has dropped in recent years and has been overtaken by *cotton* which now is the country's major cash crop. In which part of the country is cotton produced? The country's total output of cotton in the 1975–76 season was 50 500 tonnes as opposed to groundnuts' 18 000 tonnes. Not only has the quantity of cotton produced increased but the yield per hectare is now higher.

Livestock raising is vital to the economy of Upper Volta. With over 4.9 million head of all types in 1975, the country was less hard hit by the 1972–74 drought than other countries in the sahel region. Thus, on the whole, it lost only 8% of its livestock as against 40% of Mauritania's. It is also recovering fast and is expected to have 6 million head by 1990.

Live cattle are principally sold to neighbouring Ivory Coast and Ghana and now constitute 36% of the country's exports by value.

Mining has hitherto been very unimportant. Recently, however, a 12 million tonne manganese ore

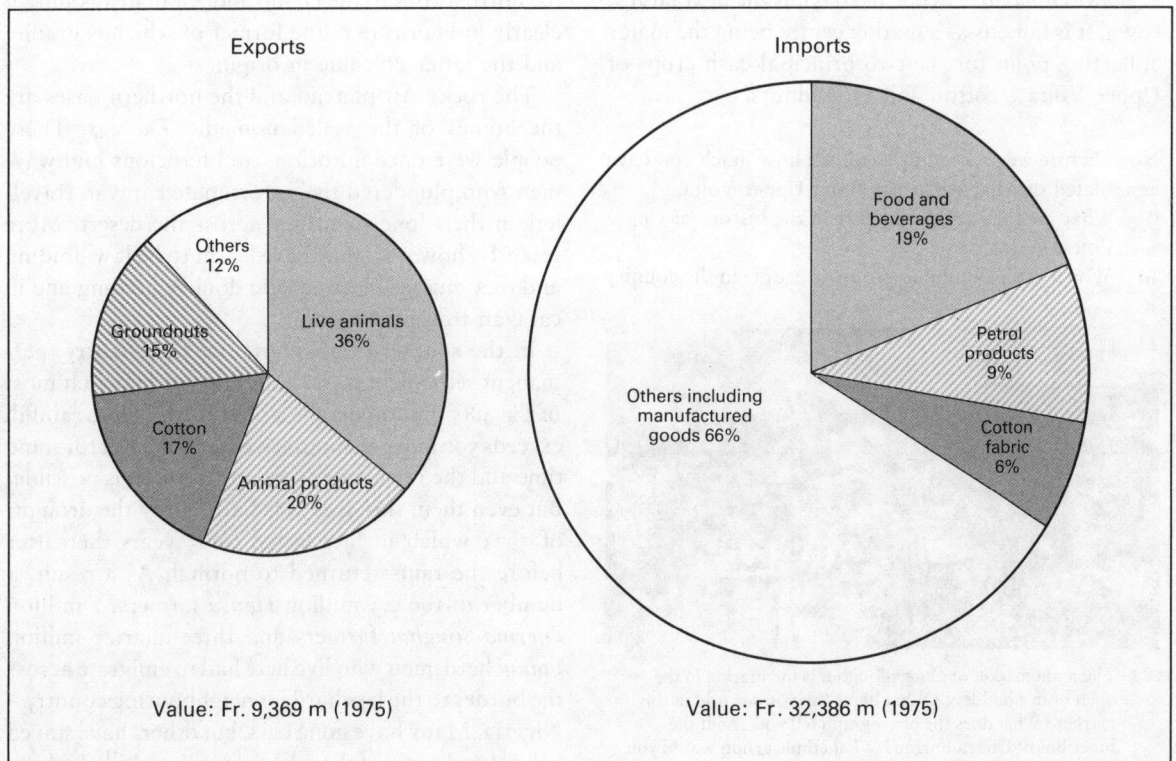

Exports

Others 12%
Groundnuts 15%
Cotton 17%
Live animals 36%
Animal products 20%

Value: Fr. 9,369 m (1975)

Imports

Food and beverages 19%
Petrol products 9%
Cotton fabric 6%
Others including manufactured goods 66%

Value: Fr. 32,386 m (1975)

18.4 Export trade of Upper Volta.

deposit was located at Tambao. A 320 kilometre railway line is now (1979) being extended to the town from Ouagadougou and mining will start as soon as the railway is completed.

Upper Volta has a vigorous internal trade, but her two greatest foreign trade partners are Ivory Coast and France which together command over 80% of this trade.

Which item in Figure 18.4 dominates her export trade? Does the country register a favourable or unfavourable trade balance? Can you give reasons for this?

Ouagadougou, with a 1975 population of 168 000, is the capital and largest town in Upper Volta. It is the current terminus of the 1 000 kilometre rail line from Abidjan, but will cease to be as soon as the extention to Tambao is completed. From here too, excellent roads plied by heavy trailers and mammy waggons radiate to the interior and also head towards Ghana and Ivory Coast in the south. Figure 18.5 is that of the main market in Ouagadougou. Describe the building, the surroundings and the traffic to the market. What do you expect to find being sold in the market?

Bobo-Diolasso (113 000 in 1975), is the next largest town. It is famous as a market centre being the major collecting point for the two principal cash crops of Upper Volta – cotton and groundnuts.

Now, before we proceed to Niger see how much you have assimilated of what we learnt about Upper Volta.
i)   What are the main highlights in the history of Upper Volta?
ii) Which is the dominant group of people in the country

18.5 The main market of Ouagadougou. Is the market in the open or in a building? What items can you see sold in this market? What does the photograph tell you about the functions of Ouagadougou? What ethnic group would you expect to find in this picture? Are they any different from your own people?

and why have they remained so?
iii) Name the three relief regions in the country. Why is the surface remarkably well drained?
iv) Which is the country's major cash crop? Describe its production.
v)   Why did Upper Volta not suffer as much as other Sahelian countries from the 1972–74 drought?
vi) Why is Ouagadougou the largest and most important town in Upper Volta?
vii) How does the country find access to the sea?

Niger

The environment and peoples

With a surface area of 1.3 million square kilometres, Niger is the most extensive country in West Africa. However, as in Mauritania much of the northern three-quarters is uninhabitable, for it is made up of a dry, thirsty plateau gashed in places by dry water courses called *dallols* or *wadis*. This plateau slopes gently eastwards to the Chad Basin but rather steeply in the southwest to the valley of the River Niger. In the north it rises to the Djado and Air plateaus shown clearly in Figure 18.6, the former of which is granite and the latter volcanic in origin.

The rocky Air plateau and the northern oases are the homes of the veiled nomadic *Tuaregs*. These people were once notorious and ferocious highwaymen who plundered the unfortunate caravan travellers in their lonely journey across the desert. More recently, however, they have learnt to be law-abiding and they engage in camel and donkey herding and in caravan transportation.

In the southern one-quarter of the country, permanent settlement is possible, and it is here that most of the 4.85 million people of Niger live. Here rainfall exceeds 500 mm per annum, wells remain wet for some time and the raising of crops and animals is possible. But even then, this area was hard hit by the drought of 1973 which in fact lasted for 3 years thereafter before the rains returned to normal. As a result, a number of the 2.3 million *Hausa* farmers, 1 million *Djerma-Songhai* farmers and three-quarter million *Fulani* herdsmen who live here had to emigrate across the border to the less hard hit neighbouring country – Nigeria. Many have gone back but others have stayed behind and some of them have found unskilled jobs in Nigerian cities. Others, women and children in particular, have remained beggers in the Nigerian cities.

Economic development

In such a bare and thirsty land as Niger, often menaced by drought, economic development, particularly agricultural, is bound to be slow, and closely and precariously tied up with the availability of water. That is why the southern part is the only agriculturally developed part of the country as Figure 18.7 shows.

i) Study this figure carefully.
ii) Why are the country's economic activities mostly concentrated in the southern quarter of the country?
iii) Why does the groundnut belt run close to the routeways?
iv) What do you think makes it possible for rice to be grown along the valley of the River Niger?

The main food crops are *millet* and *sorghum*. *Rice* is grown by the Djerma-Songhai along the irrigated riverine lands of the Niger River. But the most important cash crop in the country is *groundnuts*. These are cultivated by the Hausas particularly in the

zone stretching from Zinder in the east to Maradi in the west, and along the roadside to the valley of River Niger. Production reached a peak of 250 000 tonnes in 1967 but fell to 77 000 in 1973 as a result of drought during that year. The limited recovery to 129 000 tonnes in 1974 was again reduced to 100 000 tonnes in 1975 by insect disaster. These fluctuations notwithstanding, Niger is the second most important groundnut producer in French speaking West Africa, next to Senegal. It had been Niger's most vital export until 1973 when it was surpassed by Uranium.

Cattle, of the humpless Chad variety, are reared in the southeast. The number of cattle in Niger was estimated at 3 million in 1970, but like groundnuts, their numbers were drastically reduced by the 1972–74 drought so the total fell to 2.5 million head in 1975. *Sheep, donkeys* and *goats* are the other livestock of some importance.

Niger had been poor in mineral production until deposits of *uranium* were discovered at Arlit, south of the Air plateau in 1967. Production began in 1971 with 410 tonnes of metal, but this rose to 1 300 tonnes in 1975 with prospects of reaching the 2 000 tonne

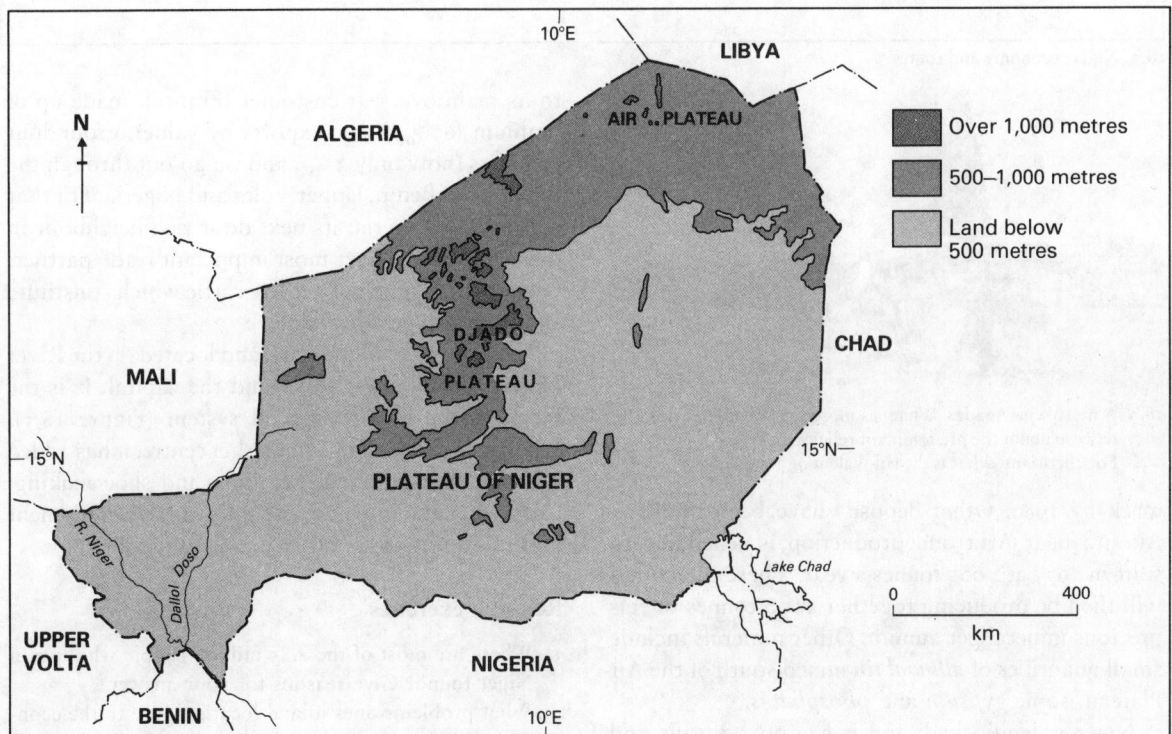

18.6 Niger: relief.

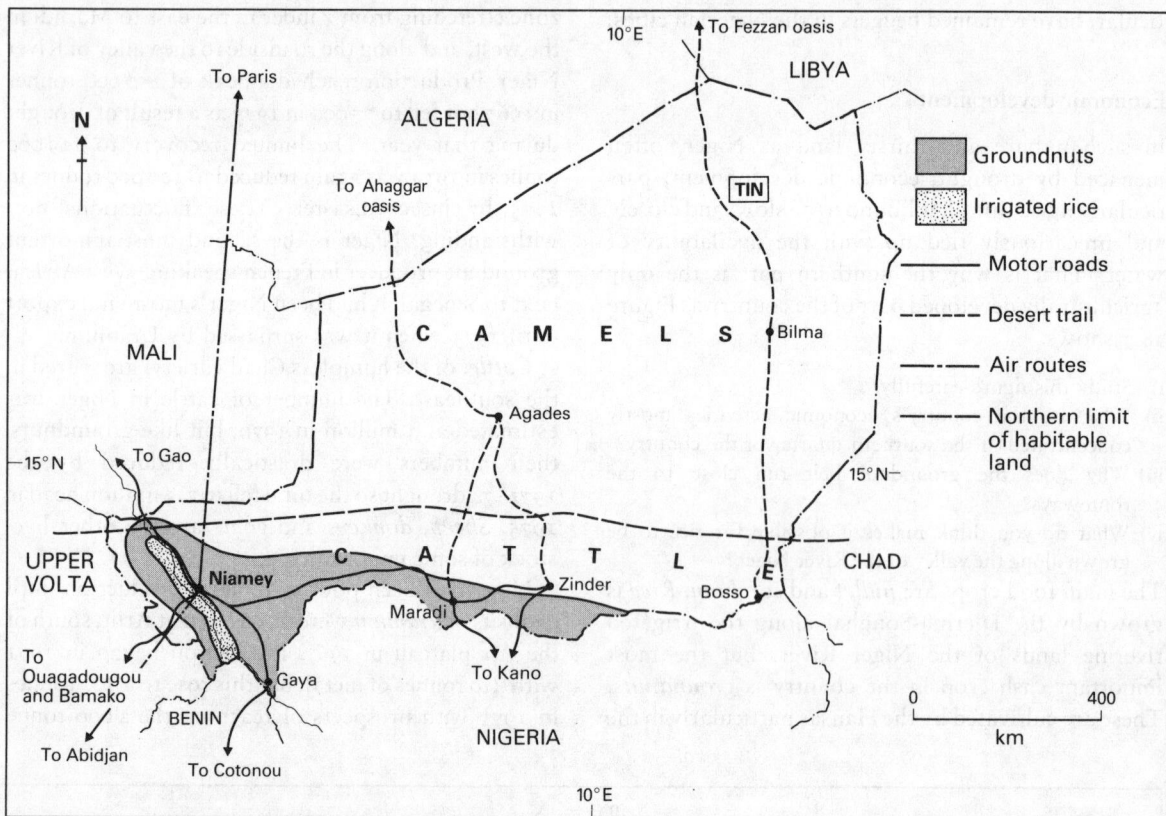

18.7 Niger: economy and routes.

18.8 A mosque in Agades. What is a mosque? What does this
tell you about the predominant religion in Niger?
For christians, what is the equivalent of a mosque?

mark by 1980. Other deposits have been found at
Akoura near Arlit and production is scheduled to
start in 1979 at 2 000 tonnes a year. These two mines
will then be producing together 4 000 tonnes of this
precious mineral per annum. Other minerals include
small quantities of *alluvial tin* mined south of the Air
Plateau, some *gypsum* and *phosphates*.

Niger is landlocked, and it has no railways and
only few stretches of navigable rivers. So its exports

to its main overseas customer (France), made up of
uranium (60% of the exports by value), groundnut
products (now only 3%), and tin go out through the
Republic of Benin, Upper Volta and Nigeria. For that
reason too, Nigeria, its next door rich neighbour in
the south, is her next most important trade partner.
Nigeria takes much of her live cattle which constitute
15% of her export by value.

Niamey (150 000 in 1975), and located on the River
Niger, is the largest town and the capital. It is the
focus of the country's road system (Figure 18.7).
Important as a fishing and market centre, it has added
brewing, flour milling, furniture and shoe making,
textile manufacture and assembly of farm equipment
and radio sets to its other major functions.

Revision exercises

1. Where are most of the 4.85 million people who live in
   Niger found? Give reasons for your answer.
2.. What problems does inland location pose to the economic development of Mali, Upper Volta and Niger?
   What efforts are the countries making to solve them.

19 The off-shore islands

The equatorial off-shore islands of West Africa are Fernando Po, Sâo Tomé, Principé and Annobon, all of which lie in the tropics and therefore experience the hot wet type of climate. There are also the islands of Cape Verde located west of Senegal and often stricken by drought. These islands happen to be all of volcanic origin, and the first set are an obvious structural continuation of the Cameroun highlands in the interior.

Fernando Po

This is the largest of the islands and politically forms part of Equatorial Guinea. Its population comprises principally the local Buli people and Creoles of mixed blood. Nigerians formerly constituted 30 000 of its 1972 population of 90 000, but as a result of the forced labour conditions under which they were working on the island, and the rather infamous rule of its president since the country became independent from Spain in 1968, they were all repartriated by the Nigerian government in 1976. Of the remaining population of 60 000, nearly 20% left on voluntary exile following the people's dissatisfaction with conditions in the country.

The island has therefore suffered economically as a result of this political unrest and the depletion of its manpower consequent on the mass evacuation of the population. So, important though its *cocoa*, *coconut* and *banana* plantations still are, output from them has fallen drastically in recent years. Cocoa is

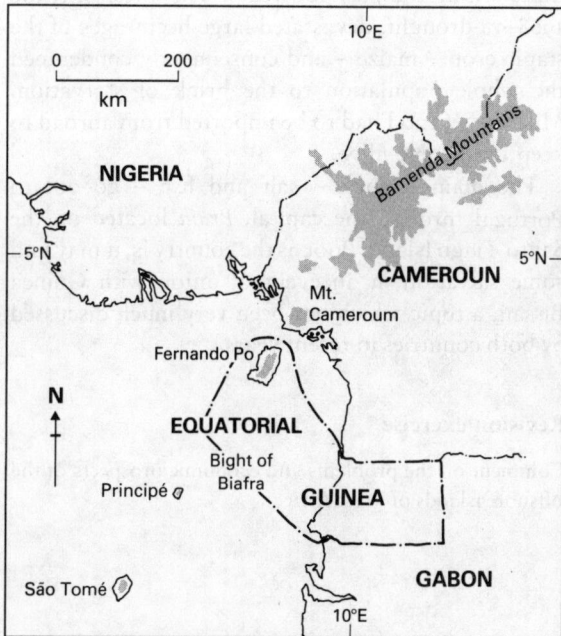

19.1 The equatorial off-shore islands.

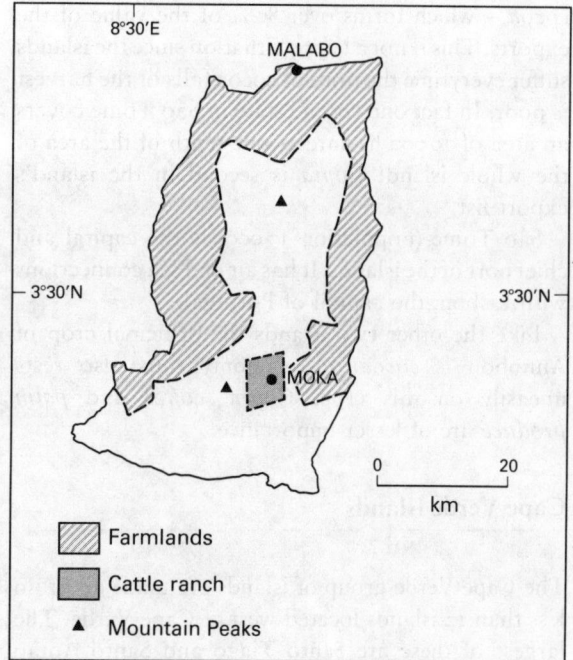

19.2 Fernando Po.

however still found in areas below 600 metres, while coffee estates and ranches are located above this level. Spain takes whatever of these products that are exported. *Cassava, yams, maize* and *fish* form the basic food items, though these have to be supplemented with large food imports since the island cannot produce enough food for it peoples.

The island's industries are mainly concerned with processing cocoa and coffee. Fish is also canned at Malabo.

Malabo (formerly Santa Isabel until 1973 when the name was changed with that of the island), is the capital. It had a population of 45 000 before the political unrest started. It is the chief commercial and industrial centre and has trade and traffic connections with Spain.

São Tomé, Principé and Annobon

Formerly Portuguese, São Tomé and Principé became independent with other former Portuguese territories in 1975. Can you name two of these other territories in Africa? The inhabitants of the islands comprise indigenous Africans, Creoles and descendants of ex-slaves, all numbering some 76 000 in 1973.

The islands depend precariously on one crop – *cocoa* – which forms over 80% of the value of the exports. This is not a happy situation since the islands suffer everytime the price of cocoa falls or the harvest is poor. In fact one cocoa estate in São Tomé covers an area of 10 000 hectares – one-tenth of the area of the whole island! *Copra* is second in the island's export list.

São Tomé (population 17 000) is the capital and chief port of the islands. It has air and sea connections with Lisbon, the capital of Portugal.

Like the other two islands the principal crop of Annobon is *cocoa*. Its economy thus also rests uneasily on this crop. *Copra, coffee* and *palm produce* are of lesser importance.

Cape Verde Islands

The Cape Verde group of islands are made up of no less than 12 islands located west of Cape Verde. The largest of these are Santo Tiago and Santo Antao Islands. They cover an area of 4 000 square kilometres

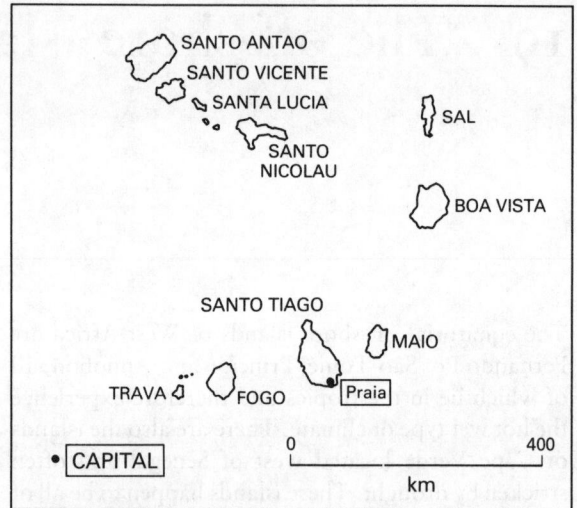

19.3 Cape Verde Islands.

and had, in 1975 when they became independent from Portugal, an estimated population of 300 000. It is relevant to note that with the final pulling out of Portugal that year from her former African territories, including the Cape Verde Islands, colonialism was completely wiped out from the political map of West Africa.

Drought has been the most serious menace to the economy of the islands. It has occurred more than five times within the past 100 years. The latest one, the 1968–78 drought, devastated large hectarages of the staple crop – maize – and consequently condemned the whole population to the brink of starvation. Much relief food had to be imported from abroad to keep the people alive.

The main exports – salt and fish – go out to Portugal through the capital, *Praia* located on the Santo Tiago Island. Poor as the country is, it may find some salvation in an eventual union with Guinea Bissau, a topic which has been very much discussed by both countries in recent years.

Revision exercise

Comment on the problems and economic prospects of the offshore islands of West Africa.

PART THREE

West Africa – a general economic review

20 Farming (1) – systems and problems of farming

Preparation

1. Visit the farm of a well-known traditional farmer in your locality.
   a) Find out and jot down in your notebook the following things about his farm:
      i) the crops or animals he raises and the quantities of each;
      ii) the tools or implements he uses;
      iii) his farm routine month by month, and
      iv) the people he employs to work for him.
   b) Estimate the size of his farm and draw a sketch showing the areas given to the different farm items.
   c) Find out from him and note down his main problems, and how he disposes of his farm products.
   d) How does your knowledge of the geography of your area help you to understand his farm routine and problems?
   e) Can you suggest solutions to the problems?
2. a) If there is a modern farm project near your school, visit it as well and do the same exercise as above in respect of the farm project.
   b) What differences do you observe between the traditional farm and the modern farm?

We studied the various aspects of farming in the individual countries in part two. It becomes necessary that we should now see them in their West African regional context. In so doing we shall touch on its major aspects – problems and systems of farming, food crop and animal production, and export crop production. We shall devote this chapter to problems and systems of farming.

West African environment, chiefly rainfall, influences farm systems and also gives us a clue to the types of problems that are encountered in the area. We shall therefore use this factor in dividing these aspects of farming into two – those found in the wet forest lands of the south and those associated with the drier savanna lands of the north.

Tradition, and level of technical knowledge, are also important in determining farm practices and the way man tackles the farm problems that confront him. This is true, for farm practice is sometimes tied up with the way of life of the people. Also, for instance, the type of irrigation man uses to water his farm depends on whether he only knows about the shadoof, or whether he can construct canals to tap the waters of the river when in flood, or whether he knows also how to build a dam to provide perennial irrigation.

Farm problems and systems in the wet forest lands

Problems

The relief, climate and vegetation in the forest lands have been described in chapters 2 to 5. Certain problems arise from their nature, and we will now discuss some of them.

1. *Leaching.* Rain water washes down useful salts in the soil to lower levels beyond the reach of plant roots. This is called leaching, and obviously occurs where rainfall is heavy. Intensive use of fertilizers is a way of restoring the plant salts lost this way.
2. *Laterite formation.* Where heavy rainfall occurs in alternation with a spell of dry weather, and where there has been chemical corrosion of rocks over a very long period, the result is a red type of soil called laterite. This type of soil is poorer in plant food than loam or humus soil. Rotational bush fallowing is a system used to prevent already poor laterite soils from rapidly losing their fertility, by allowing them rest to regain their fertility after the first year or two of cropping.
3. *Soil erosion.* Heavy rainfall gives rise to floods which washes away the soils from farm lands. The soils, normally rich in plant foods, are thus lost to

the farmlands, being carried down to rivers and eventually to the sea. This is soil erosion. There are two types – sheet erosion and gully erosion.

Sheet erosion, as the name implies, is the carrying away of thin sheets of top soil by flood. This type is hardly noticed as it does does not go deep at a time, but it is most dangerous to soil as it is spread over a large area and is never noticed in time.

Gully erosion creates deep gullies, usually at heads of streams and normally where the soils are loose and slopes steep. The gully erosion on the slopes of the sandstone Udi Plateau, or the often quoted Nanka erosion, both in Anambra State of Nigeria are good examples. The latter has not only destroyed farmlands in Nanka area but has carried away whole homesteads and other buildings which collapse on the advance of erosion gullies (Figure 20.1).

Four principal measures are taken to fight erosion in West Africa.

i) Ploughing and ridging along the contours and across the slopes. The ridges thus made, break the force of flood water and hold back the soil.

ii) Deep ploughing makes much of the rain water sink down rather than run on the surface to wash off the soil.

iii) Afforestation or planting of trees and grass afresh, and re-forestation or planting them where they had been cut down, help to bind the soils together and to break the force of flood water.

iv) Flood control, either by diverting it or building fence barrages across nascent gullies, breaks the force of the flood and holds back the soil, thus preventing the gullies from growing deeper.

There are also other measures in the fight against erosion. Can you name some of them?

4. *Pests* – These thrive under high temperatures, damp atmosphere and heavy rainfall. Examples are the nematodes which attack root crops like yams and cassava, and crickets which eat up vegetables and leaves of young plants. There are also rodents like the bush rat, or the grass cutter which eat up cassava. Chemicals and traps are used to fight these pests.

Methods and systems

Farm methods and systems are influenced by the environment and are also adapted to solve the problems it poses. Thus:

1. *Rotational bush fallowing* is common. We saw this in the Nigerian example in chapter 7, but it is popular over all West Africa, even to some extent, in the savanna lands. Annual crops are usually planted as the farm plots have to be rotated on yearly basis. Revise this example.

2. Peculiar to the forest lands, however, and as distinct from the rotational bush fallowing, is *stabilised tree crop farming*. Tree crops are planted without having to rotate the farms, and the land is devoted to a particular tree crop for several years running. We saw this system in the cocoa lands and palm belts of Nigeria and Ghana.

3. *Commercial agriculture* is also practised. This is the growing of crops (whether tree crops or annuals) and animals, using modern scientific ways and farm implements. Usually the farms have attached to them processing plants to process the products. Coffee and bananas are grown by commercial agriculture in Guinea and Ivory

20.1 Gully erosion in Nanka, Anambra State of Nigeria. Are the sides of the gully steep or gently sloped? Can you see the river at the bottom of the gully? Describe the vegetation around. What effects do you think the erosion would have on the farmland around?

Coast. Poultry and market garden crops are grown by commercial agriculture in farmlands near towns. This type of agriculture is, of course, not peculiar to the forest lands.

4. Although *plantation agriculture* is a type of commercial farming, it is different from it in that in plantations, crops rather than animals are usually raised; one crop rather than a number is grown over a single farm extending up to thousands of hectares, and wage earning labourers constitute the bulk of the farmers. Thus we have the cocoa, coffee and coconut plantations of Fernando Po (chapter 19), coffee and banana plantations of Ivory Coast and Guinea (chapters 12 and 15) and the rubber plantations of Liberia (chapter 13). Revise these.

5. In the forest lands where there are two rainy seasons a year, *double cropping* a year is possible. Thus, in the western states of Nigeria, maize can be planted in March, harvested in June or July, planted again in August and harvested in November.

20.2 One of the tragic effects of droughts in West Africa. This is one of the effects of the 1972–74 drought in West Africa. What did the cow die of? Lack of water or lack of grass or both? In which vegetational belt was this photograph taken? Why do you not find people in the picture?

Farm problems and systems in the sahel and savanna lands

Problems

The natural problems of farming in the sahel and savanna lands are chiefly soil erosion, pests and drought.

1. *Soil erosion* here is caused by strong winds which blow away the dry top soil. Sometimes too it is caused by torrential downpours immediately following a long spell of dry season. Burning of the grass by man and overgrazing by animals leave the areas bare, and trampling by them loosens these bare soils thus preparing them for being either blown away by the wind, or washed away by the torrential downpours. The inland countries of West Africa suffer from this type of erosion. To combat it, trees are planted to break the force of the wind and farmers are educated to desist from overgrazing and tree cutting.

2. *Pests* in the savanna and sahel lands take the form of locusts, birds and weevils. The first devour the crops in a matter of days but have been fought successfully by F.A.O. experts. The weevils attack the cotton bolls, blackening them and rendering them useless, while birds eat the grains before harvest.

3. The most devastating menace in these lands is of course, *drought*, or prolonged and almost complete lack of water. The problem reached alarming proportions in recent years, particularly during the drought of 1972–74. The areas mostly affected include the sahelian countries of Cape Verde Islands, Mauritania, Senegal, Mali, Upper Volta, Niger and The Gambia, and to some extent, the northern parts of Nigeria.

The drought can be attributed to three main causes:

i) changes in climate which is now becoming increasingly drier;

ii) overgrazing by animals, particularly goats, which eat the grass to their very roots making the place look bare and causing the desert to advance, and

iii) over-cultivation and cutting down of trees by man which not only make the place look bare but remove one factor which induces rainfall, i.e. vegetation.

The effects of drought are serious on livestock, crops and man:

1. Cattle and other livestock die by the millions for lack of water. It has been estimated that the 1972–74 drought caused a total loss of 6–8 million cattle and the death of an unknown number of sheep and goats in West Africa. The New York Times of 17th June 1973 estimated that Mauritania alone lost over 80% (or 1.6 million) of her 2 million cattle. Cape Verde lost over 10 000; Upper Volta being less hit, lost only 8% of her own cattle.

2. Crop yields drop steeply as harvests fail owing to lack of water. The crops most hard hit by the 1972–74 drought were cotton, groundnuts, millet and sorghum. In Cape Verde Islands maize yield tumbled down from 11 060 tonnes in 1967 to 710 in 1973!

3. One obvious effect on human beings is of course that they no longer find enough water to drink or for other domestic uses.

4. As a result of lack of drinking water, crop failure and loss of livestock, the population in these areas emigrates en masse to the southern countries. In 1973 a good number (unfortunately without any check or statistics taken of them) emigrated from Niger to Nigeria and now form a number of the unskilled workers or beggers in Nigeria cities.

5. Those who cannot emigrate face famine and death by starvation. Cape Verde Islands, more than any other country in West Africa, have suffered most seriously from this menace. The 1830–37, famine there wiped off 35% of the population; in 1860–66, 40% of the population starved to death; in 1920–22, 25% died, in 1940–43 it was 15% and the 1946–48 drought took a toll of 35%. As many, if not more, would have died during the drought of 1972–74 but for food relief brought in from abroad.

The governments of the affected eight sahelian countries have been seeking remedies for this problem. They have formed a permanent Inter-state Committee for Drought Control in the Sahel which is taking a number of steps to provide remedies for the problem as follows.

i) sinking more boreholes to provide water;
ii) building irrigation dams to hold flood water;
iii) educating farmers in better ways of grazing and cropping, to avoid mass destruction of grass, and
iv) planting more trees to check the advance of the desert.

Trees are planted along a belt running east to west to form what is called the *shelter belt*. It is so called because it shelters the areas to the south from the

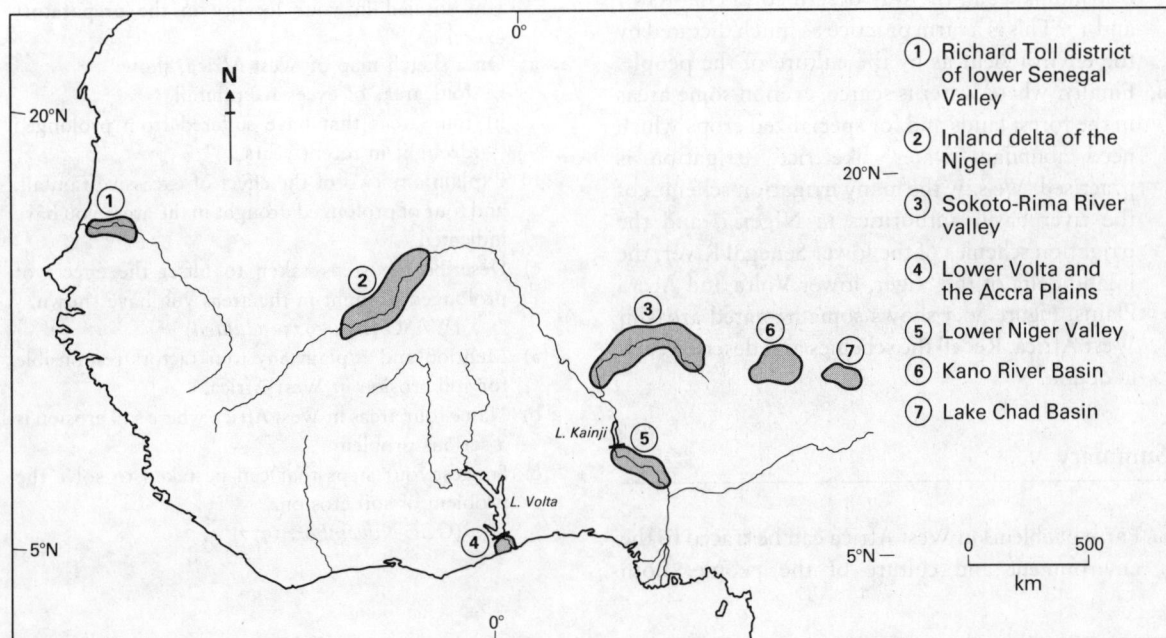

1. Richard Toll district of lower Senegal Valley
2. Inland delta of the Niger
3. Sokoto-Rima River valley
4. Lower Volta and the Accra Plains
5. Lower Niger Valley
6. Kano River Basin
7. Lake Chad Basin

20.3 Irrigated areas of West Africa.

advance of the desert. Nigeria alone planted, by 1978, a total area of over 700 square kilometres of shelter belt.

However, it is necessary that our universities too should pay attention to research into developing drought resisting species of savanna crops and into ways of generating artificial rainfall. If they can provide answers to these, then they would have gone a long way to solving a major problem in West African agriculture.

Methods and systems

Due to the problems outlined above, and the general nature of the savanna and sahel lands, a special pattern of farm methods and systems emerges:

1. Mixed farming is practised in some places. Here animals are fed on the grass grains stalks, while their droppings provide manure for the crops, and they themselves are used to draw ploughs. The Sérères of Senegal (chapter 16) and the Nangodis of Ghana (chapter 10) are typical examples of mixed farmers in West Africa.
2. Since there is only one rainy season a year in these lands, only one cropping a year is possible, except of course in the irrigated lands.
3. The Fulani herdsmen of Nigeria and Mali practise transhumance in the way described in chapters 7 and 17. This is a farm practice as much dictated by the environment as by the culture of the people.
4. Finally, where water is scarce, even in some areas in the forest lands and for specialized crops which need abundant water, like rice, irrigation is practised. We saw the many irrigation schemes of the river basin authorities in Nigeria, and the irrigation schemes of the lower Senegal River, the inland delta of the Niger, lower Volta and Accra Plains. Figure 20.3 shows some irrigated areas in West Africa. Recall the schemes and describe each in detail.

Summary

1. Farm problems in West Africa can be traced to the environment and culture of the people. Both

factors, and the level of technical knowledge, determine how these problems are tackled and the eventual farm systems in West Africa.
2. The problems in the forest lands are mainly erosion, leaching, laterite formation and pests. In the savanna lands erosion, and pests occur but take different forms, while drought is most devastating.
3. The farm systems in the forest lands are mainly rotational bush fallowing, double cropping a year, stabilised tree crop farming, commercial agriculture and plantation agriculture. In the savanna lands rotational bush fallowing and commercial agriculture are practised, but specially characteristic of the area are single cropping, mixed farming, transhumance and irrigated agriculture.

Now try the following exercises:

Revision exercises

1. a) Name the farm methods common to the forest and savanna lands of West Africa and those peculiar to each region.
   b) Describe them showing how each is related to the climate of the region and the culture of the people.
   c) For each give an example of a place where it is practised.
   d) Which of the farm methods is(are) used on the farms you studied in your locality in the preparatory exercise?
2. a) On a sketch map of West Africa, show:
      i) four areas of excessive rainfall,
      ii) four areas that have suffered from prolonged drought in recent years.
   b) Explain any two of the effect of excessive rainfall, and four of prolonged drought in the areas you have indicated.
   c) Describe the steps taken to offset the effects of prolonged drought in the areas you have shown.
      (WASC June 1975, adapted)
3. a) Mention and explain any four factors responsible for soil erosion in West Africa.
   b) Name four areas in West Africa where soil erosion is a serious problem.
   c) Suggest four steps that can be taken to solve the problem of soil erosion.
      (GCE November, 1977)

21 Farming (2) – food crop and animal production

Preparation

1. Review the preparatory exercise at the beginning of the last chapter and study the notes you took down during the exercise.
2. Name four food crops grown in your country and say where each is produced.

Environment and culture influence the type of food crops and animals raised, just as they do farm problems and methods. But these are not the only factors. Man's choice is very relevant. When presented with a number of alternative possibilities, man makes his choice, usually after considering the real and opportunity costs of all the alternatives, and knowing the one to give him maximum benefits. For example, the nature of flat land near a river makes it possible for the land to be put to a number of alternative uses. It can be irrigated and sown with rice or sugar cane, a fish pond can be built there, or in fact it can be converted to a holiday resort. Man makes his choice from these possibilities. If he chooses to irrigate it, then he must have considered the cost of the irrigation scheme (its real costs) and what he would have missed in terms of money by not turning it to a fish pond or holiday resort (the opportunity costs). It is therefore necessary to bear this factor of

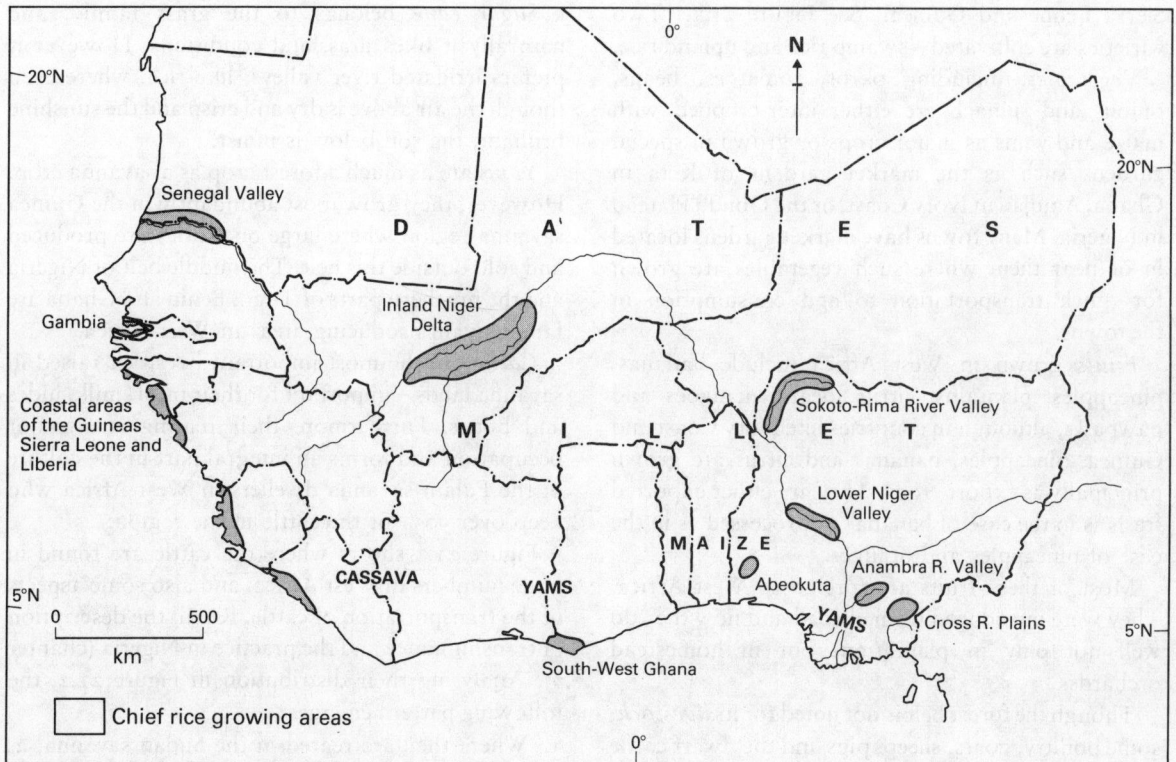

21.1 Distribution of some food crops in West Africa.

choice in mind in order to appreciate fully the rôle and limitations of environment in agricultural land use.

Here again we shall divide the food crops and animals into those found in the forest lands and those raised in the savanna lands of West Africa.

Food crops and animals in the forest lands

The most popular food crops are those which grow well under heavy rainfall and forest conditions.

Tubers, like yams, cocoyams and cassava, belong to this group of food crops. They are widely cultivated and are staple food items. Yams and cassava (in the form of garri) form items of active internal trade in the countries where they are grown.

Two important *grains* – maize and rice – are also grown in the forest lands. Maize is widespread and is inter-cropped with yams. Rice grows well in the wet flat lands of Anambra and Cross River plains of Nigeria, south-west Ghana, the fresh water swamps bordering the coasts and rias in Sierra Leone, Guinea and The Gambia, and the monsoon lands of Liberia, Sierra Leone and Guinea. (See Figure 21.1.) Two varieties are cultivated – swamp rice and upland rice.

Vegetables, including okros, tomatoes, beans, onions and spinach are either inter-cropped with maize and yams as major crops or grown in special gardens such as the market gardens of Keta in Ghana, Abidjan in Ivory Coast, or the Obudu Plateau in Nigeria. Many towns have market gardens located in or near them where such vegetables are grown for quick transportation to and consumption in the towns.

Fruits grown in West Africa include bananas, pineapples, plantains, citrus, pears, mangoes and pawpaws, although in countries like Ivory Coast and Guinea, pineapples, bananas and citrus are grown principally as export crops. They are either exported fresh as in the case of bananas or processed as in the case of pineapples and oranges.

Most of these fruits are foreign to West Africa. They were introduced from abroad and now they do well not only in plantations but in homestead orchards.

Though the forest belt is not noted for its *livestock*, some poultry, goats, sheep, pigs and the dwarf cattle are raised either in homestead farms and kraals, or on livestock farms.

Food crops and animals in the savanna lands

Cereals are the main food crops of the savanna lands, since they are suited to the dry conditions, short rainy season and brilliant sunshine of these lands. The most widespread are maize, millet and guinea corn, and there is practically no savanna country in West Africa where these are not known.

Wheat and *barley* are however being introduced with some success, particularly in the irrigated lands where they are grown in the cooler months, being themselves temperate cereals. Their production helps to cut down the importation of flour for bread making and grains for brewing beer in the countries of production, thus saving them foreign exchange.

Rice is also grown, but mostly in naturally irrigated fadama lands which are seasonally flooded in the wet season like the middle Volta, middle and lower Niger, Senegal and Sokoto River valleys. More is however produced where the land has been irrigated by the canal system as in the areas described in the last chapter and shown in Figure 20.3 of that chapter.

Sugar cane belongs to the grass family, and naturally it likes grassland conditions. However it prefers irrigated river valleys, like rice, where even though the air above is dry and crisp and the sunshine brilliant, the soil below is moist.

Yams are as much a forest crop as a savanna crop. However, they grow most abundantly in the Guinea savanna region where large quantities are produced and sold outside this belt. The middle belt of Nigeria and the northern parts of Togo, Benin and Ghana are famous yam producing areas in West Africa.

Cattle are the most important livestock raised in savanna lands – important for their meat, milk, hides and bones. Furthermore their rearing is a major occupation and forms an integral part in the culture of the Fulani savanna dwellers in West Africa who keep over 90% of the cattle in the region.

Figure 21.2 shows where the cattle are found in large numbers in West Africa, and also some aspects of the transportation of cattle. Recall the description of transhumance and the practice in Nigeria (chapter 7). Analysing their distribution in Figure 21.2, the following pattern emerges:

1. Where they are reared in the Sudan savanna, as typified by northern Nigeria or northern Upper Volta, they are found in the wide open plains

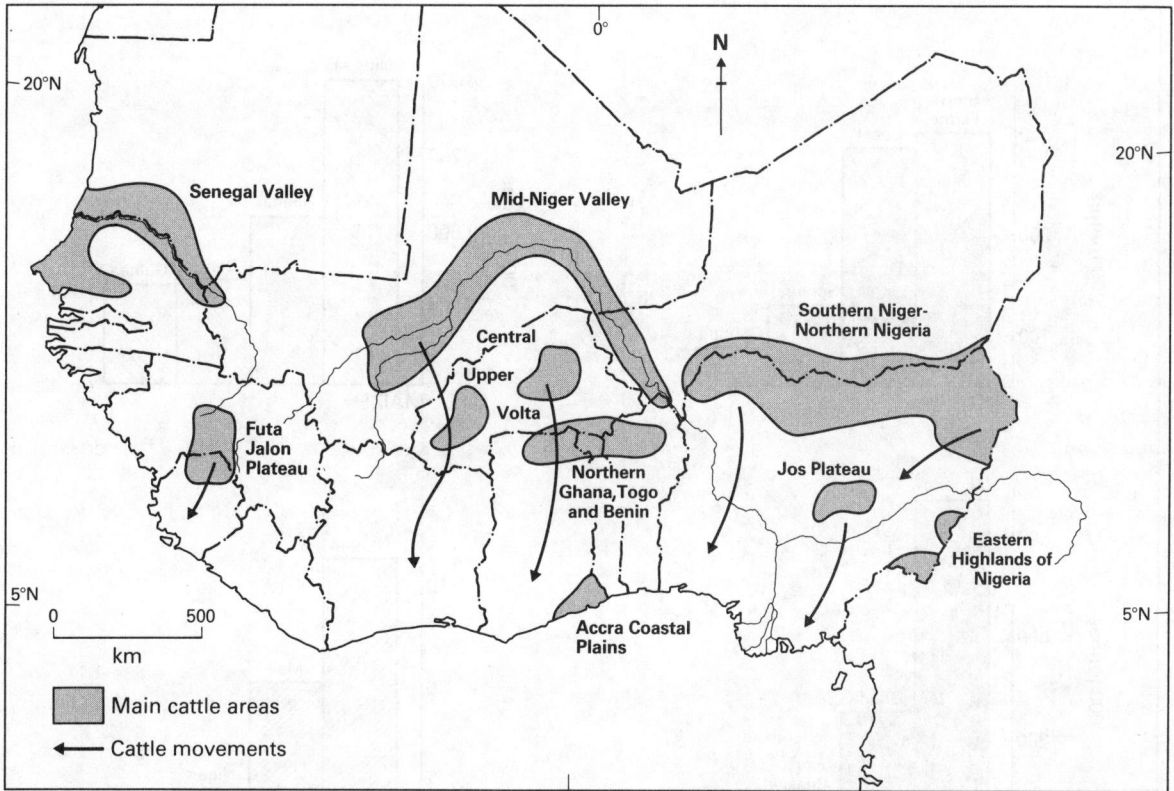

21.2 Cattle in West Africa and their movement.

where good pasture is abundant, grass reasonably short and annual rainfall between 500 mm and 1 000 mm.

2. In the drier sahel lands further north, as found in Mali, northern Senegal and Mauritania, they are restricted to the better-watered river valleys. That is why large numbers are found along the valleys of the Senegal, upper Gambia and Niger rivers.

3. In the warmer and wetter guinea savanna to the south, where trees and taller grasses grow, they are found mainly on the plateaus of Futa Jalon, Upper Volta, northern Ghana and Benin, Jos, Adamawa, Obudu and Bamenda. On these plateaus, the climate is cooler, grass shorter and surroundings freer from tsetse flies than the lowlands immediately below.

The humped Zebu cattle are confined mainly to the zones which are free from these flies, while the more tolerant Ndama breed are found in more southern and lower locations.

Can you now, from the description above, deduce the conditions necessary for the rearing of cattle in West Africa? Why, and how, do the cattle move southwards as shown in Figure 21.2?

Other livestock in the north include sheep, goats, horses, donkeys and camels. The last three are reared primarily as beasts of burden, and camels are specially kept by the Tuaregs and Arabs of Niger, Mali and Mauritania.

Summary

Three general points must be made to finalise this topic on food production in West Africa. First, some food crops discussed above are exported, just as some of the export crops to be described in the next chapter are consumed locally. But food crops are grown primarily for consumption rather than exports, with the exception of bananas and pineapples in Guinea and Ivory Coast.

Secondly, fish is also food, and so fishing is food production. However, since the occupation involves exploitation of nature's reserves we shall deal with it

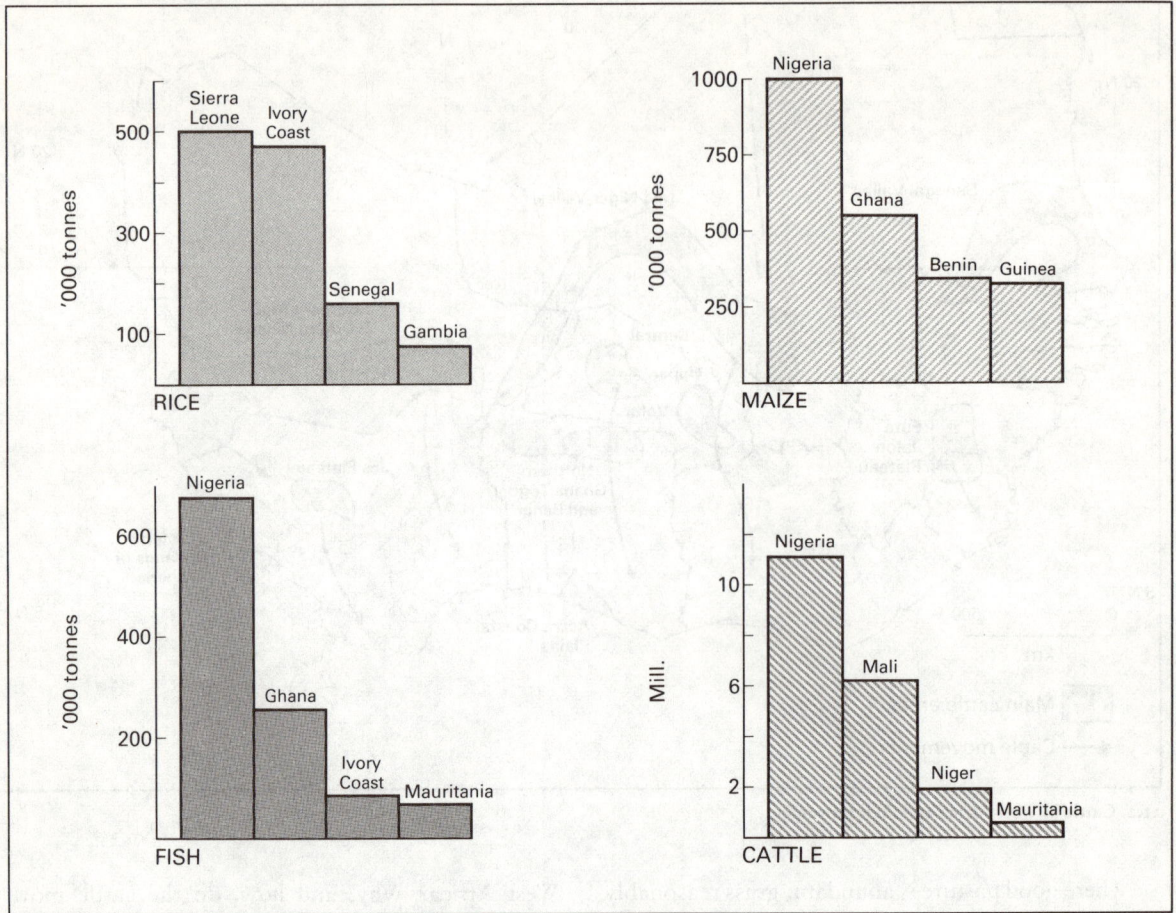

21.3 Annual production of some food items by leading West African producers (based on mid 1970–80 figures). This figure helps you see at a glance the relative position of the principal producers of rice, maize, fish and cattle in the West African region. For each item name the chief producers in order. Estimate the amount produced by each country.

in Chapter 23 on extractive industries.

Finally it is doubtful whether West Africa can any longer produce all the food it needs. Practically all the countries import large quantities of food annually. At one time it was Senegal, Guinea, Ghana and others – countries where foods constitute over 20% of the value of their imports. But now even Nigeria has joined the list of food importers. For a agricultural region like West Africa, this is an unwelcome development. Five main factors account for this unsatisfactory situation:

1. Many people are leaving the farms for more lucrative employment in the towns.
2. Potential farmlands in mining areas like Jos Plateau, the oil fields of Nigeria, Los Island in Guinea and Tarkwa in Ghana are being spoilt for farming by excavations and mine dumps.
3. Farming is not generally intensive or soils rich, so the yield per hectare is low. For example, the yield per hectare of rice in Japan is four times that of Sierra Leone, yet rice is a staple food crop in both countries.
4. Too much attention is paid to export crop production at the expense of food crop growing. Ivory Coast, Senegal and Ghana offer good examples of this situation.
5. More recently, the drought of 1972–74 devastated a lot of crops in the way described in the last chapter. Harvests were low and there has never been any full recovery since then.

Importation of foods, to which these countries have now resorted, does not provide a permanent solution to the problem. Nor does dependence on 'free' relief food from abroad which was an emergency measure during the drought years. It is therefore obvious that efforts must be made by all countries to grow more food and to promote internal trade in them so that West Africa can attain regional self-sufficiency in food production.

The steps taken to fight the problems of farming as described in the last chapter are indirectly measures taken to increase food production in the region. Government is also encouraging rural development as a way of arresting the drift to the towns and of increasing the farming population in the rural areas. Waste lands are also being reclaimed for farming. Finally governments are mounting food production campaigns.

Two food production campaigns recently embarked upon by West Africa Governments dramatise the efforts being made to increase domestic food production. One is the Operation Feed Yourself (OFY) launched by the Ghanaian Government in 1972. This was aimed at making the farmer produce more than his needs so that there would be surplus for sale, and in making many more people take up farming as an occupation. This campaign met with limited and short-lived success as the farmers were soon enticed away to more paying cash crop production. Besides, the drought of 1972–74 which set in no sooner than the programme started drastically affected crop yields.

In Nigeria a similar campaign – Operation Feed the Nation (OFN) – was launched in 1976. This was aimed at making everyone grow some food – no matter how small and even in backyard gardens. The farmer will of course grow more. When everyone produces everybody will have some to eat, there will be less rush for the limited quantities in the market, prices will fall and everyone will eventually have enough to buy and eat. This campaign met with greater success than the Ghana experiment chiefly due to the fact that everybody was involved in the programme. Prices of food actually fell between 1977 and 1980 perhaps as much due to more food that was produced as to the general scarcity of money in circulation during this period.

However, these two experiments should serve as examples which other nations could learn from and modify as locally desirable.

Revision exercises

1. a) Show on a map of West Africa the distribution of the following farm items:
      i) fruits,
      ii) rice, and
      iii) cattle.
   b) Account for their distribution and describe how the farm items are produced in the region.
2. a) Why has there been a drop in food production in West Africa?
   b) Outline the consequences of the decline.
   c) What efforts are being made to arrest the decline and increase food production in the region?

22 Farming (3) – export crop production

Preparation

1. List the export crops grown in your own country.
2. Draw two maps of West Africa, inserting the outlines of all the countries in them.

As in the case of food crops, we can divide the export crops of West Africa into those found in the forest lands and those common in the savanna areas. But before we do this, we will take a close look at Figures

22.1 and 22.2 and summarize the general features of the character and distribution of these crops.

General features of export crops

1. Both maps show that West Africa is an important producer and exporter of vegetable crops. Most of the crops, for example, palm produce, coconuts

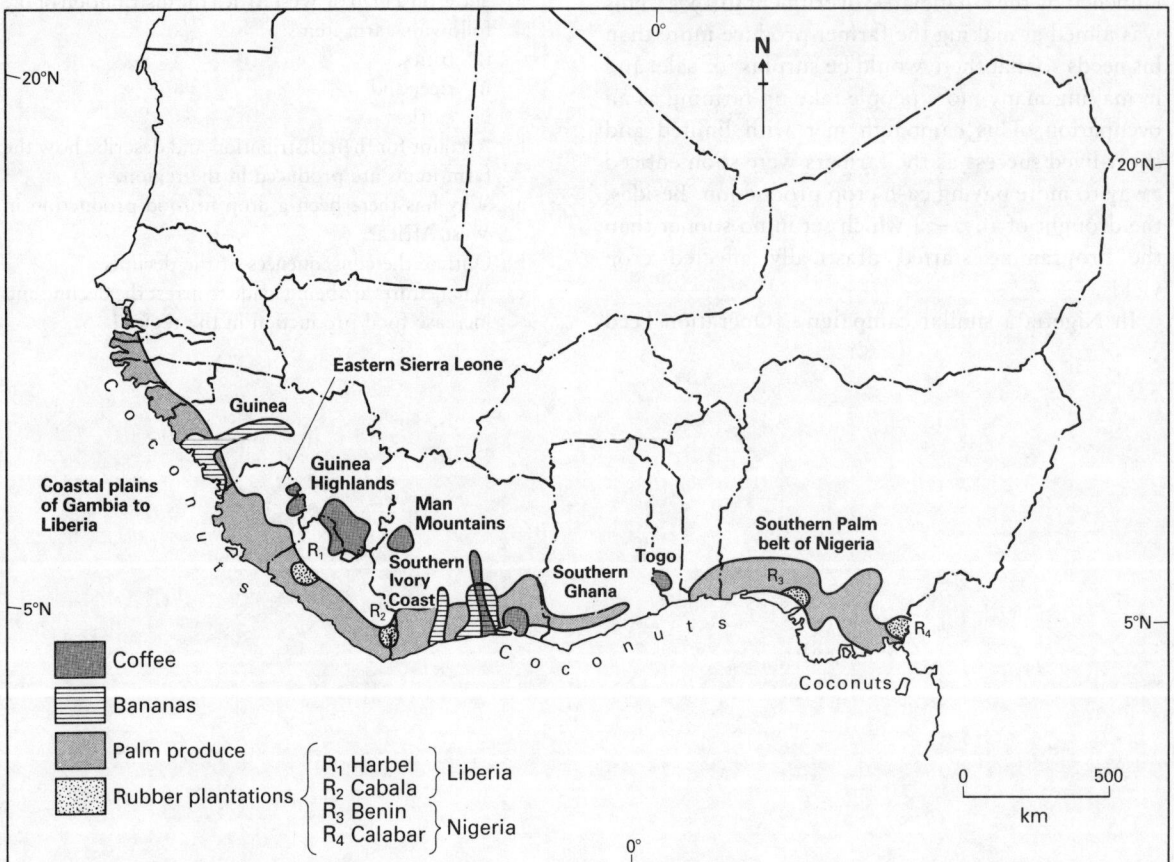

22.1 Distribution of coffee, palm produce, rubber, coconuts and bananas in West Africa.

and groundnuts, are oil producing seeds. Rubber, coffee, other fruits, cocoa and cotton are the crops not grown primarily for their oil, though oil is obtained from cocoa and cotton seeds.

2. The export crops from the forest lands are chiefly tree crops, as we would expect, since they need the heavy rainfall of these lands for their perennial growth. On the other hand annuals, like cotton and groundnuts, which complete their life cycle within the four to six months of the wet season, are typical savanna crops.

3. The French, more than the British, encouraged plantation agriculture in their former territories. So most of the bananas, coffee and pineapples and some cotton and palm produce from the French-speaking countries are produced on plantations. Only a small percentage of the crops from the English-speaking countries is produced in this way.

4. Figures 22.1, 22.2 and 22.3 show that Nigeria and Ivory Coast have the widest variety of crops, and therefore are the mot economically secure in this respect; while others like Ghana and Niger depend mainly on one crop, and therefore suffer when the price of their particular crop falls.

5. Lastly, though the maps do not show this, the production of these crops has given rise to local processing industries where the crops are either part-processed before export, or fully processed for local use. Examples are the groundnut oil mills of Senegal and cotton mills of Nigeria and elsewhere, and the pineapple canneries in Ivory Coast and Ghana.

Export crops from the forest lands

Figure 22.3 shows the relative position of each West African country in the production of the various crops. Cocoa, coffee, palm produce, coconut, rubber and fruits are the most important of the forest crops.

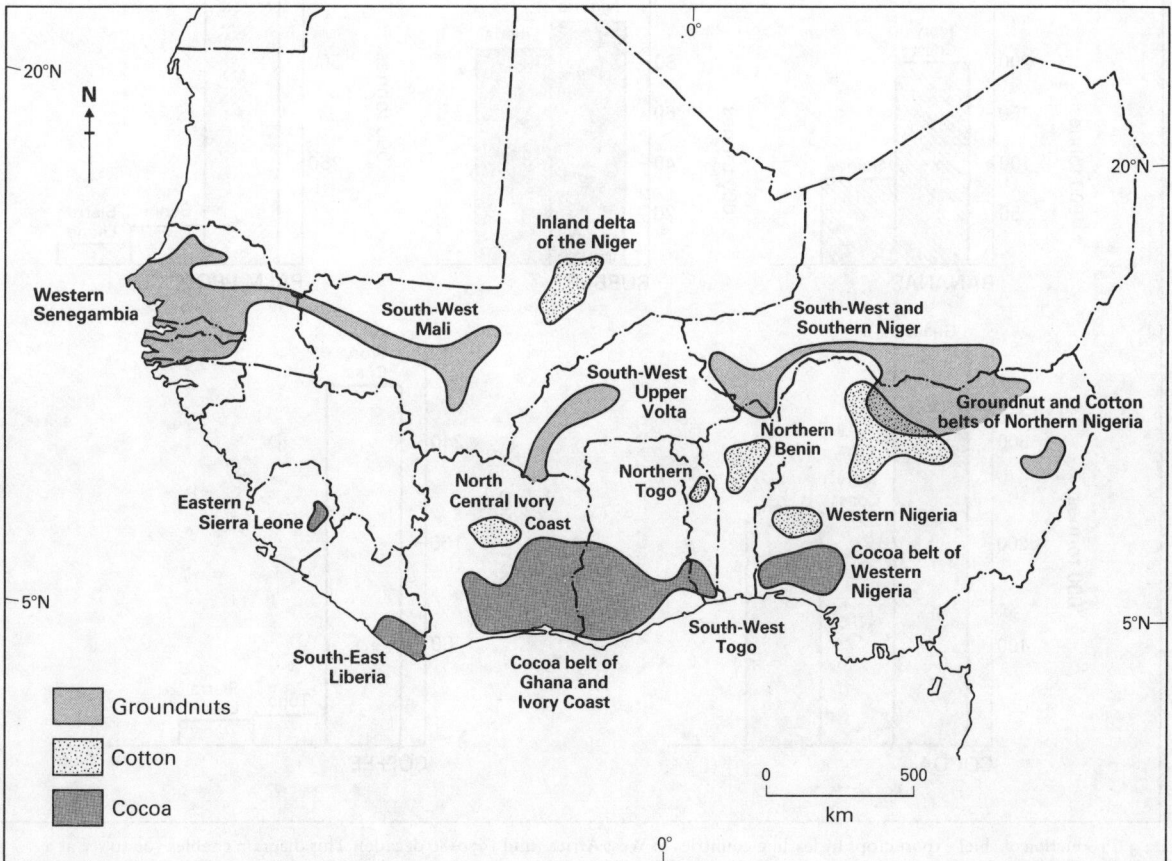

22.2 Distribution of groundnuts, cotton and cocoa in West Africa.

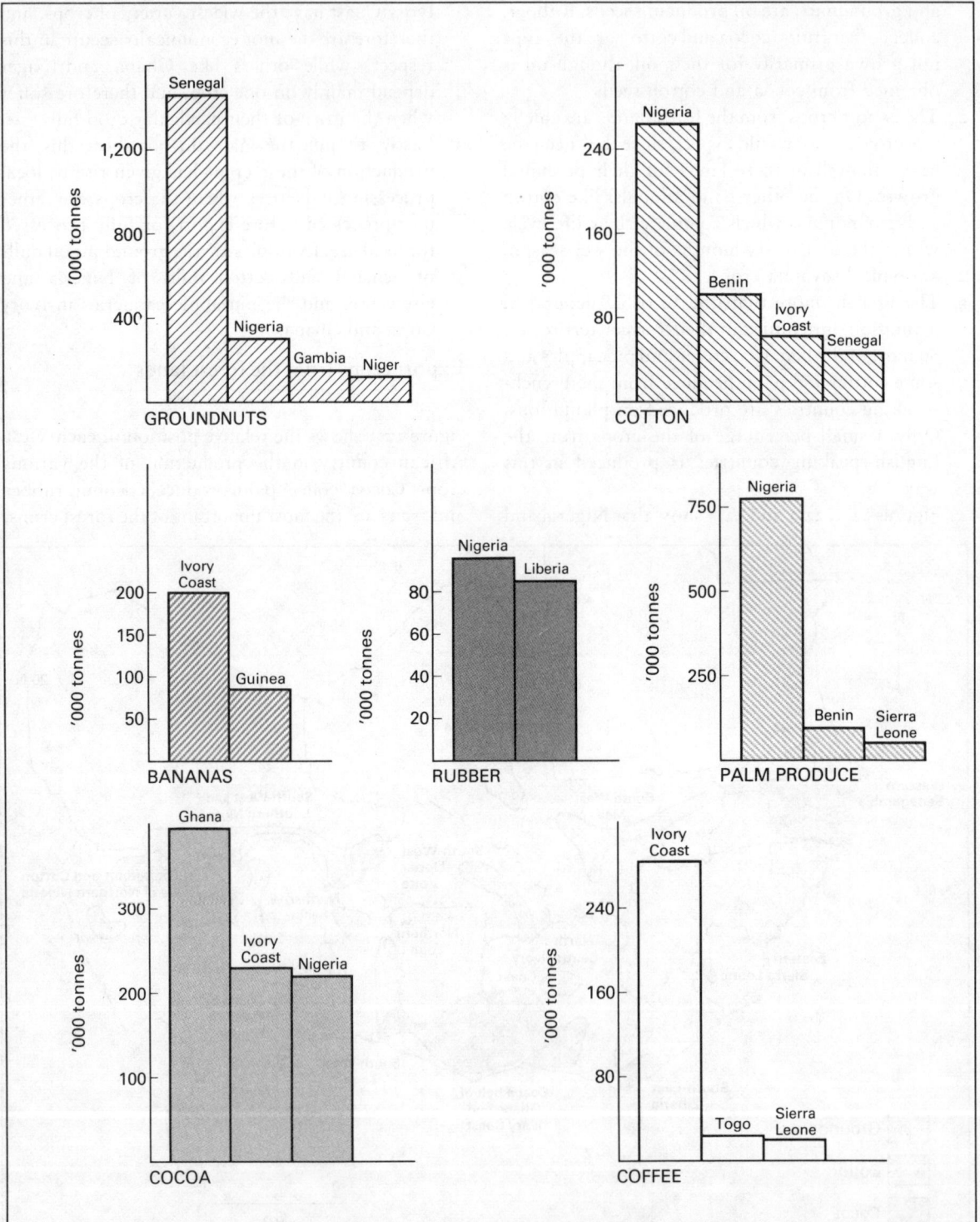

22.3 Production of chief export crops by leading countries in West Africa (mid 1970–80 decade). This diagram enables you to see at a glance the chief producers of various export crops in West Africa. For each crop name the leading countries of production in order. See how Nigeria, Ivory Coast, Ghana and Senegal dominate all the other countries. For each crop, estimate the annual production by the leading country.

Cocoa

This crop was probably introduced to West Africa from South America, but West Africa has now grown to be the largest producing and exporting region in the world. The crop was brought to Nigeria via Fernando Po in 1874, and to Ghana (then Gold Coast) in 1879. Today the cocoa belt of Ghana produces some 40% of West Africa's cocoa, Ivory Coast some 25% and Nigeria 20%. Sierra Leone, Liberia and the off-shore islands are other notable West Africa producers, which with others account for the balance of 15%.

The conditions prevailing in these areas have made the production of the crop feasible and economically profitable. For instance, consider the following advantages of the region.
1. The undulating surface ensures easy drainage.
2. The deep clay, containing some loam, found in most of the areas retains enough moisture for the plant to grow successfully.
3. The rainfall of 1250 mm to 2000 mm per annum and the high humidities of the forest belt supply the required moisture; while the very brief but dry harmattan provides ideal conditions for harvesting and drying.
4. The high, but even, temperatures, oscillating within a narrow range ensure steady plant growth all the year round.
5. The forest trees protect the cocoa plants from the direct and harmful rays of the sun while they are young, and the pods from being blown down prematurely while the trees are bearing fruit.

Now revise the way in which Mr Kyeame, the chief cocoa farmer in Mampong, Ghana, grows his crop and the problems he faces (chapter 10). Compare his methods with those of the Yoruba cocoa farmer described in Chapter 7.

Lagos, Tema, Takoradi, Abidjan, Monrovia and Freetown are the chief cocoa ports of West Africa.

Coffee

Coffee is another beverage. The original home of the *Arabica* variety seems to be Ethiopia, but some people trace it back to Arabia. The *Liberica* variety, however, is a native of West Africa, but much of the crop grown now in this region is the *Robusta* variety. Brazil in South America is however the world's largest producer and exporter of this crop. Ivory Coast has recently become Africa's leading producer and the world's third largest exporter.

We saw earlier that in West Africa the crop is chiefly grown for export in the French speaking countries, and why this is so. Thus southern Ivory Coast, Togo and south-eastern Guinea are the principal areas of production. However, the yield from south-eastern Sierra Leone and the off-shore islands is also important.

Practically the same physical conditions that are necessary for the growth of cocoa are also needed by coffee. But in addition:
1. Coffee grows well on hill slopes which provide immediate drainage for the rainfall. That is why the favoured sites for its cultivation are the slopes of the Man mountains in Ivory Coast, the Guinea highlands in Guinea and Sierra Leone, the Akwapim-Togo ranges in Togo and Ghana and the middle slopes of the off-shore islands.
2. Coffee can tolerate slightly lower temperatures than cocoa, and the mist which is common at high altitudes is particularly helpful to its growth.

When cultivated, the plant is kept down to the desired height by pruning. It bears fruits called berries, which are plucked when ripe; the seeds are extracted, dried, roasted and either packed for export or ground in local mills for local use and export.

Palm produce

Palm produce comes from perhaps the most widespread tree in the forest belt. It is a native of West Africa, and red palm oil and kernels are extracted from it.

Study its distribution in Figure 22.1, and compare it with the areas of high forest in Figures 3.1, 3.5 and 3.3, which show the temperature and rainfall distribution of West Africa. Then it will be clear why the palm belt is identified with areas where:
i) temperatures are high and over 25°C
ii) rainfall is not less than 1500 mm per annum and spread over at least eight months of the year;
iii) there is a period of brilliant sunshine which is necessary for the fruits to ripen, and
iv) the soil is deep and of the forest type.

Again, these conditions are similar to those for the growth of its forest neighbour, cocoa, except that shade is imperative for cocoa but not for the oil palm.

Also palm trees, unlike cocoa, can tolerate acid soils.

Look through the relevant section in Chapter 7 again to see how the crop is grown in the palm belt of Nigeria. The Republic of Benin is the largest producer of all French-speaking West African countries.

Both the red oil and the kernel used to be exported; now the kernel forms the major export item. It is used in making high quality soap and edible fats. Local consumption, either as food or in the soap and margarine factories, is considerable, and so trade in this commodity can thrive even when exports are minimal.

Coconuts

Coconuts are the fruits of the coconut palm which grows mainly on the coastal beaches, partly because their fruits are usually dispersed by ocean currents, but mostly because they like sandy soils and sea breezes. West Africa is not a major world producer of this crop, but its growth is consciously encouraged in order to increase the range of export crops.

The dried nuts are called copra, and this is the form in which the crop is exported.

Rubber

Some varieties of rubber are natives of the Amazon forest. A number, however, grow widely in the forest areas of West Africa

The crop grows well under tropical forest conditions. Production in West Africa started with wild rubber, but since the 1920's, plantation rubber has been growing in popularity. The Firestone Company of America started the first successful plantations in Liberia. Other companies followed suit, including the Dunlop Rubber Company which started large estates in Nigeria. Nigeria and Liberia are the leading rubber producers in West Africa, and indeed in Africa.

Read again the accounts of rubber production in Nigeria and Liberia in chapters 7 and 13. Name some of the rubber products you know.

i)   Now fill in your first map with the contents of Figure 22.1. Note carefully and fill in the areas in each country where each crop is produced.
ii) Name the areas where each crop is produced.
iii) Which countries in West Africa have the widest varieties of export crops?

Export crops from the savanna lands

Cotton and groundnuts are top of this list. Others, like gum arabic, beniseed, and soya beans are of lesser importance. Hides and skins are the principal animal export items.

Cotton

Cotton is known to have been cultivated in West Africa even before the time of the Portuguese, though later introductions, like the 'Meko' and 'Ishan' types from Asia and the new 'Allen' breed of American origin, are of much better quality than the original varieties. Cotton does well in the savanna lands, but Figure 22.2 shows that it is commonest in northern Nigeria, northern Benin, northern Ivory Coast and central Mali in the inland delta region. It grows best in these areas because:

1. They have an annual rainfall of 625 mm to 1250 mm concentrated in the growing season of six months, or possibilities of irrigation where rainfall is insufficient.
2. They have high temperatures (over 21°C) and brilliant sunshine which help the cotton bolls to ripen and break, and a dry season in which the cotton can be harvested.
3. In most of the areas, the soil is clay, containing loam, a type that retains moisture easily.
4. Great care is given to seed selection, breeding and experimentation in research stations in the cotton belts, and to spreading the results to the farmers. The Samaru Agricultural Research Station in Zaria, Nigeria, and the 'Office du Niger' in Mali have done much in this respect.

Now read again how the crop is produced and sold in northern Nigeria and Mali. Remember that local textile mills have recently grown up in the countries of production both inside and outside the main cotton growing areas, and a large proportion of the crop is sent to these factories for the manufacture of local cloth.

Groundnuts

This crop is harvested from very low creeping plants which are even more widely cultivated than cotton. But Figure 22.2 shows clearly the three areas where the crop is most heavily concentrated. These are northern Nigeria, southern Niger, and the heart of West Africa stretching from Upper Volta through central Mali to Senegambia. See how these zones lie roughly between latitudes 8° and 15° north, and generally north of the cotton belts.

You will remember that these areas have:
i) dry conditions – even drier than in the cotton areas since they record only 500 to 1000 mm of rainfall annually;
ii) a growing season of about four months followed by a long dry season when the groundnuts can be harvested, shelled, bagged and stored in the open;
iii) loose, sandy soils which are good for the crop since it grows underground, and harvesting involves pulling the fruits from the ground, and
iv) wide open plains which make cultivation easy.

Apart from these purely geographical factors, a number of economic factors have encouraged the production of groundnuts in these areas.
i) The increased demand for vegetable fats in Europe after the first world war gave a boost to production;
ii) the extension of roads and railways in these areas have provided outlets for the harvested crops; and
iii) closeness to European markets has given Senegal a lead over Nigeria in export production. In the same way it has given West Africa an advantage over other producers farther afield.

However, the drought of 1972–74 did much to reduce the quantities grown both of this crop and of other savanna crops.

The crop is sown about June, and often cultivated in rotation with grains. It is harvested about October, shelled, put in sacks and stacked in pyramids to await the journey to the coast or to groundnut oil mills.

Much of the Nigerian crop is exported to Britain in this shelled form or used in local manufacture of poultry feed, but, as we saw in chapter 16, large quantities of the crop in Senegal are processed into groundnut oil and exported to France via Dakar. Groundnut oil is a popular cooking fat in France. Exports from Senegal include groundnut oil cake.

Other crops

The other crops from the savanna lands – for example, gum arabic and beniseed – are important,

not so much for the absolute quantities exported as for the fact that, like coconuts, they help to diversify the export crops in the countries where they are raised. This helps to prevent the danger of over-dependence on the production of a single crop (monoculture) to which countries like Ghana, and Niger are exposed.

Hides and skins

The term 'hides' is most frequently use to describe the skins of cattle, while other animals are usually said to have just 'skins'. Large quantities of these are produced in the livestock belt. For many centuries, West African animal skins have been traded across the Sahara via North Africa to Europe where they have been named 'Morocco leather' simply because they come through Morocco, though they are actually a West African product. Today, trade across the Atlantic with Europe has grown considerably larger than that across the Sahara.

More factors in the distribution of agricultural products

In the above discussion we stressed the geographical, ecological and economic factors which encourage or limit the distribution of agricultural products. There are also other less obvious but equally important factors:

1. *Historical factors* play a part. Crops like cocoa, cassava and maize, a number of fruits and some varieties of cotton are not natives of West Africa. They were introduced to the region at a definite point in history. If they had not been brought in from abroad it is possible that they would never have been cultivated in the region. Palm production in Nigeria received an impetus during the early 1940's when the second world war made it impossible for Western Europe to obtain this commodity from Indonesia. It is also a fact of history that Firestone and Dunlop decided to locate their rubber plantations in Liberia and Nigeria respectively instead of in Guinea or Sierra Leone which equally have tropical conditions.

2. *Human factors* are also relevant. The Tiv population of the Benue Valley chose to cultivate the beniseed when they wanted to have a crop they

could sell for cash. On the other hand, the nomadic Fulani people would not give up cattle rearing, which is the basis of their way of life, for settled farming. Traditionally in some communities cattle used to be regarded as an index of wealth. So the raising of a crop or rearing of animal is often connected with the culture of the people.

3. *Government policy* can sometimes be decisive. Ivory Coast and Guinea cannot be the only places in West Africa where bananas can grow well, nor should the French-speaking countries necessarily be the most suitable for coffee production. The French, unlike the British, are great coffee drinkers, and lovers of the small-fingered Chinese bananas. So in colonial times they deliberately pursued a policy which encouraged the growing of these two crops in their territories. The French government has now gone in West Africa but the result of its policy still remains.

These three factors support the view raised in chapter 20, that environment is not the final deciding factor of human activities. Man makes his choice and takes his decisions.

Now use your second map, and fill in the export crops from the savanna lands as shown in Figure 22.2. Study your two maps, read through the chapter again and then do the following exercises.

Revision exercises

1. a) On a map of West Africa show by distinctive marks the areas where the following are produced:
   i)   Groundnuts   ii) Cocoa
   iii) Cattle   iv) Rubber.
   b) Describe how each of the commodities is produced and used.
2. Describe and account for recent trends in the production and export of cotton and palm produce in West Africa.

23 Extractive, power producing and manufacturing industries

Preparation

1. Name the minerals and forest products of your own country.
2. Copy and complete the table below for Nigeria, Ghana, Ivory Coast, Senegal and Mali, making use of the information given in the relevant sections of part two of this book.

Country	Major Manufacturing towns	One or more industries in each town

Five industries will be reviewed in this chapter – fishing, the collection of forest products, mining, power production and manufacturing. The first three are called extractive industries because they involve the extraction of nature's reserves.

Fishing

Fishing is very vital to the well-being of West Africans. Apart from the fact that it provides occupation to those who engage in it and to those who make the fishing gadgets and sell the produce, fish is a major source of food and protein to West Africans. Fish, whether fresh, frozen, smoked dry or salted forms an important item of internal trade among West Africans. Besides, much of it is also exported, particularly from Mauritania and Senegal.

The major fishing grounds in West Africa are the rivers, lakes, lagoons, creeks, deltas, rias and the open sea. The most important countries for open sea and coastal fishing are Mauritania, Senegambia, Sierra Leone, Ivory Coast, Ghana and Nigeria, while Mali, Nigeria and Ghana excel in river and inland fishing.

Inland fishing in Central Mali is carried on along the River Niger by the Bozo fishermen. Mopti is on this river and much of the fish caught by the Bozo is smoked here and sold to other parts of the country. In Nigeria, inland fishing is carried on principally along the Niger and Benue Rivers (but indeed along other rivers) and on Lake Chad. Both lines and nets are used and the local people use dug-out canoes. The traditional boat used by the Kanuri fishermen on Lake Chad is made from the tall papyrus reeds which grow along the shores of the lake. (See colour photographs.) Dried 'mangala' fish is traded from the north to other parts of the country. The artificial lakes behind hydro-electric dams in Kainji (Nigeria) Volta (Ghana) and Kossou (Ivory Coast) have now constituted important inland fishing grounds.

The calm waters of the coastal lagoons, deltas and rias form convenient places for fish to live and breed, and therefore offer opportunities for *lagoon and creek fishing*. The rias of Sierra Leone, The Gambia and the Guineas, the lagoons of Ivory Coast, Benin and Nigeria and the delta creeks of the River Niger are famous fishing grounds. Wicker traps and nets are used by the Ijaw and Sobo fishermen of the Niger Delta. Several tonnes of fish are caught annually in these areas, eaten locally or traded inland.

Open sea fishing is perhaps the most commercialised. Though the continental shelf, which favours open sea fishing, is narrow around West Africa (as indeed all over Africa), the waters are warm and the most important grounds occur where the warm waters meet the cold waters. Thus the major open sea fishing grounds of West Africa are found in two places:

i) The Mauritanian and Senegalese waters extending as far south as Dakar where the cold Canary Current meets the warm tropical seas, and

ii) the Gulf of Guinea, off the coasts of Nigeria, Togo, Benin and Ghana at the northern reaches of the cold Benguella Current and where the upwelling cold waters of the Ghana Coast meet with the warm waters.

The first area is largely fished by Japanese, Russian, French, Swedish, Portuguese and Spanish fishermen, who use large fleets of deep sea trawlers. Formerly they fished almost free here, but now they have to obtain permission to do so along the now extended territorial waters. The catches are landed principally in Nouadhibou and Dakar where large cold stores have been built for handling them.

The second area off Ghanaian, Togolese, Beninian and Nigerian coasts is fished principally by nationals especially the Fante fishermen of Ghana. Many use canoes, formerly paddled, but now powered with outboard engines. They go out at night using lights which also attract the fish, and come back the following morning with their boats full of fish! Trawlers have recently been introduced. Monrovia, Abidjan, Tema and Lagos have special harbours for landing fish, and large cold stores where the fish is stored and frozen or canned.

Some of the fish from West Africa is exported. Surprisingly however, the region imports fish! This is so because those countries which import fish do not produce enough for their needs, and for those countries which import as well as export, they sell in order to get foreign reserves, but buy the varieties which they do not produce.

Now do these exercises:

1. Draw a map of West Africa and locate in it the fishing grounds and ports mentioned in this section, using different colours and shadings for the three different types of fishing grounds.
2. Name the fishing grounds and ports you have located.
3. How is the occupation carried out in these places?
4. Why is fishing important to West Africans?
5. Why is it necessary to further develop this occupation and how do you think this can be done?

Collection of forest products

The forest areas, including the guinea savanna, yield a variety of other products apart from the agricultural products dealt with in the last two chapters. They include timber, firewood, charcoal, building materials, dyestuffs, gums and fibres, but the most valuable of them all is timber.

The high forest belt (Figure 5.1) is the chief potential timber producing area. But, as Figure 23.1 shows, Ivory Coast, Ghana and Nigeria are the principal producing countries. Recall what we said of the species found in each country, the methods of extraction used, the transportation of the timber and the uses to which it is put. Abidjan, Takoradi and Sapele are easily the premier timber ports of West Africa.

The chief problems of timber production in West Africa are the remoteness and scattered nature of the economic species, and the depletion of the reserves caused mainly by clearing for cultivation and reckless cutting. Remedial measures for the latter problem are, however, being taken; these include controlled cutting and the systematic replanting of trees.

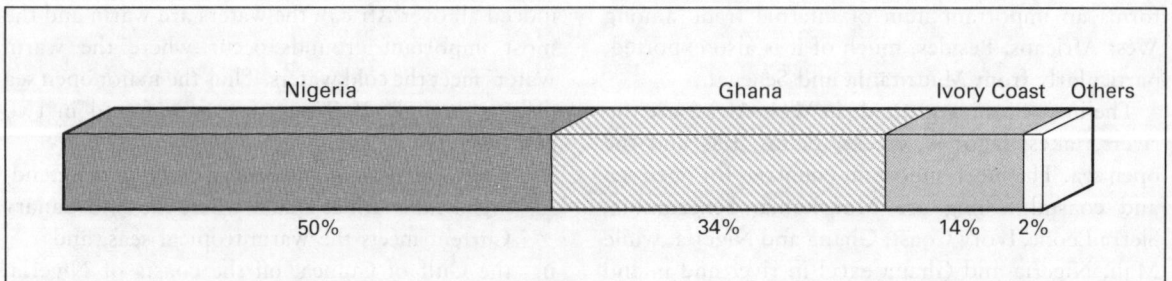

Nigeria	Ghana	Ivory Coast	Others
50%	34%	14%	2%

23.1 Timber production in West Africa (based on mid 1970–80 figures). Can you recall what areas in the three countries above produce timber? How is the timber extracted? Name the uses to which the timber is put.

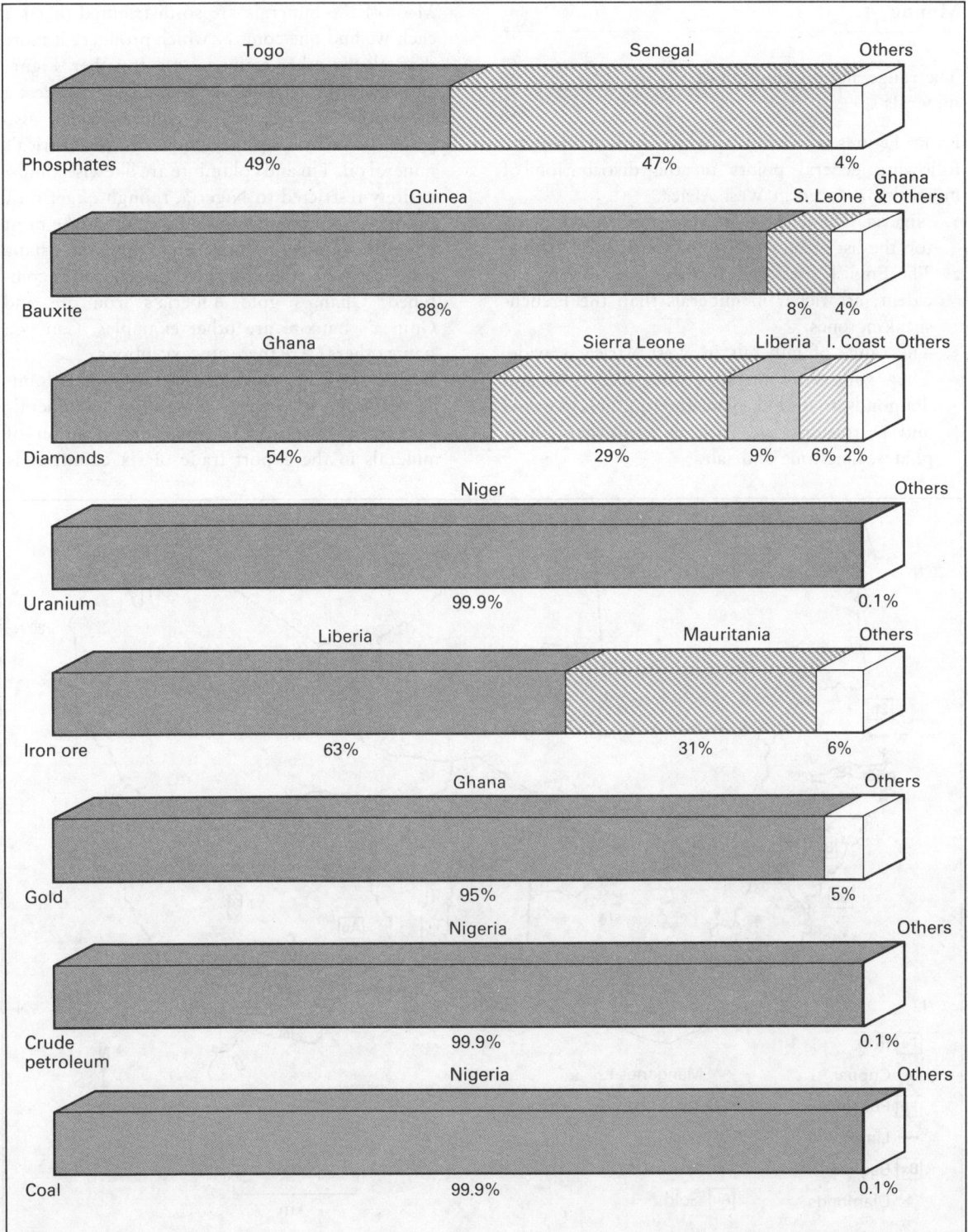

23.2 Production of key minerals in West Africa. West Africa = 100%. Percentages represent mid 1970–80 decade production. For each mineral name the country which produces most of it. What % of West Africa's production does that represent? Name the countries which are richest in minerals.

Mining

The range and distribution of minerals

From Figures 23.2 and 23.3 we can deduce the following general points on the distribution of minerals produced in West Africa.

1. Nigeria, Ghana, Liberia, Mauritania and Guinea top the list of mineral producers in West Africa.
2. The English-speaking countries, possibly by accident, are richer in minerals than the French-speaking ones.
3. The range of minerals in West Africa is wide. They vary from precious ones like gold and diamonds, to ores like iron and tin, fuels like coal and petroleum, and rock minerals like phosphates, limestone and salt.

4. Most of the minerals are so distributed that for each we find one country which produces it more than all the other countries put together. Figure 23.2 brings this out clearly. Thus, coal is almost a monopoly of Nigeria – a country which also produces practically the whole of West Africa's mineral oil. Tin and columbite are likewise almost entirely restricted to Nigeria, though Niger now produces some tin. Diamond is perhaps the most widespread mineral, but, even in this case, Ghana produces more than all the other countries combined. Ghana's gold, Liberia's iron ore and Guinea's bauxite are other examples. Can you name others? Are there any exceptions?
5. Whereas 25 years ago, agricultural produce dominated West Africa's export trade, today minerals have taken the upper hand. The position of minerals in the export trade of six countries is

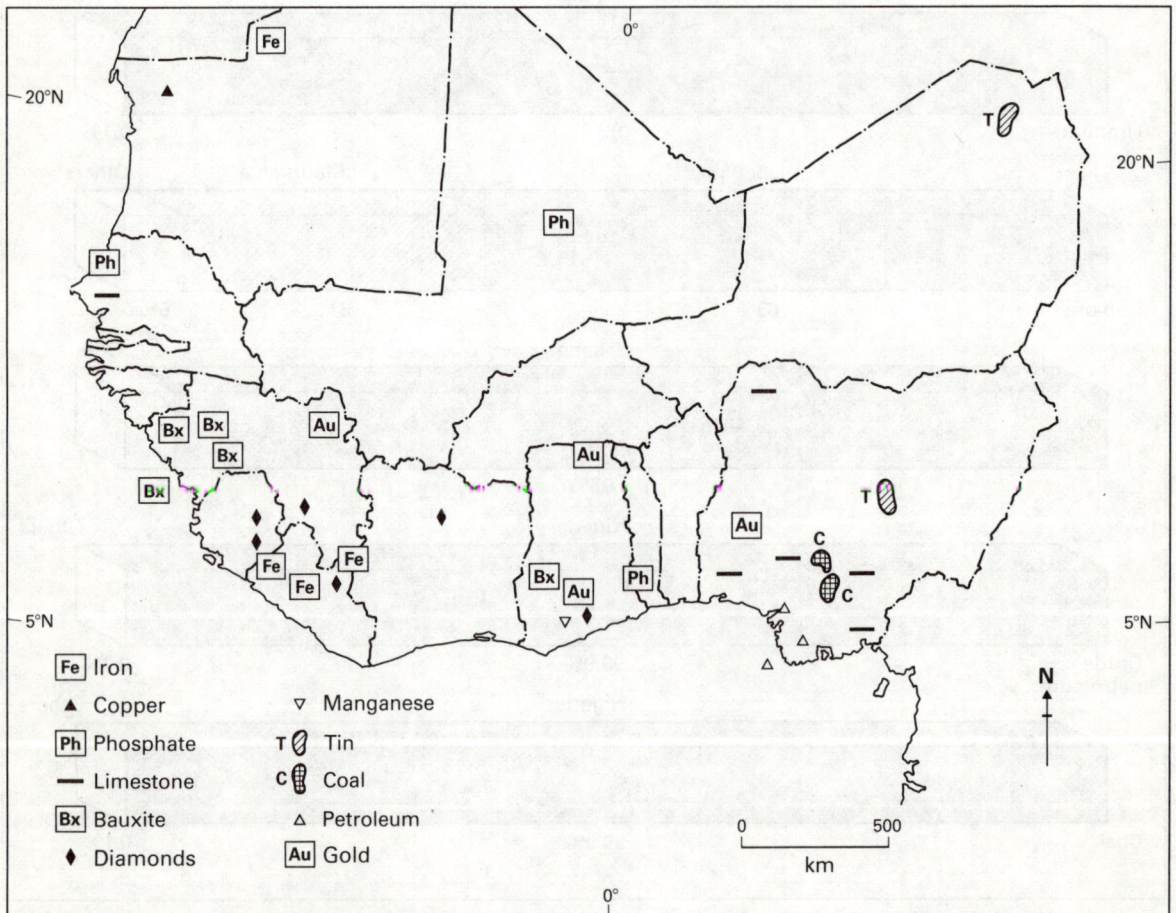

23.3 Distribution of chief minerals in West Africa.

seen in Figure 23.4. Put together, the export revenue derived from minerals in all the countries of West Africa is more than three times the revenue derived from all the other export commodities combined.

6. However, while more minerals are being located and mining areas extended; (example: the uranium deposits of Niger and the iron ore reserves in the Nimba Massif of Guinea); others, like the petroleum deposits of Nigeria, have very uncertain future, while the production of some has been completely abandoned, like the iron ore mining of Marampa (Sierra Leone) and Kaloum (Guinea), and the rutile production of Sierra Leone. Thus the mineral map of West Africa is constantly changing.

Prospecting for minerals

Two vital points need to be made on mineral prospecting in West Africa.

1. Looking for minerals and starting the production are difficult and time-consuming operations, particularly in the desert and swamp areas of West Africa. For example, oil prospecting in Nigeria started in 1937, but it was nearly 20 years before the first producing well was struck at Oloibiri in the delta region.

2. Large-scale mining is expensive, both in capital and in skilled personnel. That is one reason why mineral exploitation in West Africa has been undertaken by foreign companies who can afford these requirements or negotiate for them more easily. National governments are however taking part in the mining operations.

Mining methods

The mining methods used in West Africa compare favourably with those used in advanced countries, as they are highly mechanised. The methods used depend on where and how the minerals are located.

1. When found with sands at the beds of rivers as in the case of alluvial diamonds in Ghana, the deposits are *dredged*, the sands washed away and the precious minerals remain. This method is sometimes called *placer mining*.

2. Where the mineral is near the surface, and only covered by a layer of rocks called over-burden,

this over-burden is removed, the rock minerals blasted with dynamite and the pieces collected with huge mechanized shovels. It is then transported to where it will be further crushed and processed. This method is called *open cast mining*. As you would recall, this is the method used in the tin fields of Jos (Nigeria), limestone quarries and iron ore mines all over West Africa, manganese mines at Nsuta (Ghana), phosphate locations at Taiba (Senegal) and near Palimé (Togo), and finally the large-scale bauxite mines of Guinea and Sierra Leone.

3. When the minerals appear as out-crops at the sides of valleys, horizontal or near horizontal mines called adits are dug to recover the minerals as is done in the coal field of Enugu (Nigeria). This method is called *adit mining*.

4. Shafts, either inclined or vertical, are dug where the mineral is buried very deep underground. This is called *shaft mining*, and it is the method used in the Tarkwa Told fields of Ghana.

5. Finally, mineral oil is mined by a special method called *drilling*. Special drilling gear is used. The gear is made up of a drilling bit fixed to an end of a long pipe and mounted on a huge metal framework called a derrick.

Now turn back to the pages where photographs of some of the mining methods are shown. Identify them and describe what is being done in each case.

A sample mineral – iron ore

We will use iron ore as an example to show you how to describe the distribution and production of minerals in West Africa with the help of the material in part two and in Figures 23.2 and 23.3 above.

Iron ore, like gold and a few other minerals, was worked in West Africa even in the middle ages. Until recently, Sierra Leone was the greatest producer and Guinea also produced appreciable quantities. But both countries have now ceased to produce because they were finding it uneconomical to continue. Today Liberia is the greatest producer and Mauritania comes second. Further reserves not yet developed occur in Nigeria, the Nimba Massif of Guinea and the Sula Mountains of Sierra Leone. These are areas where future production is likely to commence. The total West African output stands at about 40 million tonnes per annum, or 10% of the world's production.

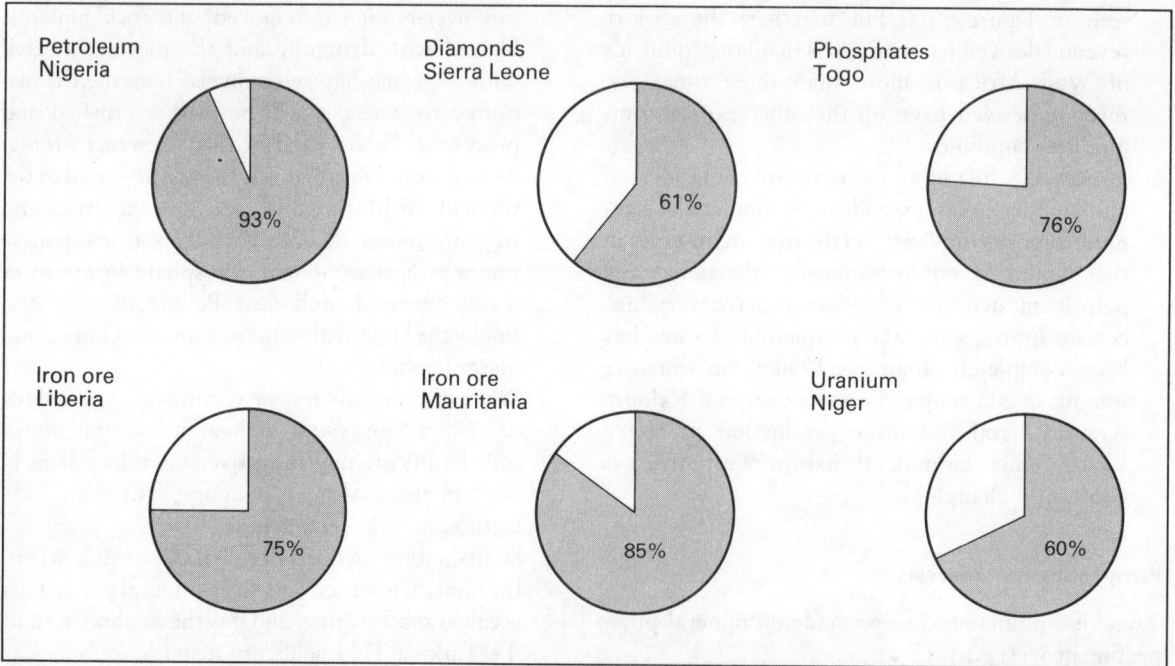

23.4 The position of minerals in the export trade of selected West African countries.

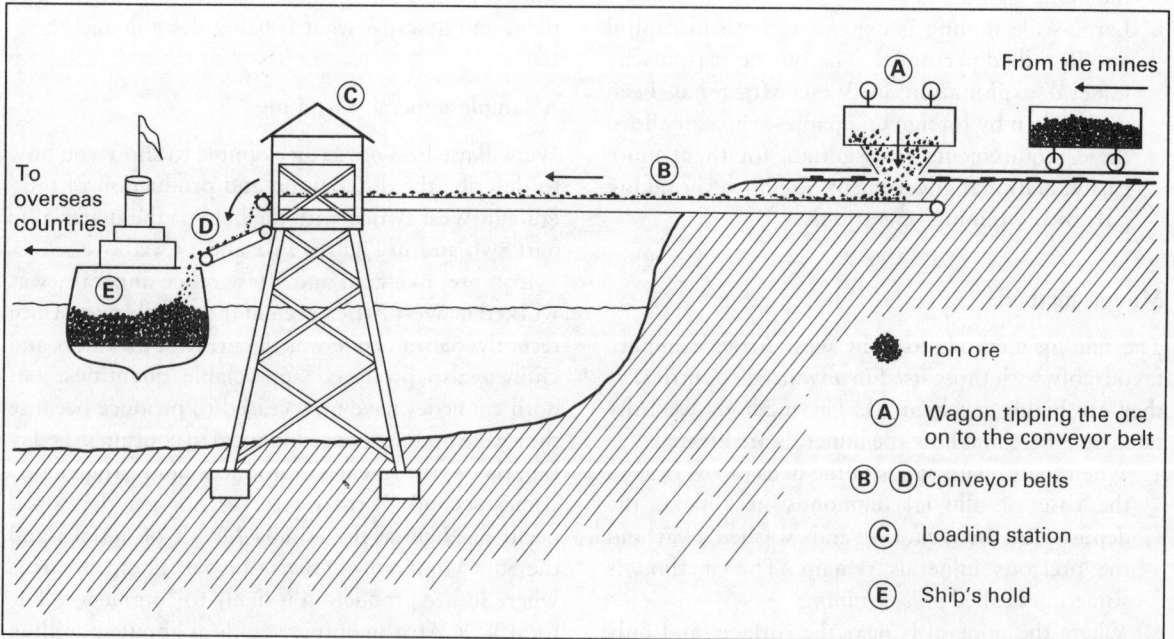

23.5 Loading iron ore at a typical West African port of export.

Liberia's yearly output of 25 million tonnes comes from five fields – the Bomi, Mano River, Mount Nimba, Bong and Bie Hills fields all opened between 1951 and 1968. The ports of export – Monrovia and Buchanan – are linked by rail to the fields. Western Germany, U.S.A. and Britain take most of the export.

Mauritania's annual contribution of 12.5 million tonnes to the West African production is derived mostly from the F'derik field which was opened in 1963. Though in the heart of the desert, it is connected by rail to Nouadhibou from where it is shipped overseas, principally to France.

In all the fields the ore is mined from the surface by open cast method. Most fields have local plants for removing the rock waste from the ore, but the ore content varies from field to field. Liberia's high grade deposits at Nimba have a 65%–75% ore content; Bomi deposits have 53%–65% and others, fall in between these limits.

Iron ore has not only stimulated the growth of railways in the countries where it is produced, it has also opened up employment opportunities, brought in more revenue and generally improved their economies. In Liberia and Mauritania where it contributes between 75% and 85% of the value of exports, it has been chiefly responsible for changing their trade balances from a deficit to a surplus.

Now study the other major minerals of West Africa shown in Figure 23.3, following as far as possible the way iron ore has been dealt with above. Then do the following:
i) Name the three most important timber producing countries in West Africa.
ii) Name the main fishing grounds in West Africa.
iii) Describe the mining methods used in West Africa.
iv) Which countries are the largest producers of the following:
   a) mineral oil,   b) iron ore,
   c) bauxite,   d) phosphates and
   e) gold?

Power production

There are four major sources of power in West Africa – coal, petroleum, water and uranium. Coal and petroleum are used in the generation of *thermal electricity*, water is a source of *hydro-electricity*, while uranium is a source of *nuclear energy*.

Nigeria is the only coal producing country.

Production is falling but the mining is being mechanised and more markets are being sought.

Though finds have been located elsewhere, Nigeria is yet the only country in West Africa which produces petroleum. It is not surprising therefore that the country has two refineries, with a third one soon to be commissioned. However, other West Africa countries realizing the importance of refined fuel, have located oil refineries within their borders.

The following table summarises the location and capacity of each refinery in terms of barrels of crude oil it can handle a day.

Table 5

S/No.	Refinery location	Country	Capacity in b/d
1.	Port Harcourt	Nigeria	60 000
2.	Warri	Nigeria	100 000
3.	Kaduna	Nigeria	100 000
4.	Lomé	Togo	20 000
5.	Tema	Ghana	28 000
6.	Abidjan	Ivory Coast	43 000
7.	Monrovia	Liberia	15 000
8.	Freetown	Sierra Leone	10 000
9.	Dakar	Senegal	15 000

The Dakar, Freetown, Monrovia, Abidjan, Tema and Lomé refineries use imported crude, and therefore have to be sited at the coast where the crude can be received at no extra cost. Except for Tema these coastal locations are also capitals of the individual countries and all are centres of dense population and economic activity. Port Harcourt and Warri refineries are located right in the mineral oil producing areas of Nigeria and can therefore receive piped oil straight from the fields.

The Kaduna refinery seems to be the odd one out. It is near an important centre of population and economic activity in Nigeria alright, but the rather distant location from the crude oil source seems to be a government decision to decentralize the refineries in the country and place one in the north.

Hydro-electricity is the other form of power produced in West Africa. Simply described, it is electricity produced from running water. Thus water is made to fall on large turbines, and on turning the turbines they operate generators which produce the electricity. Rivers are dammed to produce enough

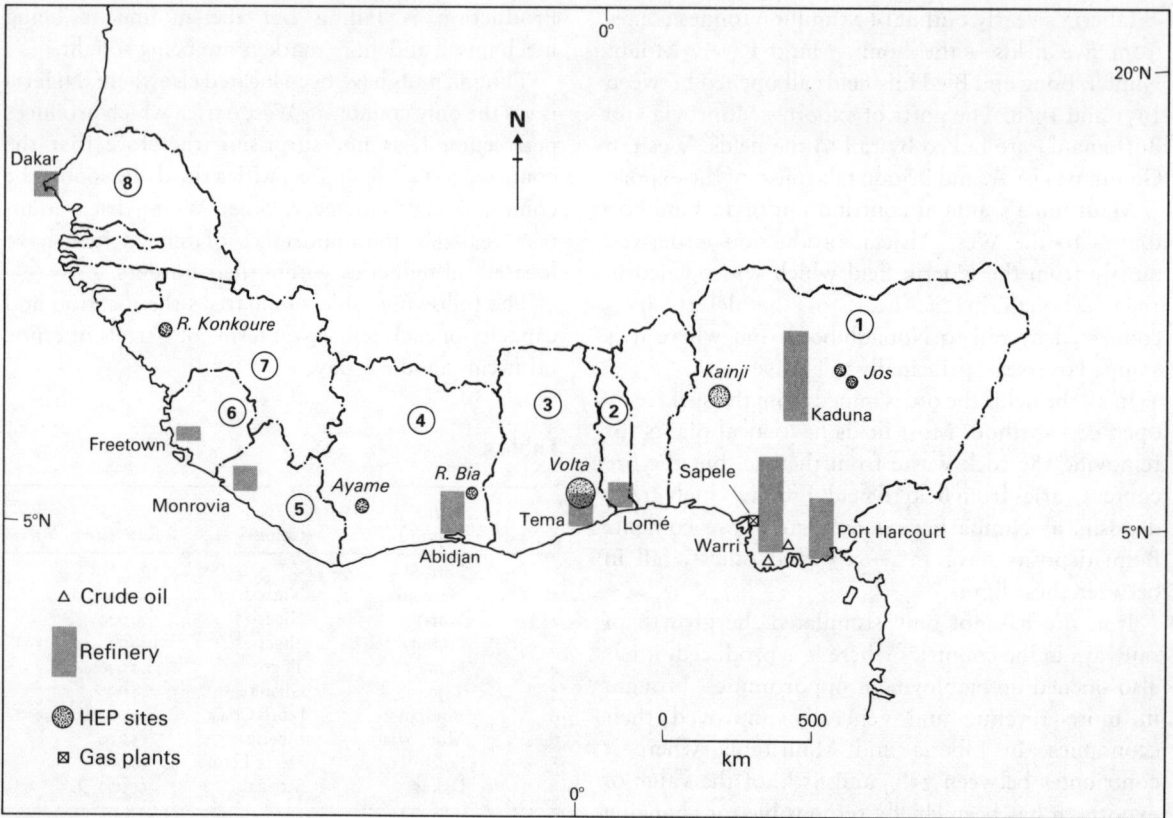

23.6 West Africa – Distribution of water and petroleum power sources.

'head' of water to turn the turbines strong and fast enough, and the Volta Dam in Ghana and Kainji in Nigeria are the largest in West Africa. Read once more the detailed description of them in Chapters 8 and 11. Figure 23.6 locates other known important hydro-electricity schemes in West Africa. Name them. How is the power from each of them utilized?

Whereas the three sources of power discussed above are tapped in producing power locally in West Africa, *uranium* is exported to support the nuclear energy programmes of foreign countries. The whole of West Africa's production comes from the two mines around Airlit in Niger which together will be producing, by 1980, some 4000 tonnes of uranium ore per annum.

As Niger has no sea port the ore is exported through Lagos, principally to France and the United States. It is likely that when Nigeria develops its nuclear programme, for which it has reached agreement with a Canadian firm, it will import large quantities of the Niger ore, and this will form another area where useful trade can be developed between the two countries.

Manufacturing industries

Local craft industries

The earliest manufacturing industries in West Africa were local craft industries now widely scattered all over the region. They are now admired, not so much for their size or mass production, as for the high artistic value of their products. Internationally famous craft industries are:

i)   the Akwette and Kente weaving industries in Nigeria and Ghana respectively;
ii) the leather and dye works of Kano (Nigeria);
iii) the metal works of Benin and Bida (Nigeria);
iv) the leather and wood carving industries of the Fulas of Futa Jalon in Guinea, and
v)   the gold and silver works of Mali.

Modern industries

There are many ways of classifying the modern manufacturing industries in West Africa. They can be classified according to size or according to type. A new way of classifying them, which will be adopted here, is according to reasons for their growth. Thus:

1. When West Africa started to produce vegetable cash crops, and later minerals, it became necessary to part- or fully- process them before they are exported or, in fact, consumed locally. Thus grew *processing industries* like palm oil or groundnut oil mills, iron ore or mineral oil refineries or bauxite processing plants. Can you recall where these are located?

2. In order to cut down on the importation of certain goods, which could otherwise be easily manufactured locally thus saving on foreign exchange, some countries of West Africa embarked on *import substitution industries*. Examples of such industries are breweries, textile manufactures, soft drink plants and cement factories. Again locate examples of these in West Africa.

3. Some West African countries, because of their special endowment of resources, have embarked on industries which not only serve local needs but produce goods for export. Such *local consumption/export-oriented industries* include power production from the giant Volta and Kainji power plants, the plywood factory at Sapele (Nigeria) and the giant iron and steel industry in Buchanan (Liberia). Why have the countries been able to support these industries? Can you say where the products are exported to? Name other industries in this class.

The table you built up in the preparation exercise for this chapter should reveal the following features on the distribution of industries in West Africa.

1. Many industrial towns in West Africa are situated close to one another, so that the area becomes a modest industrial zone. We can thus distinguish:

   i) the industrial zone of south-eastern Nigeria enclosed by Nkalagu, Onitsha, Port Harcourt and Calabar the towns of Enugu, Aba, Umuahia and others;

   ii) the industrial zone of north-central Nigeria which includes, among others, the towns of Kano, Kaduna, Jos and Zaria.

   iii) the industrial axis of western Nigeria, which links up Lagos, Ikorodu, Ibadan and Abeokuta;

   iv) the industrial zone of mid-western Nigeria, where Warri, Benin and Sapele are the chief towns;

   v) the Accra-Tema-Akosombo industrial complex which obtains power from the Volta Dam for its numerous industries;

   vi) the industrial axis of western Ghana with towns like Takoradi, Kumasi and Samreboi and the mining districts of Tarkwa, Nsuta, Prestea, Obuasi and Dunkwa; and

   vii) the industrial complex of western Senegal, including towns like Dakar, Rufisque, Thiers, Kaolack and their satellites.

2. Some industrial outliers also exist. These include the mining districts of Guinea and Liberia, where the minerals are part-processed, Abidjan in Ivory Coast, Bamako in Mali and Kainji and Ajaokuta in Nigeria to mention the major ones.

Now build up a map similar to Figure 8.1 to show the industrial zones, towns and outliers mentioned above and the railways which serve them. Review the industries associated with each area, paying attention to the types of industries, the factors which account for their location there, the sources of the raw materials and power used, and the types and distribution of the products.

The following may help you to determine the factors which account for their location:

1. Some industries are located where it is easy to obtain the raw materials, particularly if these materials are heavy, bulky and difficult to transport. Such industries are said to be *material oriented*. Many of the mineral, timber and food-processing industries in West Africa belong to this class.

2. Sometimes they are located where there is a market at hand, particularly if the raw materials are not bulky and can easily be taken to the factory site, or where the finished product is bulky and perishable and has to be sold nearby. Such industries are said to be *market oriented*. Examples are textile factories (cotton is light and can be brought down from the producing areas) and factories which make glass, drinks, ice cream or chocolate (these products are either bulky or perishable or both).

3. In cases where the source of the bulk of the raw

materials is overseas it is sometimes found more convenient to locate the industries at the ports through which the materials enter the country, to save the extra cost of transporting them inland. Such ports are called transhipment points. Lagos, Port Harcourt, Tema, Abidjan and Dakar are transhipment points and some of the industries in them are *transhipment point oriented*.

4. Most of the industries (apart from the strictly material oriented ones) are located in or near towns. For here labour, transport services and facilities for banking, insurance and advertising are available. So most of these industries are *labour and services oriented*.

Revision exercise

1. Comment briefly on one of the following:
   a) minerals and mining in West Africa;
   b) manufacturing industries in West Africa.

24 Population – distribution, trends and problems

Preparation

1. Revise what we said about the distribution of population in Nigeria (Chapter 8), Ghana (Chapter 11) and Senegambia (Chapter 16). Note in particular where most people live, where few people live and the reasons given for the uneven distribution.
2. a) Has there been a recent or a current movement of population either away from, or into, your area?
   b) Describe the type of people involved, where they were living before and where they have moved to.
   c) Can you give reasons for the movement?
   d) Has the movement brought about any change in the density of population and the type of people now living in your area?

Population distribution

In the first chapter of this book, we took a bird's-eye-view of the various peoples of West Africa and noted the numbers in each country. In the succeeding chapters we dwelt on various other aspects of the geography of the region, and from the study we learnt enough to suggest to us that the peoples of West Africa are not evenly distributed over the surface of the region. In particular, we noted that in Nigeria, Ghana and Senegambia there are areas of high densities and those of low densities. In this chapter we are going to look at West Africa as a whole, observe the broad pattern of population distribution, account for this pattern, talk on population movements and trends, and end up with a discussion of a few problems of population characteristic of the region.

Our attention is drawn immediately on Figure 24.1 to areas marked (1) to (7) where most people live. Name them. We see that they are arranged in two belts – a northern belt comprising western Senegal, central Upper Volta, north-east Ghana and north-

central Nigeria, and a coastal belt starting also from western Senegal but continuing along the coast to the coastal belt of Sierra Leone, southern Ghana, Togo and Benin, western Nigeria and south-eastern Nigeria.

In between these two, there is a relatively empty middle belt and to the north of the northern belt, there is the arid, desolate and empty Sahara. When we finally add the thinly peopled Niger Delta we complete the broad picture of population distribution in West Africa – two belts of high densities and three of low densities alternating with one another. But why this pattern? Here are some clues:

1. *Favourable physical conditions* in terms of relief, fertile soil, accessibility, congenial climate and availability of water promote population densities in West Africa. On the other hand, where these physical conditions are unfavourable few people live and may even emigrate. Recall the effect of drought discussed in Chapter 20.
2. *Incidence of disease and pests* deplete population thereby reducing the densities.
3. Population distribution in West Africa may be explained by *historical factors*. Wars and slavery reduce the population, while security offered by a strong government encourage the gathering together of people. Population movements in the past (see the section below) leave their mark on the present pattern.
4. *Economic prosperity* encourages population growth. Thus high densities are found in areas where economic crops, industries and dense communication lines exist.
5. Finally, *human inertia* which in West Africa shows itself in traditional attachment to the land, can sometimes retain high densities even when other factors may not be too obvious.

Now read once more the relevant sections dealing with the population distribution in Nigeria, Ghana,

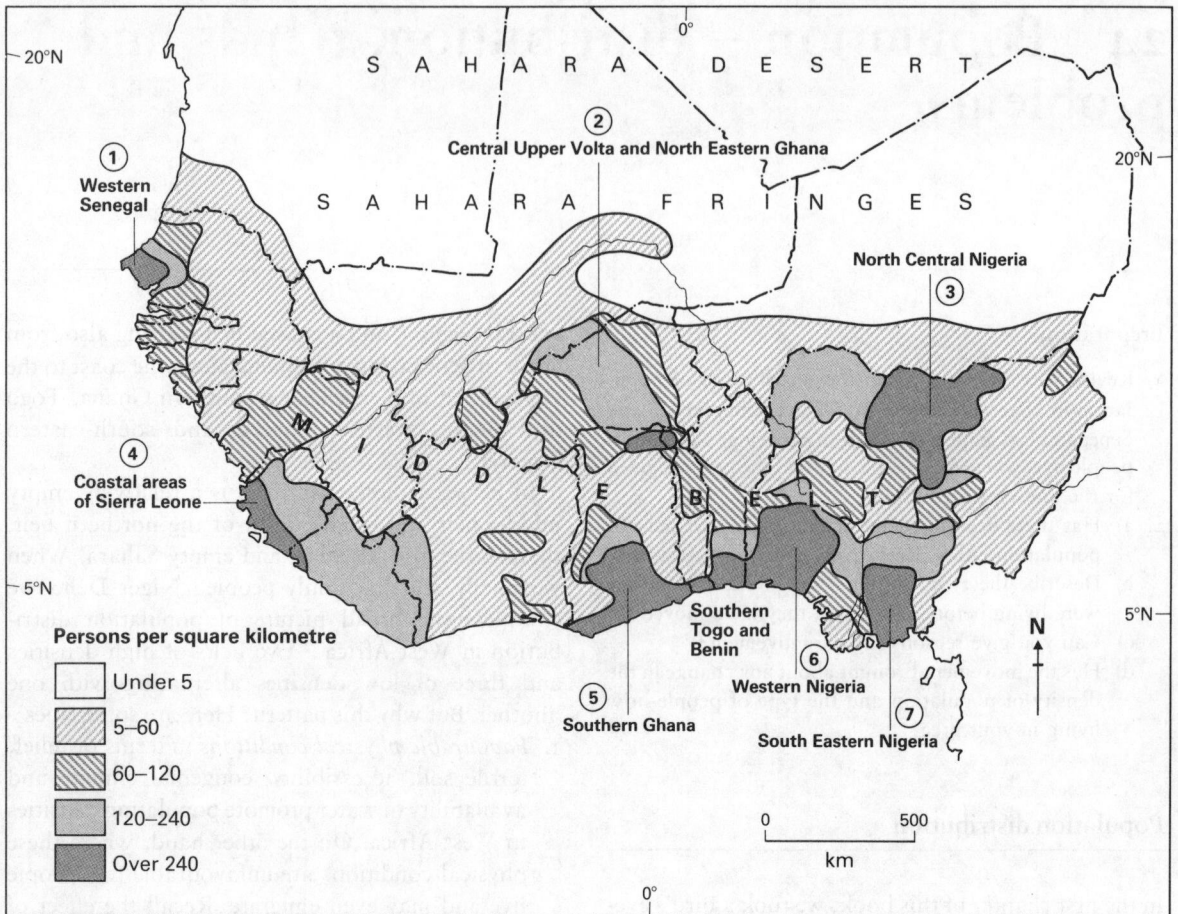

24.1 Population distribution in West Africa.

Upper Volta and Senegambia, the economic geography of West Africa and the section in chapter 20 dealing with drought. You will then be in a position to develop the points outlined above, relating them to conditions in West Africa. Then write a well reasoned account on the population distribution in the region.

Population migration

People are not static as you might have found out from the exercise at the beginning of this chapter. They are always on the move. The greatest drive giving rise to this movement is economic need – a desire for better living conditions, better employment opportunities and higher income. Past movements largely account for the present population picture as described above. In the same way, present and future movements are likely to change this picture in the future. Here we will classify the movement or migration of people according to its scope, that is how far the people have moved away from their places of origin. Thus we have:

i)   local or short-distance migration;
ii) regional migration, and
iii) inter-continental migration.

Local migration

This type involves travelling over short distances, usually a few kilometres, and mostly from a rural area to another rural area with greater economic advantage. It may take one of three forms:

1. The presence of a large town may attract people from rural areas farther afield to rural areas nearer the town so that the people can be near enough to the town where they sell their produce. Thus the Ijaws have moved from their delta home in Nigeria to the creeks and lagoons of rural areas

of Lagos State, and the Binis, Ijebus and Igbiras from the more distant parts of Bendel and the western States also to the rural areas of Lagos State. They have come here to fish and farm and sell their produce to metropolitan Lagos and other nearby cities.

2. Down-hill migration of people in West Africa belongs to this type of population movement. In pre-colonial times, some communities, frequently harrassed by enemies and slave dealers, fled to safer areas of hill-sides and hill-tops. With the restoration of peace they started to come down to the plains where in fact farmlands are more readily available. Down-hill movement from the Futa Jalon plateau in Sierra Leone and from Old Idanre to New Idanre in western Nigeria are examples. Government sometimes induces this migration as in the case of the Shendam Resettlement Scheme in northern Nigeria.

3. Where a major project is being located in an area the people living in the area can be resettled elsewhere to make way for the new project. The classic example is the movement of people away from the areas now flooded as a result of dam construction (e.g. the Volta in Ghana and Kainji in Nigeria). Over 77 000 were resettled in Ghana and 42 000 in Nigeria.

Regional migration

This is wider in scope than the local migration. People here move over longer distances, from one type of economic region to another either within the same country or across international frontiers. We can identify five types:

1. There are well established *labour migrations*, either to plantations, urban areas or mining districts in search of employment. The Malians, for instance, move seasonally to the groundnut fields of Senegal. The plantations of Ivory Coast absorb thousands of them as well as thousands of the Mossi people from Upper Volta annually. Some Mossis too travel to the mining districts of Ghana. Other mining areas of Fria in Guinea and Nimba in Liberia have attracted population from distant districts. Before the evacuation of Nigerians from Fernando Po in 1976, nearly half of the population of that Island was made up of Nigerian immigrant labourers who worked in the

plantations. People from the eastern states of Nigeria and the Ishan Plateau move to the rubber plantations of Bendel State in Nigeria to work as tappers.

2. *Rural-urban migration* of population is a common phenomenon all over West Africa. It is a type of labour migration in the sense that the migrants go to the towns or industrial centres to look for jobs, but different in the sense that it gives rise to peculiar problems which will be discussed later.

3. There is considerable *international traffic of people along the coast* of West Africa, mainly of traders, sailors and fishermen. Such migrants are found along all major coastal cities, or in fishing camps, and often in countries outside their own. The Fantes of Ghana are famous migrant fishermen. The Krumen from Liberia are adept seamen who ply along the coasts of West Africa.

4. Though *pastoral nomadism* is described as a type of farming in chapter 20, it is also a form of regional population migration since it involves the movement of the Fulani herdsmen – livestock, family, belongings and all – with no obvious aim of settling down anywhere.

5. Finally, we have *disaster migrations*. These are short-lived but intensive, and involve the movement of a whole set of people because of a disaster which has occurred in their former place of abode. Disturbances in Nigeria caused such movements of peoples in 1966–70. The mass emigration of people from Fernando Po as a result of the political disturbances there is another case in point. The drought in 1972–74 caused a wholesale emigration of people from the sahelian countries to the more southern countries where conditions were wetter. A few have gone back, but most have remained.

Inter-continental migration

This is movement out of, or into, West Africa itself. Whereas the other movements only change the pattern of population within West Africa, this either subtracts from, or adds to, the overall population, and may change its pattern as well.

1. The largest movement of people out of West Africa in modern history was caused by the *slave trade*. It is estimated that during the 400 dark

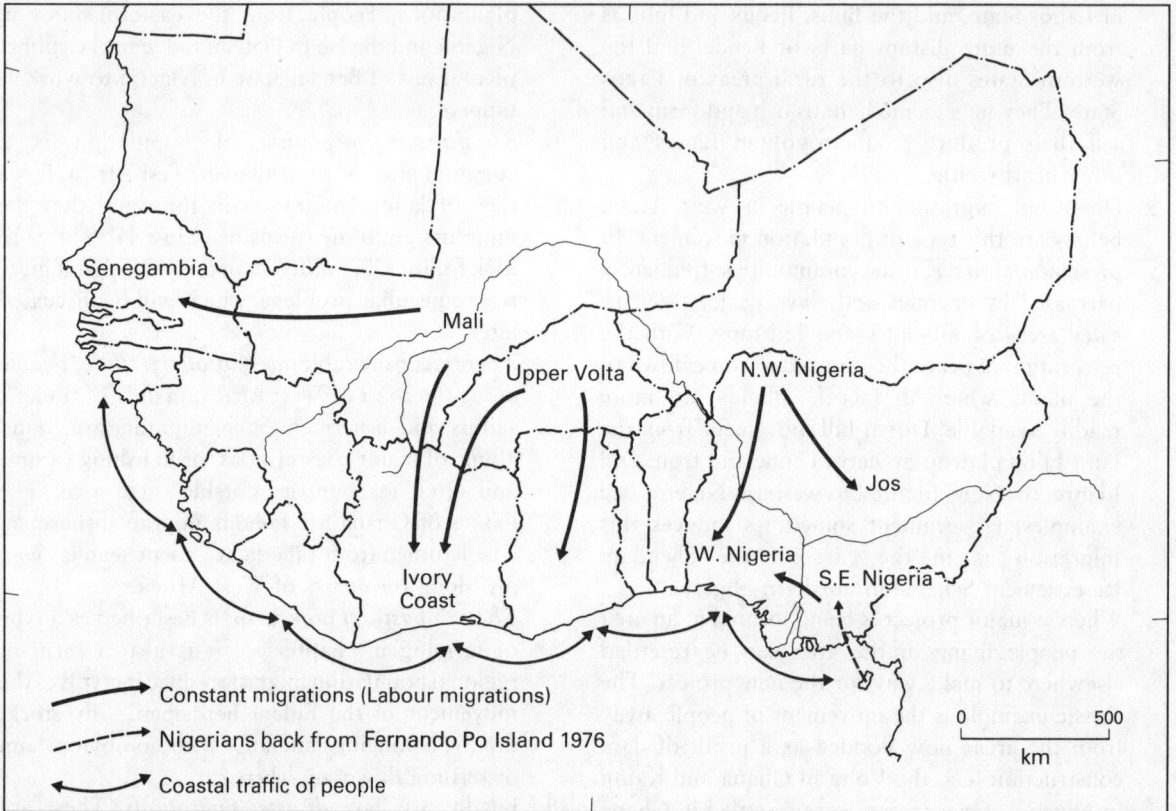

24.2 Regional migration of people of West Africa.

years of this most infamous trade, between the 15th century when the trade started and 1885 when the last slave ship sailed away from Benin Republic, over 20 million people were evacuated from West Africa to the America's and the West Indies. A few descendants of them came back to live in Liberia and Freetown after their liberation, but the bulk remained to constitute the negro population of the new world. It is also on record that the Fulani slave raiders carried an appreciable number across the desert. Their raids helped to depopulate the middle belt of West Africa.

2. There was *immigration of Europeans into West Africa* following the acquisition of the territory by the European powers. The French deliberately encouraged this movement in their former territories. Those who came were administrators, traders, missionaries and even farmers. This trend was virtually halted after independence; in some cases it was reversed. The British administrators left Nigeria and Ghana, while Guineans back-

loaded the French people 'en masse' to their home country.

3. Strangely enough, there is an unnoticed but steady drain of qualified personnel like doctors, engineers and educationists from West Africa to Western Europe and America in recent years. A few leave after they have qualified, and pick up jobs overseas. Some go as students and then stay on after their course of studies. This movement of highly qualified personnel from a less developed to a more developed country is sometimes called a *brain drain*.

4. *Pilgrimage* is another type of intercontinental migration. Many Moslems leave West Africa annually on pilgrimage to Mecca.

5. Finally, although *international tourism* is young in West Africa, there is a noticeable influx of tourists from Scandinavia and Western Europe to the coastal areas of Senegambia on holidays. This movement is seasonal and has the effect of temporarily increasing local populations.

Population trends

In the last section we talked about the movement of people. Here we are going to discuss changes in population. Some of these changes or trends may be brought about by the movement of people.

1. Since the end of the slave era, the population of West Africa has been on the overall increase. Population increases when those who are born plus those who immigrate, are more than those who die plus those who emigrate. The rate of increase is therefore (birth rate + immigration rate) − (death rate + emigration rate). This rate varies with the countries of West Africa, but on the average it lies between 1.6% and 3% and is normally taken as 2.3% per annum approximately. 108 million in 1966, the estimated population was 136.8 million in 1976.

    Now calculate what the population is likely to be in 1986, 1996 and the year 2006.

2. The growth is not even. As a result of the movement of people recorded in the preceding section, urban areas, industrial areas and mining districts show higher increases of generally over 3%, whereas rural areas record only very small increases.

3. Another trend in the population is an increase in proportion of older people to younger people. Many years back, many children were born, but because many also died for lack of medical facilities very few remained to grow to manhood and old age. Now with increased medical care many more children live up to manhood and then to old age. This means that the nations of West Africa will have to plan well for the education of many more young people, their employment after school and care at old age.

Population problems

We will end this chapter by touching on a few problems posed by the distribution, movement and trends of population described above:

1. Where the population is very sparse and homes are very few and far between as in the north and delta region of Nigeria, it is difficult and expensive to provide enough amenities like schools, hospitals and water supply.

2. Pastoral nomadism makes the taking of accurate census impossible, as the people are always on the move – here today and gone tomorrow. Without accurate census it is difficult to plan for development.

3. Too rapid an increase in population poses the problem of having too many mouths to feed. The problem is made more serious than it is now in West Africa, when food production does not keep pace with population growth. (See Chapter 21 for a full discussion on this problem.)

4. The drift to towns has a set of problems which it generates. These include congestion and the growth of slums, poor sanitation and pressure on existing facilities like houses, hospitals and schools. It increases the mouths to feed in the towns while decreasing the hands to produce the food in the rural areas. Finally, since those who flock to the towns never all succeed in getting jobs anyway, this drift leads to unemployment and follow-up problems like delinquency and crime.

5. Inter-continental migration leads to the loss of high-level manpower (as in the case of 'brain drain'), or the introduction of some unwelcome foreign cultures (as in the case of immigration of foreigners).

Summary

The population in West Africa is unevenly distributed. There are seven main areas of high densities arranged in two belts both starting from western Senegambia. Interposed with these belts are the Sahara, Middle Belt and Niger Delta, which are areas of low population densities. Physical, historical, economic and human factors are the principal factors responsible for the distribution pattern.

Population movements and trends, whether the movements are local, regional or inter-continental affect the pattern, and also generate some problems in their wake. These problems are real and pertinent and their solution should be of major concern to national governments in West Africa.

Revision exercises

1. a) Show on a map of West Africa four areas of high
      population densities and four areas of low densities.
   b) Give reasons to account for the high and low
      densities in the areas shown.
2. Write brief notes on population movement and trends in
   West Africa with special reference to:
   a) the causes of the movement;
   b) the nature of the movement and trends, and
   c) the consequences of such movements.
3. Briefly describe the problems of population in West
   Africa. What attempts are being made to solve these
   problems?

25 Transportation and trade

Preparation

1. Find out from an up-to-date map of West Africa the communication lines which link your country with its neighbours.
2. Make a list of your country's imports and exports using the following table:

	West African countries	Countries abroad
Exports to		
Imports from		

3. Prepare two blank maps of West Africa. In each insert the outlines of the English speaking countries, and insert and shade your own country.

Not all the things used in a particular country can be produced within that country. It buys its needs from other countries and in return sells its surpluses

25.1 Use of donkeys in the northern lands of West Africa. What are the donkeys carrying? Apart from the use of donkeys, this photograph suggests another means of transport in West Africa. What is it?

abroad. This transaction is called trade. But trade cannot go on unless there are means of transporting the goods. We shall therefore review the transport systems in West Africa and then say something about the trade.

Transportation

The five most important means of transport in West Africa are animal and human porterage, and rail, road, air and water transport.

Animal and human porterage

This is increasingly restricted to the remotest parts of the region. Important beasts of burden include the camel, the horse and the donkey.

The *camel* is sturdy and can go for a long time without water. So it is well-adapted to desert travel. Trans-Saharan caravan routes link one oasis with another and terminate in West African towns like Kano, Gao and Timbuktu.

The patient *donkey* and the tough *horse* are savanna beasts of burden. The former can carry great burdens but can only be used for short journeys, while the horse is increasingly used on ceremonial occasions only.

In remote villages people carry loads on their heads, their backs or their shoulders, but the distances they can cover — usually from home to the market and back — cannot be far.

Rail transport

Figure 25.2 shows the West African railway systems. The map shows that:

1. All the mainland countries, except small Gambia, Guinea Bissau, and recently Sierra Leone and poor

Niger, have railway lines. The Dakar-St Louis line was the first to be built in 1887.

2. Most of them are short; exceptions are the 1 200-kilometre Dakar to Koulikoro line, the 1 000-kilometre Abidjan to Ouagadougou line which is now being extended northwards in Upper Volta, and the Nigerian Railways, which total over 3 500 kilometres.

3. The lines head from the coast to the major mineral or agricultural producing regions, and help to evacuate the products of these areas to where they are needed for use or export. In fact, there are special mineral lines owned by mining companies and which carry minerals specifically, as distinct from the national railways owned by the government or a railway corporation and which carry passengers and goods.

4. There is no international railway linking neighbouring French- or English-speaking countries.

This is partly because the lines are short and have different gauges (rail width), but chiefly because most of them were built in the colonial days by France and Britain who had their individual – and often conflicting – interests at heart.

The lines on these railways are mostly single track and the gauge is narrow. For these reasons the trains are normally slow and therefore not always on schedule. The popular coaches are not built to a very high standard of comfort, either.

These criticisms notwithstanding, the railways have played, and will continue to play, a vital rôle in the economic development of West Africa.

Road transport

There are a number of important features about the road transport network, only the main arteries of which are shown in Figure 25.2.

25.2 Railways and major roads of West Africa.

1. The network is densest in south-eastern, western and north-central Nigeria, southern Ghana, southern Ivory Coast and western Senegal. These areas are the most densely peopled and most economically prosperous parts of West Africa, and the roads are needed there to provide the necessary transport services.
2. The longest international road artery in the heart of West Africa is the Dakar-Zinder highway. Name the towns it connects, trace its northern offshoots to the desert fringes and the southern ones to the coast. See how this French sponsored road and its offshoots steer almost completely clear of the English speaking countries.
3. Few good roads link the English-speaking with the French-speaking countries of West Africa. For example, only one road connects Nigeria and the neighbouring Republic of Benin and one links Ghana with Upper Volta. The two that lead from Sierra Leone to Guinea are bad and unsurfaced and there is not even a serviceable road from Ghana to Ivory Coast.

Road transport is very popular. The roads were built primarily to open up the interior, give government officers access to their areas of authority and supplement the railways in transporting goods. Today, however, the roads are serious competitors to the railways, since the higher speed and mobility of road vehicles make them more attractive to potential travellers and traders. In fact, in Sierra Leone, road transport has completely displaced the railway.

As a result of the growing popularity of road transport, road vehicles in the region are on the increase in number and in variety. In current use are the heavy duty mammy-waggons which are being put on the road to transport bulky goods, including cattle and imported capital goods, over long distances in the savanna and sahel regions. Smaller 5- or 7-tonne vehicles are used for shorter hauls. State government and private transport corporations run inter-urban bus transport making use of luxury coaches. Very popular for travelling between towns and their suburban locations are the smaller but less comfortable 10- to 20-seater kombi-buses. Finally, with the establishment of a number of car assembly plants (chapter 23) and the increase in income per capita, many more individuals prefer to own private cars and use them at their own convenience than make use of public transport.

Aviation

Airways provide the most convenient form of international travel; air travel is fast, normally comfortable and very practical.

Each large country has its own domestic routes and services as well as West African and international ones. Each also has at least one international airport – usually near the capital city. Identify these routes and ports in Figure 25.3.

Of the international airports, Dakar, Bamako, Kano, Accra, Abidjan and Lagos are the busiest. The first three of these airports are at the northern border of the habitable region of West Africa and so are convenient points from which to take off and fly across the Sahara or the Atlantic to Europe and North America, and at which to land on returning.

Both local and foreign air companies operate the services. The local lines include Nigeria Airways, Ghana Airways, Air Iviore, Air Guinee and Air Mali, and the most important of the foreign companies are British Caledonian, Air France, U.T.A., Royal Dutch Air Lines (K.L.M.) and Pan American Airways.

The aircraft usually carry passengers and cargo, including mail and valuable goods like precious minerals, drugs and scientific equipment.

Water transport

Water transport comprises river and ocean navigation. The first is only locally important (see Chapter 4), and the following stretches of West African waterways are navigable (see Figure 25.3):
i) the lagoons and creeks of Nigeria, Benin and Ivory Coast;
ii) the lower Niger, Cross and Benue rivers;
iii) the upper middle Niger;
iv) The Volta Lake;
v) the rias of Sierra Leone and Guinea Bissau, and
vi) the lower Gambia River.

Ocean navigation is more significant than river transport since it is vital for international trade, and ocean liners carry heavier cargoes than river craft. Sea routes connect the principal ports, and also link them with foreign countries. Both West African and foreign countries operate ocean liners.

The Development of Seaports

In our study of the various countries of West Africa in

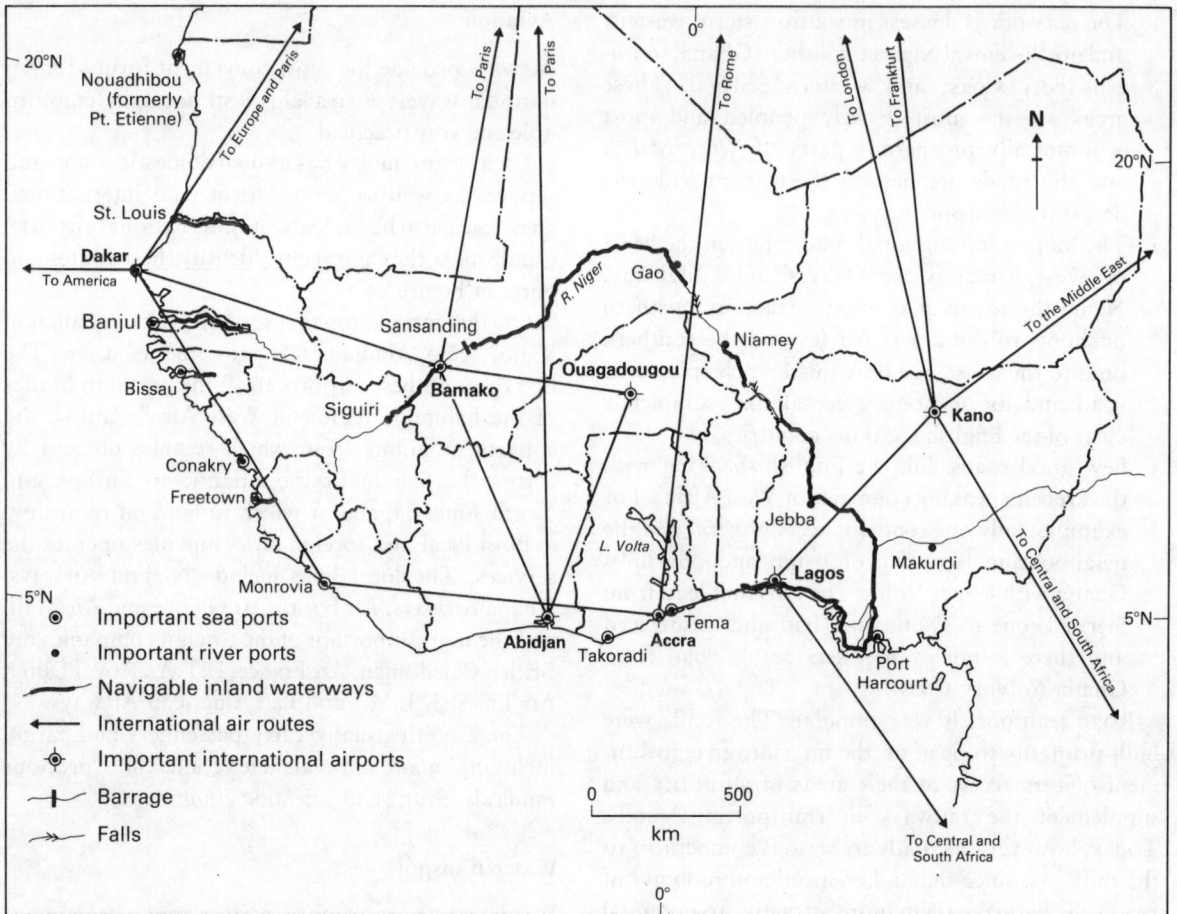

25.3 International airways and internal waterways in West
Africa.

part two we saw how the major ports in each country
grew to become important. Name these ports,
starting with Calabar in Nigeria and ending up with
Nouadhibou in Mauritania. Here we are going to
consider the *development of ports* generally in the
region and talk about the *conditions affecting their
growth*.

1. The coasts of West Africa have never had the
physical conditions suitable for maximum port
development. They are surf beaten (like along
Ghana and Mauritania); insects and pests initially
repelled permanent settlement; except for Banjul,
Freetown, Bissau and Conakry, there are few
sheltered harbours, and the coasts are washed by
long shore drift which carries tonnes of sand
along the coast. The drifts disturb shipping and
the sands are sometimes deposited as sand bars to
block the sea inlets. Lastly, behind the coastline

are mangrove swamps which naturally inhibit
port development.

On the other hand, certain other physical
conditions have given the initial advantage to the
growth of ports in the region. Fogs are generally
absent (except off the Mauritanian Coast); there
are no coral reefs as along the East African coast
to disturb shipping, and there are some rias and
other sea inlets. Dakar has a special locational
advantage. Its protrusion to the sea makes it a
convenient port of call for ships bound for South
America and South Africa. Also its proximity to
France made it an obvious choice as the cultural,
industrial and trade headquarters of former
French West Africa.

2. *Other factors* which have led to port development
in the region are *historical*. Thus ports started to
grow during the 15th century when the first

Europeans came to the region, and started the trade across the Atlantic. During this period only a few of them existed, and as would be expected, the most favoured places were the few inlets mentioned above afforded by the Senegal, Gambia Rokel, Niger and Cross Rivers.

As trade in slaves, ivory, salt, gold and later palm oil and kernels grew from the end of the 15th century to the 19th, many ports sprang up like mushrooms all along the West African coast. From a multitude of them, including Dakar, Banjul (then Bathurst) Freetown, Conakry, Cotonou, Accra, Lomé, Akassa, Brass and Calabar, these commodities flowed into ships bound for Europe and the Americas. Trading hulks were stationed at some ports (like at Calabar), and forts were built in the others (like the Elmina Castle in Accra built by the Portuguese in 1481). But these numerous small ports were found serviceable so long as the ships were small, loads light and were carried on foot over short distances from the hinterland.

As the boats became larger, the volume of trade and goods grew and railways and roads developed, it became necessary to consolidate traffic in certain ports specially favoured to cope with the increased size of ships and trade volume either due to the natural advantages they had or that artificial harbours could be built in them. Thus Freetown and Banjul survived, being on sheltered inlets while exposed Accra and Akassa declined. Artificial harbours with enclosed and dredged entrances which can receive large ships were built, first at Takoradi (1928) and later at Dakar, Lagos, Monrovia, Buchanan, Tema, Cotonou, Lomé and more recently at Nouadhibou.

3. *Economic factors* have also contributed to the growth of ports in West Africa. Of course trading with other countries is carried on in these ports, but they perform other functions as well. These functions may be political (some became capital cities), industrial (factories developed in most of them), commercial (banks, markets and shops were established) or transportation (as they formed foci of rail, road, air as well as sea routes). Consequently they also became centres of population concentration. Some of the ports also started handling the trade of land-locked neighbouring countries. Much of Mali's trade, for

example, goes through Dakar and Abidjan thus enhancing the importance of these ports. Upper Volta's windows on the south are Abidjan and Takoradi. Lagos ships out the tin, groundnuts and uranium from Niger in addition to Nigeria's own export commodities.

The size and economic activity in the hinterland of the ports have also conditioned their growth. Large ports are usually backed by large hinterlands with bouyant economic activity. Nigeria, Ivory Coast and Ghana are the richest countries in West Africa. No wonder their major ports – Lagos, Tema and Abidjan – have grown to be three of the largest in the region. Dakar another large port, serves an extensive hinterland including Senegal, Mali and part of Mauritania. Conversely, Freetown, Cotonou and Lomé, the ports of Sierra Leone, Benin and Togo have restricted growth potential because the countries that back them are small and have limited economic wealth.

Finally, and most recently, special facilities to handle special goods have been built in some ports because of special reasons or special economic advantages they have. These special facilities have enhanced the size and importance of the ports. Thus to the Lagos port has been added the Tin Can Island port specially built in 1976/77 to ease the port congestion. The new port now handles containers. (See colour photographs.) Buchanan in Liberia has been built to handle the iron ore from Nimba Mountains; Dakar has a special wharf for loading phosphates produced not far inland, and iron ore from Mauritania goes out through the special port at Nouadhibou. Tema and Dakar have special fishing ports for landing fish, while Dakar and Abidjan have special facilities for handling mineral oil imports.

It is therefore evident from the foregoing account that port development in West Africa offers a fine example of the interplay of physical, historical, man-made and economic factors. As the economic activities of the region grow, the scope obviously widens for further development of its ports.

i) Which of the means of transport described above are most common in your area?

ii) Which have you used yourself, and which did you find most comfortable?

iii) In what ways do you think that the transport system in

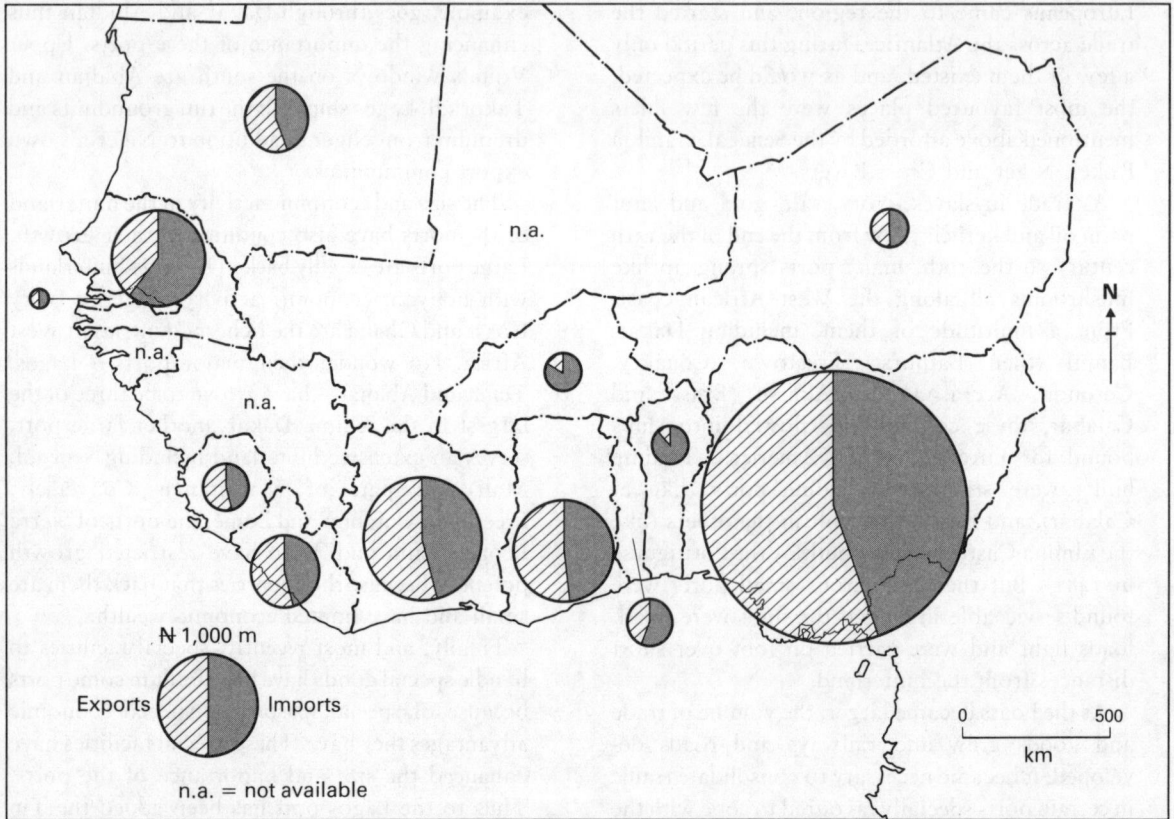

25.4 Trade in West Africa in mid 1970–80 decade. This figure shows the relative size of exports and imports among West African countries. The countries are not labelled. Name the four countries with the highest total trade value. These are the most economically developed countries in the region. Name four of the least economically developed mainland countries.
(*note*: Guinea Bissau one of the least economically developed inland countries and the offshore islands are not shown.)

your area could be improved?
iv) Name some airlines that operate in West Africa.
v) Do you live in a town with a seaport? If so your class can plan a visit to this port. Note the functions of the port and some of the new developments there. If not, name the recent developments that have occured in the main seaport that serves your country.

Trade

When we talk of trade in any particular region, we think of trade between that region and other regions, and trade within the region itself. We refer to the first as external trade and to the second as internal trade. In West Africa we can identify these two types of trade.

External or foreign trade

This type of trade is very vital to the region because it fetches more foreign money to it since those countries or regions it sells its goods to have to pay for them in foreign currency. With this currency the region can buy more goods from abroad. Thus when Nigeria sells mineral oil to Europe and North America, she gets foreign currency which she in turn uses to buy machinery and other capital goods used in developing the country.

We have studied the trade of the individual countries in part two. Look at the various pie diagrams again and recall what we said about the trade in each country. See also Figure 25.5 and the graphs in Figure 25.4 which show at a glance the recent external trade position for most of the countries. From these we can draw a number of major conclusions on the pattern of external trade in West Africa:

1. Many years back, West Africa used to be solely an exporter of vegetable commodities. Now this is no longer so. Some of the countries still export more vegetable commodities while others have

their exports now dominated by mineral products. In the first group we have Senegal, Gambia, Ivory Coast, Ghana, Benin and the interior countries. In the latter group feature Nigeria, Liberia and Mauritania. Name the chief vegetable and the chief mineral exports of the countries in each case. What proportion of the country's exports is taken by the vegetable or mineral products in each case?

2. Considering the total volume of trade, that is imports plus exports, the countries that rank highest are Nigeria, Ghana, Ivory Coast and Liberia. Lowest in this scale are the inland countries like Upper Volta and Niger, and the very small countries like Guinea Bissau, the off-shore Islands, Togo and Benin. Can you give reasons for this? Think of the countries' resources and their capacity to buy goods from abroad. This volume of trade is sometimes used to measure the degree of economic activity and prosperity of the countries of West Africa.

3. The balance of trade is also used as an index of economic prosperity of a nation. The balance of trade is the difference between exports and imports. If exports are higher in value than imports, we say that the country has a favourable or positive trade balance. If the reverse is the case, then we say that the balance is unfavourable or negative. If we consider the balance of trade in recent years together with the total volume of trade of West African countries, we see that the countries fall under four categories:

   i)   There are countries which enjoy high volume of trade and consistent favourable trade balance over the years. These countries are the most prosperous. Nigeria and Ivory Coast are in this category (Figure 25.5a).

   ii) There are others which have a small trade volume but with a favourable balance. Liberia and Mauritania are typical examples (Figure 25.5b).

   iii) Some countries have a low trade volume, and to make matters worse, an unfavourable balance as well, like the Republic of Benin, Niger and Upper Volta (Figure 25.5c).

   iv) Finally, we have countries whose recent trade balances are not steady. They oscillate from negative to positive and back again to negative. See Figure 25.5d for Ghana and Togo.

It must, however, be remembered that no country is permanently nailed down to any of these categories. Vigorous export trade may bring a country up to the group of prosperous ones, the reverse may send it down! Already there is a noticeable drop in the export trade of Nigeria due to the very recent slump in oil exports. This trend may well, in future, send it down to the category of countries with trade deficit!

4. Considering West African overseas trading partners, the various countries trade with those countries abroad with which they have had long historical association, and also long standing trade agreements. Thus, most of Ivory Coast's exports go to France and Western Europe from where it also gets most of her imports. Liberia's active trade partners are Western Germany and the United States of America. Nigeria and Ghana trade most vigorously with Britain, United States and Western Europe. However, in more recent years there have been conscious efforts made to diversify the trading partners. Featuring significantly among these new-comers are eastern European countries, Japan, the South-East Asia and other African countries.

Internal or regional trade

This is trade within the West African region. It can either be trade between one country and another in the region, or domestic trade within each country. Whereas substantial domestic trade goes on, being most active in a country like Nigeria where resources are varied, until recently regional trade among countries of West Africa themselves has been insignificant. It has been limited to livestock, and small quantities of foodstuffs and domestic crafts. This situation can be attributed to many factors:

1. The resources of the countries are broadly similar. They are mostly agricultural products which, because of the broad similarity of climate, are produced in most countries. Thus the savanna lands all over West Africa support cattle and produce maize, millet and guinea corn, and the forest lands yield palm produce. So there is little incentive to trade these products from one country to another except for supplementing existing quantities.

2. There are historical factors. The colonial masters

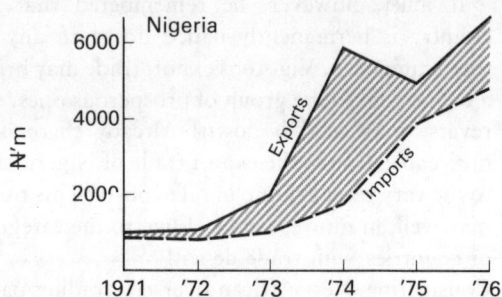

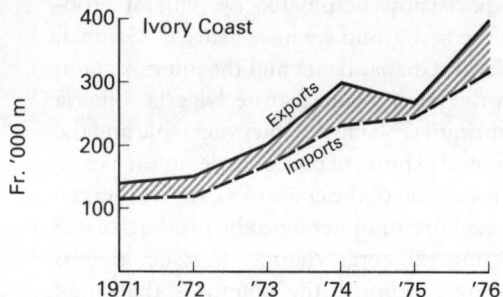

(a) Group (i). Countries with high trade volume and favourable balance

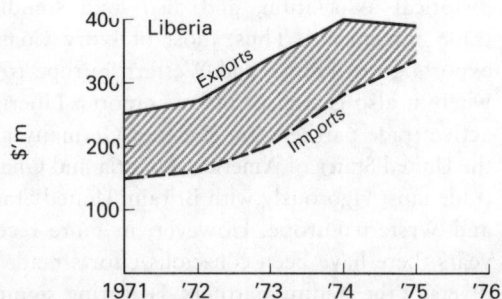

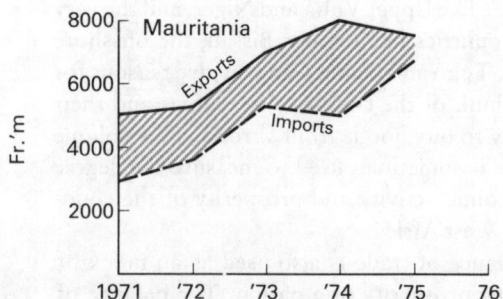

(b) Group (ii). Countries with low trade volume but favourable balance

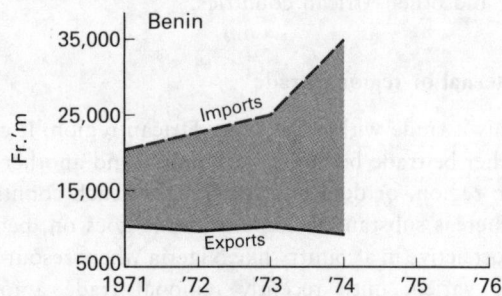

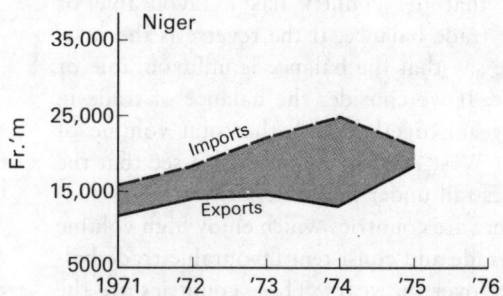

(c) Group (iii). Countries with low trade volume and unfavourable balance

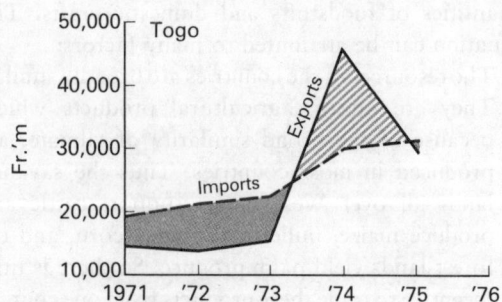

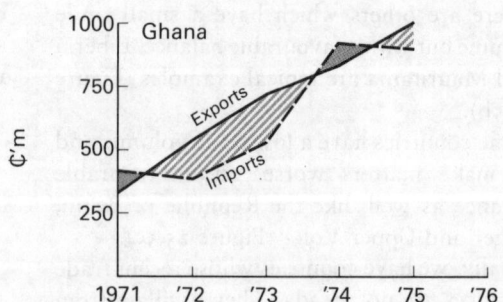

(d) Group (iv). countries with oscillating trade balance

never encouraged this trade, anyway. Instead, they channelled the commodities from their respective West African territories to their own countries, and sold back manufactured goods to them in return. Can you give examples of trade commodities that moved this way?

3. There is of course the human factor of inertia. Since independence, the countries did not immediately change over, having been used to the pattern above. This inertia has been encouraged by the preferential treatment those European countries continued to give to goods from their previous territories. France continued to give preferential treatment to coffee, bananas and cocoa from Ivory Coast and, until recently, to groundnuts from Senegal.

4. Finally, economic factors have hindered this trade. As we saw earlier on, there are few communication lines which link West African countries together. Most railway lines keep within each country. Where they cross boundaries, they keep within French-speaking countries, and all head towards the coast where the exports are emptied into ships bound for overseas countries.

Also no country in West Africa has grown to become an industrial power which will thus provide alternative markets to raw materials from the other West African countries and be an alternative source of manufactured goods.

However, the countries of West Africa are now making efforts to encourage regional trade among themselves. Specially facilitating this recent trend are the following factors:

1. Some countries produce agricultural commodities which may be needed in another country where the commodity is either scarce or insufficient to meet the local needs. Thus, before the drought, Niger used to consign quantities of cattle across the border to more populous Nigeria which has higher meat consumption capacity. Similarly, live cattle and other animals move annually from Upper Volta and Mali to Ghana, Ivory Coast and Sierra Leone.

2. Multi-national economic groupings between West African countries encourage trade. The most recent and most comprehensive of these is the Economic Community of West African States (ECOWAS). These groupings aim at removing the barriers to free flow of commodities among member states. (See chapter 26.)

3. Some countries have recently grown more than others in mineral and industrial strength. This has placed them in a position to export these products to other West African countries needing them. Thus Ghana and Nigeria now export power to Togo, Benin and Niger from their Volta and Kainji power projects respectively. Nigeria also exports crude oil to Ivory Coast which has a refinery but no crude oil, and Liberia is in a position to export its surplus iron ore and iron and steel goods from its mines and the steel plant at Buchanan to other West African countries.

4. Some countries are better placed than others with respect to receiving imported goods which are also needed by other less favourably placed countries. That is why coastal countries like Ivory Coast, Senegal and Nigeria receive imported goods from abroad and re-export them to interior countries like Upper Volta, Mali and Niger respectively.

5. Finally, there has been recent development of roads linking the countries of West Africa. An example is the Nigeria-Benin-Togo-Ghana Highway. It must however be remembered that much as these roads which cross frontiers encourage legitimate trade, they unfortunately provide routes for illegal smuggling of banned or restricted goods.

The problem of inflation

Here we shall deal with another current problem in West Africa. This is a problem of buying and selling which arises when there is too much money around chasing too few goods available. In a situation like that, prices of goods soar rapidly upwards and the

25.5 (a) Group (i) countries with high trade volume and favourable balance.
(b) Group (ii) countries with low trade volume but favourable balance.
(c) Group (iii) countries with low trade volume and unfavourable balance.
(d) Group (iv) countries with oscillating trade balance.
Recent trade in graphs of select West African countries. Study the graphs in the figure above. In which year did Nigeria record the high balance? Which comodity accounted for this high balance? Figs (a) and (b) look alike, but there is a major difference. What is this? What commodity was responsible for the steep rise of the export trade of Togo in 1974? Why did this trade fall in 1975?

value of money drops rapidly downwards. What one would have bought for ₦1 or ₵1 or Fr. 1, one pays upwards of double the price or more for. Such a situation is called *inflation*.

Inflation caught many West African countries in the first half of the 1970s. In Nigeria, for instance, prices rose by 1.5% in 1971 over the 1970 level, 2.5% in 1972 over the level in the previous year, over 5% in 1973, 12.6% in 1974, and 34.1% in 1975 over 1974 prices. This is a measure of inflation, and in countries like Ghana and Senegal, higher percentages were recorded. In Ghana it was 45.8% in 1975–76 for foodstuffs alone and 52% for all goods.

A number of factors combined to bring this situation about:

1. Too much money was pumped into the hands of people either through wage or salary increases or through paying inflated prices for contracts given by government.
2. Domestic production in West Africa did not keep pace with demand thus generated by the fact that people now had more money than before. The result was that goods became scarce and prices galloped upwards.
3. The crisis in the Middle East in 1973 halted oil exports to the industrialized countries of Europe and North America. Almost immediately after, the OPEC countries (OPEC = Organization of Petroleum Exporting Countries), including Nigeria, rapidly increased the prices of oil to enable them to recover lost sales. These meant that oil became scarce and very expensive in the industrialized countries, and they, in turn, had to increase the prices of goods they manufactured and sold to West Africa in order to make up for the high prices they paid for the oil. OPEC countries subsequently increased the prices of oil to enable them buy those goods, and so the vicious circle continued!

The years 1975–76 saw the peak inflation year in many West African countries. Since then however, it has been on the downward trend in some countries, notably Nigeria and Ivory Coast. Definite measures were taken to achieve this:

1. The countries embarked on steps to increase domestic production – of food and other goods.
2. Wages and salaries were frozen for some time.
3. The importation of certain non-essential goods was either banned or restricted to prevent unnecessary expenditure and encourage local production.
4. The OPEC countries decided to reduce the rate at which they increased the prices of oil.
5. Finally, the countries introduced measures to discipline their citizens and reduce too much spending and conspicuous consumption.

By so doing, it was possible to abate inflation at least temporarily; but since the problem is still present in West Africa, more strenuous efforts should be made in these and other directions, and more especially in countries where the grip is still firm, to get the menace completely eliminated, or at least considerably reduced.

Now attempt the following exercises on transportation and trade in West Africa.

Revision exercises

1. a) On one of the maps of West Africa you have prepared, insert the main railways lines. Insert and name the termini and two towns en route.
   b) On the other map insert the main international air-routes and waterways. Insert and name also the major airports.
   c) Comment on the services offered by the railways and airways, and assess their importance in the economic development of the region.
2. a) Describe and account for the pattern of external trade in West Africa.
   b) In what ways do you think that this trade can be improved to the greater benefit of the region?
3. a) Explain in what ways do the following hinder trade between the countries of West Africa:
      i)   climate;
      ii) distribution of natural resources, and
      iii) human factors.
   b) Explain the factors that promote trade among the various countries of West Africa.
      (*WASC June, 1977*)
4. How have physical, historical and economic factors influenced the development of ports in West Africa? Illustrate your answer with typical examples.

Before completing our review of the geography of West Africa, we must discuss three important and interesting phenomena in the current affairs of the region. First, many West African countries group or ally themselves together into unions. Second, they give help to one another when in need, or they seek help from abroad; this help is called foreign or international aid. Finally, all are undertaking planned development programmes to improve their economy and the welfare of their peoples.

These three phenomena are related to one another and to the geography of the region. Thus mutual associations and groupings between states are often the result of geographical factors – for instance, common borders, a similar culture or origin, or the presence of a common geographical feature. Other conditions for association can be a common political outlook or economic necessity – one country may possess a vital commodity which is needed by others. When two or more countries associate, they often aid one another or receive foreign aid from a common source. The aid is used to finance development programmes which, in turn, create improvements in the economic position of the countries concerned. Let us now discuss these three phenomena in some detail.

International groupings

In West Africa many of the groupings started after the independence of the countries' but not all have survived. The *Ghana-Guinea-Mali Union* was formed in 1959 on a political and economic basis. In forming the *Mali Federation*, Mali and Senegal hoped to build up a union in which each partner would provide the economic necessities not possessed by the other. But neither of these unions passed the test of time.

Of the groupings that have survived, the *West African Customs Union* (with its successor, the *West African Monetary Union*) was formed in 1959, by the French-speaking West African countries (minus Guinea). They agreed to trade freely among themselves, use the Franc as the unit of currency and to give it the same value in all the member states. The countries of the *Senegal River Union* (Senegal, Mauritania, Mali and Guinea) have the Senegal River as a unifying factor. They have formed their association in order to find ways of using the river for greater mutual benefit in the fields of fishing, irrigation, power production and transportation. This is also the motive behind the recent formation of the *River Niger Commission* and the *Lake Chad Commission* by the countries for whom these bodies of water are common geographical features. Look at your atlas and name these countries. When drought threatened the existence of the sahel countries in 1972–74, they formed the *Inter-state Committee for Drought Control in the Sahel* to fight the menace. As described in chapter 20 the Committee took steps to alleviate the effects of drought on crops, livestock and man.

The most recent and all-embracing union formed by the 16 countries of West Africa is the Economic Community of West African States (ECOWAS).

The idea of having the Community was thought out by Togo and Nigeria when in 1973 a joint mission from both countries visited all independent West African countries and obtained agreement from them in principle to join the two countries in forming the Community.

At its inaugural meeting in Lagos in May, 1975, the treaty that gave birth to the Community was signed. In November of the following year, the treaty became operative with the ECOWAS secretariat in Lagos and its headquarters in Lomé. In *the treaty* the countries agreed, among other things:

i)   to gradually remove all barriers to trade among themselves;

ii) to co-operate in other economic areas like transport, agriculture and industries;

iii) to co-operate in cultural areas like education, music and art, and

iv) to contribute to a common fund which they would use

    a) to compensate member countries for sacrifices they would make or losses they would sustain in opening their doors to free trade with fellow member countries, and

    b) to back any investment a member country would wish to make in a foreign country.

So far the Community has achieved a number of good results.

It has encouraged road development linking neighbouring member states. At a recent (1979) meeting of the Community held in Dakar, member states agreed to eliminate travel visas for visits to, and stay of not more than three months in member countries. They also agreed to freeze customs duties and develop telecommunication networks among themselves. The last will make it possible for one in Nigeria to telephone a friend in Guinea or Mali and vice versa!

West African countries also form alliances with other countries or organizations outside the region. The former British territories now belong to the *Commonwealth*. In the same way most of the former French territories are members of the *French Community*. These two groupings exist solely because their members have common ties with Britain and France respectively. The *Organization for African Unity* (OAU) and the *United Nations Organization* (UNO) are other groupings to which independent West African countries belong. The first links all independent African States together with a 'capital' at Addis Ababa; the second is a world union of independent countries with headquarters in New York.

The existence of all these groupings emphasises the fact that hardly any country can live in isolation in the modern world. Nations are inter-dependent. They have trade links or they co-operate in helping one another through international aid programmes. The groupings also provide a forum for solving quarrels between member nations. Can you name quarrels between any two West African nations solved this way?

i) How was ECOWAS conceived, and when was it born?

ii) Can you say why the secretariat and the headquarters are located in Lagos and Lomé respectively?

iii) Name some of the terms of the Treaty of the Community.

iv) Cite some examples of the success achieved by ECOWAS.

v) Name other unions to which West African countries belong.

International aid

The pattern of international aid generally corresponds with that of the international groupings. Even individuals in need of help go first to their friends – and so do nations. The different kinds of foreign aid received by West African countries can be classified according to their sources:

1. When a private foreign company or organization invests money in a country, or decides to support a project financially, it is engaging in *private aid*. It is obvious, though, that the company, in making the investment, hopes to derive profits from it. Examples of this kind of aid are the Firestone investments in the rubber plantations of Liberia, the Pamol and Dunlop investments in the Nigerian plantations and the oil companies' investments in Nigeria. German, Canadian and Swedish firms are financing the iron ore mining in Liberia. Charitable organizations also give private aid, normally on a non-profit making basis.

2. Aid is sometimes given by one government to another as a result of direct negotiation between the two. This is called *bilateral aid*. This is often granted when the country seeking aid is at the time in the spotlight of world publicity, perhaps because of the discovery there of large mineral resources, and therefore an important factor in the struggle among the wealthy, powerful nations for influence in Africa. Such aid is often said to be 'without strings'. But in reality the donor country at least maintains a more than impartial interest in the general economic development of the receiving country, and often expects to be repaid with political support. West African States are now realising this and they are a little wary in receiving bilateral aids.

The governments of Britain, France and America have the most active bilateral aid programmes in West Africa. Britain and France are the key sources of aid for their former territories, and the United States of America gives millions of dollars to Liberia and, to a lesser extent, other countries. Western Germany has attempted to revive her old links with Togo by giving her aid for her development programmes. China and other Communist countries are late arrivals in this second phase of the 'scramble for Africa'. They have given assistance to Mali and Guinea, but their aid programme in Ghana was curtailed by the political changes which took place in the country early in 1966.

3. *Multi-lateral* aid is given to a country by either a regional or world organization. A country usually qualifies for such aid if it is a member or an associate member of the organization. All West African independent countries qualify for aid from the United Nations agencies because they are all members of the United Nations.

The United Nations Educational, Scientific and Cultural Organization (UNESCO) and the United Nations International Childrens Emergency Fund (UNICEF) are arms of the United Nations Organization which have aid programmes in West Africa. The International Bank for Reconstruction and Development (IBRD), usually called the World Bank, has financed a number of projects in West Africa, including the Maiduguri railway extension in Nigeria, the Nouadhibou-F'derik railway in Mauritania, and the construction of many industries and research projects in the region. The European Economic Community (EEC) offers scholarships and makes direct loans to associated West African countries.

Methods of aid

When it is announced that one country has given another so many million dollars or pounds worth of aid, how is this sum paid to the receiving country?

The money is not just counted and transferred to the bank of the receiving country. The donor country or organization may decide to make available to the receiving country materials for constructing a project. For instance, Italy, U.K., and the U.S.A. shipped tonnes of machines and technical equipment into Ghana and Nigeria for the construction of the Akosombo and Kainji dams and power plants in the respective countries. The donor may also offer training facilities to the personnel of the receiving country, or even send their nationals (called technical aid personnel) to work there. The salaries of these people or the cost of the equipment or training provided are added up and quoted as part of the aid, which is usually given as a loan with varying percentages of interest and terms of repayment.

Development programmes

Aid is generally used to finance development programmes. However, it can only finance part of any country's development programme. Money for this also has to be raised from within the country. Let us now illustrate our whole discussion with three examples:

1. *Nigeria* embarked on the Third National Development Plan in 1975. No sooner had this Plan been launched in March of that year than a review of it became necessary. Three events led to this decision:

i) When the National Government changed in July, 1975, the new Government decided to change the emphasis in the development plan and give more attention to projects like water supply, roads, health, agriculture and housing which bear greater relevance to the welfare of the common man.

ii) Oil production, and therefore sales and revenue from it, fell in 1975. It therefore became imperative to reduce the scope of the plan and drop the prestigious money consuming projects in favour of essential ones.

iii) In February 1976, seven new states were created and the country chose a new federal capital. This development meant that the essential requirements of these new States and the new capital will have to be accommodated in the plan.

For these reasons the country carried out a plan revision exercise and came out with a Revised 1976–80 Third National Development Plan in early 1977.

The new Plan provided for a total expenditure of ₦43.3 billion by all the Government of the Federation. Of this, some 61.6%, or ₦26.7 billion, was reserved for projects in the economic sector, comprising agriculture, industries, power, mining, trade, transportation and communications; 11.5% or ₦5.0 billion for projects in the social sector like education, health, information, labour, social development and sports; 13.9% or ₦6.03 billion for regional development like development of water supplies and housing, town and country planning and community development; while security and general administration claimed the balance of ₦5.6 billion. Much of this sum of ₦43.3 billion was to be found locally and part from foreign sources through aid programmes.

Some of the accomplishments of the plan are the expressways, the Warri and Kaduna oil refineries, the port extensions at Apapa, Warri and Calabar, the new schools and colleges, and the vehicle assembly plants of Lagos and Kaduna.

2. About the same time, *Ivory Coast* launched its 1976–80 Development Plan. The plan envisaged a total expenditure of Fr. 1 400 billion or one-eleventh the size of the Nigerian Plan. Developments in transport, communication and power claimed the largest share of Fr. 588 billion or 42%; agriculture the next largest share of Fr. 560 billion or 40%, and social development Fr. 168 billion or 12%. Seventy per cent of the total sum was expected to come from within the country and 30% from abroad, principally France.

Before the plan was launched, the rate of growth of the wealth of Ivory Coast was slowing down: 8.2% in 1970, 6.8% in 1972 and 2.9% in 1974. The plan therefore aimed at increasing production so as to reverse this trend and to bring the rate up to an ambitious level of 25% per annum by the end of 1980.

3. *Togo's* 1976–80 Plan was estimated at Fr. 250.6 billion – just over one-sixth that of Ivory Coast and 1.6% that of Nigeria. Why do you think the size of Togo's Plan was less than that of either Ivory Coast or Nigeria? The investment in the plan was distributed as follows:

Industry (including agriculture) ..	Fr. 69.9 b. or 28%
Rural Development	Fr. 56.2 b. or 22.5%
Transport, Communication and Energy	Fr. 40.9 b. or 16%
Planning of Towns and Social Development	Fr. 60.5 b. or 24%
Others	Fr. 23.1 b. or 9.5%

Togo hopes, by this investment, to increase its

wealth by an average of 8% annually between 1976 and 1980.

Of the total sum of Fr. 250.6 billion, Fr. 162.5 billion was expected to come from the country's internal sources and Fr. 88.1 billion from foreign sources. Togo has a policy of diversifying her foreign connections, so she looked up both to France, Western Germany, United Kingdom, the United States and North Korea for most of the foreign assistance she needs for her development programmes.

From the above analysis, we can draw a number of vital conclusions on the nature and importance of development plans in the region. In West Africa, as in most other regions of the world:

i)   each country prepares its plan of development for a period, usually 4–5 years. In this plan it draws up programmes for developing its roads, schools, hospitals, agriculture, industry, mining and other aspects of its economic life, all aimed at increasing the wealth of the nation and the welfare of its peoples;

ii)   the size of a country's development plan depends on how rich the country is and on how able it is to find the funds to support the programmes;

iii)   in the plan the country gives greatest emphasis to areas of its greatest needs and priorities at the material time and can change its strategies as the need arises;

iv)   funds to support the programmes are obtained both from within the country and from external sources, the latter being from friendly nations and organizations;

v)   finally, when fully implemented the development programmes bring about changes in the geography of the country. New schools, roads, factories and buildings spring up, and production in agriculture, mining, industry and other areas normally shows appreciable increases.

Some practical assignments

1. Find out which international groupings West African countries belong to. What are their geographical or historical backgrounds, and which states belong to each grouping. Why were the groupings set up, and what benefits does each state hope to derive from the association?

2. If you hear of foreign aid being requested by or given to

any country you know, try to find out the type and source of the aid, the donor country or association, any previous friendly relationshop between it and the receiving country, and what the aid is going to be used for. Follow the progress of the project the aid is meant to finance and assess the changes it is likely to bring about in the economic life of the country concerned.

3. Select the major projects in your country's current development plan or in that of any other country of your choice. Find out how they are financed, their scope and the progress already made in each. Then attempt a forecast of the contribution that the completed projects are likely to make to the economic geography of the country.

4. a) Why was ECOWAS formed and how has it helped in the general economic development of West Africa?
   b) Next time you hear in the news that the ECOWAS is meeting or has met, try and find out:
      i) the venue and date(s) of the meeting;
      ii) the purpose of the meeting;
      iii) which states are attending or have attended the meeting, and
      iv) the decisions taken at the meeting.

   How are the decisions related to the general aims of the Community?

   Doing the above exercises, will help you to think not only as a modern and practical geographer but also as an enlightened and well-informed citizen.

Conclusion

At the beginning of this book we said that it was written primarily to prepare students for the West African School Certificate and equivalent examinations and to help create the seeds for better international understanding among West African countries. If you have studied this book conscientiously, you should now be well-equipped to give adequate answers, not only to the likely examination questions which follow, but also to any other examination question on the subject at your own level. If, in addition, you now understand better the peoples of West Africa, are able to see how and why their ways of life resemble or differ from those of your home people, regard their problems and achievements as yours, and are able to understand and suggest solutions to some contemporary problems of West Africa, then this book will have fulfilled its purpose.

Appendix 1

Typical examination questions

Ten objective tests

To each of the following ten questions, which are similar to those you may expect in the W.A.S.C. 'O' Level examinations, five alternative answers are provided. Select the alternative which gives the correct answer to the question:

1. Which of the following explains best how West Africa came to exist with Africa as a separate continent?
   a) sub-marine canyons
   b) plastic deformation
   c) continental drift
   d) law of supply and demand
   e) Gondwanaland
2. Which of the following peoples can you find in almost all the countries of West Africa?
   a) Asante
   b) Wolof
   c) Hausa
   d) Sousou
   e) Fulani
3. Which of the following is particularly responsible for formation of the inter-tropical front?
   a) land and sea breezes
   b) harmattan winds
   c) line squalls
   d) the meeting of the tropical maritime and tropical continental air masses
   e) convectional currents
4. Three sahel countries of West Africa are:
   a) Nigeria, Togo and Benin
   b) Niger, Mali and Mauritania
   c) Liberia, Sierra Leone and Guinea
   d) Senegal, The Gambia and Guinea Bissau
   e) Ghana, Guinea and Mali
5. Casamance woodland is most likely to be found in:
   a) the guinea savanna
   b) delta mangrove swamp
   c) high forest
   d) desert
   e) montane vegetation
6. Which of the following countries is the largest producer of coffee?

   a) Mali
   b) Nigeria
   c) Guinea
   d) The Gambia
   e) Ivory Coast
7. Match each of the commodities in list A with the country in list B which is its largest producer in West Africa.

List A	List B
Gold	Ghana
Iron Ore	Ivory Coast
Bauxite	Nigeria
Bananas	Liberia
Coal	Guinea
8. The oil refinery in West Africa which is nearest to its source of crude oil supply is in:
   a) Warri
   b) Tema
   c) Abidjan
   d) Conakry
   e) Dakar
9. Which of the following offers the most appropriate explanation for the high density of population in Upper Volta?
   a) The level land
   b) The steady supply of rainfall and water
   c) The traditional attachment of the people to the land
   d) The concentration of industries
   e) The production of cotton
10. Trade among West African countries has been retarded. Which of the following factors offers the most logical explanation for this?
    a) West African countries do not want to trade with one another.
    b) West African countries do not speak the same language.
    c) The countries do not produce enough goods to sell to others.
    d) West Africa is a region of contrasts.
    e) The former colonial masters never encouraged this trade.

Five practical exercises

11. The diagram (right) shows the temperature and rainfall graphs for a typical station in West Africa.
    a) Calculate:
       i) the total annual rainfall;
       ii) the annual temperature range;
       iii) the number of months with less than 50 mm.
    b) Account for the rise in temperature between February and April, and the fall from May to July.
    c) Account for the relatively high rainfall in March to July and again in October.
    d) Has this station single or double maxima rainfall?
    e) Name the climatic type represented by the diagram and suggest a likely station in West Africa from which the figures for the diagram might have been taken.

12. The picture (page 51) shows an economic activity in West Africa. What commodity is being mined here? Describe the activities shown in the picture. Describe the area where the photograph has been taken. How is the commodity further handled from this stage to the time it is used by industry.

13. a) Study the map and answer the questions below:
       i) What is the length to the nearest kilometre of the main stream that flows into Laka Lagoon? (4 km, 6 km, 8 km, 10 km, 12 km)
       ii) What is the elevated feature that runs westwards from the cape near Mito to the west edge of the map called? (hill, spur, ridge, cuesta,

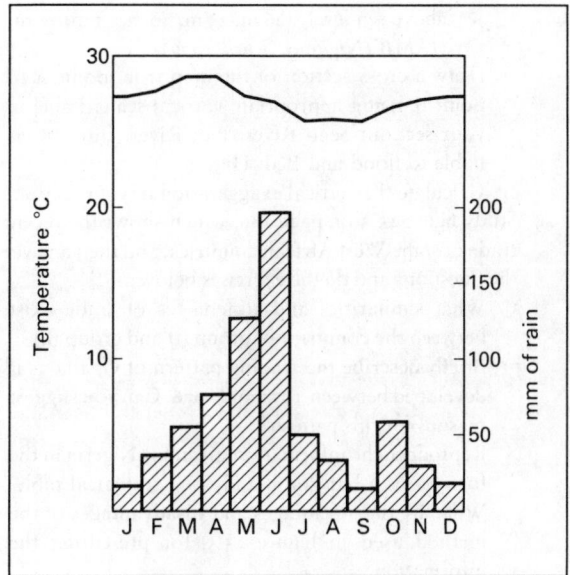

peninsula).
What is the true bearing of the trigonometrical station 54.0 m from the peak of Bedi Hill? (127°, 200°, 233°, 266°, 319°).
iv) What is the appropriate geographical term for that narrow feature east of Ela Lagoon between Ela and Laka lagoons? (lake, ocean, beach sand, isthmus, sand bar).
v) What is the approximate height of Manko

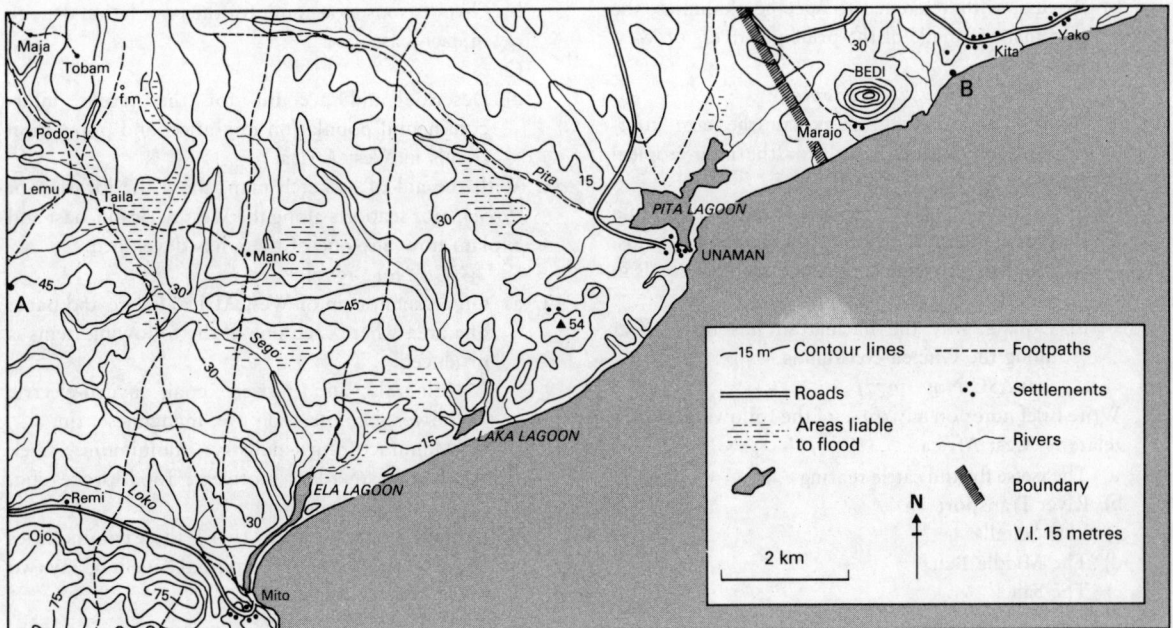

above sea level? (46 m, 35 m, 30 m, 21 m, 12 m)
(*JAMB (Nigeria), April 1979*)
Draw a cross section of the map from point A to
point B, using appropriate vertical scale. Label in
your section: Sego River, Pita River, three areas
liable to flood and Bedi Hill.
c) Calculate the vertical exaggeration of your section.

14. Study figure 25.5 on page 186, which shows the recent
trade of some West African countries, and then answer
the questions and do the exercises below:
a) What similarities and differences of trade exist
between the countries of group (i) and group (ii)?
b) Briefly describe the trading pattern of Ghana as it
developed between 1971 and 1976. Can you suggest
reasons for this pattern?
c) Reproduce the information given for Nigeria in the
form of (i) a bar graph and (ii) a statistical table.
What are the advantages and disadvantages of the
method used in Figure 25.5 for presenting the
information

15. Describe how you would make a field study of a small
area, illustrating your account fully with examples
from your own experience.
(*London GCE O.L. Jan. 1971*)

Fifteen essay questions

16. a) With the aid of a sketch map, describe and account
for the characteristics of the drainage pattern in
West Africa.
b) Discuss, with reference to specific examples, the
uses that are made of the principal rivers of West
Africa.
(*WASC Nov. 1976 adapted*)

17. a) With the aid of a diagram explain the term 'inter-
tropical convergence zone', or 'the inter-tropical
front'.
b) i) Explain why there are two crops of maize in a
year along most parts of the Guinea coastlands.
ii) Explain why there is only one crop of cereals in
a year in the northern part.
iii) Explain why the harmattan has little effect
along the Guinea coastlands.
(*WASC Nov. 1977*)

18. Write brief notes on any *three* of the following as they
relate to West Africa:
a) The tsetse fly and cattle rearing
b) River Transport
c) Line Squalls
d) The Middle Belt
e) The Sahel
(*WASC June 1977*)

19. a) Write an explanatory account of any *two* important factors that influence the climate of West
Africa.
b) With the aid of a sketch map describe and explain
the present extent of forest vegetation in West
Africa.
(*WASC June 1977*)

20. Explain any *three* of the following:
a) Vegetation belts in West Africa run generally east
to west.
b) Rainfall along the South-east coast of Ghana and
South-west Togo is generally low.
c) Trade routes in West Africa run generally north
and south.
d) Most oil refineries in West Africa are located along
the coast.
e) There are extensive labour migrations in West
Africa.
(*WASC June 1977 adapted*)

21. Explain the importance of any *three* of the following:
a) groundnuts to the economy of Senegal;
b) cattle rearing in Mali;
c) iron ore mining in Liberia;
d) the development of manufacturing industries in
Ghana;
e) irrigation in the sahel region of West Africa.
(*WASC/GCE 1975*)

22. **Either**
a) On a map of West Africa show *three* areas of high
population concentration and *three* of low population densities.
b) Give reasons to account for the population density
in each case.
Or
c) Describe and account for the recent inter-
continental population migration and population
trends in West Africa.

23. With the aid of a sketch map, show the location of
three major seaports along the West African Coast and
explain how any one of these has developed.
(*GCE Nov. 1977*)

24. a) On a sketch map of West Africa, locate and name
one area where each one of the following items is
produced:
i) Minerals and power: coal, hydro-electric
power, bauxite, iron ore, manganese, tin.
ii) Manufacturing industry: aluminium, steel,
cement, textiles, footwear, food processing,
electronic equipment.
b) Explain how trade in any two of these commodities
could be developed to the mutual benefit of any two
West African countries.
(*WASC June, 1976*)

25. a) Comment on the recent growth of manufacturing industries in either Nigeria, Ghana or Ivory Coast.
    b) How far is it true to say that the industries in these countries are dominated by ports?
26. a) On a sketch map of West Africa, insert and label the main vegetational belts.
    b) Describe the vegetational types found in the grassland areas.
    c) Comment on the problems of farming in the Sahel region saying what efforts are being made to combat these problems.
    (*WASC June, 1979 adapted*)
27. a) On a sketch map of West Africa, mark in and name:
    i) The Rivers Senegal and Niger;
    ii) the Prime Meridiam and Latitude 15°N;
    iii) the direction of the Cool Canary and the Guinea currents;
    iv) any *four* of the following towns; Dakar, Bamako, Abidjan, Niamey, Conakry, Ouagadougou;
    v) for any *two* of the following minerals one area important for each: iron ore, coal, bauxite, phosphates.
    b) Discuss, with examples, the importance and major problems of water transportation in West Africa.
    (*WASC June, 1979*)
28. a) On a sketch map of West Africa, show *five* areas (name the countries concerned), each important for the production of *one* of any *five* of the following commodities: Petroleum, Groundnuts, Cocoa, Alumina, Cattle, Rice, Diamonds. (Do not indicate more than one commodity in any one country).
    b) Mark in and name on your map *one* important town situated in each area shown.
    c) Explain how important any *one* commodity shown on your map is to the country in which it is produced.
    (*WASC June, 1975*)
29. a) On a map of West Africa shade with distinctive symbols and name:
    i) one wholly savanna and one wholly forest country;
    ii) one French speaking and one English speaking country (both different from the countries named in (i) above);
    iii) one area for the production of groundnuts and one for the production of coffee.
    b) In your answer papers describe the main features in the export trade of *either* Ghana *or* Ivory Coast.
    (*Teacher's Grade II Certificate, Enugu 1974 adapted*)
30. a) Locate on a map of West Africa:
    i) Nimba Mountains, Futa Jalon Plateau, Jos Plateau;
    ii) Rivers Niger, Senegal and Konkouré;
    iii) Lakes Chad, Volta and Kainji;
    iv) a delta coast, a ria coast and a lagoon coast;
    b) Give a concise account of how any one highland, one river, one lake and one coastline you have located are utilised by man.

Five topics for the advanced students

31. Describe the general characteristics and behaviour of air masses. Write an essay on air mass and climate in West Africa.
32. What advantages are there to be derived from the co-operation of West African states within the framework of the Common Market? What problems confront such a co-operation?
33. To what extent are raw materials an important locating factor in manufacturing industries in West Africa?
    (*Camb. HSC & GCE Nov. 1970*)
34. Examine critically, with reference to specific examples, the rôle played by foreign investments in the economic development of West African nations.
35. Describe, with the aid of a sketch map, the distribution of vegetation in any country that you are familiar with, and discuss the influence of climate, topography and soils on this distribution.
(*GCE 'A' Level, Nov. 1978*)

Answers to the objective tests

1. (c) 2. (e) 3. (d) 4. (b) 5. (a) 6. (e)
7. Gold-Ghana; Bananas-Ivory Coast; Coal-Nigeria; Iron Ore-Liberia; Bauxite-Guinea.
8. (a) 9. (c) 10. (e).

Index